I0213244

Postregional Fictions

Southern Literary Studies

Scott Romine, Series Editor

Postregional Fictions

Barry Hannah and the Challenges
of Southern Studies

CLARE CHADD

Louisiana State University Press ▮▮▮ Baton Rouge

Published by Louisiana State University Press
www.lsupress.org

Copyright © 2021 by Louisiana State University Press
All rights reserved. Except in the case of brief quotations used in articles or reviews,
no part of this publication may be reproduced or transmitted in any format or by
any means without written permission of Louisiana State University Press.

Designer: Michelle A. Neustrom
Typeface: Chaparral Pro

Cover image: Mississippi map background courtesy Frank Ramspott/iStock.com.

Library of Congress Cataloging-in-Publication Data

Names: Chadd, Clare, author.
Title: Postregional fictions : Barry Hannah and the challenges of Southern
    studies / Clare Chadd.
Description: Baton Rouge : Louisiana State University Press, [2021] |
    Series: Southern literary studies | Includes bibliographical references
    and index.
Identifiers: LCCN 2020050658 (print) | LCCN 2020050659 (ebook) | ISBN
    978-0-8071-7493-7 (cloth) | ISBN 978-0-8071-7574-3 (pdf) | ISBN 978-0-8071-7575-0
    (epub)
Subjects: LCSH: Hannah, Barry—Criticism and interpretation. | Southern
    States—In literature. | Authenticity (Philosophy) in literature.
Classification: LCC PS3558.A476 Z58 2021 (print) | LCC PS3558.A476
    (ebook) | DDC 813/.54—dc23
LC record available at https://lccn.loc.gov/2020050658
LC ebook record available at https://lccn.loc.gov/2020050659

Contents

Acknowledgments | vii

List of Abbreviations | ix

INTRODUCTION   The Storied South: Footsteps in the Snow | 1

1   The Problem of Reference in the Late-Twentieth-Century South
Geronimo Rex | 40

2   The Authenticity Paradox and the Myth of Masculinity
Airships | 75

3   The Burden of Postsouthern History
"Uncle High Lonesome" and "The Agony of T. Bandini" | 106

4   Southern Decline and the Politics of Nostalgia
"Rat-Faced Auntie" | 142

5   Authenticity and Textuality in the Postsouthern Folktale
"Evening of the Yarp: A Report by Roonswent Dover" | 179

6   Narcissistic Narrative and the New Language of the Post-South
"Get Some Young" | 206

CONCLUSION   Imagined Lacks and Literal Losses
The Post-postregional South? | 241

Notes | 257

Works Cited | 261

Index | 281

Acknowledgments

My deep gratitude goes to my family, and especially my grandparents, the now late Margaret and Leslie, who, sadly, didn't see this book's completion, and John and Mary, whose continued support I am honored to have. To my parents, Jeremy, Nicola, and (my literary confidante) Joanne, and my brother, Tom, for their backing, encouragement, and kindness across the years. Special thanks to Rachel O'Sullivan, Alice Rae, Ian, and Abi for their wisdom, solidarity, survival tips, and laughs. My thanks go to the Department of English Literature at the University of Edinburgh, especially Kenneth Millard and Andrew Taylor, and enormous thanks to Sarah Robertson, of UWE, Bristol, for her invaluable insights and guidance. Many thanks to the editors and readers of *The European Journal of American Studies* and *Mississippi Quarterly* for their support in publishing versions of chapters 3 (2018) and 5 (2016), and of course to James W. Long, Scott Romine, Neal Novak, and the team at LSU Press. Huge thanks to Joanne Allen for her eagle-eyed copyediting, and to Martyn Bone and Brian Ward for their kind help on short notice. I am ever thankful for my traveling companions in the South and those whom I had the pleasure of meeting along the way, including Jennifer and Lauren, of the University of Mississippi archives, and Tom Franklin, who so graciously shared some of his precious stories of Barry with me. Finally, my thanks go to Ken, for everything. Heaven is pals.

Abbreviations

BH   Ruth D. Weston. *Barry Hannah: Postmodern Romantic.* 1998.

NW   Martyn Bone. *Where the New World Is: Literature about the U.S. South at Global Scales.* 2018.

PA   Jon Smith. *Finding Purple America: The South and the Future of American Cultural Studies.* 2013.

RS   Scott Romine. *The Real South: Southern Narrative in the Age of Cultural Reproduction.* 2008.

SOP   Martyn Bone. *The Postsouthern Sense of Place in Contemporary Fiction.* 2005.

Postregional Fictions

The Storied South

Footsteps in the Snow

There are no stories of any merit to come out of this place.
—BARRY HANNAH, "Nicodemus Bluff" (1993)

There is a scene in the story "Even Greenland," a remarkable four-page tale from Barry Hannah's second published collection, *Captain Maximus* (1985), in which two pilots, their jet plummeting to earth in flames, calmly dispute who will have the most singular death, or at least the better story to be told about it afterwards. The first pilot, John, articulates this struggle to find an original form of contemporary creative expression as being "[l]ike somebody's seen it already. It wasn't fresh. There were eyes that had used it up some." He offers the memorable analogy that lends the story its title: "Even Greenland. It's fresh, but it's not fresh. There are footsteps in the snow" (32). His companion, the story's first-person narrator, replies with his own poetic conceit, of being the first child in the neighborhood to put fresh footprints in the rare Mississippi snow, causing John's infuriation: "You son of a bitch, that was *mine*—that snow in Mississippi. Now it's all shot to shit" (33). In retaliation, John ensures that he, the original author of the image, is the sole pilot to go down with the plane so that he might become posthumously storied, a feat later grudgingly described by the surviving narrator, visiting the scene of the wreck and John's extraordinary death, as "John's damned triumph" (34). Quickly, we realize that "Even Greenland" is a story about telling stories, an allegory for the fraught condition of modern southern writing, where the possibility of "fresh" representation has become a coveted rarity, if it exists at all.

Finding an original voice in the contemporary South is the first of several postregional challenges informing this study of Hannah's fiction. Perhaps it is inevitable that the literary output of such a singularly overrepresented or "storied" place—with "tales piling up in every holler and cove," as one of Hannah's young narrators pertinently declares ("Evening of the Yarp" 97)—should be so anxiously self-conscious. Indeed, while I do not mean to over-determine the Faulkner comparison (a familiar move in Hannah scholarship), the basic premise of "Even Greenland," John the pilot triumphing in his extraordinary death, leaving the narrator to tell the tale, is very reminiscent of the character John Sartoris in Faulkner's *Sartoris,* suggesting the persistence of Faulkner's imposing presence as a textual "father" to new southern writers. Martyn Bone points out how Hannah has "endured comparisons to Faulkner" ever since he won the William Faulkner Award for his first novel, *Geronimo Rex* (1972), and later moved to Faulkner's home-town of Oxford, Mississippi, where he lived and taught (at the University of Mississippi) for almost thirty years (Bone, "Neo-Confederate" 85). Despite the impatience Hannah has expressed with interviewers' fondness for asking him "what it's like to be an heir to Faulkner, or what it's like writing in the shadow of Faulkner" (Hannah, "Interview" 185), this concept finds memorable expression in Hannah's semiautobiographical novel *Boomerang* (1989), whose narrator exclaims that with "[a]ll of Faulkner the great" behind them, "Christ, there's barely room for the living down here" (137–38). Writing after modernism and the provocatively named Southern Renaissance, unsurprisingly several literary critics have determined a Bloomian "anxiety of influence" intensifying in the literature of the South since Faulkner, who "looms large as the local equivalent of Bloom's 'Great Original'" (Bone, "Neo-Confederate" 85). Certainly, Hannah's protagonists, who are often aspiring authors or artists (of sorts), contemplate their craft in highly self-conscious ways, dramatizing their cognizance of the inevitably belated historical standpoint from which they speak.

Beyond the apparent oedipal desire of new writers to step out from the shadow of their forebears, the problem of originality in contemporary southern writing pertains also to the wider problem of authenticity at the heart of much postmodern theory. In the wake of poststructuralism and the "linguistic turn," new rebuttals of historicity and mimesis gained significant traction from the 1960s onward, with critics and authors alike becoming increasingly concerned with ideas about construction replacing essence. How can writers attempt to represent ideas about history, place, and identity authentically when these concepts have come under such radical scrutiny? In the wake of Fredric Jameson's infamous eschewal of the historical referent in the late twentieth century (*Postmodernism* 25), when what we know may be simply a function of the aesthetic practices by which it is narrated or constructed, we are forced to acknowledge the absence of any authentic foundation for history and place (as well as for politics and ethics, perhaps). In "Even Greenland," the pilot John articulates an analogous sense of departure from what we might term the mimetic South. He admits, "I've seen a lot, you know, but I haven't quite *seen* it" (32). His predicament suggests that in contemporary southern culture, representations can consume the realities they refer to, so that places cannot properly be *seen*. John's worry that his view is marred by its prior mediations ("There were eyes that had used it up") closely mirrors a scene in Hannah's short novel *Hey Jack!* (1987), whose narrator, Homer, encapsulates the problem of Jack Kirby's famous formulation of "media-made Dixie" when he declares that "the South has been pickled in the juice of its own image" (20). Where the South has been "created and consumed" (Bone et al. ix) in this way, we are confronted again with the (ethical) issue of construction versus essence.

This notion of the mediated, simulated, or "textual" (post-)South is set at distinct odds with prior—and enduring—notions of the South's imagined otherness relative to the broader nation. It may seem obvious that any conceptualization of regional should be conceived of as part of a wider national, transnational, and global context, within which an intricate web of temporal, geographical, ideological, cultural, and material milieus operate and where no self-contained or metaphysical South exists except in relation to this larger matrix. But what does this mean for a culture that since the 1850s has been devoted to creating and upholding a palpable sense of southernness that is as persuasive as it is acutely aware of its own contingency and fearful of its own impending demise? In his 1995 survey of contemporary American regional identity, *All Over the Map: Rethinking American Regions*, Edward Ayers concluded that "from its very beginning, people have believed that the South was not only disappearing but also declining, defined against an earlier South that was somehow more authentic, real, more unified and distinct" (69). Susan Van D'Elden Donaldson maintains that "epitaphs for Dixie [. . .] are as old as the region itself" (132),[1] and Scott Romine substantiates that "surely no region, or culture, or nation, or place—whatever the South is—has been more often subjected to premature eschatology" (*RS* 1). The South (like the American West) is a region that has been mythologized and countermythologized for more than a century and a half, both locally and as part of broader understandings of American nationalism. It remains to this day a space for Americans to seek out "authentic" culture (to deploy the title of W. Fitzhugh Brundage's contribution to Bone et al.'s *Creating and Consuming the American South* [28]); at the same time, it is the stuff of legend, where (tall) tale-telling is rife and fact and fiction are often interchangeable. With such anxious trepidation of the production, consumption, and concomitant erasure of physical spaces like Greenland or Mississippi, the quandary of legitimate authorship raised by Hannah's self-reflexive narrators becomes a succinct expression of several issues within modern southern studies and an important window onto problems that have long accompanied the idea of (narrating or historicizing) the South.

Mark J. Charney, the first of only two critics to produce a single-author monograph on Hannah to date, recognized this self-reflexive quality in Hannah's writing when he aligned the stories of *Captain Maximus* with a mode of writing Raymond Federman had termed *surfiction* in 1975 (Federman 3, qtd. in Charney 70). Today this kind of writing is more commonly called *metafiction*, which Patricia Waugh defines as a style of writing that explores "a *theory* of fiction through the *practice* of writing fiction" (2). The most memorable encapsulation of this issue in Hannah's fiction comes from the story "Uncle High Lonesome" (1996), whose nostalgic middle-aged narrator ruminates on 1940s Mississippi as an imagined golden age of mimetic simplicity: "You got what you saw more, [. . .] and there was a plainer language then" (222). His words neatly capture a withdrawal from traditional conceptions of how language is able (or not) to represent. In the absence of some imagined lost referential simplicity, writers began to acknowledge with increasing candor the ways in which ideas of the real are linguistically determined, introducing a radically heightened sense of the politics of representation in which questions of authenticity become principally textual ones. Metafictional theory is integral to the larger paradigm of postmodernism; both can be understood as a specific cultural response to a contemporary sense of textual contingency, a crisis of mimesis in which, as Linda Hutcheon writes, all "reality" becomes narrative, a "form of saying" (*Narcissistic Narrative* xiv).

Here, a paradox emerges within metafiction, which remains a referential genre at the same time that its texts self-consciously subvert their own claims to authenticity by acknowledging that language is fundamentally incapable of "passively reflecting a coherent, meaningful and 'objective' world"

(Waugh 3). This tension plays out in much of Hannah's writing, inviting us to contemplate how our ideas about reality—and about the South—may be inextricable from what Mark Currie calls the systems of "referential illusion" (5). Hannah, of course, is a legatee of a tradition of American postmodernist fiction that goes back to Donald Barthelme and Thomas Pynchon in the 1960s and includes Robert Coover, John Barth, William Gaddis, Don DeLillo, Richard Powers, and Philip Roth, among others. We cannot ignore the impact of this tradition on Hannah's work, which uncompromisingly questions the relationship between word and world as well as the distinctions between fiction and the material world that fiction appears to represent. Certainly, Hannah challenges the limits of our interpretative competence; he presents scenes that profoundly unsettle conventional notions of authenticity and reality.

As much as Hannah's writing co-opts an interest in the politics of representation and the problem of authenticity that is very much of its time, it must be noted that the stories that follow are principally about the telling of the *South*. Here, the self-consciousness of Hannah's storyteller-narrators serves to illustrate the problem of postsouthern writing as a form of reference, taking an interest in the modes of production and their effect on an imagined audience and in the ways that texts and simulations can constitute truth or reality in the absence of metaphysical notions of these concepts. The cultural practice of storytelling in the South—"legending" as one character memorably calls it in the story "Evening of the Yarp: A Report by Roonswent Dover" (93)—is often directly associated with dissembling in Hannah's work, suggesting a phenomenon that has its origins in an established history of mythmaking and fabrication that long predates our attributions of the loss of (southern) authenticity to any decisive historical turn.

Hannah writes about writing about the South as a discrete region and a literary referent in ways that acknowledge the complex interaction between thinking about the region both as a sociospatial reality and as a uniquely storied place, the product of narration, mythology, and an attendant set of evolving fictions and ideas. The questions of reference accompanying postmodern writing can usefully be applied to our literary representations of the region (how is the South figured as a fiction, in fiction?), which cannot pretend to reflect a stable, coherent, or monolithic subject. Hannah's postmodernity should not be conceptualized simply in relation to other postmodern American authors of the late twentieth century, therefore; nor, indeed, would he have welcomed such a comparison: in multiple interviews he shunned the labels *postmodern* and *metafictional* (as well as *southern*, in fact). Instead, broader concerns about referential authenticity are lent an important southern inflection when the subject of Hannah's literary representation—the South—is a specific geographical region located in a particular historical moment and begetting additional problems of its own.

Thinking about the South as narrated or constructed pertains to thinking about America itself as an imagined community, in line with Benedict Anderson's ideas about "nation" as a social construct comprising subjects who must actively envision their membership (6). Apprehensions of "the South" and of "America" both have mythological origins rather than being underpinned by foundational or essential qualities that could be identified or that could have been lost (with the onset of postmodernity, for instance, if indeed we could historicize such with any real accuracy). While the search for the origin (Anderson uses *origins* in his title) of both nation and region is undoubtedly tricky, it is important to acknowledge that ideas about national or regional exceptionalism emerge, as does postmodernism, from specific sociocultural conditions. In the South's case, constructions of southern exceptionalism (occurring since the antebellum era) would increase in fervor in the post–Civil War Reconstruction era. The most influential—and the most problematic—was of course the Agrarians' role in shaping modern southern studies and white self-consciousness in the early twentieth century. The two definitive modernist texts of southern self-fashioning, Allen Tate and the Nashville Agrarians' *I'll Take My Stand* (1930) and W. J. Cash's *The Mind of the South* (1941), have underwritten decades of regional scholarship that seems duty-bound to interrogate Cash's formulation of southern distinction, where the South serves almost as "a nation within a nation" (Cash viii). This built a problematic foundation for subsequent scholars, who find themselves writing either in or against an established tradition of attempts to characterize the South and southerners as unique.

Since C. Vann Woodward's influential "The Search for Southern Identity" in 1960, scholars (including Woodward, though this has not always been properly recognized) have become rightly suspicious of the political agendas that continue to underwrite the idea of southern distinctiveness and of the reductive and often binarized mythologies such a paradigm creates: either of a fallen place steeped in (white) sin or of one that enjoys a premodern kind of lost (American) innocence. From the 1960s onward, critics have sought variously to expose the tendentious political roots of southern studies itself, a discipline that has been associated with rhetorical doctoring since Reconstruction, where Civil War and so-called Lost Cause narratives were manipulated by critics and politicians and turned into a mythology of southern exceptionalism. The mythology has proved hard to shake, despite the waning credibility of the white South's past "causes" and indeed of the very prospect of regional exceptionalism itself in a context of shifting geographical, cultural, and ideological boundaries. Contemporary cultural reproductions like *Southern Living* magazine, for example, a "lifestyle brand" that claims to "celebrate the best of Southern life [and] share authentic experiences and advance Southern culture" ("About Us"), carry alarming echoes of Tate and his contemporaries' anxious preservation of "the Southern way": one that is conservative, middle class, focused on "traditional" nuclear (and heterosexual) family values, and predominantly white.

Memory, an integral component of the self-professedly backward-glancing modernist South, is one of the most contested recent areas of an already divided field. James C. Cobb introduces his 2005 examination of southern identity with the acknowledgment that "be it real or imagined [. . .] the most common foundation of group identity is a shared sense of a common past" (*Away Down South* 6). Lewis P. Simpson's influential formulation of the postsouthern "closure of history" rests on his contention that a central aspect of Southern Renaissance writing, a preoccupation with "the mystery of history" whereby "the literary mind of the South [is] seeking to become aware of itself," no longer appeared to operate in postsouthern writing, which, in the critic's not-so-implicit view, had suffered as a result (268–69). Importantly, Simpson's understanding of the South's waning regionalism is framed in terms of its declining historical (hyper)consciousness, which he attributes directly to the loss of firsthand memories of the Civil War (Humphries ix). This speaks to the dampening of previously held beliefs that the Civil War was, as Simpson's contemporary John Pilkington put it, "the single most significant and symbolic event in the Southern past," such that "understanding the meaning of the South [. . .] and its present problems, must begin with the war" (356). Here, while the perceived diminishment of southern memory reflects broader concerns about historical crisis in the late twentieth century, once again it is lent both regional and material specificity. Such arguments fail, of course, to account for the fact that the Civil War was not the definitive experience for all southerners; narratives of white southern exceptionalism depicting the war as the defining feature of southernness reveal their considerable frailty when we consider the efficacy of their application to particular minority groups. To think about the war as a division of North and South, thereby augmenting a sense of southern regional distinction defined according to the South's alleged deviation from the North or the nation, is similarly to reduce the social and political non-uniformity of both regions.

If the past makes us who we are, how would we begin to conceive of a collective cultural memory in the South, real or imagined? Within the southern-distinction paradigm, palpable ironies and instabilities emerge in the notion of unified cultural memory when we view the region's inhabitants not only according to race (most obviously) but also according to factors such as gender, sexuality, and socioeconomic class. Nevertheless, constructions of an imagined community of defeated white southerners continue to inform contemporary southern politics, testimony to the metaphorical significance of memory and its role in shaping the ideological consciousness of specific cultural groups. We can observe this, for example, in the South's late-twentieth-century reversal from Democrat to Republican, or within the context of recent debates about the removal of Confederate iconography (the flag; Civil War statues) and the neoconservative backlash.[2] Such are the "culture wars" (Brundage, *Southern Past* 328) that have long raged over representations of regional history, where white wealth and power have traditionally enabled one version of history to become underwritten by official recognition, for example, in public memorial sites such as museums and monuments. Contested ideas about southern memory are important subcurrents in Hannah's writing, alerting us to the myriad meanings attached to any examination of southern identity in an expansive and mutable conceptual framework, notwithstanding the highly complex nature of sociocultural relations in the region today.

Despite critics' prolific and urgent efforts to eschew southern exceptionalism in contemporary southern literary, cultural, and historical studies, the persistence of the idea (if not the reality) of southern otherness has proved to be curiously static and enduring. This is apparent in Richard Grant's recent use of David L. Cohn's 1935 description of Mississippi—"A strange and detached fragment thrown off by the whirling comet that is America"—as the epigraph to his own 2015 travelogue, *Dispatches from Pluto,* suggesting that Cohn's words still resonate with contemporary experiences of the region. In this context, it is telling that the South's imagined distinction—and a feeling of being southern—should continue to exist for many. Some recent criticism, such as Christopher Lloyd's *Rooting Memory, Rooting Place* (2015), makes a case for the continuance of southern regionalism in the twenty-first century, using ideas about memory and imagined community in ways that place the region antithetically to Michael Kreyling's central contention in *The South That Wasn't There* (2010), that "the South" disappears as memories become disconnected from their origins, until the region exists only in its cultural "reproductions, narrations, and derivations" (Lloyd, *Rooting* 2–3). Lloyd maintains, conversely, that the South retains a "rootedness" (Ania Loomba's term) that the concept of the postsouthern and the attendant discourses of the global South and the New Southern Studies (discussed below) do not properly accommodate (2).

Indeed, while most contemporary regional scholars agree that regional differences are not intrinsic but constructed, that does not mean that we should stop paying attention to the discourses that have served (and continue to serve) to reify the South's imagined alterity and the ends to which they have done so. As Larry J. Griffin contends, "Each region in of the United States has a particular identity hewn from history and culture. Yet none is as distinctive as the American South, and none has been imbued with such historical weight [. . .] or afforded such metaphorical significance in its collective memory and mythological self-understandings" ("American South" 7). Most of us today would accept that the South's reputed otherness has been steadily adulterated over time, not only by the more obvious processes of globalization and late-capitalist homogenization of American regions but also by our own heightened awareness of the politics behind constructions of difference. Nonetheless, conflicting portrayals of the South, and of Mississippi in particular—the South's South, as it is still known—continue to hold sway, the state being portrayed both as the most backward, violent, racist, sexist, and homophobic[3] of all the southern states and as a "true old-timey" place with archaic graces and manners (Hannah, "The Ice Storm" 190). This is captured neatly in Joan Didion's recently published travelogue, which declares of Hannah's birthplace, Meridian, Mississippi, "It is a true earlier time" (43). Published in 2017 but written in 1970, Didion's notebooks capture the paradox (discussed herein) in which the "true" South is always already memorialized.

Even as the South's cultural borders become subject to increasing scrutiny, and despite widespread acknowledgments of the contingency of the South's distinction in both regional and national imaginaries, as well as the impossibility of any distinct or unified South existing below the Mason-Dixie line, the mythology of southern difference (notwithstanding America's own imagined exceptionalism on the world stage) continues to inform recent contemplations of the region and its people, while also resonating in global matters of cultural identity (such as trauma and memory studies), existing beyond the American South.[4] If we agree that the South remains recognizable in its strangeness, then surely our apprehensions of such must exist only in contentious or attenuated forms. This is not only in view of the worrying Agrarian origins of the concept of southern distinction itself, where ideas about a common southern identity were in fact reserved for a privileged class of southern whites. It is also, at the level sociocultural reality, when we consider the "proliferation of microSouths" (RS 15) that coexist within this not-so-singular region. Any conception of the collective South must include a plethora of individual Souths within it, including the various immigrant populations and subcultural groups (themselves incorporating ethnic, religious, political, sexual, and socioeconomic differences) that have settled in its particular locations. The South's plurality as much as its singularity has, after all, always existed, despite only receiving relatively recent and still limited critical acknowledgment.

In this context it is predictable that the difficulty of writing the South in postmodernist southern literature should find a parallel in the field of modern southern literary studies, which is similarly self-conscious, over-populated, and anxiously belated, building on the myriad attempts that have been made to define the South or southernness. As the *Atlantic* writer Benjamin Schwarz notes, "Even leaving aside the southern novelists, poets, and storywriters, since the 1850s not five years have passed without a major work seeking to explore, explain, justify, or condemn a region that the historian David Potter called 'a kind of sphinx on the American land'" ("The Idea of the South"). Between 1972 and 2001, Hannah produced eight novels and four short-story collections, with a fifth published posthumously in 2010, *Long, Last, Happy,* which includes short stories published in magazines and journals as early as 1964 as well as several new stories from the the first decade of the twentieth century that were uncollected at the time of Hannah's death in 2010. The years 1972–2001 span a significant era on the cusp of some crucial reformulations of what it is to "tell" about the region where

Hannah spent most of his life. This period witnessed an upsurge in critical interest in the South's plurality, characterized by the forces of globalization, hybridization, demographic shifts, (im)migration, cyberspace expansion, and the rise of a media-driven, late-capitalist culture, in whose light it is impossible to imagine the region as something singular, unified, or distinct—despite the manifold attempts (old and new) to construct and preserve its difference. This tension is captured in the anxiety Edwin Yoder tentatively voiced in his foreword to John Shelton Reed's indicatively named *The Enduring South: Subcultural Persistence in Mass Society* (1972): "The artist, journalist, or historian who ponders the South for a living must at times be haunted, as I am, by the fear that the regional 'differences' he traffics in are essentially obscurantist when you get down to it: elegantly so, it may be, but obscurantist all the same" (xv).

The problem of the "obscurantist" South, which had already plagued southern scholars for decades, would gain significant momentum in the latter years of Hannah's career. Partly in direct response to this issue, the late twentieth century saw the emergence of postregional studies, with eminent postsouthern scholars such as Bone, Romine, Kreyling, Matthew Guinn, and Fred Hobson questioning the very idea of regional authenticity or "southern" in its various forms, emphasizing its contingency on texts, mediation, and performance. Since the 1970s, southern scholarship has been largely focused on discourse, amid poststructuralist-informed rejections of an essential or distinctive South that operates (or perhaps even exists) beyond discourse. This is caught by the oxymoronic title of Romine's influential critique of southern authenticity, *The Real South: Southern Narrative in the Age of Cultural Reproduction* (2008). Works like Suzanne Jones and Sharon Monteith's *South to a New Place* (2002), Tara McPherson's *Reconstructing Dixie: Race, Gender, and Nostalgia in the Imagined South* (2003), or Jennifer Rae Greeson's *Our South: Geographic Fantasy and the Rise of National Literature* (2010) similarly explore how the South's narration has traditionally surpassed its material realities. As McPherson notes, the South is "as much a fiction, a story we tell and are told, as it is a fixed geographic space below the Mason-Dixie line" (*Reconstructing* 1).

It is worth acknowledging here that in the early twenty-first century the material developments of global culture were also affecting regional studies beyond the South. William Handley and Nathaniel Lewis's *True West: Authenticity and the American West* (2004), for example, a critical examination of the elusive "true" West, closely anticipates Romine's interrogation of the "real" South. Krista Comer succinctly encapsulates the sentiment of both disciplines with the declaration that "there can be no such thing as western authenticity. There can be no defensible, insider, regional discourse, [. . .] no final claim on what counts as westernness" (*Landscapes* 5). It seems that western studies, like southern studies, has experienced an identity crisis in line with Edward Casey's anticipation, in 1997, that "the fate of place" in a national and global context had "disappeared 'almost altogether'" (x). Simpson's infamous renaming the field of modern southern studies "postsouthern" in his provocatively titled essay "The Closure of History in a Postsouthern America" (1980) would mark a key turning point after which the efficacy of "South" and "southern" as meaningful conceptual scales (to borrow Bone's title phrase) was put under increasing pressure by postregional scholars. Disputes over what defines a distinctive South—when did it become, and stop becoming, distinct, and who has the power to decide?—prompted Hugh Holman in 1983 to appeal to future southernists for a greater appreciation of the South's pluralism with his famous declaration, "No more monoliths, please!" (xviii). The southern-distinctiveness dispute continued to gain purchase into the twenty-first century, with Barbara Ladd's special issue *Critical Survey* article "Dismantling the Monolith: Southern Places—Past, Present, and Future" (2000) responding to Holman's charge by undermining the idea, previously taken for granted in Ladd's view, that southern literature is "grounded in 'a sense of place'" (28). In similar vein, Bone associates Hannah's work "with the postsouthern turn in contemporary fiction" (Bone, Introduction xiv), when authors and critics turned their focus on the images and texts that inform our idea of a sense of place, rather than any essential sense of what that region really *is*, amid what Bone tentatively dubs "the social reality of 'place(lessness)' in a late-capitalist post-South" (*SOP* x). Bone makes this association despite the staunchly southern and at times self-dramatizingly parochial setting of Hannah's stories.[5]

The absence of a foundational concept of the region, and its impact on postsouthern writing, is the subject of much scholarly debate, in which ideas about authenticity again are central. In *The Southern Writer in the Postmodern World* (1991), Hobson ponders whether the characteristics of southernness identified by what he would later call the "Rubin-Simpson Generation" of southern literary scholars (Hobson, *Southern Enigma* 97)—with their hallmark themes of history, memory, place, and community—still appear in contemporary fiction such as Hannah's. Kreyling contends that the Rubin generation of literary critics "viewed southern literature as an untroubled rendition of the 'facts' of southern life" (*Inventing* xii), and Hobson characterizes southern modernist literature incorporating a tangible consciousness of place, family, community, religion, and a preoccupation with the power of the past, positing that these characteristics are no longer apparent in postsouthern writing (*Southern Writer* 4–10, 34–39). Hobson claims that "what one finds in more recent novelists [such as Hannah] is a relative *lack* of southern self-consciousness" (*Southern Writer* 6–7), and Bone writes that the "model of Southern fiction as a literature rooted in fixed ideas of place, community, and history has reached the end of the line" ("Southern Fiction" 164).[6] Those writing in the postsouthern tradition are characterized by their radical (and often parodic) interrogations of the efficacy of Agrarian-influenced terminology (*South; southern; a sense of place*), leading Robert Brinkmeyer to identify "the diminishment of place [. . .] in the [southern] literary imagination" after modernism (26). If commitment to a distinctly local sense of place and (imagined) regional community was a marker of a modernist writer's southernness, then must contemporary writers after modernism—and therefore after the South—simply abandon the region, having recognized its anxious contingency, plurality, and hybridity?

Central to such debates is the implication that postmodern aesthetics, which interrogate ideas of authenticity by stressing their textuality or contingency, not only lack a sense of place but are creatively wanting or even exhausted. This finds expression in Hannah's short story "Nicodemus Bluff," whose narrator, Harris Greeves, explicitly evokes the words of the character Shreve in Faulkner's *Absalom, Absalom!* when he ponders, "Why do people live here at all, I ask. They must know this is a filthy, wrong, haunted place. Even the trees that are left look wrong or wronged, beat up." He proceeds to deduce that "[t]here are no stories of any merit to come out of this place" (364–65). These words capture the ostensible fatigue both of a sense of place (in this postsouthern landscape even the trees look somehow unnatural or "wrong") and of southern storying, which is comparably depleted in value. Whether intentionally or not, Hobson's analogous early arguments for the attenuated state of postsouthern writing recall Simpson's more open condemnation of the post-1960s literary imagination, in which he lamented the passing of the Southern Renaissance, extolled as "the epiphany of the southern literary artist" (Simpson, "Closure" 268–69). If the literary works of the Southern Renaissance are established as the "Great Original" against which new southern writing must (unfavorably) be measured, with the existence or lack of a sense of place becoming an implicit marker of a southern writer's esteem, what can this mean if the southernness of the modernists' writing—which may be inextricable from the Agrarians' conservative agenda—was nothing more than a myth? The (ethical) problem of authenticity in southern literary studies thus reveals a concomitant problem of aesthetic value: if a sense of place is declining, can new southern literature be as venerable as its earlier modernist forms?

Kreyling's vision of postsouthern literature is informed by Hutcheon's concept of postmodernist parody, a mode by which new writers can "liberate themselves from the burden of literary history," as Bone put it ("Neo-Confederate" 86–87), by making intertextual, parodic reference to prior works. Bone characterizes Kreyling's concept of postsouthern parody as "a literary technique that, in the (post)southern context, liberates contemporary authors like Barry Hannah, Harry Crews, and Reynolds Price from a Faulknerian anxiety of influence (usually imposed on them by literary critics)" (*SOP* 43). This characterization rebukes Hobson's "theory of influence" in postsouthern literature by demonstrating how "actively postsouthern" texts knowingly reinterpret or rework modernist (and specifically, Faulknerian) literary traditions (Kreyling, "Fee, Fie" 4, 11–12), resisting modernist methods to establish their own postmodern aesthetic ground. Guinn's *After Southern Modernism* (2000) identifies nine then-recent authors (including Hannah) who establish themselves as actively postsouthern by self-consciously eschewing the "familiar [modernist] formula" (162). While Guinn notes that Hannah, unlike many of his peers, continues to write about the Civil War (e.g., in the story "Bats Out of Hell Division," one of Hannah's most frequently discussed works), he argues that this is done in a manner that the modernists "would hardly have condoned," bringing "a new irreverence to this sacrosanct topic, an iconoclastic interpretation of history that inverts the conventions of Lost Cause mythology even as his pyrotechnic prose style wreaks havoc on the reader's a priori expectations of syntax. For Hannah, the War does not serve the modernist function of ordering the present. Instead, it fully partakes of contemporary anarchy and futility; its very appeal lies in its status as the apotheosis of these qualities" (163).

For some, including Thomas F. Haddox, new aesthetics that parody and are therefore "parasitic" on the past invite suspicion. This is not only insofar as the "recycling" of prior artifacts amounts (perhaps) to a "falling off" from more estimable earlier aesthetics but also where being beholden to the past might reveal an implicit desire to preserve the "old" ways such writers purport to detach from (568); Hutcheon identifies a similar paradox of postmodern parody, which simultaneously "legitimizes and subverts that which it parodies" (*Politics* 101). Kreyling concludes more optimistically that *postsouthern* has been "an enabling word," akin to *postmodern,* that encourages subversive rethinking of the efficacy of the foundational terms *South* and *southern* (*Inventing* 153–55), but Bone insists that "postsouthern literature should not be hermetically sealed in some hyperreal hall of self-reflexive non-representations. [. . .] Instead, postsouthern parody is valuable precisely because it emphasizes the extent to which the *southern* past, and southern place, have been defined primarily through literary mediations or 'images,' rather than sociohistorical or sociospatial reality" (*SOP* 46). Despite the tensions between texts and reality, for Bone there is a real South, one that can be identified beyond its representations, a South that is anterior to mere textuality and that it is vital to retain sight of.

Romine identifies a problem in this respect where Kreyling's formulation of postsouthern parody takes as the object of its focus not a "thing" but rather a style or method of representing that thing, in this case aesthetic simulations of the South. (We are reminded of John's conundrum in "Even Greenland," where his view is obscured by its prior mediations.) The result being that the postsouthern text, which becomes an image of an image, can perhaps only parody simulations or "previous imitations of place" rather than properly referring to the region and its history in any meaningful way (Romine, "Where is" 22, 23). For Bone—whose scholarship has consistently taken a "historical-geographical materialist approach to the capitalist production of place in the (post-) South" (*SOP* 47)—this raises cause for concern: "If postsouthernism is constituted purely at the level of self-reflexive textual representations or signs, one might ask whether postsouthern literature can *ever* refer to, let alone try to represent, the 'real South'" (*SOP* 43–44). If postsouthern aesthetics relate to the concept of place only at the level of simulacra and texts, then the possibilities for authentic regional reference are deeply problematic. Is there any vestigial sense of place left for contemporary southern writers to refer to beyond the residual images, reflections, and apparitions of places and their histories?

Despite his reservations about Kreyling's work, Romine's cogent interrogations of contemporary (poststructuralist) reformulations of place and narrative theory deploy an anxious terminology of post-place that, like Bone's, perhaps unintentionally establishes a problematic relationship between a "plainer" past and a more complex and therefore dislocated present (see Romine, "Where is" 24); indeed, even some recent southernist scholarship exhibits this tension. Ania Loomba's discussion of the tricky politics of the prefix *post* is helpful here, suggesting the two types of problematic "aftermath" that the term implies: a temporal "coming after" and an ideological "supplanting" (7). Formulations of a placeless post-South might indeed posit an implicit historical rupture, between a precapitalist South that had stronger (agrarian) ties to the land and was therefore much more firmly placed and a displaced contemporary capitalist one. To subscribe to a then new lexicon of placelessness is potentially to posit an unequivocal break whereby the South, as an economic and geographical entity, "no longer exists" (*SOP* 131)—which would imply that it once did exist, in some sense that is more real than now.

To some extent, this is an oversimplification of these arguments, but it reveals a central tension between real (past) and textual (present) Souths, one that is certainly worth our continued attention because it accounts for many of the divisions that have occurred since in southern academia, most notably with the emergence of the New Southern Studies (hereafter, NSS) in the early twenty-first century. Jon Smith, one of the loudest contemporary advocates of the NSS, accuses Bone's formulation of "the postsouthern sense of place" of unwittingly employing the Agrarian and Jamesonian "terminology of a decline narrative" that "allows conservatives in the field, the very scholars against whom Bone [. . .] argues forcefully, to keep talking (in rather bad faith) about a Grand Old sense of place, just prefixing 'postsouthern' to things when we get into the 1970s or so" (J. Smith, Review 373). Smith insists that the practice of othering the South relative to the broader nation continues to be harmful to modern American cultural studies. He claims that traditional (or not "new") southern studies has been unhelpfully informed by the progressivist and neoliberalist ideology of the baby-boomer generation of American studies scholars (*PA* 1, 63, 139). Smith believes that late-twentieth-century postsouthern scholarship in fact harbors the vestiges of a regional exceptionalism that "encourage[s] the continued demonization of the South as an aberrant, inscrutable region: a permanently available and discredited 'other' that stubbornly refuses to fit the American studies community's progressive agenda and is thus exiled to a place somewhere beyond the borders of the real, or typical, or desired, American experience," as Brian Ward explains ("Forum" 692). Smith thus concludes that "an American studies that continues to rely on such a convenient southern exceptionalism is, surely, no American studies at all," and he proffers the NSS as a means of rehabilitating the discipline (*PA* 124). While Kreyling's own skepticism toward the NSS has been evident at times in his later work, he expressed similar concerns in his influential *Inventing Southern Literature* (2005), which critiques our continued (politicized) use of "the South" and "southern" as scales of conceptual analysis that can underwrite ideas about regional difference in ways that perpetuate harmful 1930s ideology.

Such accusations fail to do justice to the nuance of Bone and others' conceptualizations of the South as a product of cultural reproduction that exists *within* a historical, geographical, and material reality (*SOP* 46), just as Kreyling's arguments for the loss of the South based on fading cultural memory—where "the real thing is always already a derivation, or a derivation of a derivation" (*Wasn't There* 194)—perhaps do not fully acknowledge the intrinsic difficulties surrounding the concept of a located, or "rooted" (to use Lloyd's term), cultural memory in the first place. I remain unconvinced by Smith's interpretation of the reactionary politics of postsouthern criticism. As the NSS departs (or attempts to depart) increasingly from questions of southernness even as constructed or "postsouthern," the fact that Smith and others continue to worry about the political ramifications of the designation *post-South* and its implied distance from some more authentic precedent suggests that the problems of earlier postregional studies are still highly relevant today. If we accept that the distinguishing "southern" features of "Rubin generation" literature were simply constructed as part of the Agrarians' conservative agenda, should we cease looking for them altogether? Or by abandoning such themes do we run the risk of invoking only abstract or relativist postmodern theory about mediation and the crisis of authenticity instead of properly engaged critical thinking about regional history and culture?

Since the new millennium, southern studies can certainly be characterized by a further series of fervent remappings of the region. Besides those cited above, these include (but are not limited to) Brinkmeyer's *Remapping Southern Literature* (2000), Helen Taylor's *Circling Dixie* (2001), Jon Smith and Deborah Cohn's *Look Away! The U.S. South in New World Studies* (2004),

Jon Smith's *Finding Purple America: The South and the Future of American Cultural Studies* (2013), Romine and Greeson's *Keywords for Southern Studies* (2016), and Bone's *Where the New World Is: Literature about the U.S. South at Global Scales* (2018). The sheer profusion of recent attempts to reconfigure our understandings of southern culture in a postregional climate suggests a pivotal moment in American cultural studies, a series of radical reconstructions, many of which seek to expose the invention that Dixie always was by emphasizing the South's fluidity as well as the benefits of an interdisciplinary, transnational, and nonbinary approach. Unsurprisingly, more recent critical thinking about the South has been attuned to the project of showing what it is *not,* to reject the (Agrarian) notion of a distinct or uniform South.

The turn of the twenty-first century witnessed what many consider to be a second paradigm shift in southern studies, the emergence of the above-mentioned "new" southern studies, so named by Houston Baker and Dana Nelson in "Violence, the Body, and 'The South,'" their contribution to the 2001 special issue of *American Literature,* which built on these late-twentieth-century revisions of the terms for the study of southern literature. (For what it's worth, Smith identifies the beginnings of the NSS in 1999, with Romine's *The Narrative Forms of Southern Community,* Deborah Cohn's *History and Memory in the Two Souths,* and Greeson's "The Figure of the South and the Nationalizing Imperatives of Early United States Literature" [J. Smith, "Response" 43].) The early NSS purported to "[surrender] its traditional claim to regional and historical distinctiveness, [find] a common language in public debates over globalization of identities, and [take] its chances in the dangerous, new, postmodern world where construction replaces essence" (Kreyling, "Toward" 16). It promised to situate the South in a transnational framework, asking how "globality" had shaped a region within a nation when that region had typically been defined according to its alleged distinction from the North, in apparent isolation from wider global forces (*NW* 3), while promoting "interdisciplinary approaches to the American South in comparative global or hemispheric frameworks that challenge narratives of regional exceptionalism" (B. Ward, "Forum" 692). Amid mounting tensions surrounding the concepts of collective cultural identity, uncontested historical memory and its documentation, and indeed historicity per se, this purportedly new discipline launched a thorough attack on familiar (modernist) constructions of the South and southern identity, promising "to exorcise the ghost of southern exceptionalism and add nuance to analyses of the region" (B. Ward, "Forum" 691).

As laudable examples of the NSS, Baker and Nelson cited a series of then-recent studies, including those by Patricia Yaeger, Richard Gray, Anne Goodwyn Jones, and Susan Van D'Elden Donaldson, which sought to address previously overlooked dimensions of the southern literary canon to reveal a reformulated sense of place that was not monolithic, which is to say homogenous, timeless, or, significantly, white, middle class, and male. Bone, Ward, and William A. Link's *Creating and Consuming the American South* (2015) is one of the more thorough recent attempts to examine our literary mediations of the South and to find productive common ground amid radical disputes over what "southern" means when it is embedded in a much broader global framework, encompassing also a plurality of hybrid Souths within the region. Other adroit attempts to articulate the heterogeneity that exists within any concept of the local include Jones and Monteith's *South to a New Place*, whose contributors discuss the various micro-Souths that have been systematically subjected to "the historical exclusion [. . .] from the category 'southern'" (28); Michael P. Bibler offers here an extensive (and nonexhaustive) list of the various coexisting demographics within the region, such as queer Souths, Latino Souths, swamp Souths, rural Souths, urban Souths, and mountain Souths (153).

These studies explore the possibilities for deploying the concept of southernness to thinking about other underrepresented cultures both in and beyond the region. For example, when we consider how the backward glance of Vietnamese Americans living in the South might turn more meaningfully toward Vietnam rather than the Civil War (Jones and Monteith 251–52); or where the Great Depression, rather than the Civil War, might represent the pivotal southern experience for those whom Sarah Robertson calls poor whites. Contemporary southern writers such as Rick Bragg and Dorothy Allison have explored this; take, for example, the peculiar verb phrasing of the title of Allison's 1992 novel, *Bastard Out of Carolina*, whose protagonist's coming not securely from but awkwardly "out of" her birthplace reveals the antipathy of poor whites to Agrarian-influenced myths of a grounded sense of place wrought from Civil War memory and a united white southern cause. Indeed, the relative exclusion of "Grit Lit" writing (about the "Rough South") from the mainstream southern literary canon and its critical reception reinforces Robertson's argument, in her latest book, *Poverty Politics* (2019), that "the hesitancy to engage with class has certainly been a defining aspect of much [southern] literary criticism" (xiii).

Contemporary studies of indigenous and immigrant cultures such as instructive work on the Native South by Melanie Benson Taylor, Eric Gary Anderson, Annette Trefzer, and Kirstin Squint mark analogous attempts to redress the conspicuous absence of indigenous southern voices from contemporary literary and cultural studies after overdue attention had, since the 1960s, started to be paid to the Black/white racial binary and the exclusion of African American accounts from mainstream southern cultural representations.[7] Such studies pursue a reconstructed, multicultural account of the region, acknowledging inhabitants' claims to (or denials of) southern spatiality, as well as the political purchase that such claims would afford or deny; Squint identifies here, for example, Eric Gary Anderson's problem of "the South before 'the South,'" which forces us to acknowledge the "layers of colonial history" that still work to erase Native presence from these sites (Squint 37). These efforts to expand our conceptualizations of "South" and to remedy the absence of different demographic accounts (an absence all the more conspicuous in a supposedly overrepresented culture) all speak to an ongoing (and now perhaps ironic) imperative to find more authentic ways of talking about the region.

Another related paradigm shift occurring during the early twenty-first century is characterized by Paul Jay as the "transnational turn" (1). More recent attempts by southern studies scholars to grapple with what Katherine Henninger calls the "death of the South" (10) can be partly attributed to their writing in the wake of this turn. Documenting the possibly irreconcilable tensions between material and discursive souths, Jay's influential *Global Matters: The Transnational Turn in Literary Studies* (2010) discusses the implications of transnationalization for literary theories that foreground the intrinsic correspondences between regional, national, and global. To conceive of a transnational America is to query its internal demarcations, such as the region. As Henninger explains, "As the South becomes increasingly 'Americanized'" and "America becomes transnationalized" (11), the concept of the region invariably is called into question. This call for southernists to reject southern distinctiveness and situate their work more usefully in relation to the global currents of history, commerce, and culture can be seen in the emergence of new journals such as *Southern Spaces* and *The Global South* or with new book series, including the University of Georgia's New South-

ern Studies and the University of North Carolina's New Directions in Southern Studies. In their preface to *Global Contexts, Local Literatures: The New
Southern Studies* (2006), a sequel of sorts to Baker and Nelson's 2001 article,
Kathryn McKee and Annette Trefzer argue that the NSS redefines southern
studies by foregrounding the global contexts of the purportedly local. In
the early twenty-first century, studies such as James C. Cobb and William
Stueck's *Globalization and the American South* (2005), James L. Peacock and
others' *The American South in a Global World* (2005), and Smith and Cohn's
Look Away! each attempted to articulate the present "new global phase [as]
a crucial turning point in the South," where "transnational and postcolonial
perspectives yield a field of study fundamentally different from previous approaches" (McKee and Trefzer, "Preface" 680).

This is not to say that neither transnational studies nor the NSS has been
consistent or coherent bodies of work, as the definitive article *the* (NSS) perhaps unhelpfully implies. Quite the opposite, in fact, appealing as the NSS
does for continuously new approaches to be brought to bear on the field. The
early NSS was largely hemispheric, which is to say almost entirely concerned
with the relationship between region and nation, but more recent work has
moved in other transnational directions, whose beginnings are difficult
to place and which some are now impatiently calling "old and redundant"
(Thompson 1083, qtd. in *NW* x). It has also attracted increasingly multidisciplinary methods, partly in an effort to establish more productive dialogues
between southern historians and southern literary and/or cultural studies
scholars. It is also important to remember that when talking about the *new*
southern studies, it is now some twenty years since Baker and Nelson called
for the abandonment of a southern exceptionalism that we were allegedly
still talking about; as Matthew D. Lassiter and Joseph Crespino would ponder in *The Myth of Southern Exceptionalism* as late as 2010, why does "region"
remain "the most popular but also the most imprecise scale of analysis" (12)?
In a field that is expanding and morphing as fast as it is arguing for the demise of its own subject, of course it is difficult to imagine what such a new
discipline would (continue to) look like. Yet these twenty-first-century developments certainly forced the question whether the infamous region had
been rendered finally redundant. Can we continue to talk about the South
at all when it is so imprecise? If we acknowledge its impreciseness, can we
reconstruct more meaningful ways of conceptualizing it? Compounded by
more recent proliferations of transnational and transcultural theory in the

early twenty-first century, the South's conceptual borders had demanded some thorough rethinking in the period of Hannah's career and after.

In the wake of these ideological shifts, Romine writes, "I believe that the idea of the South has been mostly a bad idea" ("MoonPie" 63), and Greeson admits, "I am not even sanguine that the notion of a monolithic South can be recuperated in U.S. cultural studies in a useful way" (*Our South* 10). Smith calls "the South" an "unhelpful scalar unit" ("Toward" 75) and, extending these more cautiously articulated suspicions of the idea, "a meaningless term, naming nothing but fantasies: either a great, 100-million-resident void at the heart of American studies, or a ridiculously strained attempt at identity politics at the heart of southern studies"; he claims that the NSS is therefore "neither a 'critical regionalism' (yawn) nor a rebellion against old southern studies (yawn), but an attempt to fix a broken American studies" (*PA* 22, ix). Extending Kenneth Warren's earlier declaration that "southernness, as a political concept, has rarely if ever portended a broader democratization of American life" (67), Leigh Anne Duck, editor of *The Global South,* famously pronounced in 2008 that we need a "Southern studies without 'The South'" ("Nonidentity" 329), words that have since come to encapsulate the NSS doctrine. The fissures in contemporary regional studies thus turn upon the hotly disputed question whether in today's transnational culture, America's southerly states can still be considered distinct enough to warrant continued critical attention using terms like *South* and *southern* without subscribing to a reductive or simplistic essentialism.

Part of the contention here has to do with ideas about white male southern nostalgia. The NSS came three years after Kreyling, in *Inventing Southern Literature,* had "melancholically declared the field dead," in Smith's view (J. Smith, "Response" 43). The frequency of academic southernists' convening to "kis[s] southern distinctiveness good-bye one more time" has been attributed to what Cobb and others have identified as the white South's apparently "uncontrollable urge to self-obituarize" (216). Smith views this as symptomatic of the boomer-influenced cohort's implicit reluctance to leave behind a nostalgic image of the South that perpetuates notions of white supremacy in American culture. Smith calls this "White Southern Melancholy" or "the crisis fantasy [. . .] about 'forgetting'" the "traditional" South (*PA* 34, 4), in which, supposedly, even seemingly progressive southernists (such as Ladd or Kreyling) inadvertently reinforce (Agrarian) exceptionalism by focusing on memory and not forgetting the past (*PA* 30). For those in the NSS camp, the worry is that simply acknowledging the South as a construct or an invention (as has happened from at least as early as the 1970s, for example, with Michael O'Brien's *The Idea of the American South*) does not properly undercut those aspects of southern studies that demand more radical overhaul. Drawing on Slavoj Žižek's conception of the "pure ideology" we gain by establishing our ironic distance from something (*End Times* 3), Smith contends that postregional discourse about the constructed South "has almost functioned to preserve [the complacencies of old southern studies] under the putatively hipper sign of the 'postsouthern,' where 'post' in practice denotes not 'after' but something like 'ironic and self-aware.' But an ironic approach to one's ideology does not detach one from it" ("Toward" 75). A problem emerges, perhaps, where the poststructuralist approaches that lend themselves very well to thinking about the South as a construct are prone to turn inward, thereby (potentially) fostering a political relativism that can be deployed in the service of conservative political agendas.

Recent scholarship from Smith, McKee and Trefzer, Duck, and McPherson reveals a concerted, even impatient move away from the poststructuralist approaches of the late twentieth century (indeed, those that informed the early NSS itself) because of the problems posed by highlighting the South's construction at the expense of the "real bodies" (J. Smith, "Toward" 75) upon whom the inequities of imperialism, globalization, and labor exploitation in the rise of industrialist capitalism have been and continue to be visited. For some historians, including O'Brien, "postmodern" literary scholarship lacks sufficient focus on the material contexts of history because it appears simply to favor ideas about how the South has been thought about (*NW* 19). Such thinking remains open to criticism from those skeptical about a postsouthern sense of place that exists in "purely textual form," whose literary output might, as Romine ponders, appear to turn inward and "dispense with reality all together" ("Where is" 23, 25). (Analogous charges have been leveled at the metafictional literary genre, unfairly in my view.) Such an exclusively textual South would exist perhaps only in its self-absorbed reflections. To counter this possibility of southern studies turning ineffectually inward by focusing on the symbolic or imagined South, several contemporary critics argue for sustained attention to what Bone (drawing on Paul Giles and David Harvey) calls "historical-geographical materialism," through which the contexts of "economic globalization, immigration, and the South's long [regional] history of labor exploitation" are revealed (*NW* x). These sentiments are echoed in McPherson's avowal that "our readings of southern culture need to be more materialist and less southern, pushing beyond representation and narrative to conditions of production and the flow of capital" ("Afterword" 320); or when Smith and Cohn described the NSS's attempt "to redirect the critical gaze of southern studies outward, away from the nativist navel-gazing that has kept mainstream southern studies methodologically so far behind American studies" (*Look Away!* 13).

Again, we can situate the developments of late-twentieth-century postregional criticism within the context of changing conceptualizations of authenticity in a postmodern moment. Lewis begins his interrogation of the postregional literary West by describing the relationship between authenticity and memory as a case where "authenticity is often freighted with the burden of the golden past, a nostalgia for an earlier age that seems, in retrospect, more real" (5). It is fallacious to construct the nostalgic past as more real than the present if authenticity is a quality that we attribute to places only in retrospect. Meanwhile, the elusive concept of authentic place, despite its known contingency, inevitably continues to occupy our thinking about regions, as Romine and Abigail Cheever have argued. Exploring the persistence of (southern) authenticity in the face of the dampening of American regions in a globalizing culture, Romine observes: "The U.S. South [has a] tortured and complex relation to contemporary economic pressures and to flows of culture that are increasingly global and dispersed in nature," while the South's "acute absorption and production of declension and progress as culture-stories" speaks to its "fraught and anxious relation [. . .] with authenticity" (*RS* 3). In a similar vein, Cheever claims that the culture stories constituting places like the South are intrinsically preoccupied with "the concept of authenticity," which becomes "an index to and an instantiation of this culture's negotiations of the changing terrain of the self and its constitution" (18). These invaluable studies come at a critical moment in our thinking about American regionalism and of the concept of the region more broadly conceived, where a vital tension emerges between the idea of regional authenticity on one hand (the distinctive South, of which nostalgia for its demise appears to be a crucial part) and, on the other, the weakening of this notion in a contemporary global culture that threatens the very concept of authentic place and indeed authenticity itself.

The nostalgic search for authenticity has certainly played a key role in the white South's own mediation, which has been integral to ongoing disputes about southern distinctiveness and about the disappearance of the putative region. A sense of the contemporary decline of authentic places is lent memorable expression in Hannah's work. We can observe this in the short story "Rat-Faced Auntie" (1993), whose elderly character Hadley laments the passing of "Old Savannah" in the 1920s as an era "[w]hen men were realler" (176), anticipating the narrator's earlier cited yearning for "plainer" old times in "Uncle High Lonesome." Or in "Even Greenland," when John the pilot articulates a sense of tragic departure from better times past when he declares, "I haven't had a 'good time' in a long time. There's something between me and a good time since, I don't know, since I was twenty-eight or like that" (32). If it seems anachronistic that John should bemoan the dampened freshness of his (writerly) perspective at the age of only twenty-eight, then this phenomenon is apparently worsened in Hannah's last novel, *Yonder Stands Your Orphan* (2001), whose fictional Mississippian population is made up of "men and women nostalgic by age eleven" (40). Nostalgia, it seems, is an inevitable part of being white and male and southern in Hannah's stories, to the extent that Romine interprets *Yonder Stands Your Orphan* as "an elaborate meditation on the production and consumption of space," where "local consumption is dominated by the nostalgia industry" and its duplicitous construction of desirable "authentic" spaces ("Orphans All" 168).

In her afterword to *Creating and Consuming the American South*, McPherson tackles the problem of constructing southern authenticity by calling for the cessation of our "circling around Southern authenticity." Authenticity, she claims, is (possibly) as bad an idea as "the South" itself; she wonders whether "authenticity is something, like the Agrarians, that we shouldn't be talking about at all" (312). Similarly, if we choose to emphasize the South's phoniness, as something storied or constructed, is this to create a sense of departure from an implied authentic South, such that we are inadvertently perpetuating Agrarian nostalgia for its inferred loss? By the time of Hannah's last publication during his lifetime, in 2001, developments in the NSS had thoroughly divided scholars over whether to continue to incorporate *southernness* (as well as *authenticity*) in our critical vocabulary is to perpetuate a harmful mythology that we ought to have abandoned long ago. Earlier I cited Ayers, who sustained that apprehensions of the South's disappearance have circulated from the very earliest conceptions of thinking about southern regional identity, almost as a defining feature of the region and its critical reception. In such a pathologically nostalgic and powerfully me-diated culture as the South, it is difficult to imagine where subjects might find an unsullied and authentic sense of place, if indeed it ever existed. We might say that the South has always been "metafictional," in the sense that it was consciously created as a response to its own self-inferred demise.

In "Where is Southern Literature?" (2000), Romine asks whether the terms *southern* and *place* can endure in a postsouthern age that lacks "mimetic reference at the economic or ideological levels" (11), exploring the possibility that "postsouthern literature will become less real" or even hyperreal (23). This question is crucial, as it pertains to a tension between material and sto-ried Souths that accounts for the impasse whose effects have been reverber-ating in southern studies since the new millennium. The NSS's call for the removal of "the South" from the discipline is not to argue that the region has gone from being simply "post" to having disappeared altogether; it is more about stressing the overdetermined (and thus conceptually useless) nature of "the [singular] South" than about saying that it does not exist in some sense. Yet here, I think, is where the NSS's rebuking of post-1960s, discourse-focused criticism has become counterproductive. I would argue that such an approach can lose some of its critical purchase when it assumes that the con-cepts of locality, the South, and southern are synonymous with the *mono-lithic* region. Did late-twentieth-century postregional studies ever make such a claim, and do these concepts need to be abandoned to emphasize the globality of ostensibly local cultures and their literary productions? While neo-Agrarian images of "autochthonous, organic communities and fixed, defined societies" (*NW* 26) of course speak to a problematic white male nos-talgia and conservatism, and while the southern literary canon has tradi-tionally tended to marginalize certain social and ethnic groups in similarly contentious ways, attending to elements of the local in contemporary south-ern literature need not amount to the reification of the region.

I do not agree (with Smith) that self-reflexive acknowledgments of the constructed South cannot be politically subversive and enabling, nor that postsouthern literary studies cannot detach from prior ideology. To ac-knowledge the South's mediations, as self-reflexive writing inevitably does, is not simply to remove it as a meaningful historical referent or conceptual scale. In agreement with Bone as well as the majority of the contributors to *Creating and Consuming the American South*, I believe it is unhelpful to pro-pose that we can separate the storied and real Souths in any simple way, because how the South is narrated has very real sociopolitical consequences, for example, when culture stories are produced that authenticate monolithic versions of the region at the expense of other micro-Souths. Bone quotes Wimal Dissanayake and Rob Wilson's assertion that "the local need not embody a regressive politics [. . .] where locality becomes some backward-gazing fetish of purity to disguise how global, hybrid, compromised, and unprotected everyday identity already is" (Wilson and Dissanayake 5, qtd. in *NW* 26). As Paul Giles declares, "Transnationalism [. . .] is not the anti-thesis to regionalism but crucial to its constitution: it is precisely the ways in which any given region configures itself in relation to the world around it that determines its internal sense of its own identity" (Giles 222, qtd. in *NW* 26). Bone concludes that while to some extent "the South" is an unhelp-ful scalar unit (Jon Smith's words), "ultimately, (new) southern studies and (transnational) American studies would benefit from a fuller mutual under-standing of how [southern literature] represent[s] both region and nation as inextricable from the capitalist world-system that, circa 1981 or so, we came to call 'globalization'" (*NW* 214). To continue to question the efficacy of the concepts South and southern (rather than to deny their continued utility after the NSS) can tap into (and problematize) the real-world systems from which these concepts come.

Hannah's work may be postregional, but it is less obviously "global," at least insofar as ideas about global labor exchange and migration are not at the forefront of these often seemingly "parochial" stories. This, in fact, is part of my point. While I am not locating Hannah in relation to (or against) the NSS in terms of the global bent of his work, his fiction offers a produc-tive terrain between the local and the global in ways that usefully anticipate the more recent turns in (new) southern studies. I agree (with Bone) that we should pay attention to the dialectical relationship between regional, na-tional, and transnational as scales of analysis, and not simply abandon the concept of regionality when acknowledging that the old ways of thinking about regional distinctions are no longer tenable. By asking critics to aban-don ideas about southernness (as nostalgic fantasies or constructs), the NSS begets the same ethical problems that it identified in earlier postregional scholarship, by suggesting a tangible break from a regionally distinct history of labor relations that, as Bone points out, continues to resonate today (*NW* 24–26). (The charge leveled at "traditional" southern studies, that it focuses on and has not forgotten the continuities between old and new Souths, rests on the same ground.) Bone argues that while "the present era of capitalist globalization and mass immigration constitutes a transnational 'turning point' for (the study of) the South," such phenomena must still be considered as "continuous with regional histories of exploitation": while "the South" may be a flawed and contradictory scale of analysis, "ever more intwined with rather than distinct from local, national, and global scales," we must still attend to the local in literary representations of the South (*NW* 26).

McKee and Trefzer have usefully complicated the distinctions between regional, national, and global, asking, "What happens when we unmoor the South from its national harbor, when it becomes a floating signifier in a sea of globalism? How does the South participate in the global networks of culture and economy? How have the South's culture and history always already been global? What are the global gestures in literary texts that we were formerly interpreting as regional or national issues?" ("Preface" 678). Part of my similar contention here, and of my arguments for Hannah's significance, is that some constructions of postregional culture do not properly account for the ways that any antecedent, "conventional" sense of place will have been similarly contingent and *always already* global. It is not the South's regional authenticity that is diminishing; rather, our *interpretations* of local and global have changed (and are continually changing) in ways that suggest that our former conceptualizations of what is regional (or national) were never so localized or contained. Certainly, we can note the difficulty critics have had in pinpointing precisely when the pivotal transitions to a New and then post-South occurred. Likewise, the proposed turns into a newly transnational culture and an accompanying "new" mode of scholarship (without "the South") are themselves just points in a constantly reformulating continuum of ideas.

Attempts to historicize the South's transition from placed to placeless can be upset in various obvious ways. For instance, while early postregional criticism may be attributed to the collapse of the referential South coincident with the 1960s linguistic turn, itself informed by the cultural commodifications and new cybertechnologies that contribute to our culture of signs and simulations, in fact the waning of the South was already a concern in the earlier 1940s, when capitalist consumer economy replaced rural agriculturalism.[8] Further, while the postbellum transition to the so-called New South saw the first upsurge of nostalgia for the *Old* South—with the Agrarians' attempted preservation of the "traditional" character of a declining (white) culture necessitating the systematic exclusion of African Americans and other key ethnic groups—concurrently, the end of the Civil War coincided with the first rise of the South's industrialization, "northernization," or Americanization. This is somewhat ironic, because these material changes mark the beginnings of a "modern" phenomenon we can associate with the late-capitalist culture scrutinized in the late twentieth and early twenty-first centuries and in our more recent interrogations of global material cultures. This suggests that the challenges of the postregional South were in place far earlier than has been typically acknowledged.

This difficulty of placing the origins of southern authenticity, by which to designate contemporary writing as southern or otherwise, pertains usefully to the problem of historicizing the moment of the South's alleged removal and to questions about whether to continue to conceptualize the South is to subscribe to nostalgic melancholy for its putative loss. Ayers, Romine, and Van D'Elden Donaldson's earlier mentioned proclamations of the South's demise from its very beginnings make apparent that the problem of its disappearance has always accompanied thinking about the South, and not just in the shadow of recent postregional criticisms. This explains the complexity of locating the moment of the South's withdrawal, a process that has proved to be curiously enduring, with critics well into the twenty-first century still announcing their efforts to dispel the myth of southern exceptionalism. The challenge of historicizing the South's disappearance is caught in Benjamin Schwarz's earlier cited words: the issue of defining the real South is not simply a postmodern problem but has preoccupied those writing about the region since at least as early as the 1850s, and therefore it cannot be attributed to the respective postsouthern and transnational turns.

Perhaps the slippery concept of when exactly the South "turned" postsouthern can be most thoroughly complicated when we consider the history of the Old South and its participation in colonial practices already operating on a transatlantic scale. Recalling McKee and Trefzer above, Charles Raegan Wilson asks, "Does a postmodern South equate to a postsouthern one? [. . .] The South, after all, emerged during the same historical moment we now associate with the emergence of modernity itself, within an already global network of commerce, capital, and labor that linked the entire Atlantic rim and found its great ideological engine in the colonial plantation" (145). The cultural practice of colonial slave labor has its own roots in British imperialism and the global exchange of human capital, as W. E. B. Du Bois, in his perceptive study "The African Roots of War," acknowledged as early as 1915. David L. Carlton and Peter A. Coclanis's *The South, The Nation, and The World* (2003) discusses southern economic development and confirms that like the rest of British North America, the South was "born capitalist," with the North-South divide also beginning as early as the late seventeenth century. Again, this upsets neat distinctions between the supposedly distinctive premodern economy of the South and the modern North. As Ladd argues in "Dismantling the Monolith," the "impact of colonial experience in the Deep South has been and continues to be experienced" in a much wider web of national and transnational influence than previous understandings of the South as "marginal" or singular have acknowledged (34). It is possible to attribute the nascent beginnings of the end of the South—and the beginnings of the global post-South, though this language was not yet available—not only to the American Civil War and the end of slavery in the South but also to the antebellum Slave South and its place in modern transatlantic commercial exchange. In these ways the South has been "global" always, not just in recent understandings, just as contemporary studies of the American West have acknowledged the ways in which the Old West was already "new" (Handley and Lewis 5). Distinctions between old and new pertain largely to our interpretations of different historical moments (including anxieties about the present predicaments that we seek to attribute to particular turning points); the global new has always existed, whether people were articulating it or not. Again, we might ask how far back we can go in pursuit of an authentic origin from which we believe we have tragically departed.

Hannah's stories make a conceptual problem of the southern backward glance by revealing how regional cultures have been thought to diminish at key moments, each of which locates the authentic (or not-post) South differently. The process of regress becomes vertiginous, extending all the way back to prebiblical origins in some stories. In having these stories derive a significant part of their drama from questioning when exactly the pivotal removal of "South" can be thought to have occurred, Hannah makes a vital contribution to contemporary postregional theory, which has been similarly preoccupied with how, when, and whether the distinctive South has disappeared as a meaningful category of analysis. Here, my claims about the political value of Hannah's work are, broadly speaking, that it challenges simple ideas about the decline of regionalism in postsouthern literature by simultaneously refuting the notion of waning historical consciousness in the pu-

tatively disappearing South (with a coterminous decline in southern literature) as well as the very prospect of definitive place or history. These stories'
focus on forms of white male southern nostalgia can be usefully deployed in
observing the danger in southern studies of critical recourse to visions of a
more authentic, nostalgic past.

Born in 1942 in Meridian, Mississippi, Hannah grew up in the small town
of Clinton, near the state capital, Jackson. He studied in Mississippi and
Arkansas and taught at several southern universities, including South Carolina, Alabama, and finally, for many years, the University of Mississippi, in
Oxford, Mississippi, where he remained until he died. Hannah's stories are
situated almost exclusively in the South: in the Deep South and the Sunbelt
states, in the suburbs and small cities, in the Mississippi Delta, and (once)
in the Ozark Mountains. Donald Noble, the first to publish a scholarly article on Hannah, in 1982, commends Hannah's focus on the "relatively unused
material" of "'Sunbelt' characters, not Old South or New South people," in
testimony to the fact that Hannah is not, in Noble's view, "trying to recreate
some traditional Southern literary landscape" (38) such as we would find in
textual precursors like Margaret Mitchell, Walker Percy, Eudora Welty, or
Peter Taylor (as well as Faulkner). With his voice-driven narratives in the
mode of Mark Twain's tall tales, as Brad Vice points out (19), Hannah paints
a new kind of Southscape by locating in specific sociospatial contexts previously underrepresented micro-Souths that depart from prior literary representations of the region, while also recalling older modernist formulae so
as to thoroughly complicate static conceptualizations of Old, New, Sunbelt,
modern, and postmodern Souths.

I am not suggesting that to be called southern, literature must choose
the South as its fictional locale; Hannah's writing upsets this simple de-
marcation of the regional. However, with the exception of *Never Die* (1991),
Hannah's "postmodern Western," as Mark Graybill called it ("Peeping Toms"
120), the careful southern geographical placing of Hannah's stories marks a
key tension that emerges in the author's work, between the region he valorized and refused to abandon as setting and subject and a growing sense
that regions in contemporary America are part of an increasingly plural and
transnational culture that changes the concept of the region dramatically.
Hannah has proclaimed in interview that "I couldn't exist without the South.

My voice couldn't start without the South that I adore. It's wretched. I know almost everything that's wrong with the South, and I also know everything glorious that's never really spoken about in *Southern Living*. Just the familiar ease with the earth is never spoken of. I mean, I think Southerners [. . .] move with the earth better than other people, but they don't need to write it" (Hannah, "A Conversation" 227). We have already seen such claims to "natural" southern spatiality being undercut in Hannah's own work (recall Greeves's suspicion of the southern landscape in "Nicodemus Bluff"), just as southerners, it seems, *do* feel compelled by a need to write about the South in Hannah's stories. Such tensions help to illustrate my contention that Hannah's fiction is usefully situated between southern and postsouthern.

In a postregional culture that seems obliged to acknowledge the absence of an authentic sense of place, Hannah's fiction certainly performs a compelling interrogation of regional authenticity. But it does so in a manner that acknowledges how the region's unique properties *can* be articulated or enacted, in ways that might yet render its literatures distinctively southern at a time when *southern* was such a highly contested term. For example, as if in direct reply to the charges above, the story "Through Sunset into the Racoon Night" (1996) features an aspiring author, Royce, the most self-conscious narrator in the collection, who is deeply preoccupied both with the nature of his native South as a region and with his own status as a writer of regional literature. Minrose Gwin contends that "[s]outherners have always maintained that place makes us who we are and that the stories we tell ourselves about 'home'—the places we come from—are the means through which we negotiate identity" (437). In a fitting parallel Royce ponders, "I have lately thought about my birth place, St. Louis, and what is wrong there" (110). Royce's belief that "[e]minent creeps," a demographic in which he includes himself, "have issued from there as by some necessity of environment" (110) reveals that his contemporary vision of the South is just as perceptibly bound to the region's unique geography and history, therefore offering a strong claim in favor of the persistence of the idea (if not the reality) of a tangible and distinctive South.

The imagined "necessity" or inevitability of the regional environment expressly informs the character Royce's own writing ("Why else am *I* writing?"), which he describes as a "willingness to go public with hideous disease" (112). Hannah's tales, which William Grimes calls "darkly comic" and which are at times absurdist, violent, and grotesque, are full of self-confessed creeps and "losers" like Royce who both perpetuate and poke fun at the tradition of southern "weirdos" telling stories about themselves ("Through Sunset" 123). While we know that Hannah rejected being labeled Faulkner's successor, echoes of the comic grotesque are integral to his contemporary take on the Mississippi tall tale—just as Hannah's own influence can be observed in the stories of Charles Portis, Mark Richard, George Singleton, Lewis Nordan, and Jack Pendarvis, who, as the new novelist Jamie Kornegay argues, continue to "take the perversity, humor, and outrageousness of Southern Gothic and shape it into something alive and fantastic which speaks to the current situation of the South." In "Through Sunset," Royce concludes that "[p]laces *do* make people" (111), and the South of Hannah's stories certainly appears to make storytellers who are inherently anxious about the efficacy of their craft—such was John and the narrator's quandary in "Even Greenland." This apparent compulsion to continue to talk about the "diseased" South comes even though Hannah's storytellers, surrogates for his own authorship, are acutely aware of their own place in an anxiously overrepresented white culture where contemporary identity feels like something of a belated historical footnote to the past.

The South's heavy bearing on both subjects and writers alike is a key trope in Hannah's short novel *Ray*, whose publication in 1980 neatly coincides with Simpson's opposing arguments for the diminishment of regional historical consciousness in postsouthern fiction. Like Royce, the eponymous Ray laments that the problem for contemporary southerners (Royce's speculative "what is wrong there") is not the closure of history or the amnesiac lack of cultural memory but its crippling abundance. Using language that could have come directly from Faulkner's Gavin Stevens in *Requiem for a Nun*, Ray declares, "I live in so many centuries. Everybody is still alive" and "There is no forgetting with me" (41, 51). Time is a slippery concept in Hannah's fiction just as in Faulkner's, with memory acting in curiously anachronistic ways, as if this were still a defining feature of the southern imaginary. Again, this is caught by Didion's identification of the "time warp" that is still operative in the South, where "the Civil War was yesterday, but 1960 is spoken of as if it were about three hundred years ago" (104). Noble's characterization of Hannah's unique style—"Not only is there no conventional narrative flow, there is no regard for *time*, much less chronology" (43)—neatly articulates this sense of (modernist) historical anomaly enduring in postsouthern writing.

Hannah's decision to continue placing his fictions firmly in the South is matched, then, at the thematic level, where a tenacious and imposing sense of place is revealed. Such fiction stages "southern" themes and stylistic devices that invite interpretation as recognizably modernist, but these are creatively reworked in ways that bridge the two periods and complicate neat distinctions between them. This notion, that the idea of the South survives in postsouthern literature even while it troubles the very notion of an authentic sense of place remains unacknowledged in some early contemplations of the distinctions between modernist and postmodernist southern writing, though it is essential to my arguments here. The productive coexistence of regional and textual in Hannah connects to my core thesis that a kind of aesthetic authenticity—as well as a form of the South—endures, even though (or precisely because) his fiction foregrounds the construction and narration of the concepts of the South and authenticity.

This book attempts neither to obituarize the distinctive South nor to reinstate or preserve it in any full or final way. I am not "judging" the authenticity of the South but rather exploring how the idea of authenticity is deployed in its cultural representations. I am less interested in evaluating the designations *authenticity* or *southernness* than in understanding the politicized forms of their applications. Thus, this book is an attempt to dislocate the putative origins of the South's demise by identifying those Hannah texts that convey a deliberate suspicion of the politics behind nostalgic ideological constructions of a once realer South in ways that subvert the declension narratives to which some of the stories might appear to subscribe. In part, my objective here is to show how Hannah's writing emphasizes the tensions implicit in the idea of an earlier golden age, a purer historical origin, whose loss becomes palpable only in retrospect. Such writing not only reveals the politics surrounding all constructions of the authentic South. It also suggests, in fact, the paradoxically heightened importance of regional authenticity at a time when the concept was scrutinized most. If the concept of the region has been dismantled in significant ways, then what comes after the South? This book attempts to explore what such an "after" would look like, partly to facilitate more productive responses to the fissures in contemporary southern studies.

Hannah's fiction has not received the close attention that it warrants in what remains a conspicuously sparse field of criticism despite the author's substantial output and wide (if still a little cultish) acclaim. While they are informative and valuable, the Hannah monographs by Mark J. Charney and Ruth D. Weston, *Barry Hannah* (1992) and *Barry Hannah: Postmodern Romantic* (1998), do not pay Hannah's writing the detailed attention required to uncover its vital place among postregional debates. Even Bone's instructive edited volume *Perspectives on Barry Hannah* (2007) is now also more than ten years in the past. It is my belief that only sustained close readings of individual stories can reveal the nuanced simultaneity of southern and postmodern in Hannah's writing, and this is the approach taken here. A degree of textual exegesis, which may seem forensic at times, will therefore be necessary to tease out the remarkable subtleties of Hannah's style and reveal the critical currency of this fiction and the important revelatory window it offers on a series of challenges within modern southern studies in ways that have not yet been properly recognized or appreciated. My arguments do not attempt to provide comprehensive "coverage" of Hannah's fiction; his writing is so dense, so richly intertextual and allusive (with many short stories not only approximating the author's shorter novels in length but also resonating with the complexity of much longer works), that this would be impossible. Instead, the following six chapters examine Hannah's postregional fictions in relation to a discrete conceptual paradigm, asking how Hannah situates the South in terms of categories such as language's referentiality, masculinity, history, nostalgia, storytelling, and ideas about aesthetics and performance.

Each chapter's line of inquiry poses a significant challenge to the concept of authenticity in ways that pertain not only to the historical moment of Hannah's writing but also to contemporary debates over the continued efficacy of regional studies. In order to encourage some important rethinking of the (literary) South in ways that are useful beyond the temporal confines of Hannah's career, the stories discussed herein are identified for their value in reconceptualizing those issues in recent southern studies where a standoff is imagined between regional (southern) and global (postmodern) that continues to divide scholars in the field. While the key strands of my analysis center on textual and aesthetic concerns rather than socioeconomic or political ones, exploring the textual elements of (post)southern authenticity is integral to thinking about its broader political significance, if we agree that texts are inextricable from the wider sociopolitical conditions that produce them. My arguments for Hannah's significance as a postsouthern writer may begin at the level of close reading, but the value of his work emerges in the broader currents and issues in modernism and postmodernism, vis-à-vis the South and southern writing, in which his creative formulations of the region are situated. Textual and aesthetic concerns take precedence herein, not to downplay the material realities but to show how Hannah interrogates ideas about authenticity by stressing their textuality, even as throughout his work we see the authenticating potential of performance. It is not my contention that this fiction (or the South) can be finally *understood* (the crude reflective model) but rather that thinking about the post-South in relation to specific cultures of authenticity (to use Cheever's title phrase) facilitates compelling ways out of the simple impasse that postregional theory appears to offer between southern and postmodern, perhaps partly in terms of ideas about creative agency and the legitimized performance.

This concept, akin to Cheever's paradox of the real phony, is evident in Hannah's story "The Ice Storm" (1996) when a fraudster called Hood enacts the persona of fallen artist-hero by donning cloak, cane, and beret in what the narrator observes to be "a lot of costume for early fall" (192). Despite its flagrant charlatanism, Hood's ersatz performance stimulates the grudging admiration of the narrator, an aspiring but defeated artist himself, who admits upon beholding the theatrical spectacle, "I'd had in mind one of the great wounded artists of the fin de siècle" (192). Hood, whose "art" really consists in making pornographic films full of "lively girls" (191), has suffered mild injuries in a domestic accident that he allows people to think he sustained in Vietnam. The narrator, a self-confessed "aging creep," has been shunned in his own analogous attempts "to shoot scenes of [his] wife naked or nearly so in compromising positions" (190). Yet the ultimate success of Hood's costume—and in parallel, the artfulness of the narrator's story itself—suggests the enabling and curiously authenticating possibilities of the phony performance in this postsouthern culture. Hannah's characters are performers, just as their textual accounts, the stories themselves, are a performance: both require a persuaded audience to testify to their authenticity. Authenticity created in the interaction between a performer and a witnessing audience can elevate the most banal or even abject of circumstances.

At the metalevel, feats like these also reveal an affirmative belief in the power of language to authenticate or redeem ostensibly moribund southern aesthetics, providing a powerful counter to the fallacy of (critical) yearning for the authentic past that many of these stories first appear to evoke. Kenneth Millard articulates this paradox succinctly. He argues that while "The

Ice Storm" seemingly "laments the poverty of its own creative strategies" by evoking "a nostalgic desire for the language of the past," it also "fashions its own unique creative enigmas as characteristic of the language of the present, [which] is offered as the distinctive crossroads of the old South and the new South" (*Contemporary American Fiction* 191). As with "Even Greenland," the self-consciously bastardized languages of Hannah's writing and the ostensibly sullied nature of the South's contemporary artistic output (such as Hood's and the narrator's above) may appear to feed off the purer aesthetics of the past, which are now "shot to shit" (in John the pilot's words [33]). But on closer inspection these stories dispute nostalgic appraisals of the past by making compelling art from the aesthetic conditions of the *present,* and this art can gain significant power from the issue of its historical belatedness or derivativeness.

These crucial moments in Hannah's stories profoundly trouble distinctions between authentic and performative to suggest that a contemporary sense of authenticity may be principally an aesthetic concern. The staged moments of drama in Hannah's stories that carry the potential to transform a raptly attentive audience with something that becomes curiously authentic are testimony to Hannah's vital place in revisiting postregional disputes over whether a simulative South can retain its critical purchase. This is not to argue that these narratives convey a Baudrillardian realm of pure performance that erases any referent beneath. Instead (and contrary to some accusations of the NSS), critical formulations of a region that exists in a performative condition are only contentious if one accepts the fallacy that the South was ever *not* performative or if one believes that a nonperformative South (should that be possible) would be more authentic. Thus, while Hannah's writing does not engage in the same game-playing as the high postmodernisms of Coover or Barth, it is a useful synthesis of modern and postmodern, southern and postsouthern, not least because it complicates these disputed theoretical distinctions. This "in between" quality of Hannah's writing allows his fictional characters to explore how a paradoxical sense of authenticity might persist in a postsouthern culture that dispels this very possibility.

Confounding simple understandings of authenticity in relation to each paradigm discussed, these stories offer no easy answer to the sphinx on the American land that is the South nor to the question whether the South of Hannah's fiction has survived the death of the region. The following texts resist simple interpretations as narratives and in terms of the broader conceptual parameters within which we might understand them, where the dual concepts of authentic reference and authentic place are scrutinized. Hannah's late collection *High Lonesome* (1996) derives the most creative force from foregrounding the (metafictional) complexities that reveal the contingency of the referent South, while upsetting its narrators' abilities to represent it authentically; hence my dedication of two out of six chapters to its stories. Again, my aim here is not coverage for its own sake but rather to locate moments in Hannah's stories where the dynamic coexistence of authenticity and textuality is most apparent and where Hannah's peculiar interest in performance, and in the concept of the South as a performance, is revealed. These moments recognize the contingency of authenticity beyond its textual constitutions while simultaneously staging a new form of southern self-reference that paradoxically becomes authentic by way of this very recognition.

My arguments are broadly in favor of preserving some aspect of the regional while complicating rigid understandings of regional authenticity. To some extent I am indebted to postregional theory and its emphasis on the South's construction; at the same time, I seek to showcase elements of the southernness of Hannah's work that some NSS scholars would urge us to steer clear of. Hannah's writing is acutely conscious of the tensions between southern and postsouthern, and it thoroughly complicates ideas about authenticity in a postregional culture at the same time that it upholds a renewed sense of the importance of the regional in a postmodern culture that demands we reconceptualize it. As one sifts through multiple and competing narratives in Hannah's texts, the monolithic South becomes more elusive; yet the stories and performances that make up the contemporary region have the power to become vitally enabling and, paradoxically, authentic, or southern. Rather than offering a simple solution to the problem of postregionalism, Hannah makes hermeneutic challenges about the infinitely regressive South integral to the drama of his texts, which derive significant power from the collision of postmodern theory and the idea of a real or authentic region worthy of study and representation. If our concept of authentic place is a condition of how that place is represented, then it is in the very processes of aesthetic production that putative authenticity lies. Hannah suggests that it is entirely possible to have it both ways, to be authentically southern while fostering a self-reflexive awareness of the anxious contingency of this very designation. This self-consciousness about how south-ernness is created and consumed—as part of a long and *unfinished* history of performance—is characteristic of the new postregional aesthetic in the author's making. Thus, I am offering a new reading of Hannah's fiction that I hope might find its place in a still evolving field of postregional theory, a reading based on an appreciation of Hannah's own vital place at the inter-section of southern and postmodern.

1

The Problem of Reference in the Late-Twentieth-Century South

Geronimo Rex

This chapter offers a reading of the problem of reference in Barry Hannah's first novel, *Geronimo Rex* (1972), both as an illustration of the shift from modernism to postmodernism and in the context of some specific late-twentieth-century concerns about the problem of the postregional South as a referent. Hannah's novel occupies a pivotal moment in American fiction, acknowledging the forms and philosophies of earlier modernist writing (James Joyce especially), while simultaneously displaying a marked awareness of the postmodern linguistic turn that would question the very possibility of language's referentiality. Where poststructuralist theories of representation have made authenticity profoundly problematic, *Geronimo Rex* hinges on the issue of mimesis, exploring its limits—such as we would find, for example, in John Barth's *The End of the Road* (1958) or Thomas Pynchon's *V.* (1963).[1] Meanwhile, the problem of late-twentieth-century reference can also be applied to wider cultural issues of authenticity in the American South, issues that remain integral both to the politics of thinking of Hannah as a southern writer and to the putative authenticity of that very label.

Adopting a typical bildungsroman structure, *Geronimo Rex* follows the narrator, Harriman (Harry) Monroe, from age eight in 1950, small-town Dream of Pines, Louisiana, to age twenty-three, newly married and enrolled in a graduate English program at an Arkansas university. A parallel *Künstlerroman* narrative simultaneously reveals Harry's development as an artist, which involves contemplating the possibility of an authentic articulation of subjectivity in writing after Harry fails as a jazz trumpeter. In the transition from music to writing, how might Harry's subjectivity be expressed through different signifying aesthetic media, the relative efficacy of which he interrogates as he establishes himself as a new southern writer? *Geronimo Rex* problematizes the referential capacity of language in important ways, asking how, and indeed whether, language refers. It also anticipates some useful transformations in our approach to the bildungsroman genre at a time when critics were increasingly associating the concept of identity formation with postmodern ideas about textual constitution rather than with a simple, organic unfolding of both subjectivity and narrative.[2]

This chapter discusses three different signifying media: (jazz) music, (Joycean) epiphanies, and proper names, each dramatizing Hannah's interest in the problem of (southern) reference. Within the broader paradigm of Harry's (and by extension, Hannah's) writing, I explore the aesthetic conventions of narrative epiphanies and proper names—as linguistic media—as well as those of music as a nonlinguistic conceptual foil. Hannah seems bent on undermining the concept of referentiality in key ways, until authentic subjectivity may be nothing more than a function of the languages in which it is expressed or simulated. In addressing this problem—the authenticity paradox mentioned herein—I will attempt to determine whether *Geronimo Rex* posits a putative sense of authenticity that exists beyond its textual mediations and an attendant form of southern self-reference that can properly refer to it. These arguments can be extended to thinking about the concept of postregional authenticity: how do we articulate an authentic language of the region in a postregional moment, and is a South that is textual simply unreal? While critics have touched upon the significance of music, epiphanies, and names in Hannah's work, they have not considered these things collectively or in relation to *Geronimo Rex*. By interpreting *Geronimo Rex* partly as a metafictional disquisition on the problem of authentic southern reference, this chapter reveals Hannah's continued relevance to postregional debates. The problem of Harry's selfhood becomes a problem of southern language, pertaining to a paradigm shift in contemporary critical thinking from regional to postregional, authenticity to performance.

Harry's bildungsroman concludes with his coming of age, having defeated two oedipal rivals: "Whitfield" Peter Lepoyster, former psychiatric inpatient and white supremacist uncle of Harry's college sweetheart, Catherine Wrag, and Dr. Gregory Lariat, Harry's graduate literature teacher, who has condemned Harry's writing style. Harry shoots Lepoyster and demands a better grade from Lariat. In this latter seminal moment Harry finally declares, "I could speak" (368), overcoming a persistent anxiety about verbal expression manifested in such statements as "I didn't have the words yet," "I expressed myself so badly" (144), or "some days [. . .] I wouldn't speak at all" (249). Revealing its indebtedness to James Joyce's *A Portrait of the Artist as a Young Man,* Harry's *Künstlerroman* becomes partly about language acquisition, and once he has found his voice, the narrative concludes when Harry begins telling Lariat the story that we immediately recognize as a nascent version of the book we as readers are about to finish. This novel-within-the-novel dimension allows the ending simultaneously to resolve Harry's *Künstlerroman,* because Harry becomes the implied successful author of the completed retrospective novel. *Geronimo Rex's* denouement further coincides with the date of Harry's publishing "my first poem" (368), another artistic triumph over Lariat, whose conservative theory of aesthetic value Harry repudiates. Thus, writing and becoming are coterminous: the production of Harry's first poem and Hannah's own completed novel conclude both Harry's fictional search for a proper language of subjectivity and Hannah's own metafictional inquiry into the nature of the novelistic language of *Geronimo Rex.*

As a new *southern* writer, Harry (Hannah) has overcome the oedipal conundrum of writing from a historically belated standpoint (hence the novel's title), one in which new writers are almost paralyzed by awareness of their own literary lateness, as discussed earlier with "Even Greenland" and the problem of postsouthern originality. While Harry's narrative is told retrospectively from the position of his fully realized adult self, importantly, it is Harry's mature status as a *writer* that has been testimony to his coming of age. Within this narrative is the conceptual problem of authentic reference that underwrites Hannah's novel and dually complicates Harry's subjective and artistic *Bildung,* therefore further challenging us to fit Hannah's novel into traditional expectations of the genre. The unique circumstances of Harry's coming of age imply that subjectivity is achieved only after concluding the difficult search for an aesthetic theory from which Harry's writing and *Geronimo Rex* have both come. Despite the precedent it finds in Joyce's *Portrait of the Artist,* the language Harry acquires is beset with a metafictional anxiety that persistently undermines its own ostensible authenticity—perhaps as a key part of its southernness.

This metafictional dimension of writing about its own composition prompted John Updike to designate Hannah's first novel "a fresh angle" on an established formation-novel tradition. This sort of writing explicitly foregrounds what Ruth D. Weston calls "the subtext of writing and the writer," which "debunks the illusion of the story as mimesis in the traditional sense" (*BH* 89). Drawing attention to the processes of writing and reading alike, Harry's narrative is certainly full of self-reflexive interjections, moments of palpable awareness of the contrivances of writing, such as "There are others who will say I was honest in all the wrong places in this book" (134). Michael P. Spikes takes this literary self-consciousness as evidence of *Geronimo Rex's* postmodernity because its narrator "prompts the reader unmistakably to notice that [it] is just a particular arrangement of words, not a direct and unmediated presentation of reality" ("*Rides*" 415–16). Clearly authenticity is an issue. In fact, Harry's authorial self-consciousness in seeking the "right" language is an integral feature of the self-reflexive aesthetic theory that Hannah implicitly formulates, one that is partly informed by a knowledge of its own "late" appearance in an overcrowded field. The self-conscious elements of such an aesthetic become increasingly pronounced as Hannah's career progresses: a heightened awareness of the contingency of southernness on language is also a key part of Hannah's unique style. This style involves first questioning which forms of expression can be said to be artful, original, and authentic, then applying these to the aesthetic performances one encounters in the text, including, not least, our apprehensions of the text itself as an aesthetic performance. By scrutinizing what the terms *artful, original,* and *authentic* can even mean in the heavily storied, narrativized or "imagineered" South (Charles Rutheiser's term), *Geronimo Rex* questions whether such vocabulary is losing or has lost significant critical purchase for thinking about the postsouthern bildungsroman in 1970s America.

Hannah's stylistic decision to narrate Harry's coming of age retrospectively further inflects the traditionally future-oriented nature of the bildungsroman with a backward-looking southern twist. This marks a departure from a national mythology of American innocence, where the perpetually youthful American Adam in the New World begins from a point of historylessness, unlike southerner Harry, who is already burdened by a regional mythology of (original) sin, which he expresses as "the past history that sucked you down" (302). In the context of the South and southern identity, ideas about forward linear progression toward self-understanding and social responsibility are always intrinsically regressive to historical origins that might have already mapped out what (limited) possibilities for subjectivity are available. Franco Moretti interprets retrospection in the classical bildungsroman as indicative of "a refusal to see the future still 'open'" that is coincident with the protagonist's maturity and thus the conclusion of his *Bildung* (68). But here, I would argue that Giovanna Summerfield and Lisa Downward's more recent reconfiguration of the genre—where looking back is not simply indicative of a closed future but rather is "a crucial step in moving forward, in opening up what the future has to offer" (107)—resonates much more appropriately with understandings of the backward-looking South after modernism, where going back to go forward has been, for good or ill, integral to critical apprehensions of both (Black) cultural trauma and (white) cultural guilt.

Geronimo Rex occupies a valuable position in the history of debates about linguistic reference when we consider its emergence amid a series of radical reappraisals of referential authenticity. Recognizing the early 1970s as a turning point, David Schalkwyk argued in 2004 that "for the past three decades, the intellectual world has been divided between two sharply conflicting conceptions of reference. One, arising from [. . .] philosophical empiricism and realism, [. . .] takes an interest in reference chiefly as a path from language to the world. The other, rooted in Saussure's diacritical view of language, [holds] that, at best, any reference to a world beyond language is conditional on self-referential relations that make up language itself" (13). This issue of mimetic crisis is an integral feature of post-1960s literary theory, which, with Saussurean structuralism fueled by Derrida's deconstructive turn, increasingly questions whether the names and symbols we use to represent reality can faithfully represent it or, indeed, whether we can even access or refer to some reality outside text. Harry's search for a worthy form of written self-representation in *Geronimo Rex* must contend with the notion that the linguistic turn has rendered the gap between signifier and signified so great that no clear "path from language to the world" exists at the time of his writing—if it ever did. So, while of course "a world beyond language" remains, any perfectly authentic or mimetic form of referential access to it is deeply problematic. This anticipates a moment in Hannah's later *Hey Jack!* when its orator, Homer, exclaims that "talk destroys. Your mouth emits a thing like a furnace. What you meant was already burnt up" (83). After Saussure's challenge to a rationalist approach to language, an approach that assumes that language is a process of attaching names to objects via intrinsic links, we are left with a condition Geoffrey Hartmann referred to as the "scandal" of referentiality (74), in which the mimetic referentiality of texts gives way to an infinite network of textual (re)interpretation.

In his study of contemporary southern literature, Michael Kreyling formulates an analogous notion, that the world occupied by Hannah's character-narrators is merely an intertextual web, a "set of mediated representations" (*Inventing* 163). In an apt dramatization of Kreyling's vision, Harry declares his own textual entrapment, saying "I was sure I was sealed up in a cartoon farce which was bound to explode with me inside it" (373). Indeed, Harry performs many such farcical acts throughout the story, which superficially pertain to the theatrical and hyperbolic nature of adolescence—"I must have seemed a wild pop-up dummy" (244)—and to the bildungsroman context, whose developmental subject is characterized by exploration and experimentation. Harry's outrageous acts and guises also suggest the possible inauthenticity of selves, or at least of writing about them; they imply the fundamental contingency and mediation of subjectivity through texts. We might infer Hannah's full participation in a postmodern introspective turn, where the real is immersed in the textual, or where there is no authenticity anterior to its textual representation. However, *Geronimo Rex* also reveals its self-conscious relationship to modernist figures such as Joyce and T. S. Eliot even while questioning and moving beyond their narrative conventions. For example, schoolboy Harry is inspired by Eliot's "The Love Song of J. Alfred Prufrock" to write a version of it in his own first poem (44); at college he claims Joyce explicitly, as "one of my masters then" (248). Indeed, echoes of Prufrock's imagining himself as "a pair of ragged claws / Scuttling across the floors of silent seas" (73–74) resound throughout Harry's narrative as he conceives of himself using the same crab metaphor (248, 354–56). A key aspect of the aesthetic style Harry develops is to draw attention to his own literary indebtedness, his own entrapment in an intertextual "web" (or "farce") of prior representations, and to the artful ways that certain writers have tried to capture contemporary subjectivity.

I am not attempting a simple comparative reading of Joyce and Hannah here, nor of modernism and postmodernism. However, I do question the extent to which Hannah subscribes to Joyce's epiphany as a means of expressing Harry's subjectivity to argue that Hannah employs Joycean methods partly to question their contemporary value. This helps situate *Geronimo Rex* at a watershed moment toward the end of modernism's motivating energies, yet not participating fully in experimental postmodernism. Its publication coincides with a shift in linguistic theory that it seems tacitly aware of and eager to exploit and explore, partly in order to articulate a new form of creative aesthetic value. Hannah's work is itself so richly intertextual that it is difficult to compare him to a single author, but thinking about its relationship to Joycean epiphany is key to establishing the vital place that Hannah's writing occupies, in the early seventies, at the intersection of modern and postmodern, European and American, American and southern. This liminal quality of Hannah's work is partly evident in the rejection of the Joycean epiphany, even as music and names remain putatively privileged aesthetic categories that could circumvent the apparent crisis of linguistic referentiality.[3]

If we accept that modernist writing was largely concerned with how to express some ideal authentic subjectivity, existing beyond language but which might be capable of being articulated in language, then for Eliot or Joyce there was a sense of radically new textual ways to express (adolescent) subjectivity. Tobias Boes captures this in his claim that Joyce's *Portrait of the Artist* marks a key contribution to the bildungsroman genre because it frames its subject "in a new rhetorical vocabulary" (235). Laurent Milesi argues similarly that Joyce's "experiments in literary languages" reveal the author's "need to transcend the barriers of expressiveness set by the systems of existing languages" (1). Saussure's early-twentieth-century *Course in General Linguistics* was a likely influence on the modernists' attempts to manipulate linguistic reference, because Saussure's initial formulation of language was of a structural system that could be known and controlled. Challenges posed to the concept of mimetic verisimilitude in the early twentieth century provoked literary modernism's revolutionary attempts to make it new, to surpass those existing systems of linguistic expression found wanting by contemporary linguistic theory. Underpinning this era of literary experimentation is the possibility of a more authentic relationship between art and reality, gained by pushing the boundaries of existing referential systems to reveal transcendent signifying moments otherwise obscured.[4] Therefore, Joyce's striving for a transcendent new language—a practice constitutive of modernism itself—is based, implicitly, on a belief in (pure) mimesis, which, though elusive, might yet be sought via the formulation of this new lexicon. If language is deployed to best effect, subjectivity could be discovered and expressed more authentically.

While modernist epiphanies aspired to new forms of authenticity and more authentic articulations of subjectivity, Hannah seems to be abandoning such a claim as he moves beyond modernism by scrutinizing the idea of authentic reference and suggesting that this is only a function of language. Comparing the different signifying "languages" available to Harry—music, epiphany, names—*Geronimo Rex* implies that moments of Joycean linguistic transcendence give way to purely aesthetic gestures in which all expression comes only from the language available, and the authentic is itself but an aesthetic contrivance. Thus we can see the passing of the high modernist moment in Hannah's novel as it interrogates the putative authenticity of subjectivity and the different means with which it can be represented.

The opening scene of *Geronimo Rex* and its last word ("Music!") establish music as the benchmark of aesthetic value against which Harry's writing can be measured. Harry's decision to write follows his fall from grace as a prospective musician: having naively believed "that playing hot music on a trumpet might be an exciting thing to do all one's life" (47), he comes to realize that "I sounded like a cow stepping in its own pies" (196–97). Within this vital subplot, music is established as an elusive, pure form of aesthetic expression that Harry abandons to become a writer. Harry's failure as a musician haunts his search for a substitute but equally estimable form of literary expression from which to make the story, leading him to question the validity of all linguistic reference, including his own. This is summed up by the novel's last line, Lariat's "Good, good heavens. We're in the wrong field. Music!" (381), a reference to those, like Lariat and Harry, in the field of writing. In a sense, Harry wants to write a language of subjectivity that aspires to the condition of his first love, music. If music is established as a more authentic aesthetic register than writing, this is because it epitomizes a referential form not contingent on language to articulate meaning nor reliant upon learning a language to interpret it. This is signaled when as a young boy Harry possesses some intrinsic knowledge of the language of music—"I had the music, but not the words yet" (144)—or when he ruins "the best jazz" he "ha[s] ever played" by "becom[ing] a thinking person, right in the middle of [it]" (227). These examples imply that music directly speaks to some prelapsarian realm of inward subjectivity that bypasses verbal language and consciousness and thus might be more authentic.

Ideas about language acquisition are commonplace in Hannah's narratives, which often describe an author's first act of storytelling as a pivotal, fall-from-grace moment. For example, *High Lonesome* contains Hannah's most self-conscious narrator, Royce, an aspiring writer who declares that he is "condemned to my own story like somebody already in an Italian hell" ("Through Sunset" 123–24). Royce's anxiety about his artistic condemnation directly evokes both Dante's *Inferno* and Milton's *Paradise Lost,* disquisitions on the fallen condition of human language as a secondary or absent form of reference. Harry's above reflection on the immediacy of music (compared with writing) is further corroborated by Royce when he declares of his writing, "I am slow, I am windy" (123–24), invoking not only Harry's suspicion of the secondary nature of verbal reference (which impedes rather than aids subjectivity) but also the fraught belatedness of new southern storytellers. The suggestion is that writing in general, and southern writing especially, lacks the immediacy of signification enjoyed by music as a nonverbal form of expression.

Brad Bucknell examines how some major modernist writers, including Joyce, engage with music as a distinct mode of artistic expression in their writing. They do so because, as Mallarmé phrased it, music represents to writers a "self-succeeding" aesthetic with a special ability to convey with perfect reference, because it does not "translate [. . .] into any language save that of the listener's ideas." Thus, it conveys a "direct and fitting" message (qtd. in Bucknell 31), in purely abstract terms, without secondary recourse to the words or symbols that were proving so problematic in the modernist period. If other arts, especially writing, are representational and symbolic, music can so completely unify form (the sound made) and content (the sound heard, the emotional response produced) that it refers outside the conventions of verbal meaning. Meaning inheres in the sound alone, and while this may "mean" differently to different auditors, it means directly, making music a self-present form of reference with signifier and referent perfectly coincidental.

While this is an oversimplification of the "language" of music, it is worth briefly considering Daniel Chua's scholarship on the history of music's relationship to the word in *Absolute Music,* which argues against the notion of "absolute music" as the paradigm for most musicological studies. Chua's arguments are partly indebted to Deryck Cooke's controversial study *The Language of Music,* which proffers that such "language" is readable in properties identified as consistently referring to specific psychological or emotional states that composers and musicians exploit when they want to evoke different moods in an audience (Cooke 199–211). Chua contemplates not only how meaning is actively constructed in music but also what structures of knowledge are presupposed (philosophical, ideological, cultural, social) for such meaning to exist.[5] He contends that the structures of musical reference do not exist in absolute or autonomous form (it is just as contextually contingent as language), contrary to Harry Monroe's initial impressions. *Geronimo Rex* establishes the presence of music as a point of "absolute" aesthetic comparison with Harry's writing, therefore, but ultimately the hierarchical relationship between music and writing (like that between speech and writing) cannot be upheld in any simple way.

Harry's formative introduction to jazz music is described in a language of awe and enraptured witness repeated whenever he encounters this aesthetic. In the first instance, an eight-year-old Harry reveals that it "was the best music I'd ever heard, bar none. [It] made you want to pick up a rifle and just get killed somewhere. [It] went deeper than what before my heart ever had room for. And I just didn't know what to think" (14). Years later, despite having gained a technical knowledge of the nonabsolute language of music and believing that "now my heart had room for it," an older Harry admits similarly, "The verities are that I was washed away again, ripped off, out, away, and that for me to even *name* the march [the band] let loose is impossible, the same as it's impossible for a man drowning, waves blasting him, to pronounce the name of the ocean he's in" (188). The significance of both scenes is made apparent when they transcend Harry's narrative as heightened instances of drama, epiphanic moments that halt the temporal unfolding of events. The language of these scenes' articulation is something to return to, but for now it demonstrates the artistic significance that Harry attributes to the jazz aesthetic, captured when Harry's trumpet teacher, Livace, quotes Walter Pater's claim that "[a]ll art aspires to the condition of music" (165).

Christopher Griffin has noted Hannah's use of the metaphor of jazz to articulate "authentic being" in his fiction (173), just as Hannah has conceded regarding his own writing that the "tone I want is sometimes just a kind of confluence of music" (Hannah, "Spirit" 326). Here, *Geronimo Rex* betrays an indebtedness to the Beat writing of the 1950s and 1960s, discussed in Preston Whaley's *Blows Like a Horn: Beat Writing, Jazz, Style, and Markets in the Transformation of U.S. Culture.*[6] It also reveals Hannah's further debt to Joyce, who, influenced by Mallarmé, similarly exploited the musical or "rhythmic potential of English" in his search for a revolutionary language of subjectivity (Attridge 136). In *Geronimo Rex,* therefore, jazz signifies an enigmatic realm of pure reference—the best, bar none—to which Harry's language will aspire. Music informs Harry's implicit formulation of a literary aesthetic that might still incorporate some of its qualities, captured neatly (albeit problematically) by his college roommate, Bobby Dove Fleece: "You [Harry] think you can make music breed with language and you end up sounding like Edgar Allan Poe playing the tuba" (337).

The hope here is that Harry's writing would achieve "the possibility of romantic transcendence [and] the potential space of the fullness of expressivity" (Bucknell 24) identified by many in the language of music. The quintessential aptitude for musical expression, if this could be applied to one's writing, would solve the problems of reference addressed by Hannah's novel at large. Of course, the novel *is* written, and Harry's art, like Royce's, is condemned to the "wrong" field. Therefore, Harry seeks to integrate the aesthetic characteristics of music into a literary aesthetic that he suspects might be deeply inadequate. Because he has established language as a primary conceptual distinction between music and writing, something that may seem paradoxical given our narrator's decision to write, Harry's written narrative must therefore consider the ways in which reference can occur beyond, or differently from, conventional verbal language. Here, Harry's narrative turns its attention first to epiphanies, then to proper names, as two discrete types of linguistic reference that appear to aspire to the seemingly worthier condition of music, and the aesthetic features of music are a vital influence on Harry's exploitation of the creative potential inherent in each.

Harry's adolescent subjectivity emerges in a series of epiphanic dreams and visions—"It was a stunning dream I couldn't do anything with" (215)—that are integral to the style of self-expression realized in *Geronimo Rex.* This section addresses how epiphanies appear in the novel, expounding its author's relationship to previous literary constructions of epiphany in coming-of-age narratives. This will involve first comparing Hannah's aesthetic construction of epiphany with Joyce's, then contrasting different occasions of epiphany within Harry's own narrative. My aim is to undermine a simple notion of the true epiphanic moment in *Geronimo Rex* as something properly transcendent, absolute, unmediated, or "musical," to distance Hannah's late-twentieth-century formulation of narrative epiphany from Joyce's.

Harry appears to devise an implicit narrative technique of epiphany in which qualities of intellectual and verbal failure consistently emerge in dramatic revelatory moments. Epiphanies are singled out aesthetically as exceptional even though (or because) their meaning remains unclear, not only in the original instance but also when Harry recounts them years later. Because they continue to resist reduction into explanatory or representative language, epiphanies stun Harry's sensibility in the present as much as in the past, recalling conceptualizations of the South as a site of unresolved historical trauma, the past impinging on the present with gothic immediacy and incomprehensibility. Part of the reader's interpretative difficulty here comes from Harry's inability to comprehend certain episodes in his narrative even with the benefit of writing retrospectively. Harry's epiphanies briefly suspend signification because they are verbalized in a language that evokes the curiously nonlinguistic qualities identified in jazz music and Harry's awestruck response to hearing it. He can neither "think" nor "name" in the face of the music, just as he cannot "do anything with" these stunning revelatory images. Therefore, epiphany becomes a strategy whereby the "mimetic" possibilities of music might be directly incorporated into language.

It is unsurprising that crises of expression and thought accompany instances that apparently represent the most "honest" (to borrow Harry's word) events in Harry's bildungsroman. Epiphanies provide moments of true insight through which the significance of the moment becomes paradoxically clear, with a different kind of meaning emerging in the musical qualities of hermeneutic *obscurity* that accompany these moments. Dramatizing a gap between powerful emotion and the language that fails to express it imbues the epiphany with a sense of (aesthetic) legitimacy, while simultaneously rendering it inassimilable into the language of Harry's articulation or fully conscious comprehension. An apt analogy might be the difficulty we have grasping and then articulating the essence of dreams despite being sure that they mean something significant. Harry echoes this notion by saying, "I'm the sort of fellow [. . .] who isn't inclined to ever bring himself fully awake" (51–52) and who (like his father) "would have to *dream* an answer before he knew it was right" (24). By revealing the epiphany's significance despite the limitations of the lexicons in which it must be verbalized, Harry's narrative can approximate, or at least simulate aesthetically, moments of truth in the story that either are obscured by or will not be articulated in conventional fallen language.

This recalls Milesi's view of Joyce's transcendent language, and Hannah also explores epiphany's potential to extend the limits of linguistic reference. In this respect Hannah's technique is explicitly redolent of Joyce's then radical narrative strategy of epiphany, whereby singular moments of genuine understanding on behalf of character and/or reader suddenly appear to transcend the narratives in which they are expressed. This accords with the etymology of *epiphany* (reconfigured in the secular context of Joyce's writing) as a sudden revelation, a literal "showing forth," as Morris Beja notes (15). Given both Joyce's and Hannah's conceptual interest in music, epiphanies, while they are inadequately re-created in language, are established as authentic precisely because they resist full incorporation into the structures that characterize linguistic reference. Because they will not be fully assimilated, they cannot be mediated or copied, and this testifies to their authenticity, or "absoluteness," relative to the secondary simulations of text. Harry must prove himself unable to logically understand or unequivocally describe his epiphanies, because he wants to invest this mode of expression with a sense of legitimacy that might be lacking elsewhere. The value of Harry's epiphanies lies precisely in his ability to interpret them rationally, because they pertain to the characteristics of music rather than to verbal signification.

An example of this strategy (which is just an aesthetic performance, as I will explain) comes when Harry visits the site of the Battle of Vicksburg and experiences an epiphany of sudden overwhelming sadness: "Jesus mercy, I was sad" (218). The revelatory moment is accompanied by a catastrophe of words and thought that perfectly recalls Harry's dumbfounded reaction to hearing jazz music and to the incompressible dream that stuns him: "The strange *silence,* then, is what got me—as if you walked in a dream of refracted defeat. The horror was, *I could think of nothing to say. I couldn't even think of anything to think.* I could not get 'Dixie' or 'The Battle Hymn of the Republic' to play in my mind. Vicksburg simply weighed on my heart like lumber: all the old history [. . .] seemed like a boat rotting up in a bayou nobody would ever find" (218, second emphasis mine). The epiphany is the unspoken realization of southern historical entrapment as a result of past ills, history resurfacing as in "a dream of refracted defeat." This epiphany facilitates the kind of visionary, dreamlike state that ushers supernatural insight into the nature of external reality, in this case, Harry's intuitive recognition of the region's "rotten" history, weighing heavily on present inhabitants, who are "landlocked" (302) between conflicting but equally bogus mythologies about the Confederacy ("Dixie") and the Union ("Battle Hymn of the Republic"). It is a half-articulated insight into the burden of Harry's own southernness.

Joyce argues that whereas reality lies outside the rhetoric that enshrouds it and that is presently silenced, the epiphany, at least in its most literal sense, directly connects us with the "whatness'" of a thing (*Stephen Hero* 218; *Portrait* 212). It expedites an astute vision of things as they really are. This is further redolent of Stephen Dedalus's reappearance in Joyce's *Ulysses*, as if to counter the idea of the "[i]neluctable modality of the visible" (37), where we can apprehend only forms (signs) and not substance (referents). Therefore, Harry's narrative strategy appears to align him with Joyce, suggesting that epiphany is a worthy aesthetic medium for legitimately expressing fleeting moments of transcendent, authentic subjectivity in the contemporary southern bildungsroman. Indeed, Harry's epiphany can be imbued with further "whatness" when we consider that as above, it is Harry's status as a southerner that engenders the revelation at Vicksburg, the symbolic site of the fall of the Confederacy. It is not simply the existential expression of dispossessed adolescence, therefore. Rather, Harry's alienation at Vicksburg has a specific sociospatial basis when he is unable to place himself among an older regional discourse of southern manhood; it is a "southern" site of epiphany.[7] The alternative epiphany, perhaps, is that this overbearing mode of heroic white southern masculinity is a nonstarter. Harry feels displaced among the old rhetoric of the heroically defeated white South ("I could not get 'Dixie' or 'The Battle Hymn of the Republic' to play in my mind"; the lofty "old history" becomes distinctly bathetic when it is transposed onto a boat rotting in a swamp that "nobody would ever find"), but the harmful ("rotten") mythology continues to be "refracted" upon contemporary white masculinity in detrimental ways.

Harry's epiphanies also conspicuously subvert their own seeming legitimacy or exemption from the problem of reference. We can see the beginnings of this in the scene above, where what we might term Harry's *southern-burden* epiphany is itself a common aspect of southern mythologizing (discussed in chapter 3). While Stephen Dedalus's epiphanies may be difficult to identify in Joyce's writing, once the genuine epiphany *has* been identified, it does not seem to originate in something that the author so pointedly establishes as ersatz; we are not invited to suspect its authenticity in the same way. Despite the mentioned similarities between Hannah and Joyce, when we look closer, *Geronimo Rex* subtly undermines its own formulation of the epiphany as a genuine or unmediated revelation. This deviation from the Joycean epiphany is one vital way in which *Geronimo Rex* distinguishes itself from its generic precursors even while it appears to follow some of their conventions. This becomes evident if we now compare a set of what I call "true" and "false" epiphanies in Harry's narrative.

The *Oxford Dictionary of English* defines *authentic* as something "of undisputed origin and not a copy; genuine" ("Authentic"), and this notion of undisputed origin is key to determining the relative legitimacy of Harry's epiphanies. The modernist premise that epiphany is the emergence of some authentic subjectivity, existing before and becoming suddenly separated from language, is subtly reformulated in *Geronimo Rex* when it becomes clear that Harry's (southern) epiphanies have no genuine foundational basis or undisputed origin. This is intimated in the scene above, when Harry's melancholy sympathy with the "defeated" South has roots in suspicious Lost Cause and neo-Confederate mythology. The possibility is raised that the genuine ("musical") epiphany has not simply become phony through the act of its reconstruction in language; rather, the epiphany was already bogus to start with. By emphasizing the mediated nature of Harry's subjectivity through text, as well as the frequent incursions of "simulacra" that challenge the very notion of some delineable, authentic original (Baudrillard, *Simulations* 14), *Geronimo Rex* brings to a modernist problem of mimesis the added complications of copies and text. Harry's epiphanies often stem from highly dubious origins, and thus their authenticity by merit of a Joycean transcendence of language is implicitly undercut.

Take the example of an ostensibly true epiphany emerging from a moment of spontaneous intimacy between Harry and Catherine Wrag in a scene at the Ross Barnett Reservoir in Mississippi. The episode occurs after Harry and Catherine's relationship has ended, and it will haunt Harry's narrative, particularly after Catherine is killed shortly thereafter. Harry recalls the scene thus: "I still think about that—perhaps—two minutes [. . .]; the odd, sudden affection she had for me—'Honey'—and [. . .] my own love for her [. . .] reviving instantly, damn near tears. This surprising butterfly of sentiment with both of us [. . .] I remember, even after the disasters, as one of the strangest interludes of my time" (308). The implied epiphany is Harry's recognition of the mutual love that has been wasted. Later, the reemergence of this scene sparks a second epiphany, more tragic in its posthumousness. This occurs when Harry suddenly "grow[s] sick" on a plane to Jackson, on his way to participate in a dramatic showdown with Whitfield Peter. Harry's epiphany of grief ("She's dead, dead") comes from the sudden intrusion of vivid flashbacks, first of the scene at the reservoir and then of his final date with Catherine: "I began seeing in my mind [the scene] at the reservoir. [I saw] it again and again. Then Catherine, [. . .] Doing it again and again. [. . .] I saw it over and over. I began heaving and sobbing. [. . .] When I sat down I saw her all dolled-up for the last date, her foot in the shoe with one strap across it. [. . .] 'She's dead, dead'" (374). Harry's inability "to forget" (308) or make sense of this "strangest" of episodes directly aligns it with the sense of profundity attached to the unforgettable jazz music he has witnessed: "There wasn't any forgetting that" (47). Thus, we might infer that the epiphany generated by this scene has a genuine origin. Seemingly, the reservoir epiphany stands out among the realest "interludes" in Harry's narrative, a moment in which the true significance of his and Catherine's lost affection is suddenly and gut-wrenchingly felt and revealed. The revelation draws attention to itself, true to form, by resisting the narrative languages with which Harry would more fully elucidate or make sense of its impenetrability or strangeness.

Compare this with what looks like a straightforwardly false epiphany transpiring between Harry and his soon-to-be wife, Prissy Lombardo. Toward the end of the story, the failure of this marriage is imminent, arguably traceable to the fact that Harry's initial compulsion to propose comes from a specious moment of *false* epiphany. In what first appears to be a genuinely epiphanic moment, Harry gazes at Prissy lying on the beach and enigmatically declares the inevitability of his action (the proposal) by saying, "I saw it, and I suppose that did it" (342). But what Harry "saw" was in fact only a version of one of the formative *texts* encountered in his youth (below), of a "Revlon model picture [that] stung me in the guts" (116). Based on an image, a replica, Harry's epiphany is conspicuously textually wrought, from a prototypically artificial source. The texts and images assimilated from past encounters inform the experiences to which Harry attributes significance and value in the present, such that meaning is made not from the real experience but from the texts with which that experience is (falsely) invested with meaning.

Harry recognizes that the romantic moment with Prissy above is the exact aesthetic facsimile of the scene depicted in the Revlon advert, which featured "a skinny thing lying supine" in silver makeup "with a high-heeled shoe dangling off her toe [and] lying on a pillow of sand [. . .] in twilight" (116). On Biloxi Beach at twilight, nineteen-year-old Prissy, like the Revlon poster girl, "had hardly any bosoms at all, [and] she wore silver shoes, [. . .] and dangled one of the shoes on her toes" (342). This near-perfect reproduction of an original scene in a subsequent one prompts Harry's action: "I *had* this scene with her [Prissy], asked her to marry me" (117). Harry invests the duplicate scene with a metaphysical weight ("that did it") that in reality it lacks, and therefore the marriage is doomed. It is an epiphany of sorts, then, but a sham one, contingent on a staged scene or simulacrum. Interestingly, Harry knows this, once it is too late, and he is angered by the fact, though this anger is never fully explained: "Prissy didn't quite have the body of the Revlon gal. The beach was white and rippled, but not the Sahara. It was the beach of Biloxi, Mississippi. [. . .] [It] was then the longest manmade beach in the world. It may be still, for all I know. Doesn't take away any of my anger" (117). The spectacle of Prissy on *manmade* Biloxi beach is not only a secondary, lesser version of the (authentic?) image of the "Revlon gal" on the Sahara; worse than that, it is a copy of a copy, the original itself not only being one of countless reprints but having been photographically contrived, presumably, in imitation of the real Sahara, which Harry misidentifies in the image. Harry arbitrates his experiences, including his romantic epiphanies, through textual (mis)interpretations, thereby severely threatening the concept of a Joycean epiphany transcending the mediations of texts.

In *Geronimo Rex*, epiphanies that might once have seemed authentic insofar as their textual origins could not so easily be traced become inseparable from copies, which not only obscure but perhaps even obliterate their originals. Harry's epiphanies cannot ultimately be viewed as transcendent moments that involve some measure of genuine experience that is unmediated, because they explicitly arise from texts or simulations rather than from lived experience, and this corrosive element can be brought into relief by contrasting it with how epiphany operates in Joyce's work. In problematizing its own conception of genuine epiphany, Harry's narrative sabotages its own formulation of what is authentic. Because these epiphanies are mediated and staged (and at the level of Hannah's self-reflexive metafiction they are very self-conscious of the fact), they deny Harry the opportunity to comprehend their full significance or to transform his present experience; we can observe this in the character's retrospective inability to understand or outrun his own history. Aesthetic staginess—and this is a concept that can be brought to bear on much of Hannah's fiction—infects all epiphanic moments in *Geronimo Rex* to the extent that it subverts the modernist epiphany's efficacy in the contemporary southern bildungsroman. Again, this marks Hannah's participation in an existing conceptual issue of the postmodern (stagy) epiphany, such as Harold Bloom identifies in Pynchon's later work (Bloom 101, 197).

Here, Harry's love for Catherine is also dubious from the outset. It is a romantic fantasy that bears little relation to reality or to its subject. Harry dramatizes the contrived nature of his self-professed love when he ponders, "But yes, that *love*. How was that doing? My Catherine! I couldn't quite get those words in my mouth" (248). Furthermore, Harry cannot reconcile the fact of Catherine's poor literacy—"*her* words, her voice, [. . .] this bad whining illiteracy, not even good Alabama English"—with a "sense of the exquisite [. . .] in grammar" he has acquired from a knowledge of texts, having "read so much good English poetry and prose" in high school and college (248). Once again, texts have hindered Harry's authentic relationship with reality, with Catherine, and with the epiphanies that might have revealed their narrator's true feelings in a Joycean bildungsroman. Harry's questionable "*love*" for Catherine originates in another worrying set of texts: a set of stolen, illicit love letters written by Whitfield Peter to his estranged wife, a textual doppelgänger of sorts who is also named Catherine. Contrived with "a lot of art" and "good grammar" (212), the letters aspire to Harry's self-confessed sense of the exquisite. Yet they are clearly suspect, not only being written but coming from a patient of the colloquially named Whitfield asylum, a man known to speak a "baroque stream of fraudulent melodrama" (247), surely not an apt basis for a relationship that would stimulate a legitimate epiphany. It becomes ultimately impossible to verify or void Harry's love for Catherine because *Geronimo Rex* subtly foregrounds the textually determined nature of its narrator's seemingly candid moments of self-revelation. Harry's epiphanies persistently reveal the limits of their ostensible transcendence because they have no origin that is not contingent on the tricky and infinitely regressive interpretation of texts.

This becomes further evident if we consider the reservoir and Biloxi epiphanies together. Closer comparison blurs the distinction I have established between the apparently sham nature of the Biloxi epiphany and the seemingly more trustworthy nature of the reservoir one. This undercuts the real-phony dichotomy between Harry's feelings for Catherine and Prissy, observable in moments of true and false epiphany. This is epitomized when the scene that begets Harry's ostensibly genuine epiphany at the reservoir in fact contains an exactly comparable image to that which annuls his epiphany at Biloxi: Catherine, like Prissy, alarmingly recalls the Revlon picture when she too has "her foot in the shoe with one strap across it" (374). In turn, this undermines any neat opposition between the seeming authenticity of Catherine's spontaneous and uncontrived expression of affection at the reservoir, "Honey"; Harry notes that "she was never so easy with me" as in this moment (304) and the hackneyed nature of Prissy's forced attempt at romantic language, once again underpinned by a (written) text: "Once, she called me 'Darling,' but forced, like reading from a magazine article on love" (344). The perceptible recurrence of texts in each case questions the notion of an original or unmediated articulation of self, such as we might expect from an epiphany, since we cannot trace it to some nontextual origin.

This blurring of genuine and contrived is complete when, having begun sobbing and repeating "She's dead," Harry responds to Lariat's "Did you love the girl?" with an anticlimactic affirmative that is distinctly discordant with his putative grief: "For a few weeks" (374). By contrast, in a sudden visionary moment during a party, Harry unexpectedly declares, in a language perfectly echoing that of both the reservoir and Harry's episode on the Jackson flight, "I loved her [Prissy], never before in this full and humble way loved her. [. . .] I was damn near sobbing" (362). The interchangeable echoing of one scene's lexis in another (recall Harry's earlier "damn near tears") implies that we cannot unequivocally designate one epiphany as more or less faithful or fraudulent than any other. Thus we might question whether any of the narratives formulating individual subjectivity may ever in fact be called authentic. Ultimately, the foundations of Harry's "real" love for Catherine reveal themselves to be no more "easy" or authentic than the circumstances underpinning his apparently disingenuous, "forced," and loveless marriage to Prissy (304, 344).

The complex interweaving of truth and falsehood in Harry's emotional epiphanies suggests that Hannah's novel is evolving beyond the concept of authentic epiphany formulated in much modernist writing. The text stages moments of epiphany that appear to be sincere but that on closer inspection reveal their departure from ideas about genuine epiphany in favor of foregrounding how the *quality* of authenticity is merely the product of a convincing aesthetic performance. Harry's epiphanies are purely performative and more self-consciously so; they are a function of the many texts and historical languages that produce and express them. Inverting the premise of Joyce's transcendental language of the self, Harry's subjectivity is created by his interactions with the texts he consumes rather than described by a transcendent language of epiphany that is just an illusion. Again, this acknowledges the problem of the South's own referentiality, not simply in recognition of the *purely* textual nature of regional identity ("the South" may have become conceptually useless, but the region and its inhabitants continue to exist) but also in recognition of its staged and therefore contingent status.

The novel itself only comes once Harry has gained "the words" in which it is realized (144), which troubles the notion that any truly authentic expression of the self would be possible in this context. Writing is a performative attempt to approximate the real or authentic with narrative strategies like epiphany while recognizing its elusiveness. The metafictional dimension of Hannah's writing augments this problem, when the textual inscription of Harry's life is the very text we are reading and the circumstances of its production are those its narrator describes. If we accept the implication that epiphanies fall short of aspiring to the more perfectly referential condition of music, then what, besides music, might be authentic in *Geronimo Rex?* In the late-twentieth-century American South, is there is any other linguistic form that is not flawed in this way? The answer, perhaps, lies in the proper name.

This final section identifies a poetics of naming in a series of naming acts and events, including the passage that imparts *Geronimo Rex*'s title. Names denote another possible way for language to circumvent the problem of reference accompanying the "wrong field" of writing (381), something epiphany partially failed to do. Harry's narrative is full of noteworthy incidents concerning proper names—the most paradigmatic of these is Harry's finding his "own" name in the name "Geronimo" (below)—which form an integral part of Hannah's conceptual interest in referentiality. If names can be established as some uniquely authentic linguistic register in *Geronimo Rex*, then this would certainly offer an interesting foil to the problem of reference that the novel has subtly exposed elsewhere, as well as a triumph, perhaps, for writing over music.

As mentioned above, the 1970s and 1980s witnessed a surge of attention to what critics called a "new theory of reference" (D. Schwarz 9), marking a significant turn in twentieth-century thinking about the philosophy of language. This theory is attributed primarily to the American philosopher and linguist Saul Kripke and derives from his book *Naming and Necessity* (1980), based on three lectures given at Princeton University in 1970. This influx of critical thinking about names and naming in language, and about language and subjectivity, coincides almost perfectly with the publication of *Geronimo Rex* in 1972, making it an obvious context in which to situate Hannah's novel, whether or not Hannah was aware of such developments. Yet, as an interpretative paradigm names remain notably absent from existing Hannah criticism, with the exception of Spikes's reading of Hannah's *Ray* in his *Mississippi Quarterly* article "What's in a Name?" (1988). While I am not suggesting that *Geronimo Rex* appears to uphold the premises of Kripkean language theory in any simple way, the significance of "proper" reference generally and of proper names specifically is conveyed in a discernible interrogation of naming and names in Harry's narrative, reflecting usefully on some key aspects of late-twentieth-century critical debate.[8]

David S. Schwarz contends that Kripke's theory holds "a special place in any theoretical discussion of natural language" because it reconfigures the way that naming terms, and specifically proper names, refer (xi). Christopher Norris agrees that in the wake of Saussure and the attendant linguistic turn, Kripke's theory "asserts the case for determinate reference," which provides "a fairly drastic critique" of (post)structuralism's central premise, namely, that the sign "lack[s] any natural bond between signifier and signified" (156, 170, 171), and Spikes has extended Norris's central contention to posit, tentatively, that Kripke's insights on (proper) names "may be extended to all of language and thus [can] actually work to controvert poststructuralism" (Spikes, "Saul Kripke" 301). Saussure's "diacritical" principle suggests that words expose the limits of meaning, because words mean only in a differential system, relating to one another rather than to something beyond themselves; recall the image of Harry's being "sealed up in a cartoon farce" (373). Kripke's account of how proper names signify *directly,* however, offers an alternative to this narcissistic element of linguistic self-referentiality where "there is no direct or one-to-one relation between word, concept and referent" (Norris 159). For Kripke, the name is a unique sign of authenticity because names refer in a discrete singular way, such that his (disputed) theory has been understood by some to amount "to a denial of the 'arbitrary' nature of the sign, and a move to re-establish the referential function of language denied to all language in all varieties of post-Saussurean discourse" (Norris 169).

Kripke argues that proper names function as "singular referring terms" that "denote an essence of the object they designate in all possible worlds"; names therefore possess the power to fix determinate reference to something external (48). Key to this is Kripke's concept of rigid designation. Recalling Joyce's formulation of the elusive "whatness" of things, Kripke writes, "A name conveys a thing-in-itself meaning which can be known apart from the meanings represented by the properties associated with the name." Names function as "*rigid designator*[s]" since they designate the same object in every possible world (48). While of course a name's referent has properties that can also be used to identify it, Kripke contends that this referent can be identified nonetheless as a self-contained "*it*" that can be known on its own (52). Where it is functioning as a rigid designator in this way, a name can designate an object in its essence, fixed and coherent, which can be known distinct from its properties and descriptions; it is both descriptional *and* nondescriptional. If names do function as rigid designators, then their referents can be understood to have a stable and unified identity quite apart from their (descriptive) properties, which may of course be shifting, multiple, and contradictory. This challenges the descriptivist theories of Russell, Frege, Wittgenstein, and Searle, which argue that names mean only in their reference to descriptions implicitly associated with the name's bearer, or some sum thereof (Kripke 27–30). In different possible worlds a name's bearer might be described differently (according to different behavioral attributions the person could possess in alternative worlds, for example), but if the name's bearer as a referent remains constant across contexts, then *that* name refers to *that* person, regardless of the name, the person, or of any detachable descriptions or properties upon which the name is not, in fact, contingent. Names, perhaps uniquely, are signs that point directly, singularly, to their referents, and Kripke contends that our names can and do represent things independently of the incursions of language or text.

While it is an oversimplification to argue that Kripke occupies a simple "realist" position, as Spikes notes ("Saul Kripke" 304), his theory of names preserves a link between language and reality that deconstructionists would deny. I am not claiming that Kripke's controversial theory is not ambiguous; indeed, it has bred multiple interpretations (Norris), challenges (Plantinga; Clarkson), and revisions (Kaplan). By his own admission, Kripke's theory of proper names cannot be extended to all reference (though it has been applied to some common nouns), and not all words function as rigid designators (48, 145). But his arguments certainly prompt us to ponder what Richard Rorty has called a form of "linguistic essentialism" (17), a reference to the essential one-to-one signifier-signified relationship missing from post-Saussurean linguistic theory, where nothing is signified outside (con) text. While this onomastic exceptionalism, as one might term it, would not be accepted by many poststructuralists (whose theories inform many of the arguments herein), in *Geronimo Rex* names certainly appear to signify in a unique way, allowing aspects of Kripke's theory to be applied to our readings. If we accept Kripke's claim that a name has a value in itself, not just in relation to other signs, then this peculiar linguistic unit might offer a unique way out of Harry's textual entrapment, and a significant victory for his writing.

In the novel's most important scene, Harry discovers a set of "books on Geronimo, the Apache" in the college library (230). It is perhaps unsurprising that Harry, who like many of Hannah's narrators is desperate to become a storied figure, encapsulated when he exclaims, "Someone record me" (129), should be so enamored with the literary figure of Geronimo, one of the most mythologized figures of Native American history. Yet there is more to Harry's identification with Geronimo. He admits explicitly that the books "caught my eye" because "I went for the name, *Geronimo*" (159). Shortly thereafter, Harry's identification with the Native American comes from a second notable acknowledgment of Geronimo's name: "At the same time my eyes fell on the word, name, *Geronimo,* again, and I realized that *my* last name could be found mixed up in it. It was silly but true. Monroe could be found in Geronimo. I was delighted [. . .]. [I]t was all a high throb" (160). Later still, Harry declares a third time that "[a]h, Geronimo! [. . .] All the letters of *Monroe* could be found in his name" (302–3). Mark Graybill claims that because Harry discovers Geronimo through library books, he "has no access to the real Apache leader, only the versions of him inscribed in language" ("Fall of the West" 681). In a sense, Harry's sympathy with Geronimo is purely textual—and even more so when we consider how Harry's reading his own name in the other's is merely anagrammatic and therefore arbitrary. However, the strong emphasis placed on Geronimo's *name* in each case suggests that there is something as vitally enabling in terms of Harry's masculinity in identifying with the name itself, as a word, as in his perception of the name's bearer, or the textual versions of him inscribed in the books that Harry reads. In this context *Geronimo* does not work in quite in the discrete singular way Kripke suggests names do, perhaps partly because this is a figure whose mythology supersedes any direct access to the referent. But I would certainly concede that given the three examples presented above, Harry identifies with Geronimo the name as much as with Geronimo the man or the myth.

Having acquired Geronimo from his name, Harry proceeds to enact a persona he deems worthy of it. This act of "playing Indian," to borrow Philip J. Deloria's title phrase, speaks of course to more troubling issues of race and imperial ambition and acquisition that it is worth initially pausing on before resuming my exploration of how names function in these scenes. Harry appropriates a costume of "action boots," pistol, and neckerchief to simulate the Apache, even proceeding to declare facetiously, "I am an Indian" (232, 166). Several critics have interpreted Harry's obsession with Geronimo in terms of the performative formulation of adolescent male identity, of idealized masculinity and a kind of simulated model of manhood, seeing Harry's theatrical staging of "authentic" Apache masculinity as underwriting his adolescent exploits and fantasies, which often romanticize violence, as Mark J. Charney notes (8–9; see also Madden 311 and Noble 40). However, we cannot ignore the political agenda behind this staged persona, where white southern masculinity defines itself against multiracial others, in keeping with Deloria and others' insights into the duplicity of white America's mythologizing of disenfranchised ethnic groups, American white men exploiting the idea of the "Indian" to fashion their own national identity in ways that have contributed to the maintenance of a mythology of Native Americans as savage other.

Melanie Benson Taylor identifies here two problematic "general categories" into which Hannah's Native American characters fall, most notably in *Geronimo Rex, Ray,* and *Never Die.* The first appear as "elegiac ghosts serving a nationalist agenda through which a still-shaken (white) South can inspire and re-empower itself"; the second are depicted as "actual" southern Native Americans actively *"made* into ghosts, denied existence and respect, another 'race' altogether" (Benson Taylor, "Southern and Western" 142). Benson Taylor thus argues that Hannah's fictional representations of Native Americans can be understood "in a somewhat reactionary tradition of southern self-interest," contrary to then recent criticism from Kreyling, Bone, Guinn, and others who have situated Hannah in an actively *post*southern and thus more politically subversive context (143). While I would argue that Hannah's foregrounding this troubling dichotomy is not necessarily the same as subscribing to the reactionary politics underwriting it, nor an attempt (as Benson Taylor charges) to absolve "colonial culpability" for the absence of more authentic Native American representation even in contemporary southern fiction (Benson Taylor, *Reconstructing* 40), certainly Harry's oppositional depictions of Native Americans in *Geronimo Rex* fit worryingly into the two categories Benson Taylor identifies.

The first category is discernible in the romanticized figure of Geronimo, epitome of Apache masculine power, serving as inspiration, benevolent ally and even starting to represent Harry's moral conscience in key moments, sanctioning acts of violence and vengeance in the name of romance and righteousness (below). The second is revealed when Harry encounters real Choctaw people and is shocked and sickened by them, or rather, by his perception of the spectacle of them. The latter encounter comes when Harry, a twenty-two-year-old medical student in Mississippi, witnesses a group of impoverished Choctaws awaiting medical aid. In a passage that might have come from Conrad's *Heart of Darkness,* Harry describes Choctaw women in childbirth (whether from memory or fantasy is not clear) with a thinly veiled attitude of white superiority: "Their vaginas were fossileums of old blood. Their babies came up in a rotten exhumation; [. . .] It almost belied the germ theory of disease. The mothers did not cry out for Jesus like Negro women. They bawled [. . .] as if in direct, private accusation against some little male toad of a god. It made my blood crawl" (281). The corporeal reality of the sick Choctaws' bodies disgusts Harry, and the picture he paints of these bawling, subhuman creatures is a far cry from his eulogized vision of Geronimo the Apache. Neither does it fit into the "standardized" biracial social order of the South after the Civil War; Benson Taylor notes Harry's failure to compare the Choctaws to "Negro Women" here (*Reconstructing* 50–51). Benson Taylor is right to point out the conspicuous absence of any more authentic, nuanced, or developed characterizations of the Native Americans who feature sporadically in Hannah's stories, just as recent scholarship on the Native South (from Benson Taylor, Eric Gary Anderson, Kirstin Squint, and others) seeks to redress the still problematic exclusion of the Native South from southern literary studies. Harry's interest (as a white southern male) in Geronimo certainly appears to bear out Benson Taylor's arguments for exploiting Native Americans for the first purpose above, the duplicity of which is brought shockingly to the fore in the scene with the Choctaws.

Attending to the troubling politics of Hannah's portrayal (or Harry's perception) of Native American characters, vital as this is, does not fully account for Harry's peculiar interest in the formal properties of the *name* Geronimo nor for the broader significance of names throughout *Geronimo Rex*. For example, Harry's first experience of Catherine Wrag is when he recognizes her name, written in a text: "Fleece passed a [theater] program down. He had underlined her name in the cast. *Catherine Marie Wrag*. [. . .] Fleece had encircled *Catherine*. Yes, I'd read it often enough in the letters [Whitfield Peter's]" (240). The boys read Catherine's printed name in the program of a college musical she is performing in and recall having initially encountered her namesake in Peter Lepoyster's letters. Just as the name Geronimo signals such "a high throb" to reader Harry, so too is Catherine's mere name equally significant: reading it, Harry declares, "I fell for her before I was certain who she was [and] I loved her purely" (240). On the surface, Harry's finding *Monroe* in *Geronimo* is essentially counterfeit, just as Harry's infatuation with Catherine, based purely on her written name (and it is not even her own name), seems rather questionable, like imitating Geronimo. While of course Harry does gain access to the real or uninscribed Catherine, his identification with Geronimo is entirely contingent on text. But this does not detract from the comparable value Harry invests in the name Geronimo.

There are many other instances in the novel where names, and the act of naming, take on a heightened significance. As a child, Harry is aware that his own father "has the name of a bayou poet—Ode Elann Monroe" (18), and in order to simulate "a hot and ancient mental life" (17) that would be appropriate to his name, Harry guesses that his father sits each night in his study "writing his own name over and over in different scripts until he bores himself into a coma" (18). While this may be a farcical act on Ode Elann's part (and Harry admits that "I've *inherited* a major bit of the farce from him" [18]), and although the name he shares with the bayou poet does not refer singularly to him, the *act* of naming—specifically, writing one's name—is therapeutic nonetheless. Harry will later perform his own act of self-repair via writing his own name when he reasserts his threatened white male authority against the group of pregnant Choctaw women by writing "*Harriman Monroe, M.D.*" on one of the women's medical-aid forms after he has failed medical school (281). Despite the fraudulence of the act, Harry realizes that "[m]y signature had helped," and he admits that "[s]ometimes, even now, I'll put *M.D.* after my name when I sign a check and get a warm old kick from it" (282). Writing the name, as a text, on an authoritative document (here, a check) lends temporary authority because it *passes* as authentic.

In contrast and pertaining to an implicit class politics underwriting the novel, both Harry's father and his new father-in-law conspicuously misname each other. On Harry's wedding day, Prissy's wealthy father, Ted Lombardo, comically effeminizes Ode Elann by drunkenly calling him "Old Elaine! Old Elaine!" (346). In retaliation, we learn from Harry, his own father will make a political point of *not* naming the other man: "The old man gave Lombardo a negligent scan, as if he would never be troubled to learn *his* first name. I wasn't sure of it myself until we got the checks from him in Fayetteville. He had a hard and vigorous signature: *Ted Lombardo*" (346). Again, the name is crucial, written on the authoritative document. It is likely that Lombardo's signature serves the same performative function here, of reasserting his own sense of (hard and vigorous) masculine virility, that Harry's signing checks with *M.D.* serves. These brief examples—and there are many—signal the important subjective function attached to certain acts of (self-)naming, and in fact this finds expression in the language of Harry's narrative self-reference itself.

Harry chooses to refer to himself in the third person at various formative moments, most notably when he resolves finally to face up to his nemesis, Whitfield Peter: "The next time he saw me, he would meet Harry Monroe and all that that boy really was" (253). Writing the name proves curiously enabling in terms of southern masculinity, which, paradoxically, becomes legitimized when it gains the anchoring power of inscription. Spikes discusses Hannah's *Ray* using Kripke's theory of names in similar terms, arguing that Ray's referring to himself in the third person acts as a means of psychological grounding, unifying Ray's fragmented psyche in a sea of protean and confusing signifiers compounded by Ray's mental illness: "The name's meaning is its referent, that object which the name designates, and that object is *one* thing"; where the name Ray functions as a rigid designator, Ray the "referent" can be "*both* a man of contrary thoughts and actions *and* a unified self" ("What's in a Name?" 77, 79–80). This concept of the grounding power of self-naming adds nuance to Harry's wish to achieve the legendary status of Geronimo. The special power that Harry identifies in the names Geronimo and Catherine (and indeed in proper names in general) comes, then, from his status as a would-be *writer* and his recognition of the constitutive power of words and text, especially in the South.

This notion of names' inherent significance, or power, reflects usefully on Kripke's theory, because Harry's heightened interest in names allows Hannah's novel to play with, if not fully subscribe to, the concept of names as special instances of signification that mean in an altogether more authentic way than conventional language. This is epitomized when Geronimo's very name assumes totemic power: the name's potency is such that Harry invokes Geronimo's spirit at various times in his narrative, for example, when imploring the Apache's sanction in shooting Whitfield Peter. It is interesting that Harry should say "Help me, Indian!" (377) rather than "Help me, Geronimo!" in this crucial moment. More than being simply indicative of white men's suspect appropriation of Native American culture to serve their own ends, it could be a working example of Kripke's rigid designation occurring with an interchangeable pronoun. That is, *Indian* refers singularly to Geronimo (or an idea of him) in Harry's mind. One obvious difference I would identify here between names and other signifiers is that names have a much narrower function and are therefore less susceptible to referential slippage. They are also much more limited and limiting, a more direct experience of subjectivity, perhaps. Whatever a name might mean to us, we could not articulate that meaning to another person using the name alone. But the name, as well as the other names that could be substituted for it (here, *Indian* for *Geronimo*), would nonetheless signify to us directly because of this potentially unique, one-way referential capacity embodied in names. Signifying beyond the normal workings of linguistic (self-)reference, then, names become important not just in relation to a signifying web but also for their own sake. They have an inherent meaning and value without any *real* reference to the named (Catherine or Geronimo), such that *Geronimo Rex* certainly appears to hypothesize that names carry the noncontingent properties of singular referring terms whose absence has been so widely lamented in the concept of reference after Saussure.

Several passages in Harry's narrative support these arguments. For example: "I pronounced the name, *Ge Ron I Mo*. Two iambs, rising at the last with a sound which might be blown forever through some hole in a cliff in Arizona by the wind. A name which in itself made you want to cast off, even being landlocked, and kick off the past history that sucked you down" (302). Again, this scene can be read in terms of Harry's involvement with Geronimo and the "imperial fantasies" it reveals. Benson Taylor points out the "white southern narcissism" implicit in Harry's subscription to the western fantasy of "casting off" to unchartered lands (Geronimo's Apache Arizona), a fantasy especially appealing to the historically burdened white southerner. Likewise, the image of being "blown forever through some hole in a cliff in Arizona" pertains chillingly to the process of Indian removal, which remains unacknowledged in the white (southern) fantasy of "going West" ("Southern and Western" 155). Once again, however, we must note that symbolic power is vested in the name *in itself* rather than in any secondary description or symbolic reference to the name's bearer—just as authentic descriptions of the Native South are conspicuously lacking here as elsewhere in mainstream southern fiction.

Harry's claim that Geronimo's name instinctively compels action ("made you want to cast off") explicitly recalls his reaction to hearing the jazz music that similarly made him feel "washed away [. . .] ripped off, out" and made him "want to pick up a rifle and just get killed somewhere" (14). This not only directly connects music, names, and (violent) masculine agency. It also establishes an explicit link between the name as a linguistic unit and how close it comes to musical reference. The *sound* of the (written) name—which might be blown through a hole by the wind (302)—becomes literally like a sound played on a trumpet. Figuratively, therefore, the name has successfully achieved the condition of music. It is the phonetic properties of Geronimo's name, more than its referential meaning (be that the real referent, the man Geronimo, or the warrior mythology that has been retrospectively applied), that imbues the word with aesthetic promise, affording it a share in "the non-linguistic aesthetic properties of music," to use Nathan Salmon's formulation of rigid designation (23). This would explain Harry's distaste for the (musical) tone of Catherine's "whining" *voice* as much as for her vocabulary and "bad grammar" (248). And as we know, these pre- or metalinguistic properties are those that Harry implicitly associates not only with meaningful masculine action but also, and perhaps more importantly, with artistic value. This epiphanic moment in which the word (*Geronimo*) *becomes* the sound or thing not only implies the "absolute" referential condition of music but also subtly evokes a test case for some perfect word-to-thing correspondence in which language functions properly or with mimetic verisimilitude.

Quoting Jameson, Romine argues that Hannah's *Yonder Stands Your Orphan* reveals a postmodern aesthetic that departs from a modernist belief in "some 'pure' work or form [that] can emerge from the process" of "burn[ing] away, like slag," the "noise" of postmodern signification (Jameson, *Seeds of Time* 36, qtd. in Romine, "Orphans All" 179). Again, these putatively postmodern problems find a precedent in the oversignified South. Romine argues that *Yonder Stands Your Orphan* "inverts the scenario precisely: it is purity that cannot be assimilated in the novel's messy domain, one dominated by cultural noise against which 'music' can be posited only as an 'exquisite hypothesis,' and against which only silence can be brought to bear as a practical measure" (179). *Geronimo Rex*, however, hypothesizes that certain types of *linguistic* reference carry the potential to approximate the "exquisite" condition of music. This resonates with the convergence of music and words Hannah claimed to have sought in his own writerly "tone" (Hannah, "Spirit" 326), and it anticipates Hannah's later bluegrass-influenced collection of stories, *High Lonesome*. While (logocentric) ideas about exquisite or pure forms of reference are challenged more than they are upheld in Hannah's fiction, his stories certainly derive significant creative energy from conflating traditionally antithetical ideas about music, speech, and writing in ways that challenge preconceived distinctions between the authentic and the merely textual.

Christopher Eagle describes modernist theories of "the perfect language" as attempts to recover, or at least to understand, the condition of language in a prelapsarian state, one in which, on the basis of Adam's (proper) naming in Genesis 2:19 ("Thou hast rightly named"), the name signals a prototype for language's lost ability to refer or to name rightly. Eagle explains that the "perfect" language would "possess the virtue of clarity, through which we can be made to see objects distinctly, due to some quality, whether pictorial or phonetic, inherent to the form of the word itself" (7). In the above example from *Geronimo Rex*, *Geronimo* generates a symbolic referential transcendence that is captured neatly when the name enables Harry to metaphorically kick off "landlocked" place and time, arguably because the "pictorial or phonetic" qualities inherent in the word *Geronimo* similarly extend the word's meaning beyond the workings of ordinary language and invest it with a paradoxical clarity or rightness of meaning. This is much like what music does, and what epiphanies have tried to do.

Harry's interest in the audible "iambs" and visible syllables of the written name *Geronimo* invites parallels with Joyce and Nabokov. Harry's *"Ge Ron I Mo"* perfectly echoes the opening lines of Nabokov's *Lolita,* and it is possible that Hannah is directly beholden to Nabokov here: "Lo-lee-ta: the tip of the tongue taking a trip of three steps down the palate to tap, at three, on the teeth. Lo. Lee. Ta" (9). In the *Dubliners* short story "Araby," Joyce's adolescent narrator declares similarly: "The syllables of the word *Araby* were called to me through the silence in which my soul luxuriated and cast an Eastern enchantment over me" (24). Furthermore, the magic of the word *Araby* is echoed in the unspoken name of the narrator's infatuation (known only in the story as "Mangan's sister"), over which Joyce's narrator, like Harry Monroe and Humbert Humbert, similarly fixates: "her name was like a summons to all my foolish blood" (22); "Her name sprang to my lips at moments in strange prayers and praises which I myself did not understand" (23). Therefore, certain words, including but not limited to proper names, communicate a near-spiritual meaning to each narrator in a curiously immediate but unconventional way. In each case, the name refers without the need for recourse to secondary descriptions about, or knowledge of, either the named object or the name itself, as a word. Recalling the language of music and epiphany, highlighting the individual tonal and formal components that constitute words has the effect of slowing our interpretative processes and making them refer in a different or nondescriptional way.

This is evident not only in the way that Hannah, Nabokov, and Joyce have emphasized the *syllables* of *Geronimo, Lolita,* and *Araby* but also in the strikingly similar way in which foreign words appear in *Geronimo Rex* and indeed in Hannah's narratives more broadly, with italicized French words appearing in moments that draw attention to their unique (aesthetic, musical) significance, a technique similarly deployed by Joyce (see, e.g., *Dubliners* 63 or *Portrait* 279). Take, for instance, Harry's consideration of "[t]he word *ricochet:* what Frenchness, what powerful romance, I remember when I first heard it back in 1951" (113), or when he imagines Geronimo being "bored extremely [by] most language and English especially" (303). Because to nonnative speakers foreign words do not make sense according to the normal rules of the language system (which nonspeakers do not know), they become curiously nonreferential. Foreign, newly heard, or exotic-sounding words can easily be exploited for their creative or musical possibilities, because only the pictorial or phonetic qualities of their shapes and sounds are accessible to nonspeakers; they mean in an exclusively visual or aural way. Foreign words exist beyond the mediations of text that would inevitably come with the outsider's initiation into the previously unknown language system: a fall moment where meaning becomes merely a matter of context and (re)presentation. Thus, the meaning of alien words can be communicated to their auditors in a curiously innocent or perfectly direct way, as names might. This is much like having an immediate reaction to hearing music or being struck by an image or scene, both of which we have witnessed Harry doing in *Geronimo Rex*.

If singular reference is inherent in a proper name, it is not generated from the word's meaning-making from a (post)structuralist perspective, in which reference occurs only via the differences between words and not from any directly referential word-to-thing correspondence. Rather, the Kripkean name-as-referent "can be identified as just itself, as an *it* with an identity distinct from its [linguistic] properties" (Kripke 52). Interestingly, *Geronimo Rex* contains a good working example of Saussure's diacritical principle, when Harry engages in a curious wordplay with Catherine's surname: "I am your rag, my name is Wrag" (250). This reveals the significance of Catherine's name to Harry, who obsesses over it while simultaneously highlighting the conventionally meaningless nature of the word, which means only in a system of phonetic and formal difference. At first glance this seems like a perfect example of the failure of poststructuralist signification to refer finally or unequivocally. But taking Kripke's position, *Wrag, Catherine,* and Catherine are in fact perfectly united, at least in Harry's mind. Access to one breeds access to the other, such that the named person is personified (and signified) singularly in his or her name. This is captured succinctly when Harry declares that merely reading the written names *Geronimo* and *Catherine* makes both figures "c[o]me alive" (160) "in my hands" (249). This tension between word and world (and, more subtly, speech and writing) is furthered when Harry considers Catherine's four names—"Catherine Vinceen Marie Wrag"—and concludes with, "And so what? You live, my Catherine, and you were so much when I first saw you, language couldn't do you right, and you're worth four different names at least, if language ever tried" (249). Crucially, while in this case Catherine initially appears to outrun the capacities of a fallen system of language to name her "rightly," it is nonetheless through recourse to Catherine's name(s) specifically that Harry imagines language's best attempt. Thus, Harry subsequently implores, "Would you [Catherine] say your whole name for me?" (252), and in so doing further implies some intrinsic value that lies in the name and the act of naming. Meanwhile, by revealing the musicality of names as living speech (Harry likes to *say* the syllables of the written name *Geronimo;* he wants Catherine to *say* all of her names), *Geronimo Rex* both pertains to and complicates (reductive) understandings of Kripke in which the name establishes some pure or singular relationship between sign and referent.

Harry's fascination with names as words subjugates a traditional notion of textual meaning to the formal components of the language of the text itself, to the extent that *Geronimo Rex* certainly entertains the prospect of names as a special linguistic register that transcends the normative workings of verbal reference. This is not to say that Hannah's novel unequivocally dramatizes Kripke's new theory of reference, much less that it (nor indeed Kripke's theory itself) fully or finally resolves the challenges posed by poststructuralism's arbitrary sign. These issues are thoroughly compounded by Harry's (Hannah's) status as a writer of a highly represented and mediated place. What it does show, however, is a vital conceptual nuance that extends the intellectual significance of Hannah's work beyond the parochial southern culture it depicts. It makes a significant and in many ways remarkably prescient contribution to ongoing metaphysical debates about the problem of reference, at a pivotal historical moment when contemporary problems of mimesis and representation began to overtake prior notions of what is authentic in art and in contemporary regional studies after modernism.

The circularity of *Geronimo Rex*'s ending, concluding with its own nascent beginnings, not only reveals Hannah's metafictional preoccupation with the circumstances from which his novel (a finished work of art) could emanate but it also constitutes part of the text's own self-staged southernness. This suggests that the South has always been in a sense postmodern, mindful even from its earliest conceptions of how "South" and "southern" have been mediated, contrived, or "arranged" (Spike's term). While Hannah's "meta" moments force us to consider the strategies of interpretation and the competence of our own reading practices in a way that pertains to contemporary ideas about postmodernity—both Weston and Spikes have taken this as evidence of Hannah's postmodern departure from presenting the *real* South in his writing—they also speak to Hannah's self-reflexive acknowledgment of "South" as a narrative contrivance or function of text.

If *Geronimo Rex* speculates that there is no authentic southern subjectivity that can be articulated in writing and, by extension, no writing that we can call authentically southern, then what is left for new southern writers to do? Must they simply play with the now worthless fragments of a more authentic past, or is there something paradoxically valuable that can be wrested from acknowledging the contingency of (regional) authenticity? The Persian poet Rumi said that "real men dance and whirl on the battlefield; they dance in their own blood" (qtd. in Nachmanovitch 53), and I think there is something of that here. Hannah having been obliged, in the literary battlefield of the late twentieth century, to dramatize some serious contemporary problems with the concept of authentic reference and even (regional) authenticity itself, it is to his immense credit that he can reach this potentially nihilistic conclusion in his very first novel, and then proceed to "dance" in it by creating original and exciting works that retain a deep-rooted interest in an older concept of authenticity while also challenging and evolving beyond it. On the one hand, it seems that the authentic has become so inextricably bound to ideas of the textual that the concept of mimetic verisimilitude would be better relinquished in the late-twentieth-century (southern) American bildungsroman. On the other, apparently something paradoxically real and authentic can come from a self-reflexive undermining of these very concepts in contemporary southern writing.

As with much of the author's subsequent writing, new kinds of conceptual paradigms appear to be required to interpret *Geronimo Rex*, if not to reconcile its contradictions, then at least to better appreciate its conceptual complexity. The small-town southern culture described in *Geronimo Rex* is not the realm of the experimental game-playing of high literary postmodernism and its portrayal of a Baudrillardian crisis of meaning. Instead, Hannah's novel preserves a tangible sense of southern authenticity, which may have been reconfigured but certainly is not lost. For some scholars, especially after the New Southern Studies, no such recovery of the real and authentic is possible, yet this paradox certainly remains viable in Hannah's fiction during the early seventies and beyond. Hannah suggests that in some (aesthetic) contexts things are best represented with names, while in others they are best represented with epiphanies or with music; no matter that all forms of reference, including our attendant apprehensions of the region, may be lacking a foundational basis in authenticity. The last word of the novel is "Music!" but in the end (and contrary to Romine's arguments for "silence" in *Yonder Stands Your Orphan*), the final victory may be for language and writing in *Geronimo Rex*. If this triumph has been wrested from Hannah's early exposé of the problem of authentic southern reference, in an already overpopulated field that might have prevented the text's very existence, then arguably, success is all the sweeter. And we writers may be in the right field after all.

2

The Authenticity Paradox and
the Myth of Masculinity

Airships

In *Real Phonies* (2010) Abigail Cheever describes a critical paradigm that resonates with Hannah's fiction when she writes, "There are probably few books
written in the past half century in which questions of authenticity and its
opposites are not in some way raised, if not resolved" (17). I argued in chapter 1 that in his first novel Hannah abandons faith in a belief in the concept of authentic reference, partly by exposing how the ostensibly Joycean
epiphanies in narrator Harry Monroe's narrative were founded on forms
of counterfeit simulation that complicate their interpretation according to
what Matthew Guinn terms "the familiar [modernist] formula" (162). Meanwhile, Harry urges us to believe in the value of his own writing according,
paradoxically, to a concept of authenticity that he suspects to be a sham.
Where Harry was a writer in *Geronimo Rex*, Hannah's first short-story collection, *Airships* (1978), hosts a gallery of artists, whose stories signal sophisticated inquiries into the nature of aesthetics and the conundrum of
representing subjectivity, in which the question of authenticity remains vital, though the concept appears to have been lost. *Airships* takes up this
challenge of the "authenticity paradox" by further engaging with the cultural problem of authenticity, in ways that reflect usefully on a contemporary, late-twentieth-century shift away from authenticity to performativity.

The two *Airships* stories discussed in this chapter, "Testimony of Pilot"
and "Midnight and I'm Not Famous Yet," examine this relationship between
real and counterfeit, authenticity and performance. The stories are intensely
homosocial, being conducted in almost exclusively male arenas, including
the Vietnam battlefield and the sports field (golf, tennis). They explore how
ideas about masculinity (what makes a real man?) are formed from the rela-

tionships between men, in unique contexts of spectacle, performance, and witness. More than simply interrogating what constitutes heroic masculine action in the late-twentieth-century South, the stories question what kinds of aesthetic qualities need to be present for masculinity to be created and consumed, where masculinity is an issue not of ontological certainty but of (social and aesthetic) performance. The analysis of white southern masculinity in stories like these is somewhat familiar, and these stories are among the most analyzed works in Hannah scholarship. My approach here, therefore, is to show how the construction and narration of authentic masculinity can be better understood by emphasizing how the stories themselves make visible the production and performance of authenticity.

Having identified a problem with masculinity related to performance, Hannah's texts also interrogate the notion of authentic *art* by exploring their own methods of aesthetic staging, acknowledging their artificial contrivances as literary products, and challenging us to determine their integrity and merit. By exploring what aesthetic value might consist of in different performative contexts, the stories question not only what sorts of masculine performance might be designated meaningful and authentic but also what conditions are necessary for good art to be produced. While these stories are concerned with the idea of masculinity as a performance, they are also self-reflexive about the performative nature of (written) stories. They dramatize their own performativity alongside that of masculinity, until the two become inextricable. Consequently, this becomes fiction about fiction, even while it is about the idea of masculinity as a kind of fiction, or myth. This is the sophisticated level of conceptual duality in *Airships,* which considers the circumstances in which the quality of authenticity might be, if not determined finally or metaphysically, then staged or performed.

In this chapter, first I explore how "Midnight and I'm Not Famous Yet" dramatizes a concept of authentic masculinity (the myth of the "real man") being formed in the homosocial relationships between men that are crucially performative. Then, I extend this to an analysis of "Testimony of Pilot," where the concept of authentic art (music and writing) is forged similarly in the bond between performer and audience, rather than being inherent in the art form itself. I interpret Hannah's heightened interest in staging, performance, and simulations, as well as what sorts of things lend a performance credibility, as the basis for an interrogation of a concept of representation that at the historical moment of Hannah's writing has become removed or separated from what we might conventionally have designated *the thing itself.* Comparing the figures of soldier, artist, and "gentleman" sportsman, as well as the different forms of aesthetic expression the story presents (music, photojournalism, writing, and noncombat sport), I identify key scenes that include an audience witnessing a staged spectacle of drama and testifying to its authenticity. This chapter does not attempt to establish what authentic southern masculinity, or authentic southern art, in this period really *is,* but to investigate the terms on which such things might be imagined in a contemporary culture characterized by what Cheever calls our "[re]negotiations of the changing terrain of the self and its constitution" (18). Hannah's stories foreground an interest in the staged contexts in which the investigation into authenticity might be conducted. As anticipated by *Geronimo Rex,* such an investigation appears to be superseding crude or reductive understandings of the real. This might mark part of a transition from modernism to postmodernism, but as I have stressed elsewhere, this is a contested historical distinction that is not my focus here.

If it seems incongruous to be writing about authenticity while arguing that Hannah's writing destabilizes this sort of critical vocabulary, it is because these stories continue to worry over what is authentic even while they reconfigure or temporarily abandon the notion in its older, more conventional sense. In examining a masculine mythology of romantic individualism, the stories valorize certain types of male behavior and criticize others, even while they recognize the contingency of what makes a real man in any given context. In Hannah's stories, to discover the authenticity of something, the quality of authenticity must, paradoxically, be staged or performed, even while staging and performing would appear to undermine the putative claim to authenticity to which the stories appear to be devoted. If both authentic masculinity and authentic art are a performance, Hannah implies that there is no authentic (essential) masculinity and no pure (unmediated) art. Despite acknowledging authenticity as a form of simulation, however, these stories also seek to persuade an implied reading audience of their own legitimacy *as* aesthetic performances, whereupon some vestigial sense of authenticity can be identified. It is this paradox, and its engagements with late-twentieth-century southern masculinity, that these stories are dedicated to dramatizing (if not resolving), asking us to consider whether it is possible to have it both ways.

While Hannah's texts characteristically resist interpretation according to

any neat paradigm shift from authenticity to performativity, his work usefully anticipates some recent ideas about masculinity as a myth and a performance. Such ideas would gain purchase from the early 1980s onward, not
only amid challenges posed to the concept of authenticity in the global West
but while the concept of the American region was itself similarly undergoing a series of important transitions. While the questioning of essentialist
mythologies of gender was something of a staple of American fiction of the
1960s and 1970s, Hannah's work is valuable because it entwines the concept
of performative masculinity with postregional thinking about how "South"
and "southern" are performed, while also incorporating metafictional ideas
about writing as a performance.

   Among the more influential twenty-first-century studies of the "problem" of American masculinity is James Gilbert's *Men in the Middle* (2005).
Gilbert identifies the 1950s as a formative period when modern conceptualizations of the "masculinity crisis" (16) first gained a language and the
widespread critical attention of sociologists, anthropologists, psychologists,
historians, and literary critics, who have attributed the challenge of American masculinity in the 1950s to some key sociocultural developments of
the time. These include the rise of the nuclear family, with responsibilities
shared between the sexes, the entry of females into a previously all-male
workforce after World War II, and the imminent rise of feminist criticism
in the 1960 and 1970s, inspired by the civil rights movement. Gilbert is indebted here to a series of prior studies, including David Riesman, Nathan
Glazer, and Reuel Denney's *The Lonely Crowd* (1950), Joseph Pleck's *The Myth
of Masculinity* (1981), Mark Gerzon's *A Choice of Heroes* (1982), and David
Gilmore's *Manhood in the Making* (1990); further contributors to the field
include Michael Kimmel, Robert Griswold, Roger Horrocks, and Gail Bederman (Gilbert 17–25). Despite the obvious problems with projecting cultural
crisis onto a precise era (Gilbert is careful to trouble the practice of historicizing any kind of crisis point, as well as the designations *crisis* and *masculinity* themselves), the midcentury masculinity crisis continues to be cited
by scholars as a pivotal moment when prior assumptions about masculinity
and male behavior were being challenged in specific new ways.

   From the 1960s onward, poststructuralism and performance theory
posed a further series of challenges to the notion of unified subjectivity and
the concomitant possibilities for authenticity. Contemporary theories of
performativity such as Judith Butler's poststructuralist-informed *Gender*

Trouble (1990) imagine subjects to be constructed by and within cultural institutions, where they are "actors" performing roles that are not essentially authentic. Todd Reeser acknowledges the crucial role poststructuralism has played in dismantling an ontological concept of (authentic) gender: "it assumes that masculinity has no natural, inherent, or given meaning, that it does not have to mean something predetermined, and that whatever meaning it has is in constant movement" (11). In the absence of any essential core of gender, performance theory suggests that we consider masculinity to be solely a matter of social performance. While we can debate whether there remains a difference between a performative and a true self, where the very concept of a fixed, stable, and unified subjectivity (that can be known) is understood to be itself a fiction or myth the notion of authentic masculinity (and gender in general) comes under scrutiny.

The work of E. Patrick Johnson and John Howard is useful here. Johnson's *Appropriating Blackness: Performance and the Politics of Authenticity* (2003) marks an important critical intervention in both performance studies and Black American studies. Central to Johnson's arguments is the claim that Blackness has no essence, but rather, understanding notions of ethnic and/or racial difference through performance theory reveals the constructed nature of difference, lending Blackness the appearance of a naturalized category through constantly reiterated performances that are, essentially, bogus. This process can be both productive and problematic (E. Johnson 4–8). Howard introduced regional history to existing studies of the field of gay and lesbian history, more commonly associated with the East and West Coasts of the United States and with urban settings. His groundbreaking *Men Like That: A Southern Queer History* (1999), the first book-length study of the queer South, challenges nominal understandings of the small-town rural South and post–World War II America as (geographical and historical) sites where queer life was supposedly precluded. Also key to Howard's arguments are ideas about performance and the narration of oral histories stemming from the critic's ethnographic approach. Howard refers to what he calls "twice-told stories" or "hearsay," by which (queer) histories are constructed and by which they can be recuperated, provided we retain a "self-reflexive" approach (5). Attending to the performativity of storied histories destabilizes notions of *the* truth in favor of authenticity experienced in the act of storytelling; it is a process simultaneously fictional and real. Howard's related claim that "performance becomes a vehicle through which the Other is seen and not seen" (7) resonates with Bone, Ward, and Link's notion of the "created and consumed" South, where "the South" has become such a highly charged concept as a contested vehicle for performances serving particular political agendas across history.

Similarly, the myth of masculinity is contingent on performative constructions of what is "manly" in any given moment, staged through acts and role-playing in different contexts of social performance. Such performances are themselves adaptable to contemporary cultural ideologies, which are inherently changeable. Mary Chapman and Glenn Hendler acknowledge the fallacy of a supposed historical shift in thinking about masculinity, from regarding it as something that is essential to regarding it as something that is staged or mythologized. They argue that "American masculinity has *always* been in crisis, in the sense of being constantly engaged in its own redefinition" (9, my emphasis). Thus, where late-twentieth-century apprehensions of masculinity were engaging in a process of redefinition that was newly emphasizing the ways in which "authenticity" is critically performative (it is a case of acting like a real man rather than *being* one), we should ask which cultural mythologies or social conventions were determining which actions pertain to an accepted *idea* of masculinity at this time. How viable is it to talk about authentic masculinity (or authenticity generally) in this context, as prior lexicons of authenticity were being systematically repudiated? As Gilbert writes, "Throughout the twentieth century, at repeated intervals, the remaining pockets in which older concepts of masculinity still prevailed were further undercut" (16). In the cultural moment of Hannah's writing, the denomination *authentic* seemed to demand a major conceptual overhaul if it could continue to account for subjects understood in performative rather than essentialist terms.

What happens to the concept of masculinity in the American South in this period? Much southern scholarship has explored the concept of masculinity in a regional context, with several critics advancing the South's special relevance to contemporary apprehensions of masculinity. Jason T. Eastman, for example, discusses southern "rebel" masculinity and contends that "Southern men occupy a contradictory place in American culture as the rest of the country stereotypes them as backwards and deviant, yet simultaneously celebrates Southern males as quintessential exemplars of American manhood" (189). Numerous others have argued that the various national studies of American masculinity have downplayed the importance of region-alism when considering how masculinity operates in recent American cul-ture. Craig Thompson Friend and Lorri Glover's *Southern Manhood* (2004), Friend's *Southern Masculinity* (2009), and Lydia Plath and Sergio Lussana's *Black and White Masculinity in the American South* (2009), for example, ex-plore how the concept of "Southern uniqueness" can inform national dis-cussions of masculinity as a cultural construct, where "gender ideals [. . .] have taken their own distinct form in the South" (Plath and Lussana 2). Such studies focus on distinctive elements of the South's social, cultural, economic, and military history. These include (but are not limited to) the historical prolongation of a predominantly rural economy relative to the American North, the perpetuation of "old-fashioned" patriarchal values and religious practices, and the indebtedness of the South's problematic class and race relations to a much more "recent" racial history, given the region's belated removal of Jim Crow laws relative to the rest of the nation.

The South's material differences aside, a key element of the region's sup-posedly distinctive gender politics comes from the ongoing legacy of Lost Cause and neo-Confederate mythology. Angie Maxwell explains how histori-cally, "southern masculinity [has] focused on studies of antebellum southern performances of male honor and chivalry, both of which were cemented in the code of the Confederacy" (*Indicted South* 23). While of course we should be wary of framing *all* forms of white southern masculinity within this sin-gular mythology (at the expense of other micro-Souths within which differ-ent gendered mythologies may operate), Thomas Bjerre and others have con-vincingly applied these arguments to Hannah's work. Drawing also on R. W. Connell's ideas about hegemonic masculinity (below), Bjerre writes that "as a southerner Barry Hannah grew up surrounded by myths of the valiant he-roes of the Lost Cause," and much of his fiction contains contemporary male characters inevitably failing to "live up to the burden of the Lost War and the masculine codes of honor and heroism it connotes" ("Heroism" 46–47). In the wake of postbellum Reconstruction and the more recent movements toward racial and sexual equality in the 1950s and 1960s, the narratives that had once underpinned the concept of white masculinist supremacy in the South—U. B. Phillips claims this as "the central theme of southern [modern-ist] history" (qtd. in Wilson 144)—were losing or had lost their cultural pur-chase. New discourses inflecting the multicultural and often divided voices of the region rendered antebellum myths about gender, which romanticized "gentleman" plantation culture as a time of white "mastery and independence," suddenly obsolete (Maxwell, *Indicted South* 23).

Here, the challenge of white masculinity in the New South (and, more recently, the postmodern South) finds at least partial origins in this collapse of traditional means of defining white southern manhood against subjugated racial others; recall bell hooks's condemnation of white cultural appropriations of Blackness, which she poignantly terms "eating the other." Historically, race has been central to southern constructions of male dominance. As Maxwell writes, "Masculinity is inextricable from southern whiteness, particularly during the early twentieth century, when both constructs were wholly dominant" (*Indicted South* 23). Several critical studies have focused on the intersections between southern masculinity and race, and between southern masculinity and American masculinity. Joel Williamson's *The Crucible of Race* (1984), Trent Watts's *White Masculinity in the Recent South* (2008), and Angie Maxwell's *The Indicted South: Public Criticism, Southern Inferiority, and the Politics of Whiteness* (2014), for example, explore the unique interrelations of myths about masculinity and myths about race, both of which are performative constructs whose authenticating (or denigrating) narratives have given historic rise to dominant groups while oppressing others.

If white southern masculinity has traditionally been constructed by methods of opposition (defining it against nonsouthern or nonwhite masculinity, for example), then the question what makes a real southern man cannot be understood except in relation to this complex web of myths about race, gender, region, and nation. However, while antiquated patriarchal ideals have been systematically challenged by hegemonic masculinity's interactions with various forms of otherness, they nonetheless run the risk of becoming even more entrenched in the face of putative outside threat. Studies of southern masculinity by Glenda Gilmore, Stephen Kantrowitz, and Nancy MacLean have documented the impact of these tensions, where perceived threats posed to "traditional" white masculinity in a northernizing or Americanizing culture have manifested in social antagonism. In addition to the obvious examples of public lynching of Black men or Jim Crow laws, the "crisis" of white southern masculinity continues to reveal itself in subtler but equally harmful and systemic ways, for example, with white men emerging as the dominant figures in the professional classes or young Black men accounting for a disproportionate number of those incarcerated or convicted of crimes in the region (see, e.g., Maxwell, *Indicted South* 24). Performances (of white masculinist superiority in this case) have the power to become paradoxically real when they are underwritten by cultural narratives, which lend them power.

In similar fashion, despite the discursive nature of both white southern masculinity and even southernness itself, stereotypes from the Old South have endured in the southern imaginary, holding significant political purchase despite being only myths. As Gerzon argues, men living in the contemporary South "are likely to consume certain images of manhood even though the world from which they are derived may have disappeared—if it ever existed" (5). My following interpretations suggest that to recognize masculinity as a mythopoetic concept, the product of fiction and cultural mythologizing, carries significant political purchase. The stories discussed are strongly influenced by old myths of "ideal" southern manhood, but in ways that subtly complicate what Connell called "hegemonic manhood" (77). The nuance of these stories, then, is in their revealing how the construction (if not the reality) of authentic masculinity (and, by extension, the authentic South) has functioned across different historical moments, and to what ends.

The narrator of "Midnight and I'm Not Famous Yet" is an ex-Army officer named Bobby Smith, a disgraced veteran of Vietnam whose public shame and private melancholy debunk both regional and national myths of antebellum southern chivalry, Lost Cause "rebel" masculinity, and the innocent American Adam of pre-Vietnam America. Written before the end of the Vietnam War and first published in *Esquire* in 1975, Hannah's story forestalls some important reconfigurations of American masculinity after America's military defeat in Vietnam threatened a traditional mythology of American innocence and triumphalism—one from which the South has been traditionally excluded. Hannah's prescience in this respect might be explained by his familiarity, as a southerner, with the concept of cultural failure as a white southern man. If we accept that Lost Cause mythology has been responsible for shaping a sense of defeated southern masculinity for many, as Bjerre's, James B. Potts's, and Martyn Bone's contributions to Bone and others' *Perspectives on Barry Hannah* argue, then the nation's defeat in Vietnam problematizes preestablished myths about the differences between northern and southern masculinity. Indeed, Owen W. Gilman Jr. argues, in his chapter on Hannah's *Ray* in *Vietnam and the Southern Imagination*, that in the southern imagination the nation's fall from grace with Vietnam had already "been prefigured in the history of the South" (87). With the figure of the "fallen" soldier and southerner, "Midnight and I'm Not Famous Yet" foregrounds how the myth of masculinity has been constructed historically, complicating accepted fictions about American manhood and seeking out alternative contexts of action in which (southern) masculinity might be performed.

"Testimony of Pilot" is the story of the social bond between two men: the narrator, William, and his former schoolmate and fellow high-school band member, Arden (Ard) Quadberry, a talented saxophonist turned Navy jet-fighter. This bond was broken when the latter was killed during an operation to repair spinal injuries sustained in a flying accident in Vietnam. The story is therefore William's testimony to this pilot's life and, more importantly, to his talent as an accomplished musician, a talent tragically wasted after Quadberry abandoned music for the military career that killed him. William explains that his story has been motivated by a sense of guilt, having encouraged his friend to take the "gamble" on the operation, which proved fatal. Despite the favorable odds, we are given the shock revelation at the story's close that "[t]he brilliant surgeon lost him," and our narrator dramatically concludes, "This is why I told this story and will never tell another" (44). Like *Geronimo Rex,* "Testimony" ends by describing the moment of its own conception, revealing how the story we have just read came about.

Ostensibly, this strange ending (why should our narrator urgently declare the impetus for his storytelling in this way?) emphasizes the story's origins in an unforgettable emotional experience involving loss, guilt, and the death of a friend (remarkably similar circumstances to those in "Midnight and I'm Not Famous Yet"). More subtly, these features lend William's story the qualities of urgency, spontaneity, and uniqueness (it is the first and last of its kind), by which it establishes authenticity. I argue that William's implicit need to validate his tale stems from a different kind of survivor's guilt, comparing himself, the surviving artist, with the deceased Quadberry. William's narrative is imbued with authorial anxiety that the lesser man survived, and his sense of his own masculinity (his merit as an artist) is measured against the idealized other's. It is through this homosocial relationship that the narrator's sense of himself as a fallen man is conceptualized. (Importantly, it is also how it is redeemed: in the act of writing, William proves his artistic worth, as I will explain.) Thus, the story performs a sophisticated disquisition on the relationship between masculinity, authenticity, and the artistic performance.

"Midnight and I'm Not Famous Yet" is the story of Smith's relationship with his peer and military comrade Ike "Tubby" Wooten. Tubby, an Army photojournalist, also dies, shot in Vietnam after being encouraged by Smith to join his military unit in combat. Toward the end of the story, and invoking the fame to which its title alludes, Smith reveals a similar impetus for telling his story. Haunted by a sense of loss or guilt related specifically to the deceased's talent as an artist, he confesses, "It's Tubby's lost fame I dream about" (117). Smith is referring to a photograph Tubby took of the captured Viet Cong general Li Dap, a likely doppelgänger for General Vo Nguyen Giap, a mythologized figure of national celebrity known as the "Red Napoleon," who led Vietnamese forces to victory over both France and America.[1] Smith knows that this unique photograph would undoubtedly have made Tubby famous had he not himself subsequently killed the imprisoned general and caused the military scandal resulting in Smith's being demoted and sent home to Vicksburg, Mississippi. As a result of this disgrace, the photograph has been confiscated to hush up the tale of Smith and Li Dap—until we read its account here.

Both Tubby's lost fame and Smith's lost honor are recovered in the act of Smith's telling his storied account of "the truth" (117). Ostensibly, "Midnight and I'm Not Famous Yet" provides the true, firsthand account of the circumstances surrounding Li Dap's murder and our narrator's subsequent dishonor. Contrary to the public narrative of Smith's "unheroic action in Vietnam" (*BH* 77), Smith's account reveals that he shot Li Dap in honorable circumstances, to protect one of his own young soldiers (Oliver) from an encroaching attack. In the absence of a weapon capable of targeting discriminately, Smith had no choice but to "[burn] them all up" (116). In this respect, and in tandem with William's "testimony," the word evoking authentic witness, "Midnight and I'm Not Famous Yet" (like "Even Greenland") becomes a parable about what makes an authentic story. It posits a hidden authentic core that selected initiates can witness and know. This is evinced when, despite the scandal, our narrator is privately solaced: "That's all right. I've got four hundred and two boys out there—the ones that got back—who love me and know the truth, who love me *because* they know the truth" (117). This is the truth that readers are privy to, such that both Smith's masculine honor, and the story itself may be redeemed and validated. This is a common theme in *Airships,* established by its lead story, "Water Liars," in which several critics have discerned the redemptive power of the truth (Klevay 133; Thoreen

227; *BH* 34). In "Midnight and I'm Not Famous Yet," Smith's literary confession carries the power to transcend popular discourse, because the "official" narrative—"The story got out to the UPI and they were saying things like 'atrocity' with my name spelled all over the column" (117)—is *not* the truth that he, his "boys," and we readers share. Similarly, at the end of "Water Liars," a truth-telling stranger makes a confession that publicly shames him— a hostile audience exclaims, "Is that the truth? I wouldn't've told that" (6); "This ain't the place! [. . .] Tell your kind of story somewhere else" (6–7)—but the act proves privately grounding and redemptive. Like Smith, "The old man who'd told his story was calm and fixed to his place" (7).

True stories are authenticated by a sense of emotional weight, and in the act of their telling we might recover something vitally important. In "Water Liars," the defeated man's abject tale of the "[w]orst time in my life" (he witnessed his teenage daughter having sex with a much older man [6]) incites public dishonor but private victory, described in an epiphanic moment of religious transcendence with which the shunned narrator claims affinity: "We were both crucified by the truth" (7). Here as in "Testimony of Pilot," there is something heroic in confessing male abjection, a sense of honor in the shame of being disgraced and white and male in the "indicted" South (to use Maxwell's term), where southern masculinity (re)emerges from a point of crisis. While of course this claim invokes a questionable mythology of heroically defeated southern masculinity, in more subtle ways it challenges traditional ideas (patriarchal, martial) about what constitutes heroic male action in the South.

In this respect, "Testimony of Pilot" and "Midnight and I'm Not Famous Yet" are both relatively conventional as narrative confessions that establish authentic emotional bonds between two men, their narrators writing directly from a sense of personal loss. Both narrators' aims seem candid initially, their tales symbolizing a form of reparation with which to recover what both they and the deceased have lost. This establishes an authentic relationship between the teller and his tale, caught when both Smith and the truth-telling stranger in "Water Liars" are privately solaced by the truth that they know and have told. *This* is the authentic moment of a narrator's testimony. However, this simple interpretation misses something vital that this chapter will explore, namely, that these stories problematize this surface reading by challenging the putative concept of authenticity they seem to be dramatizing. First, the stories establish masculinity as something staged, drawing attention to its performative nature and complicating the images of authentic manhood ostensibly promoted. Then, by dramatizing their own performative contrivances as works of art, the stories establish themselves as staged artifacts that challenge us to authenticate them as true moments of testimony. Finally, a third level of complexity is introduced when we extend these arguments to thinking about the South itself, as a complex mix of reality and performance. By staging a concept of masculinity, the stories proceed to stage the process of their own artistic staginess. This creates *two* levels of counterfeicy, masculinity and artistic contrivance, in which Hannah is invested. Both are related to the concept of performance and to Hannah's broader conceptual interest in the problem of the postregional South.

"Midnight and I'm Not Famous Yet" entwines masculinity and aesthetics when it posits golf as an artful form of masculine action, an alternative to war. The presence of the celebrity golfer John Whitelaw in Hannah's story facilitates two epiphanies that contribute both to Bobby Smith's reconfigured conceptions of authentic southern manhood and to his apprehension of which types of aesthetic performance warrant "fame" in their artfulness. At the level of self-reflexive metafiction, the epiphanies also inform the story's own examinations of what makes a narrative—or a certain type of narrative confession—seem authentic, or true. One of Smith's epiphanies occurs in the final scene, when Smith attends the John Whitelaw vs. Whitney Maxwell playoff in his hometown, Vicksburg. Having become infatuated as a child with Whitelaw and having recently been shown a memorable photograph of the golfer by Tubby in Vietnam (below), Smith is awestruck by this serendipitous occurrence, exclaiming that "[i]t was a piece of wonder" and thanking "God or whoever [. . .] brought that fine contest near enough by" (117). While Whitelaw loses the tournament, Smith scorns the despondency of the home crowd: "Fools! Fools! I thought. Love it! Love the loss as well as the gain. Nobody was killed," and he achieves the epiphany with which his story ends: "We saw victory and defeat, and they were both wonderful" (118).

The celebrated fact that "nobody was killed" recalls Kimmel's observation that after Vietnam the figure of the soldier was transformed in the public imagination from the personification of "manly virtue" to its very opposite, "a failed man," because he was accused of enacting an "excessive and false hypermasculinity" (263). With a generation of American men allegedly experiencing a symbolic wholesale emasculation upon the nation's military defeat in Vietnam in 1975, it is interesting to see these ideas played out in a story published contemporaneously. If America became more "southern," or the South more "American," after Vietnam—which is to say, defeat and shame became part of a national narrative of fallen masculinity that had formerly been reserved for the othered South—perhaps Smith's renouncing the hypermasculine image of the American soldier is tantamount to a recognition of the contingency of both regional *and* gendered identities, a recognition in which both are revealed as the products of cultural discourse. (Indeed, Guinn's arguments for the absence of the Civil War from postmodernist southern fiction center on the idea that "the appeal of Confederate history has waned in an age that is suspicious of grand narratives and that has also endured the disillusionment of the Vietnam War," resulting in "a profound post-Vietnam skepticism of military glory" [162].) When the hypermasculine illusion is shattered, alternative mythologies of masculinity become available; sport is proffered as an alternative arena in which masculinity can be expressed. To the disillusioned soldier Smith, the appeal of Whitelaw's peaceful sportsmanship lies in his offering what Bjerre calls "a surrogate but non-violent form of war" ("Heroism" 52). Smith believes Whitelaw is wonderful even in his defeat, and by extension, so might Smith's own defeated manhood, sustained both as a disgraced soldier (individually and as part of the collective historical discourse of Vietnam) *and* as a white southerner, be at least partially restored.

There have been multiple multidisciplinary studies of how hegemonic masculinity, a concept popularized by Connell in 1985, underwrites the prevalence of violence in sport by sanctioning a dominant (hegemonic) form of masculinity centered on aggression, violence, and force. Importantly, because golf and tennis (below) are noncontact sports, this model does not apply to them. If sport is a different kind of "war," then golf and tennis are specifically gentle and more artful versions of it. While Hannah writes in relation to an established American tradition of sportswriting in relation to masculine frontier mythology and "boys' own" fiction—where writers such as Hemingway, Fitzgerald, Faulkner, and Ring Lardner have written about (and against) the hegemonic figure of the American sportsman—the ironic difference here is that golf is not hunting, bullfighting, football, or boxing.[2] It is a different kind of mastery and independence that might appear to pertain to the hegemonic figure of the southern gentleman: as the most noncontact of sports, golf gets its masculinist credentials from its "play-by-the-rules" sense of its own propriety.

One of the story's most significant scenes features a photograph of the golfer John Whitelaw playing at the Augusta Masters Tournament, and we cannot ignore the significance of Augusta itself here. The Augusta National Golf Club, whose public image is fiercely policed, has been widely criticized for presenting a phony, sanitized version of (white) southern hospitality culture. As Curt Sampson notes, "Put aside whatever images of the South that you may have gleaned: *This*, we are assured, is what the South is all about—a place of propriety, tradition and fellowship, holding fast to vanishing aristocratic graces" (6). *This* image, of course, conceals a history of racism, sexism, and elitism that is still very much present. The traditionally all-white club did not allow its first Black player until 1975, and its first Black member until 1990; its first female members were admitted as recently 2012. The luxury and exclusivity afforded to the club's select members sits uncomfortably with the predominantly working-class mill-town setting of Augusta, Georgia, as well as the club's having been built on cheap (and predominantly nonwhite) labor. In the context of Hannah's war fiction (in relation to "rebel" Confederate masculinity), the significance of Whitelaw's craft may be that it is not underwritten by violence. However, with the backdrop of Augusta and its own violent underside, along with this problematic allusion to the Old Southern chivalric code, Hannah simultaneously invokes and rebukes existing myths about (white) southern masculinity.

Weston argues that the character of the celebrity tennis player French Edward in Hannah's *The Tennis Handsome* (1983) is a "mock-heroic" character who in his handsomeness and theatricality signifies "style over substance" (*BH* 76–77). Weston cites a line from Hannah's novella to illustrate the point: "He had more style losing than L. or N. or S. did winning" (*Tennis Handsome* 3, qtd. in *BH* 77). However, since Edward and Whitelaw, and tennis and golf, are interchangeable in Hannah's fiction,[3] I would argue that there is more to Edward's artful losing than Weston allows. It symbolizes a pleasurably "effete" form of masculinity that opposes the hegemonic American mythology of the victorious sportsman (or war hero), confirmed when Whitelaw and Edward are described as "a beautiful man" and "the prettiest" man on the court ("Midnight" 108; *Tennis Handsome* 3). Male tennis players appear variously in Hannah's fiction in special moments of enamored male witness, described in a language of otherworldly grace (a word used directly) that evokes the biblical transcendence wrought by the emergence of the truth in "Water Liars." Thus, the artful style that these men possess is not simply parodic or lacking in substance as Weston suggests; rather, regardless of its theatricality, it carries the power to transform a raptly attentive male audience.

Whitelaw's embodiment of what might be termed effeminate masculinity is, of course, also a performance—on Smith's part as much as Whitelaw's, since he is mediating the spectacle of Whitelaw into a counterimage of masculinity as a means of cultural resistance. Tristan Bridges and Cheri Pascoe offer a useful insight into the nature of the Smith-Whitelaw interaction when they discuss the phenomenon of *hybrid masculinity*. The term refers to men's "selective incorporation of performances" associated with other or nondominant forms of gendered behavior; hybrid masculinities "symbolically distance men from hegemonic masculinity" (Bridges and Pascoe 246). Once again performativity is key, with masculinity emerging from social performance. Bobby Smith identifies Whitelaw's masculinity as "other," and he will emulate it in his unspoken decision to become an artist (the implied author of the tale we read) rather than conform to the damaging "mythology of war and the myth of the warrior" (*BH* 72). Masculinity is a performance that is staged for the affirmation and appropriation of others, who not only testify to but actively *create* its legitimacy. Recalling Michael Kreyling's scholarship on the "mythopoetic" nature of masculinity and the ways in which the idea of southern manhood has been mediated through literary texts (*Figures* 29), here the staged spectacle of manhood gives rise to a particular narrative of maleness that is not intrinsic to the thing itself.

The first of Smith's abovementioned epiphanies comes from seeing the photograph of Whitelaw at Augusta in Vietnam. It provokes Smith's sudden realization of the damaging effect that subscribing to the cultural image of the hypermasculine soldier has had on his own masculinity: "I started crying [with] hard sobs coming up like rocks in my throat. [. . .] I'd killed so many gooks. I'd killed them with machine guns, mortars, howitzers, knives, wire, me and my boys. [. . .] They were lying all around me [. . .]. The picture of John Whitelaw at Augusta was jammed in my head. There was such care in his eyes, and it was only a golf ball, a goddamned piece of nothing. But *it was wonderful and peaceful. Nobody was being killed.* Whitelaw had the [. . .] beloved American right to the pursuit of happiness. [. . .] All we had going was the pursuit of horror" (113–14, my emphasis). The realities of war have exposed to Smith the pointlessness of the hypermasculine role of officer-soldier. Comparing his own violent awakening with what he perceives to be the life of the other unfallen man (Whitelaw), Smith comes to the harrowing realization: "It seemed to me my life had gone straight from teen-age giggling to horror. I never had time to be but two things, a giggler and a killer" (114). Rather than war making a man of him, his subjectivity has been undercut in the act of his becoming a soldier, as Tubby's death dramatizes quite literally. Smith exclaims, "I shouldn't ever've seen that picture of John Whitelaw. I shouldn't've" (115), and it is in this seemingly odd exclamation that the story dramatizes how the counterimage of the noncombative sportsman has crystalized Smith's realization that because of his having gone straight from childish innocence to a hellish realm of adult horror, his own masculinity has been afforded no approximate process of becoming. The nullifying effect that war has had on Smith's masculinity directly recalls retrospective critical understandings of the Vietnam War as a pointless conflict, with "no discernible telos, no apparent shape or function beyond large-scale carnage" (Guinn 162). As a historical narrative, Vietnam fails to produce anything meaningful beyond the "giggler-killer" trajectory that curtails male subjectivity. Compared with our disillusioned veteran, who "hadn't loved anything for nigh three years," Whitelaw is established as a symbol of male integrity who "*cared* so much about what he was doing" (108). Because his pursuit has purpose or meaning in this way, Whitelaw is afforded a share in the American "pursuit of happiness" that Smith's experiences as an American soldier have, ironically, excluded him from.

Tubby's photograph of Whitelaw depicts the golfer poised, "in agony," about to strike a ball under a "heroic deficiency" at the Augusta Masters tournament (108), suggesting again that southern masculinity centers on a point of crisis, or a point where old myths about victorious male heroism are suddenly undercut. (The word *agony* is further significant in its reference to a neo-Confederate rhetoric of stoic defeat, discussed in chapter 3.) The spectacle profoundly affects Smith: "But the picture of John at Augusta, it moved me" (108). Subsequently, it provokes a lengthy narrative regression dedicated to Smith's memory of his first real-life encounter with the man, in Baton Rouge, when "I was ten, I guess, and he was twenty" (108). The formative nature of this episode is caught in Smith's revelation that "I got my whole idea of what a woman should look like that day . . . and what a man should be" (108), and the scene proves vital to the alternative (but equally performative) vision of manhood Smith identifies in the conspicuously southern notion of "heroic deficiency" or defeat.

The decisive childhood encounter happens when Smith, his father, and his grandfather are attending a major southern ballgame, "a classic that makes you go goo-goo eyed when you're a full-grown man," and "in the middle of it, this feeling, I [Smith] saw Whitelaw and his woman" (108). Whitelaw is described in a (homoerotic) language of aesthetic perfection: "a beautiful man" with "muscles [. . .] bulked up plain as wires," a face framed "by that wild hair the color of beer; his chest deep, just about to bust out of that collar" (108). Beholding the other, Smith concludes, "The way John Whitelaw looked, it sort of rebuked yourself ever hoping to call yourself a man" (108). Looking on the *spectacle* of another man who signifies the personification of authentic male being (Smith gets an idea of what a woman should only look like but of what a man should *be*), Smith becomes suddenly aware of his own nascent masculinity in a coming-of-age moment: "The girl he [Whitelaw] was with woke up my clammy little dreams about, not even sex, but the perfect thing" (108). In this moment of subjective realization, our narrator establishes a relationship between an idealized man—a figure to emulate and aspire to—and himself (or his ten-year-old self) as a lesser (rebuked) or fallen version. Pertaining to Butler's idea of the performative, according to which subjectivity may be performed but the subject is *created* by the performance and does not exist prior to it ("Performative Acts" 520), Cheever explains her title conceit of the "real phony" thus: "If you really believe the fakery, then there is no discernible authentic self to which the performative character can be compared" (15). In a similar way, the fact that Smith's empathy with Whitelaw is only his empathy with an image, that "real men" are only simulations of authentic manhood, is of no consequence: the *idea* of authentic masculinity (what a man should be) is created in the homosocial relationships between men. Recalling postregional formulations of the created or "constituted" South from Kreyling, Romine, and Bone (see, e.g., *RS* 59), the fakery is indistinguishable from the reality, which does not exist prior to it.

These arguments become especially pertinent when we consider General Li Dap as a version of Giap, himself a version of Napoleon and indeed also of the Confederate legend J. E. B. (Jeb) Stuart, whom Kenneth Seib notes was viewed as "the very embodiment not only of the fortitude and determination of the Confederate fighting man, but of the ideal of Southern manhood" (43). Guinn (with Kreyling and Bone) acknowledges that Jeb Stuart appears at least tangentially in most of Hannah's war fiction, as exemplar of the southern chivalric myth (Guinn 163), and indeed, a firm correspondence is established between Li Dap and Jeb Stuart when Smith explicates, "Li Dap wants to be Jeb Stuart" ("Midnight" 110). Smith's encounter with the Vietnamese general is vital to the story's disquisition on masculinity, therefore, because Li Dap embodies the image of hegemonic masculinity under Smith's scrutiny. Initially, several factors in Smith's narrative establish Li Dap as the true offering of masculinity in the story. Declaring that "[a]ll this hero needed was a plumed hat" and "[w]e had a *real* romantic here" (113, 112, my emphasis), Smith portrays Li Dap as an archaic military authority (in his proximity to Napoleon), a man to respect and admire. If (as the story ostensibly suggests) Smith sympathizes with the captured general because he embodies some older, more authentic masculinity, then it is severely problematic that Smith should shoot and kill the man. However, if the soldier represents a model of masculinity whose emulation is *detrimental* to male subjectivity, as Smith has realized, then this explains his symbolic death in the story. The general, in his proximity to Jeb Stuart, symbolizes the oedipal father whom Smith must vanquish, not only so that he might finally come of age but also to make way for a new form of nonhegemonic masculinity (Whitelaw's), one that is not underwritten by ruthlessness and aggression. The curious transposition occurring between these mythologized historical warrior figures (Giap, Jeb Stuart, Napoleon) suggests that old ideologies generate only dead-end narratives of male becoming. Therefore, they must be exposed and renounced in favor of a new masculinity that cannot be realized until the old illusion has been removed.

This tension between old and new, hegemonic and hybrid, is enacted in Smith's memory of his actual boyhood encounter with Whitelaw, which further dramatizes the absence of some pure or absolute masculinity. In this scene, three generations of men in the family—Smith, his father, and his grandfather—behold the same spectacle of Whitelaw, but their reactions are diametrically opposed. While Smith views Whitelaw as the perfect embodiment of manhood, his conservative grandfather sees the very opposite, describing the man as "that little peacock who left football for golf [who] ought to be quarterbacking" (108). Similarly, Whitelaw's mixed-race girlfriend ("Johnny got him something Cajun," says Smith's father [108]) represents to the older generation an unwelcome symbol of modernity characterized by waning masculinity, while the youngster applauds the modernity of the spectacle he beholds: "It struck me as something deep, brave, mighty and, well, modern" (107).[4] Unlike the elders, with their thinly veiled racism (and classism), our narrator views Whitelaw's "gypsyish girl" as the very image of perfection (108). These profoundly oppositional reactions to the same spectacle reveal that Whitelaw's masculinist credentials (or lack thereof) are simply the product of an audience's interpretation, or mediation, which is culturally and historically contingent. There is a certain democracy in the fact that because there is no essential masculinity, the spectacle is open to multiple (re)interpretations.

Masculinity is a cultural construct that is performative and mutable; hence the contrary interpretations of old and new. Smith's grandfather intends his designation "little peacock" to effeminize the golfer because he construes the man's appearance and profession—noncombat sport, with all its costume and manners, appears effeminate to the elder—as symbolic of a diminishing southern patriarchy. Arguably, in the grandfather's South the cultural markers between masculine and feminine behaviors were much more clearly delineated. If we conceive of masculinity as something that can be "read" in a man's appearance, then it follows that the signifiers of southern masculinity will change across different interpretative cultures. Here, the grandfather's inability to interpret Whitelaw's masculinity (he perceives only its absence, or the absence of an older version of it) suggests that an older language of southern manhood has lost its critical currency or meaning. We can anticipate the exchange between mother and son in Hannah's later story "The Ice Storm," where the elder simply cannot comprehend her son's use of the word *bitch* in relation to another man (191). The signs of masculinity, then, are not somehow fixed and discoverable beyond context. Smith interprets Whitelaw as the epitome of southern manhood, while his grandfather reads the scene oppositely. On the one hand these interpretations are in keeping with notions of postmodern textuality, where signs and simulacra are all there is. However, we can also contextualize Hannah's dramatization of the myth of masculinity in a specifically American, and specifically *southern*, way. As noted, the crisis of post-Vietnam American masculinity reflects usefully on thinking about the defeated (white) South. Weston argues that the concept of "a truly unified self" (*BH* 72) is unavailable to Hannah's postsouthern men because they have (rightly) dispelled the cultural illusion of southern manhood with which they identified historically. We can extend this claim, in fact, to argue for the illusory and wholly performative character of the conception of southern manhood from its ante-bellum conceptions.

In "Midnight and I'm Not Famous Yet," arguably the most important function served by Li Dap and Whitelaw is to alert us to the ways in which constructions of masculinity, revealed in narrative mythologies of valorized romantic individualism (the "real romantic hero"), come solely from cultural images of authentic maleness rather than from authentic masculinity per se, which does not exist outside its stagy simulations. This is encapsulated in Li Dap's performative impersonation (he "wants to be," but he is *not*) of Jeb Stuart. He is not only a copy of a real historical figure; more importantly, he is a copy of a *mythology* that was not real to begin with. Indeed, it is Li Dap's romantic appearance and the *stories* circulated about him ("He went to the Sorbonne and [. . .] speaks French very well"; he "had studied Napoleon"; "He knows Robert Lee and the strategy of Jeb Stuart" [110]) that appeal to the southerner Smith. The masculinities performed by both Stuart and Li Dap are heavily reliant upon narratives and images that render them profoundly textual, contrary to initial impressions of these men as figures from a true earlier time. This notion of textuality subsuming the reality is furthered when Smith later ponders on Tubby's *photograph* of the captured general, admiring such aesthetic aspects as Li Dap's "wild hair while he's making a statement full of conviction" (117). While this statement ostensibly recalls Smith's infatuation with Whitelaw as a man of real purpose, in fact Smith is only imagining Li Dap's "conviction" here, which complicates in turn Smith's earlier conjecture that Whitelaw was a man who "*cared* so much about what he was doing" (108). In both cases, the spectator is transposing a meaning on the image that he cannot really know.

Indeed, when we return to Smith's encounter with the authoritative figure of Li Dap, we realize that it is characterized by communicative and interpretative *failure,* rather than by any meaningful mutual exchange by which Smith could have apprehended the sentiments of Li Dap's proposed statement of conviction. For example, Smith implores the imprisoned general to "[s]peak English" because "[m]y French isn't too good," but this request is met with hostility: Li Dap "wouldn't say anything" at all, nor was "[h]e [. . .] hearing much" either (112). That being the case, Smith can only retrospectively speculate on Li Dap's previously spoken French, translating it in disjointed and nonsensical phrases such as "Asshole of the mountains,"

"Fortune's ninny," or *"something like that"* (112, my emphasis). Crucially, then, it is the pictorial simulations of both Whitelaw and Li Dap with which Smith engages primarily and returns to, perhaps because, paradoxically, his real-life encounters with these men prove less illuminating. While he encounters both men "in the flesh" (108), the idea of masculinity that Smith consumes comes primarily from his interaction with an image. His sense of the other, from which his sense of his own manhood comes, is mediated heavily until there is no discoverable authentic masculinity, which disappears entirely in its ontological sense.

This contention is corroborated when we acknowledge Hannah's strong emphasis on aspects of the visual. It is the picture of Whitelaw that provokes Smith's epiphany. It is the picture of Li Dap that embodies Tubby's lost fame. It is their appearance that Smith fixates upon when he meets these men. Hannah's foregrounding of ocular aesthetics is augmented when Tubby's photographs are described in a curious language that renders their subjects somehow even more textual or unreal: "In the picture he [Whitelaw] wore spectacles. [. . .] [H]e had to have the eyeglasses on him to see the mighty thing he was about to do. Maybe I sympathized too much, since I have to wear glasses too, but I thought this picture was worthy of a statue. Tubby had taken it in a striking gray-and-white grain" (107–8). In evoking eyeglasses, the statue, and the formal contrivances that make up the image itself, this scene confirms that it is the *spectacle* of authentic masculinity from which the notion comes. Much as statues reduce the complexities of lived history into a single memorialized image (a highly charged practice in the context of ongoing disputes over southern Civil War memory), masculinity exists only as a matter of performance, in the homosocial bonds between performer and audience.

The significance of Smith's "giggler-killer" epiphany increases here in terms of how art relates to the concept of performative masculinity in Hannah's fiction. Importantly, not only has the war cut short Tubby's career as an artist (hence the lost fame that haunts Smith so deeply) but it has denied Smith's pursuit of art in place of a hypermasculine world of military violence. As the story progresses, Smith's heightened interest in matters of artistic contrivance (much like Whitelaw or Edward's perfected craft) is revealed. Art, like masculinity, is a performance, and it demands the affirmation of an audience to testify to its worth. The issue of stylistic contrivance accompanying this idea of performance is best exhibited in Tubby's photograph of Li Dap. Smith recognizes the artifact's celebrity value: "It'll change your whole life, Tubby," Smith says, and Tubby admits the contrivances of his not so spontaneous work: "I tried to get nice touches in with the light coming over his face. The pictures could turn out awfully interesting. I was thinking about the cover of *Time* or *Newsweek*" (115). The suggestion here, if we agree that the military has harmed Smith's masculinity, is that the partisan images of storied historical figures (Whitelaw or Li Dap; Jeb Stuart, the "Red Napoleon" Giap, or Napoleon himself) have the power to affect real-world masculinity, for good and ill alike. It is telling that the white southerner Smith should berate North Vietnam as "a land full of lousy little [. . .] robots" and "[a] place of the worst propaganda and hypocrisy" (114), given the white South's fraught mythologizing of historical violence and indeed America's own political whitewashing of history more broadly conceived. The suggestion here is that "official" doctrine from any nation presents a series of duplicitous images for unthinking (robotic) national consumption in the service of its own political agendas. Hence Li Dap's comparison to the legendary figures of Napoleon or Jeb Stuart, a mythology that supersedes him and that Smith, it seems, is initially taken in by— before killing the general, that is. The political impulses underwriting propagandist myths about war heroes are called sharply to the fore.

These scenes dramatize how masculinity is forged via one man's relationship to the staged spectacle of another man's masculinity, which is itself inherently performative. In choosing to emulate the figure of the sportsman over that of the soldier, Smith reformulates a concept of white southern manhood, while acknowledging (with the story itself) the arbitrariness of this practice. Emphasizing the stagy contingency of the male characters whom the text appears to establish as authentic, the concept of a real man, like that of the real South, is constantly emerging and evolving. It is determined by sociocultural context, and it is consumed by different audiences to different (politicized) ends, but it means nothing inherently. That said, if we agree with Guinn that southern culture has *always* been "predisposed to narrative" in this way (165), then the storied, image-driven or constitutive nature of southern masculinity need not simply negate its meaningfulness or value—so long as we remain mindful that what is authentic is a matter of performance, not being. Hannah's self-reflexive writing implies that any claim to authenticity in this context derives its integrity from its own recognition of this paradox, where a new kind of authenticity inheres in art that emphasizes its own performativity. This would explain Hannah's keen interest in methods of staging and narrative contrivance, elements that become even more crucial in "Testimony of Pilot."

"Testimony of Pilot" extends the conceptual problem of southern masculinity to the concept of what makes art true, original, or authentic. Artistic integrity might be, if not determined in any metaphysical or foundational sense, then staged or contrived, both at the narrative level in a set of key scenes and at the metafictional level of the story itself as an aesthetic performance. This occurs again in a homosocial context of masculine performance, with the narrator, William, formulating an ideology of aesthetic value in exclusive relation to the male subject of his testimony, the pilot and saxophonist Ard Quadberry. Much of William's narrative returns to his youth and adolescence, describing formative encounters not with Quadberry as a person but with Quadberry as an *artist,* much as Bobby Smith's masculinity was contingent not on any real empathy with Tubby Wooten or John Whitelaw but on the *spectacle* of Whitelaw or the *idea* of Tubby's vetoed fame. Among William's remembered episodes, one is vital: the day he and Quadberry performed Ravel's orchestral piece *Bolero* while competing in the Mississippi State high-school band championships, Quadberry on saxophone, William on drums. I claimed earlier that William's relationship with Quadberry engenders a sense of the former's inferiority. It is from the position of defeated artist that William's story originates, driven by an unspoken impetus to emulate Quadberry's wasted musical talent. Just as Smith valorized Whitelaw's alternative or nonhegemonic masculinity, William's urgent story attempts to approximate the superior qualities he has attributed to Quadberry's lost craft, until the perfect aesthetic performance becomes, by implication, William's story itself. The very existence of the tale, a self-proclaimed one-off, simulates the conditions of the perfect aesthetic performance the narrator has observed in Quadberry's saxophone playing—specifically, his take on Ravel's *Bolero.*

The first time an eleven-year-old William hears Quadberry play the saxophone, he is initially ambivalent about the (heterosexual) manliness of the act, admitting, "Quadberry began sucking and licking the reed. I didn't care much for this act, and there was too much desperate oralness in his face when he began playing. One had to engage himself like suck's revenge with a horn. That was why I chose the drums" (21). However, William soon concedes that "what Quadberry was playing was pleasant and intricate. I was sure it was advanced, and there was no squawking, as from the other eleven-year-olds on sax in the band room. He made the end with a clean upward riff, holding the final note high, pure and unwavering. 'Good!' I called to him" (21). Describing Quadberry's playing as "advanced" denotes a maturity that belies his age and authenticates his performance; indeed, Quadberry's playing is later characterized as "sound[ing] like a very troubled forty-year-old man [. . .] who had had his brow in his hands a long time" (25). Unlike the boys' schoolmate Radcleve, who dismisses and effeminizes Quadberry's playing ("Sounded like a girl duck") and responds with an immature act of violence, almost blinding Quadberry by firing a mud cannon at him (22), William identifies in this moment the potential for masculinity to be expressed differently (and nonviolently), through art.

Radcleve's juvenile antagonism to Quadberry recalls Bjerre's discussion of the ambivalent relationship between art and masculinity. Drawing on Peter Schwenger's scholarship in *Phallic Critiques*, Bjerre argues that "a 'real man' is supposed to be a man of action" and that writing is traditionally considered "a feminine activity" ("Heroism" 48). While the scene above ostensibly explores the potential for masculinity to be expressed via *music* rather than via writing, as noted, in fact William's narrative establishes an important set of parallels between Quadberry's music and the story itself, as a piece of writing, whereupon William's retrospective inquiry into his friend's talent is transposed onto his own emerging talent as a writer. That Quadberry is visually impaired and William is hearing impaired (having deafened himself drumming) sets the two in important dramatic correspondence: one occupies the aural realm of music (and speech), and the other, the visual realm of writing.

This subtle doppelgänger effect is sustained throughout. We can see it in the scene above, when the "troubled" mature voice ventriloquized through young Quadberry's playing pertains to William as the tormented adult author of the tale, an author who explicates the "fit of nostalgia [. . .] I am having right now as I write this" (31). This curious transposition between Quadberry's music and William's writing is furthered when William describes Quadberry's playing in a lexis normally reserved for describing forms of linguistic communication: "When he played, I heard the sweetness, I heard the horn which finally brought human *talk* into the realm of music" (24); "He was, as I suspected, a genius. [. . .] I could hear the *voice* that went through and out that horn" (25, my emphasis). Therefore, while William's reminiscing about Quadberry's talent establishes his own comparative deficiency as a musician, concurrently, the interchangeability between Quadberry and William, music and writing, and music and speech establishes William's *story* as an alternative artistic pursuit to his drumming. His drumming, while accomplished, can never compare to Quadberry's saxophone playing. But the implication here is that perhaps his story can, especially when it comes from a moment of masculine crisis. William becomes the *heroically* defeated artist who, paradoxically, creates high art from his own professed abjection, a trope common to Hannah's as well as Southern Gothic writing. This idea of art being wrought from and elevating forms of damaged masculinity is captured by the image of Quadberry playing the horn and "loving the wound in a private dignified ecstasy" (24).

This notion is corroborated toward the end of the story. Quadberry has returned to their hometown of Clinton, Mississippi, from the war in Vietnam for a final time, a hero of sorts, but he is "sick" (37), injured, and no longer able to continue his military service nor play the saxophone. This moment of Quadberry's masculine crisis provokes an epiphany in William, who suddenly acknowledges, "I'm just a deaf drummer, too vain to buy a hearing aid. Can't stand to write the ad copy I do," and he implores the other man, "Wasn't I a good drummer?" (43). Once more, William's drumming, as an artistic concern, is extended to the matter of our narrator's worth as a writer, and as a (vain) man. In this revelatory moment, William's anxiety about his drumming is transposed onto the question of his authorial efficacy, both as a writer of bogus advertising copy *in* the story and, at the metalevel, as the implied more authentic writer *of* the story. This confessional heart of William's narrative reveals his true purpose, his desire as a "rebuked" artist (to use Bobby Smith's term [108]) to create something more authentic than the drumming that has deafened him and the advertising copy he admits he cannot stand to write. His relationship with Quadberry's masculine crisis facilitates an understanding of his own baulked coming of age as an adult male artist and, by extension, a rebuked southern man. Thus, while both "Midnight" and "Testimony" purport to be told in testimony to the honor of dead men, their function is to recover a sense of personal integrity that both narrators, defeated southern men and artists, feel has been compromised.

The *Bolero* scene is the story's most significant moment because it establishes the conditions of the archetypal aesthetic performance, setting the benchmark against which the value of William's writing can be measured. Quadberry steals the show in this scene, not only by performing a brilliant sax solo but also by successfully directing "a weeping herd" of bandmates through the piece after their beloved director, Dick Prender, is killed in a freak motor accident on his way to the show (27). We have already been told that "*Bolero* was exactly the piece to make the band soar—now especially as we had Quadberry, who made his walk into the piece like an actual lean Spanish bandit" (25), but now this unique set of chance circumstances surrounding the performance (recall Tubby's photograph of Li Dap) lend it a special significance. Like William's urgent story, *Bolero* will be a singular occurrence, a one-off, and to play becomes a matter of urgency especially for Quadberry, who implores his reluctant bandmates: "Don't you dare quit [. . .]. You've got to be heard. *I've* got to be heard" (27). In an "unbearable" "mixture of grief and superb music" (30), what transpires with *Bolero* is a transformative experience for band and audience members alike. It is a formative moment for William, who declares, "Boys became men and girls became women as Quadberry directed us through *Bolero*. I even became a bit of a better man myself" (28). We are not given an account of the piece itself (this is vital, and something to return to), because our narrator is preoccupied with keeping time on the drums. Importantly, William's impaired hearing and the distraction of his own drumming mean that he relies on the testimony of *others* to validate Quadberry's performance: the first-chair clarinetist, for example, responds to William's inquiry "Was Quadberry good?" with "Are you kidding? These tears in my eyes, they're for how good he was. He was too good. I'll never touch my clarinet again" (29). Thus, it is only in the aftermath of the performance that its merit is determined by the reaction of an audience that has been affected profoundly, much as "southernness" is a quality that writers and critics have created only in retrospect.

Initially, the absence of William's narrative from the description of *Bolero* accords with theoretical notions of epiphany as something that resists rational language and comprehension. There is something incommunicable about religious awe, something here beyond representation. Martin Bidney argues that while critics have long debated definitions of literary epiphany, they generally agree on what epiphanies are *not*, that is, insights of knowledge arrived at in a rational or straightforward way. They oppose rational linguistic definition (Bidney 4; Beja 15). This argument formulates the epiphany as something granted from "above" rather than as a product that has been (or can be) constructed (Bidney 5). "Testimony of Pilot" certainly appears to support this sense of magical transcendence accompanying "the miraculous way he [Quadberry] had gone on with *Bolero*" (30). This is sustained further when Quadberry, having been asked by William to testify to his performance, declares enigmatically, "I was walking downhill in a valley, is all I was doing. [. . .] Another man, a wizard, was playing my horn" (29–30). A very particular kind of aesthetics is functioning here, *Bolero* signaling an outstanding feat of artfulness whose unique context is a miracle that, *like the story itself,* will never occur again.

If we recall William's concluding words ("This is why I told this story and will never tell another"), then the story, as a second instance of artistic performance, simulates the exact aesthetic qualities of *Bolero*. William's having told his singular tale implies that our narrator means to invest his story with an urgency and uniqueness that testify to its own approximate value. Further comparison can be drawn between the performances of *Bolero* and William's story; for example, the latter emerges following the death of its subject, just as Prender's death preceded *Bolero*. More subtly, if we recall the clarinetist's claim that because he has witnessed the superlative musical performance (Quadberry's playing was allegedly *too* good) he will never play again, then perhaps the implication here is that William's story, similarly, will never be retold, because it has already achieved the quality of artistic perfection lauded in Quadberry's *Bolero*. Thus, the distinctive aesthetic characteristics that appear to legitimate *Bolero,* as well as the peculiar material circumstances of its origins, are extended to the qualities of the story itself and the conditions from which it came.

Interestingly, however, William's reliance on audience testimony to validate Quadberry's performance (and, by extension, his own) serves a dual purpose that is integral to my understanding of how the authenticity paradox functions, both in Hannah's texts and in my broader understandings of the postregional South. On the one hand, it establishes a sense of the extraordinary nature of the performance that transcends William's narrative capacity (it exceeds description) and accords with theoretical notions of (literary) epiphany being beyond linguistic contrivance. On the other hand, it emphasizes the key role of audience, of mediation, in evaluating or legitimizing the performance—which of course offsets the notion of epiphanic transcendence. The legitimacy of the romantic epiphany is called into question when it becomes entirely contingent on an audience to authenticate it. But crucially, it *can* be authenticated by measuring its *effect* on that audience (it is clearly fake, but it is real to them), until it becomes real once more. Essentially, authenticity is not lost, but it becomes a quality that is determined or applied retrospectively (rather than inhering in the thing itself), therefore seriously complicating the putative claim to authenticity that William's story (and the epiphany within it) initially appears to advance.

The story's most direct dramatization of this conundrum involves William's deafness. He cannot describe Quadberry's *Bolero* solo, admitting, "I have no idea what Quadberry sounded like on his sax ride" (28). He relies on the testimonies of more able auditors, such as the clarinetist, in a way that pertains to the trope of "bad journalism" that resounds variously in Hannah's fiction. As noted, the value of Quadberry's performance is observed via its effect on an audience, but importantly, this is an audience from which our narrator is excluded, the irony being that William describes an auditory experience when he has no auditory capacity, lacking in the one sensory ability that is absolutely required to bear proper witness and to testify authentically to the musical performance. Because of *Bolero*'s extraordinary nature, the witnessing audience must retain a sense of incredulity; at the same time, we have to take their word for it that this really happened: we are given no mimetic window on the events from our narrator directly, as we might have expected. While this partly corroborates notions of epiphany as resisting worldly language and mediation, it simultaneously troubles the very notion of bearing authentic witness *to* the epiphany, because an audience by necessity mediates (invalidates?) that which it witnesses.

To return briefly to "Midnight and I'm Not Famous Yet," some of the same conceptual problems apply. The notion that Smith's tale, like the stranger's in "Water Liars," possesses an integrity derived from its privileged share in a private truth is open to the same interpretative challenges as the scenes above. This is captured most distinctly by the fact that Smith's memories of the circumstances in which he killed Li Dap are hazy and poor: he introduces the scene with the admission that "I don't remember too well," and this sense of dreamlike uncertainty is sustained throughout the ensuing episode (111). First, "Midnight and I'm Not Famous Yet" establishes masculinity as something authentic, and then it reveals it to be performative. Then, we can apply this paradox to the story itself, whereupon the very notion of a true story becomes tricky and contingent, and it is difficult to attest to the authenticity of Smith's badly remembered account of "the truth" that he and his "boys" (and we readers) supposedly share (117). We can question whether his story represents a record of the truth or a duplicitous textual copy that has been staged, perhaps as a means to fame for its *author,* who, as the title suggests, intends to be "famous *yet.*" Ultimately, just as Whitelaw and Li Dap staged the putative qualities of "real men," which were essentially arbitrary, so too does Smith's story, like William's, simply stage the (contingent) qualities of an authentic story. While it is convincing, it remains purely performative, if we accept that authenticity can only be determined by a believing audience.

Several further instances in "Testimony of Pilot" corroborate the paradox of the authentic performance, in which a sense of legitimacy is established despite obvious duplicity. First, the description of Quadberry's being "*like* an *actual* lean Spanish bandit" while performing *Bolero* connotes a possible contradiction in terms: how can one simulate (be *like*), and thus be a copy of, the *actual* real thing? Second, Quadberry leads *Bolero* by assuming the role of director, which originally was intended not for him but for Prender. Finally, even the *Bolero* piece itself was composed not by a Spaniard but by a Frenchman (Maurice Ravel), who was himself originally commissioned by a *Russian* actress and dancer (Ida Rubinstein) to compose the piece. Its authorship—and even its nationality—cannot be pinpointed conclusively. Quadberry's performance has from its outset been built on various levels of mediation from which no authentic origin is extricable. And where *Bolero* is a copy, William's story becomes a copy of a copy, further removed from the putative authentic origin, which is just an illusion, caught neatly when William admits, "I was stealing for my art" (31). The performance *of* the story mimics the performance *in* the story, until mimesis has gone; there is nothing inherent in either performance from which authenticity could finally be determined. This is the remarkable sophistication of Hannah's writing: when close readings of the *Bolero* scene subvert the very notion of authentic performance, it appears at first to be dramatizing, against which the value of William's own artistic performance (his story) would also have been measured. Thus, just as "Midnight and I'm Not Famous Yet" ultimately undermined its own ostensible offerings of authentic masculinity, so too does "Testimony of Pilot" come to destabilize the seemingly paradigmatic instance of true and original art emerging from a moment of epiphany. In dramatizing these conundrums, Hannah creates a compelling artistic performance of his own, stemming from his metafictional interest in the contexts in which authenticity can be created, while dramatizing how authenticity in such contexts is merely the product of convincing aesthetic staging, simulation, or copy. In the relationship between mediation and performance, mediation, paradoxically, authenticates the performance. This suggests that authenticity exists, but the ethical imperative of these texts is to lay bare the devices by which it has been staged. This is testimony to the valuable contribution that Hannah's fiction makes, both to contemporary theoretical apprehensions of epiphany and authenticity and to conceptualizations of postsouthern masculinity and the postregional South.

Close readings usefully tease out the wider philosophical and sociocultural contexts in which Hannah's fiction can be placed, revealing not only how ideas about authenticity (gendered, socioethnic, aesthetic, regional, historical) are created and consumed but also how the authenticity paradigm gets deployed in the service of particular political agendas. It is only at a deep conceptual level that these stories reveal the performative nature of authenticity; on the surface, the performance seems real because it is so convincing. Arguably, the creation of a persuasive sense of authenticity is the success of Hannah's narrators, the real stimulus for their stories, or what they seek their art to achieve. Cheever writes that while contemporary critics "generally correlate the emergence of postmodernity with a declining interest in authentic selfhood," in fact "authenticity is resurrected [. . .] by reconfiguring the terms" (16). In a similar way I would posit that Hannah manages to have it both ways, resurrecting a concept of authenticity, while subverting its traditional romantic origins. If an audience is thoroughly seduced by something staged and the quality of authenticity is produced, then what, these stories seem to ask, is the difference? Emphasizing the performative nature of authenticity is not tantamount to the *removal* of authenticity, dramatized most compellingly at the metalevel of Hannah's stories in which acknowledging the counterfeicy of writing paradoxically becomes authenticating. A new sense of literary authenticity can emerge from a story's self-reflexive interrogation of the efficacy of story.

3

The Burden of Postsouthern History

"Uncle High Lonesome" and
"The Agony of T. Bandini"

"Uncle High Lonesome" and "The Agony of T. Bandini," two remarkable short stories in *High Lonesome* (1996), invite analysis as postmodern inflections of the southern modernist "burden of southern history" paradigm (hereafter called *southern burden* for simplicity). Both stories explore ideas about "inherited" burden as a form of white cultural guilt, ideas that also extend beyond conceptualizations of American regional culture. Like much of Hannah's fiction, these texts frame themes of inherited historical memory, haunting, and trauma as distinctly regional phenomena to suggest that the concept of southern burden endures in contemporary literary constructions of the South. Matthew Guinn argues that southern fiction after modernism has departed from the southern-burden trope as a modernist ideology. In this proposed shift, literary dramatizations of the South's historical legacy, bearing more heavily on its subjects than on the "lighter" North's, is eschewed in favor of a postmodern dismantling of historicity (Guinn 162). Hannah's typically complicated attitude to regional authenticity, however, resists drawing rigid conceptual distinctions between modernist and postsouthern literary cultures. In Hannah's fiction, the burden of southern history and the problem of historicity coexist.

This chapter identifies a series of moments in Hannah's writing that propose a dynamic relationship between modernist and postmodernist formulations of southern burden, thereby challenging mutually exclusive conceptualizations of "southern" and "postmodern." Countering the notion that a simple historical break accompanies the transition from southern to postsouthern, each story conveys a sense of the post-South emerging as part of a (constant) process, a process in which the critical discourses of different historical moments can be mutually informative, even retrospectively. While distinctions between *modern* and *postmodern, southern* and *postsouthern,* are hardly ones on which critics agree, Hannah's contemporary literary dramatization of what might be called *postsouthern burden* certainly encourages our critical reengagement with these terms, suggesting the persistence of the regional after the alleged postsouthern turn.

My title derives from C. Vann Woodward's influential *The Burden of Southern History* (1960). Written in the face of growing nationalization and globalization, Woodward's study makes a case for continued regional exceptionalism after modernism because of the defeated and dispossessed South's radical distinction from its national counterpart. In fact, Woodward's study simply attaches this new lexis of historical burden to preexisting (Agrarian) formulations of the historically preoccupied South in the 1920s and 1930s, ideas that contributed greatly to the so-called Southern Renaissance. Indeed, one of the most memorable modernist literary encapsulations of the southern-burden trope comes from Faulkner's *Requiem for a Nun,* when Gavin Stevens reproaches Temple Drake's declaration of the death of her past, saying, "The past is never dead. It's not even past" (85). Benjamin Widiss characterizes Faulkner's "perennial preoccupation with inheritance, guilt, and other determinations bequeathed by the past," and he attributes Faulkner's strong literary influence to "the continuing project of bringing literature to bear on the haunting burden of historical violence and dispossession" (149)—a project that resonates far beyond contemplations of the South. Allen Tate had already prefigured this sense of the dependency of regional identity on narrative when he acknowledged that "the Southern legend [. . .] of defeat and heroic frustration was taken over by a dozen or so first-rate writers and converted into a universal myth" (*Essays* 592). Ideas about the sudden gothic resurfacing of past traumas that refuse to be buried are certainly rife within Hannah's stories, further protracting a sense that southernness is a quality used and created by writers who convert it into an accepted mythology. If the concept of southern burden was from its earliest conceptions beholden to narrative and performance, then this does not detract from its centrality to constructions of the South. As Woodward argues, the mythology of a distinctive South endures in both regional and national imaginaries despite the contingency of the regional-national distinction.

Hannah's "Uncle High Lonesome" and "The Agony of T. Bandini" both stage and revise aspects of Agrarian and modernist narratives about the "fallen" white South, its inhabitants burdened by guilt from past sins. The stories are a compelling dramatization of the theme of historical determinism subsuming individual agency in an environment where defeat and the passive acceptance of fate seem inevitable, captured by the eponymous Tiger Bandini, who describes southern history as a case of "Nothing could stop it, nothing" ("Agony" 136). In a dramatic enactment of this phenomenon, the title figure of "Uncle High Lonesome," Uncle Peter Howard, is intermittently struck by what the narrator, Howard's nephew, calls "the high lonesomes," compulsive bouts of depressed alcoholism that result from an unpunished historical crime (murder), eventually culminating in the man's death: "he seemed to be intent on destroying himself in episode after episode when, as he would only say afterwards, the high lonesomes struck him" (226). Robert Brinkmeyer explores the association of (Westward) mobility with freedom in America's national imaginary (14–15), a mythology from which the South, a region of imagined stasis and backwardness, has been excluded. In parallel, Uncle Peter's shameful past carves a path of self-destruction that proves finally impossible to deflect: "he seemed unable to reroute the high lonesomes that came on him" (226). The high lonesomes, therefore, serve as a fitting trope for the difficulty of dealing with historical guilt and trauma, portrayed as an enduring and distinctly southern problem.

The contemporary merit of Woodward's southern-burden model had come under radical scrutiny by the late twentieth century, as new postregional criticism sought to disband the idea of regional exceptionalism or even the concept of "southern" itself. Toward the end of Hannah's career, globalization and the rise of a media-driven culture were also affecting regional studies beyond the South, compounded by more recent conceptualizations of a (newly?) transnational American culture. In such a context, where *southern* burden could easily be dismissed as part of an outdated southern-distinctiveness paradigm, we might ask whether Hannah's contemporary South can be considered distinct enough to deserve continued critical attention using such terminology without critics subscribing to a reductive and unhelpful metaphysics of place.

Aside from the encroachments of late-twentieth-century postregional criticism on the idea of "southern" per se, amplified by more recent apprehensions of an increasingly globalized and hybridized South, Woodward's paradigm was also being challenged in the wake of the widening distance emerging from the supposedly formative event of Black and white regional history alike, the Civil War. For those who accept that the South's burden derives from this defining event, the passage of time could annul the efficacy of the southern-burden paradigm as a means of understanding contemporary regional identity. As Jefferson Humphries argues, most contemporary southerners "may lack the powerful sense of southern history that came from [their] elders from temporal proximity to the Civil War, and that was so essential for their strong sense of southern identity" (ix). While Humphries replaces the immediate influence of the Civil War with that of the civil rights movement (and while we should dispute the contention that the Civil War is essential to all southern identity), this idea that the South's historical burdens simply diminish in the absence of temporal proximity to events makes for a reductive interpretation of Woodward's view of memory as a complicated and nonlinear process that does not necessarily diminish in intensity with the passing of time. With its very resistance both to linear temporality and to "essential" conceptualizations of identity (Humphries's word), as well as to reductive understandings of definitive historical events affecting a monolithic South, there is still room for Woodward's model in contemporary apprehensions of southern regionalism. Likewise, at the level of literary discourse, engaging with this established "southern" trope in recent southern writing—rather than abandoning it as some in the New Southern Studies camp would insist—opens up this kind of writing to the wider social and political realms in which it is situated.

Brinkmeyer chastises Humphries for ignoring the vanguard of new southern writers, including Barry Hannah, Frederick Barthelme, and Josephine Humphreys (Brinkmeyer 373), despite Humphries's claim to bring the field into a more up-to-date dialogue with a post-Rubin generation. Guinn's more recent study of contemporary southern fiction, however, concurs that the literary period "after southern modernism" (Guinn's title) has produced very little on the Civil War and its attendant mythology of historical haunting, supposedly because contemporary writers have no living access to what Lewis P. Simpson called the "resource of memory" (qtd. in Guinn 162). According to Guinn, the trend of historical retrospection Widiss discerned as a central preoccupation of Faulkner's writing was becoming increasingly scarce in southern fiction after modernism, recalling Simpson's infamous declaration of "the closure of history in a postsouthern America" (268). Conversely, Houston Baker pointed to the nonlinear intensity of memory in 2001, when he declared with Dana Nelson, "I live in a haunted place" (231).

Again, this refutes Humphries's proposition of the South's diminishing burden with the demise of living memory. Surely the legacy of slavery and racism is far more problematic, entrenched, and indeed current than such a model allows. Arguably, had the legacy of the Old South and the Lost Cause simply died out with firsthand experience, then the push for racial equality with the civil rights movements in the region would have occurred long before they did (and indeed, we can imagine that they might have been more successful). Similarly, it seems unlikely that the South—or Western cultures in general—should forget the cultural implications of the civil rights movements even as the immediate bystanders of the 1950s and 1960s diminish, because in many ways the problems, divisions, and injustices these movements sought to abolish more than half a century ago remain unresolved.

The issue of the alleged decline (or persistence) of historical burden, regionalism, and therefore the South is not only psychological, which is to say concerned with southern identity, but also aesthetic, regarding the political status and cultural merit of contemporary southern art. For some, the weakening of firsthand memory of the South's determinative historical events generated nostalgia for a prior time when the word *southern* had meaning as a cultural collective and could be discerned, moreover, in regional literature. Echoing Richard Gray's characterization of Faulkner and his contemporaries' writing as "the literature of memory," Simpson writes of the "southern aesthetic of memory" developed by the modernists (67–71), which he believed was being menaced with the inevitable onset of time: "The literary imagination cannot remedy the fact that the southern writer born in the 1960s has had to find out about Gettysburg from a textbook rather than from the memory of an uncle. [. . .] At best by the 1960s personal links with the memory of the Civil War had become insubstantial" (251–52). Words and phrases like "cannot remedy," "at best," and "insubstantial" convey a distinctively nostalgic sense of not only a regional identity but also a literary culture declining in the face of cultural amnesia. Simpson's pessimistic diagnosis reveals how the perceived waning of historical-burden literature signaled a concomitant decline in its value. As Simpson put it bluntly, "The epiphany of the southern literary artist will not be repeated. The Southern Renaissance will not come again" (268–69). Likewise, Fred Hobson compares Hannah's generation of writers to the lost Southern Renaissance and declares it "lacking the tragic sense, devoid of Faulkner's high seriousness and social consciousness," and exhibiting "a relative want of *power*" (*Southern Writer* 34,

10). For these critics, the supposed deterioration of historical memory after southern modernism had impacted unfavorably on postsouthern art, which was left both historically detached and aesthetically depleted.

Several postsouthern scholars agree that Faulknerian themes of deterministic historical inheritance have begun to fade from contemporary southern writing. For example, Guinn argues of Hannah that southern writers after modernism chose to symbolize history as an "open field," a "triumphant reply" to claustrophobic modernist images like Faulkner's of the burdened (and anxiously overrepresented) South (Guinn 176). If Faulkner and the modernists asserted that the past was not even past, Guinn claims that Hannah and his contemporaries eschew "the familiar [modernist] formula of understanding the present through the past" by asking instead, "but what *is* the past?" (162, 179), his words echoing Donald Noble's aforementioned identification of the unique temporal convolutions of Hannah's narratives (41, 43). However, this historical distinction in southern literature has been challenged by others, including Cleanth Brooks, who argues that as much as history is central to a modernist "sense of place," in fact Faulkner's work also constitutes "a persuasive commentary upon the thesis that much of 'history' is really a kind of imaginative construction" (34). Importantly, Brooks contends that to acknowledge the constructedness of history is "not to maintain that it is necessarily untrue" (34). While Hannah certainly appears to scrutinize the concept of historicity (what *is* the past?), as well as to mark his distinction from textual father Faulkner, it simply does not follow that southern history is conceivably now "past" in Hannah's contemporary fictional constructions, as Simpson, Humphries, and Hobson infer.

Many contemporary southern writers self-consciously shun Faulkner's influence by locating their fictions at a decisive distance from the South. Hannah, however, not only locates his fictions staunchly within the region but frequently explores themes of cultural stasis and entrapment, often dramatized in subtle formal patterns of temporal circularity or in odd transpositions of youth and age. Hannah's characters, like Faulkner's, feel the palpable presence of the past; they are often haunted by memories of private fall-from-grace moments to which they return compulsively, in a manner strongly redolent of the "peculiarly heightened consciousness" and habitual "backward glance" that Tate identified as characteristic of southern modernist literature (Tate, *Essays* 292). This is caught by the retrospective narrator of "A Creature in the Bay of St. Louis," who declares of a pivotal moment in his past, "I would return and return to it the rest of my life" (51). Explicit textual parallels suggest that this story shares a narrator with "Uncle High Lonesome" and therefore offers a conceptual foil; indeed, the narrator's promised regressive return is fulfilled by the circular aesthetic of Hannah's collection at large, which returns in its last story's last scene to this formative adolescent memory of coming of age in the old Bay of St. Louis. In *Ray*, the eponymous narrator similarly declares that when it comes to historical memory, "[n]othing is hazy" (51), thus perfectly recalling the predicament of the narrator in "Water Liars," who admits, "My sense of the past is vivid and slow. I hear every sign and see every shadow" (4). In each case, the past is curiously alive to these contemporary white southern men, as if the mythology of southern retrospection has become entrenched enough to become paradoxically authentic, though it may have detached from more direct apprehensions of the (spurious) shared legacy of the Civil War.

Rather than testifying to Hannah's eschewal of the southern-burden model, the antilinear temporal reworkings of his narratives strongly suggest its endurance. These stylistic devices offer a distinct echo of Widiss's account of Faulkner's modernism even while they form a key part of Hannah's postmodern interrogation of historicity. It is ironic, perhaps, that those critics who commended southern modernist writing and its emphasis on the "never dead" past should have inferred its contemporary demise in postsouthern literature. The post-South's alleged departure from fixations upon its formative past signals precisely what Faulkner imagined the South was incapable of doing: forgetting or laying the past to rest. When we return to Faulkner's memorable encapsulation of the hauntingly present southern past as Widiss describes it, it is apparent that in this earlier literary formulation of history and memory an equal dismantling of chronology inhered. There is a sense of history malfunctioning, as if this epitomic modernist trope were already in a sense postmodern, though this critical language was not yet ready to apply to it.

Hannah's male protagonists often fall from grace in ways related to their inheritance or memory of the Civil War. The war is central to constructions of white southern masculinity in much of Hannah's work, as Ruth D. Weston, Melanie Benson Taylor, Thomas Bjerre, James B. Potts, and Martyn Bone have pointed out in relation to Hannah's Civil War stories specifically; Hannah's character Ray dramatizes this succinctly when he cries "Oh, help me! I am losing myself in two centuries and two wars [Vietnam and the

Civil War]" (*Ray* 45). This sense of the South's history being still unresolved is testimony to Hannah's attitude toward the past in much of his writing. Perhaps it accounts for the continued interest in the Civil War, which distinguishes Hannah from many of his peers, as Guinn, Weston, Bjerre, Potts, and Bone have each noted. However, because in "Uncle High Lonesome" the Civil War is not an obvious concern, it becomes apparent that ideas about southern burden can continue to inform contemporary creative interrogations of southernness in more subtle and unexpected ways. Because Hannah's protagonists' personal falls from grace are subsumed in a broader public discourse of southern history—for example, southern burden manifested as white shame—even in stories where the war is not an explicit focus the mythology of the Lost Cause is never far away. By focusing on those Hannah stories in which the Civil War is not a direct theme, we can better appreciate how the idea (if not the reality) of a sense of postwar burden bears out on the construction of contemporary white southern masculinity even where direct proximity to the war has vanished.

While late-twentieth-century postregional scholarship typically questions the force of history and memory in postsouthern literature and identity, several recent critics have championed the persistence of Woodward's model, extending its relevance to twenty-first-century American identity politics. In Angie Maxwell, Todd Shields, and Jeannie Whayne's aptly named *The Ongoing Burden of Southern History* (2012), for example, the South's ongoing burden is figured as both a political consideration and an ethical imperative. Similarly, Larry J. Griffin's "Southern Distinctiveness, Yet Again, or, Why America Still Needs the South" (2000) reworks Woodward's model into accordance with twenty-first-century discourses that problematize modernist conceptions of southern distinctiveness framed in regional historicist terms. While Griffin points out the obvious political tensions inherent in proposing that all southerners are burdened by white guilt, he argues for the continued efficacy of Woodward's historical-haunting paradigm and indeed its ethical merit once it is detached from its dubious Agrarian origins. This recalls Maxwell's acknowledgment of Woodward's "private goal" as a self-professed "activist historian": to expand the definition of southern identity and "refocus southern whites on elements of their identity that did not rely solely on the maintenance of white supremacy and segregation" (Maxwell, "Introduction" 79). This more nuanced appreciation of Woodward's model allows it to encompass the many divisions and micro-Souths that exist within any concept of southern burden (and thus distinction), while also providing a framework for thinking about how the South's alleged burdens might have much broader resonance.

For example, the concept of historical haunting directly recalls contemporary thinking about the historical transference of guilt or trauma at the heart of much psychoanalytic and literary theory, which incorporates ideas about second-generation trauma and the inheritance of historical burdens not experienced firsthand. Cathy Caruth (along with Ruth Leys, Dominick LaCapra, and Michael Roth) explores the relationship of trauma, history, and representation, arguing that while immediate traumatic memory remains unspeakable or beyond representation, belated representations of collective historical trauma have the capacity to transform past ethical failings (Caruth calls this "the failure to have seen at the time") with the "imperative of a speaking that awakens others" (18). Several studies of southern cultural memory, including Anne Goodwyn Jones and Susan Van D'Elden Donaldson's *Haunted Bodies* (1997), Patricia Yaeger's *Dirt and Desire* (2000), and Lisa Hinrichsen's *Possessing the Past: Trauma, Imagination, and Memory in Post-Plantation Southern Literature* (2015), explore in this respect how trauma studies, with its emphasis on inherited memory and the politics of witness, testimony and silence, can help us to comprehend the South as a contested site of public and private conflict. Contemporary representations of historical traumas help commemorate those traumas in ways that one hopes prevent their repetition in the future, returning to the past to imagine a tacit alternative future. In the context of the South's past ethical failings, new formulations of the region's ongoing historical burden can exist as insurance against silence and forgetting if we remain mindful of the Agrarian influence on constructions of southern distinction and its problematic backward glance.

The concept of the ethics of historical memory is key to interpreting "Uncle High Lonesome" because Uncle Peter's high lonesomes are the manifestation of guilt from an unatoned crime. As a young man, he killed another man but was never punished for it. As the story unfolds, we learn that this formative historical event was the result of hurt pride following a lost game of poker and a fight with a stranger in a bar. Having been publicly humiliated in both respects, Uncle Peter returned in a rage to kill the man who "shamed [him] real bad" (220), astonishingly proceeding to escape (capital) punishment because in this small town in the Deep South, it was the "out-of-towner" victim who "was sentenced to remain dead," while homegrown killer "Peter was let go" (230). The story suggests that Peter was spared because he acted according to a locally accepted code of southern honor that was operative "back in the '20s" (230). Discussing issues of southern masculine identity and how "Hannah's [male] characters are driven by inherited ideas about honor, shame, and vengeance" (*BH* 46), Weston draws on the work of the historian Bertram Wyatt-Brown, who argues that shame and honor "cannot be understood apart from [each] other. [A southerner] was expected to have a healthy sense of shame, that is, a sense of his own honor. Shamelessness signified a disregard for both honor and disgrace. When shame was imposed by others, honor was stripped away" (viii, qtd. in *BH* 46). These arguments certainly appear to pertain to the events in Hannah's story, when we consider that Uncle Peter's vengeance was the result of a humiliation. Further, since he had reacted violently to the initial humiliation as a young man, the older man's high lonesomes signal a retrospective acceptance that his youthful *reaction* was disgraceful. Subsequently, Uncle Peter's self-imposed shame in the form of the high lonesomes signals a redoubling of "southern" shame and as such, a paradoxical recuperation of lost (old) honor from a kind of defeat.

Perhaps because of this paradox, Uncle Peter is described recurrently by his nephew as exhibiting "a savage grace" (214), unlike the man's own rather innocent brother, the narrator's father. Comparing him with Uncle Peter, "the man who could do things" (214), the narrator repeatedly describes his father as well-meaning but "childlike" (222), "an infant at a number of tasks" (216), and a man who "didn't know how to do things. He had no grace" (222). Persistently, the father's naïve ineptitude is contrasted to his brother's mature wisdom and proficiency at masculine "tasks," and it is the narrator's uncle rather than his father who facilitates the boy's passage into adulthood: "He taught me to fish, to hunt, to handle dogs, and horses" (218). This seeming incongruity, in that Uncle Peter, a murderer, should be the one who not only acts as a role model for the narrator but is described as living in a condition of prelapsarian grace, can be better understood in the context of the inherited primal honor code described above.

Individual masculinities and personal histories are subsumed in a mythology of honorable southern shame in which innocence and grace are not coterminous concepts. There is the sense that a proper coming of age and even a paradoxical state of attendant grace are inherent in the fall, as part of the South's unique historical legacy. If this version of white southern masculinity has its origins in sinfulness, then perhaps it is unsurprising that Hannah's narrator should profess that he has inherited his uncle's (not his father's) sin in his own white male coming of age. Uncle Peter provides the proper textual father in this story, which interrogates the malfunctioning of oedipal narratives in the South. The idea of the uncle as ersatz father transposes onto a much more generalized concept of inherited burden, of the sins of historical fathers visited on future generations of southern sons. This well-worn theme circulates widely in Hannah's work and finds its most obvious expression in *High Lonesome*'s lead story, "Get Some Young." Thus, Hannah continues to engage with established mythologies about southern masculinity and historical determinism, adapting ideas about inherited sinfulness and shame such as we would find, for example, in the stories of Faulkner's *Go Down, Moses*.

"Uncle High Lonesome" is written from the perspective of a middle-aged author who has gained posthumous insight into his uncle's dark past: "When he was dead I discovered that he was also a killer and not a valiant one" (214). It is the unearthing of this gothic family legend that drives the narrator's storytelling. By revisiting the formative scenes of his childhood and adolescence to try to comprehend his uncle's more violent loss of innocence, the nostalgic adult narrator attempts to make retrospective sense of his beloved but elusive subject by performing a backward historical excavation of his family history in the light of the recent shocking revelation of "the whole truth of where he [Uncle Peter] had come from [. . .]. That night [of the murder]. From there" (217). The narrator seeks recourse to this explanatory point of historical origin, which he imagines would aid a better understanding of the shame at the core of his uncle's life and then, strangely but seemingly inevitably, his own. It is this search that motivates his storytelling. However, if we accept that our narrator is performing a version of the modernists' backward glance, then his method becomes distinctly postmodern when the search becomes tricky and ultimately futile. The more the narrator attempts to approach the focal point of his story, the mysterious Uncle Peter, the more this focus becomes a vanishing point of historical reference that might be ultimately unknowable or unexplainable. Much of the narrator's retrospective narrative preserves the innocent perspective of his child self (acting as a surrogate for the naïve reader), even while it purports to be written by the knowing adult self. With the narrative operating simultaneously on both levels, the problems of interpreting the story generate from the formal interplay between these dual perspectives inhabiting a single narrative voice. Typically, it is in these interpretative challenges—what Weston calls the "unsettling shifts, gaps, and disavowals of [the story's] own truths" (*BH* 47)—that the text's remarkable subtleties reside. And it is in these "gaps" that the nuance of Hannah's own contemporary reworking of southern historical retrospection can be properly recognized.

In performing his storied excavation of history via a series of remembered scenes and images, Hannah's narrator foregrounds some distinctly postmodern ideas about reality, textuality, and performance. Because of the sustained incomprehensibility of memory augmented by the proliferation of conflicting images of the past, the narrator fails to piece together some coherent, explanatory narrative wrought from the illuminating knowledge of the posthumously unearthed truth of Uncle Peter's history. Instead, the title figure is described only in a series of isolated "scenes" or "episodes" (226, 218); in keeping with the lexis of performance, he inhabits various theatrical guises that prove strikingly incompatible with one another. For example, we learn that sometimes Uncle Peter would resemble "the criminal writer Jean Genet, merry and Byzantine in the darks of his eyes" (214). Sometimes he would "survey" the land in a manner redolent of "Napoleon" (218), or "he could also look, with his ears out, a bit common, like a Russian in the gate of the last Cold War mob; thick in the shoulders [and] with a belligerence like Kruschev's [*sic*]" (214). The language of Hollywood accompanies many descriptions of the man: "his face was spreading and reddening, almost as in a fiend movie" (219); he dresses dramatically and performs a set of chameleon costume changes, for example, wearing polo boots, a necktie, and fedora and later "dressing *up* [. . .] for [his nephew's] puppet shows" (226). After each high-lonesome episode, the melodrama of Peter's appearance is temporarily quietened, but the contrivance remains, as he dresses plainly in the style of an ashen-faced, humble deacon (221). Finally, at the end of the story we are told rather incongruously that he "now looked somewhat like Versace, the Italian designer" (227), and "in the last curious scene when I [the narrator] recall him [Uncle Peter] whole" (226) the narrator imagines that his uncle "was enduring a sea change" (227), the reference to Shakespeare's *The Tempest* intensifying this sense of the man's volatility or foreignness.

These descriptive recollections produce no single, coherent picture of a character whom the narrator describes, ironically, as having come from a bygone era when "[y]ou got what you saw more" and "there was a plainer language, then" (222). On one hand, Uncle Peter, a performer, is presented as a spectacle to behold, a proliferating succession of wildly mismatched and protean images that combine in their diversity to render him a fundamentally impenetrable signifier. On the other, his various attempts to reinvent himself in the image of other men (Genet, Khrushchev, Versace)—whom he can imitate or be "like" but never truly *be*—prove ultimately unsuccessful, and his true self prevails: "He remained the same, and [it] killed him" (226). With this curious intrusion of the modern on the postmodern, the suggestion is that Uncle Peter cannot escape the crime that has shaped his history irrevocably; the violent visitation of the past on the present results ultimately in his own death, as if in rightful reparation for the stranger's life he took. The ability to perform different roles only provides temporary escape, perhaps because this modern character possesses a real, tangible link to the historical trauma that defines him. Indeed, it was Uncle Peter's enactment of what Hannah elsewhere calls a "true old-timey" honor code ("The Ice Storm" 190) that catalyzed the murder, precisely what has caused the man to assume these different personae subsequently. While Uncle Peter's theatrical mutability signals an attempt to release himself from a distinctly southern sense of shame, however, the character resists neat categorization as either southern or postmodern, thereby also suggesting the conceptual unhelpfulness of thinking about these concepts in neat opposition.

Equally problematically, even the simple notion posited above, that Uncle Peter's heroic masculinity results (paradoxically) from his shameful past, is contrasted to the narrator's early charge that his uncle was *not* a "valiant" killer (214). This troubles any easy application of an old honor-code paradigm even while it implies that such a code is still operative in the South. On close inspection, sudden declarations of hermeneutical uncertainty invade the narrative throughout, with the adult narrative voice penetrating the childish perspective that dominates much of the story and ultimately corroborating, rather than alleviating, the child's sense of interpretative ignorance. These include: "I did not know there were women involved in the [high lonesome] benders, but there were" (221); "I [. . .] could not decide what the man, my uncle, *wanted* from this episode" (218); and most significantly, "I don't know if the dead man in his past urged him toward the final DT's and heart attack, *nor will I ever know* how much this crime dictated his life" (226, my emphasis). Self-reflexive attempts to enlist our collusion in reading for putative authenticity (where perhaps there is none) pepper the narrative ("You could see him—couldn't you?" [228]), betraying the narrator's continued incomprehension and powerlessness to know this phantom from the past. This belies the implicit objective behind the narrator's act of storytelling, which is not simply to get to "the whole truth" (217) of Uncle Peter's shadowy history but to determine the extent to which the past has "dictated" the present.

Hinrichsen writes that trauma escapes our ability to rationalize or analyze it, hence the language of the "supernatural and the spectacular" frequently used to describe it through the popular metaphor of "haunting" ("I can't believe" 233). In parallel to the narrator's obsessive mining of his own coming-of-age memories, each of Uncle Peter's high-lonesome episodes compulsively repeats the pivotal trauma when he killed the man. Again, both pursuits have a temporally regressive element characteristic of Southern Renaissance fiction—Tate called it "a literature conscious of the past in the present" (qtd. in T. Young ix)—whose characters (and authors) are compelled to revisit the past in order, paradoxically, to move forward. In this respect "Uncle High Lonesome" is perceptibly reminiscent of Kentuckian Bobbie Ann Mason's *In Country* (1985), which similarly reworks distinctly modernist ground in its exploration of how we make sense of the present (or not) by gaining an understanding of the past. With Hinrichsen, Alison M. Johnson interprets Mason's novel according to the historical transference of trauma. Mason's protagonist, Sam Hughes, believes that the "stress of the Vietnam War [. . .] was her inheritance" (Mason 89) because the war killed her father, even though this event transpired before her own birth. Like Uncle Peter's nephew, whose story is parasitic on the legend of his uncle's past, Sam seeks posthumous recourse to her father's history in an attempt to write herself into an all-male war narrative that excludes her. The novel culminates in a performative act of historical appropriation, with Sam finding "her" name on the Vietnam Veterans Memorial in Washington, DC. Gray reads this climax as a successful act of historical recuperation that places Sam "on the threshold of knowing the past—and starting [. . .] to accept [it]" (*Southern Aberrations* 365). Elsewhere Gray argues that in this moment Sam becomes "inscribed in history," having "come into reality, out of hyperreality" ("Afterword" 223–24). Yet for others, including Hinrichsen ("I can't believe" 246) and Kenneth Millard (*Coming of Age* 150), the strong sense of textual duplicity inherent in this putative epiphany reveals that Sam's imaginative inclusion in American history is a reflection on a misreading according to which texts continue to occlude reality, thus resisting any simple resolution.

In "Uncle High Lonesome," the narrator's historical reexamination creates a vital point of tension between the (imagined) truth of Uncle Peter's violent past and the narrator's naïve recollections of the man he adored as a boy. Thus, like Mason's problematic epiphany, the story cannot be understood as simply a contemporary recycling of a traditional southern modernist trope in which the present is understood through the past. Which is to say, while the mature narrator's newly gained knowledge has called for a revisiting of the past, the act of historical revival does not encourage resolution in the familiar modernist way. Nevertheless, the *compulsion* to revisit the putative historical origin remains, in a manner that retains a distinct echo of Guinn's southern modernist formula (162), and therefore suggests that postsouthern history might not be such an "open field" after all (Guinn 176).

Uncle Peter's disgrace, the ostensible origin of the man's present malaise, offers an important perspective on several other losses of innocence occurring in the story and bears further testament to the endurance of the southern-burden literary trope. Persistently, the uncle's shame impinges on his nephew's childhood, imbuing a series of the narrator's remembered boyhood experiences with a heaviness incongruous with each scene. None of these episodes in themselves denote the boy narrator's lost innocence, but in each one the biblical language of original sin resounds at the exact moment when Uncle Peter's mediating gaze is acknowledged by the narrator (225, 226, 227), suggesting that the present is dictated by the sins of the past. This sense of historical entrapment is compounded in a memorable scene on the beach at Bay St. Louis (226). The moment occurs after the narrator (who has just turned thirteen) falls prey to a stinging verbal assault by a "street-mouthed" teenage girl from New Orleans, who screams "Hey Cracker, eat me!" at him as he plays in the water (228). Observing the encounter, Uncle Peter flies into a disproportionate rage, instilling an epiphany of sorts in the boy narrator, who suddenly "understood there was a huge tragedy in my uncle, regardless of anything" (229). The mature adult narrator proceeds to offer a retrospective explanation for the man's odd behavior, interpreting it as an instance of historical foresight: "Could it be [. . . that] he saw my fate coming to me in my teens as his had, when he killed the man?" (229–30). It is no coincidence that the story's narrator, Peter Howard Jr., or

"Little Pete," is the namesake of his double: symbolically, the elder's shameful inheritance is conferred to its successor, as if to suggest that the boy's own fall from grace has already been predetermined, his own fate coming to him just as his uncle's had come to *him*. When the narrator himself pronounces the New Orleans youth "[a]lready deep into sin, weathered like a slut at a bingo table, from a neighborhood that smelled like whiskey on a hot bus exhaust" (229), a moment of transference occurs, with Uncle Peter's darkened perception of the girl's sinfulness transposed onto his now grown nephew. The intergenerational bestowing of the South's burden is therefore dramatized in Hannah's creative adaptation of the gothic convention of textual doppelgängers.

The concept of the passive inheritance of second-generational guilt is best dramatized in the climax of "Uncle High Lonesome." The story ends with an extraordinary confession from its narrator (corroborating the sense of oedipal predictability above), who professes to have inherited a strong and tangibly felt guilt for Uncle Peter's crime as if he himself had committed the murder: "For years now I have dreamed I killed somebody. The body has been hidden, but certain people know I am guilty, [. . .] and I know, deep within" (230). Then, equally mysteriously, Uncle Peter's shameful legacy is bequeathed in turn to the narrator's own nephew: "My nephew was nodding the whole while I was telling him this. He has dreamed this very thing, for years" (230). Many Hannah stories may be read as articulations of original sin, and indeed, quite fittingly, "Uncle High Lonesome" comes full circle when the certainty of historical recurrence is realized in its closing lines, these nephews apparently fated to inherit guilt from a prior generation's crime. Providing a neat analogy for the shame of both the antebellum and the pre–civil rights South for subsequent generations, white male coming of age in Hannah's fictional family is therefore microcosmic of the South's public mythology, its present inhabitants bound to repeat the region's shameful past even while they are not related to it directly.

Caruth's work on historical transference pertains again to discussion here, in line with a body of contemporary scholarship on the passing down of trauma onto subsequent generations. Marita Grimwood explains her own broad conception of the term *second generation* (a term gaining purchase in America following Helen Epstein's 1979 *Children of the Holocaust*) to encompass "the consciousness of later generations and communities" not necessarily ancestrally related but including children, grandchildren, and those living in close proximity to Holocaust survivors, who "tend to address the issue of growing up with the profound sense that their [predecessors'] experiences are inescapable and somehow their own" (3, 8). While thinking about the inherited trauma of the violence experienced by Holocaust survivors most aptly applies to the victims of racism in the South (cue the men's decreeing the sinfulness of the New Orleans girls above, who we assume is Black), the notion of "inescapable" postsouthern burden across generations might also be applied to Hannah's white characters' self-professed inheritance of their forebears' guilt. The ending of "Uncle High Lonesome" confirms that history does not simply die with its living memories. It is kept alive by historical transference and by the stories and mythologies (familial and cultural) that have been borne from its events. Partly, these ideas within contemporary trauma and memory studies are in keeping with the modernists' understanding that the burdens of the past can never be alleviated.

While the transference of cultural trauma (such as war or the Holocaust) is a widely discussed phenomenon in the global West, the prospect of cultural *guilt* transcending the immediate community can be usefully explored in relation to the South. Of course, the notion of white southern guilt lasting generations can be troubled by contrasting it with Black cultural trauma and the (surely more pressing) ongoing legacy of racism, providing an interesting dynamic between thinking about the white South's cultural failure to move forward and an ethically motivated compulsion to revisit past failings.[1] But if we accept that historical trauma need not always be experienced personally for its pressures to be felt, then the sort of amnesiac historical rupture some have identified after southern modernism is a misconception. Hannah's postsouthern protagonists feel the weight of the past as much as their elders, although their direct experiences are not the same, because the South's historical narratives—from both sides of the racial divide—are not easy to escape or reroute. Further, because historical memory in many respects is indistinguishable from story, historical burden retains its usefulness as a formula for thinking about certain kinds of cultural identity, even in a contemporary moment that questions the very notion of authentic cultural history as distinct from its representations. Hannah's postsouthern aesthetic seems bent on muddling oppositional distinctions between the haunted modernist South and the amnesiac postmodernist one in ways that complicate some of the more straightforward arguments of this chapter's opening pages.

Within the self-consciously southern paradigm of historical entrapment, a further twist is added in Hannah's story, a distinction between old and new ideas about how historical burden functions in contemporary formulations of southernness. It rests on a concept of performativity that appears almost uniformly in Hannah's fiction (gaining momentum in this last collection) whereby the author's vision of postsouthern burden reveals its true complexity. When we compare Uncle Peter's historical burden with his nephew's, it becomes clear that if the older generation's guilt is real (insofar as Uncle Peter's guilt comes from an actual crime he committed), then the younger generation's is only imagined or dreamed, removed from what we might term the *authentic* historical event, twice removed in the case of Uncle Peter's great-nephew. While he was never physically imprisoned, Uncle Peter exists in a state of stasis that is as literal as it is psychological: he is as unable to leave his hometown as he is to forget "the dead man in his past" (226). Meanwhile, his nephews' final confessions of their own felt culpability may seem authentic enough "(I know, deep within"), but of course *we* know that neither has committed the crime outside the fantasy realm. The guilt has become increasingly detached from its historical origin, and the new generation appears to gain a historical agency, committing the crime by proxy, as it were, because of the performative freedom this detachment from the actual crime has afforded. Occurring only at the level of performance, it is the narrator's creative *enactment* of southern burden that recovers a sense of agency that at first would seem incongruous, given its basis in previously established ideas about historical determinism and the passive acceptance of fate.

This performative aspect of postsouthern burden lends Hannah's fiction its distinctive currency amid debates about the contemporary efficacy of regional studies and of southernness per se. In parallel to the nephews' professed burden as a creative adaptation of the past, we can appreciate the performative aspect of Hannah's own creative modification of a modernist southern-burden trope. The narrator's guilt may be purely textual in Hannah's story. But while it is freed from the uncle's guilt, which is debilitating and imprisoning, the concept of southern burden remains, regardless. Like Sam Hughes's questionable epiphany at the end of *In Country*, Hannah's narrator's guilt is phony, but it is felt authentically enough. Playing with our expectations and with the modernists' formula in this way, Hannah's new take on a familiar theme defies us to distinguish, finally or fully, between what is authentic and what is merely performative. This suggests that the concepts of authenticity (southern) and performativity (postmodern) have always been as essentially symbiotic as "Uncle High Lonesome" suggests, though again, it is perhaps only more recently that the critical language to articulate this phenomenon has emerged.

The capacity for freedom in performance distinguishes Uncle Peter's original burden from its subsequent copies, and it can explain Hannah's visible sidestepping of traditional oedipal narratives by way of uncles and nephews (not fathers and sons). Uncle Peter cannot escape the burden of history, because he cannot invest the roles he plays with the semblance of authenticity. The narrator, meanwhile, has inherited something from his namesake, but it is not his guilt so much as his dedication to performance. This is implicit in such narrative revelations as "I was not the same person [. . .] after that afternoon" (225) or "These were my teen years when I was altogether a different person" (226). The relative mutability of these two male characters is a seemingly minor detail in the story, but it is crucial to Hannah's creative adaptation of the modernists' theme, exploring the possibilities for contemporary white southern masculinity to reside in historical mutability, in performance, and in the phony image.

The concept of performance as a vehicle for (masculine) agency is captured in a scene where the narrator recalls his uncle being oddly captivated by the puppet shows he would perform as a boy, inspired by the television show *Howdy Doody*. The scene's unique significance is revealed when its memory continues to trouble our adult narrator long after Uncle Peter has died: "I still don't know what the hell went on with him and the puppets, the way he watched them, then me" (226). Like the fishing episode (224), the scene is described in a curiously biblical language of enraptured witness, with childish innocence replaced by sinfulness and shame: "The puppets seemed to worry him [. . .]. He looked at me as if I were magic, operating these little people and speaking for them. He had the stare of an intense confused infant. When I'd raise my eyes to him, he'd look a bit ashamed, as if he'd been seduced into thinking these toys were living creatures. He watched my mouth when I spoke in a falsetto for them" (226). The special appeal of these shows lies in the child's successful execution of a performance, one that seduces its audience into thinking he has conjured these inanimate toys to life. While the boy is empowered by this feat (momentarily the roles are reversed, and the adult is infantilized), history excludes his uncle from such possibility. As a man from an older world, Uncle Peter remains unable to carry off a truly cogent performance: "You'd have thought he was star-ing into a world he never even considered possible, somewhere on another planet, something he'd missed out on and was very anxious about" (226). Thus, the scene can be framed in terms of Hannah's exposition of the rela-tive agency in performance available to uncle and nephew.

The level of alienated (high lonesome?) detachment from authentic his-tory achieved by the postsouthern generation can be further explained by recalling how Hannah's second-generation characters have inherited a *myth-ology* of southern burden in place of the experience itself by creatively ap-propriating elements of southern regional discourse in a manner that in this sense is entirely simulative. Within Hannah's imaginative reworking of the southern backward glance is the possibility that new generations' ex-periences are merely echoes of their forerunners', coming from texts rather than from real events. Not only is "Uncle High Lonesome" parasitic upon a previous generation's authentic historical experience but it is underwritten by a prior narrative, the family legend its narrator has become privy to as an adult. Storytelling therefore becomes an acquisitive act, appropriating the secondary tale of another man's fallenness, gleaned from the partial ac-counts of others in the absence of any direct account from the man himself. As the real thing becomes a distinctly elusive concept, the story is reduced to a mediation on a mediation. Simultaneously (and typically of Hannah), the performative appropriation of story proves oddly enabling in terms of the narrator's own masculinity.

The narrator's imaginative but essentially ersatz appropriation of Uncle Peter's real history, the true story, is epitomized in the scene in which the nephew describes his imagined account of "[t]hat night" (217), with Uncle Peter awaiting his fate in the cells, having killed the man. A change in lexis marks a visible turn in the narrative, whose retrospective voice is brought sharply into the present tense, conveying a sense of urgency and panic with a visible lack of punctuation amid a rapid succession of thoughts and im-ages. The episode is described as if it were the narrator's own experience, or as if Uncle Peter's authentic historical voice were being ventriloquized through his conduit nephew: "the chair legs he ground in your face all over you, and the crashing truth of your sorriness in gambling and drink so loud in your head they might be practicing the trapdoor for the noose over and over right outside the door. That night. From there" (217). Something com-plex and intriguing regarding the symbiotic relationship between authenticity and performance occurs here. The repetition of *you[r]* establishes a bond between performer and audience, the implied you, as if to suggest that if we readers are seduced into believing the performance (as Uncle Peter was by the puppets), it is paradoxically authenticated, no matter that of course we know this purportedly firsthand account is entirely speculative and contrived. At the metalevel, the boy's puppeteering anticipates the grown narrator's performance of the story itself: as the implied author of the story he intends his audience, *you* readers, to be similarly persuaded of its authenticity. A performance depends on the audience that consumes it (a trope deployed widely in recent southern studies) to testify to its aesthetic merit as much as its historical veracity; both are created, not inherent.

Despite his later skepticism toward elements of the NSS, Michael Kreyling was one of the first to indict modern southern literary studies in favor of a "new" southern studies that critically rejects the idea of a South that exists outside its discursive constructions. In *The South That Wasn't There*, Kreyling seeks to trouble rigid distinctions between history and memory, ultimately positing that the "future" of "southern memory" resides in "simulacra" or the forms of its textual mediations (194). Kreyling's title denotes his interest in "place/time narratives" in postsouthern writing "when the author has (as yet) no firsthand experience of being there: no ground literally" (121). These words not only evoke contemporary thinking about historical transference as dramatized in Hannah's postsouthern narratives; they also offer an apt summary of what Hannah's narrator, Uncle Peter's nephew, achieves with his story, writing from a "groundless" position where authenticity is inextricable from narrative. We can observe this in the transcendent language of scene above, evoking a tangible sense of immediacy that legitimizes the younger generation's claim to genuine inherited guilt, even though we know that the memory described is not the narrator's own, however urgent or firsthand it appears to be. The narrator thus underwrites a sense of the transference of southern memory, while demanding that we reconceptualize it, in a postmodern moment, as a function of the forms of its mediation.

On first impression, this move from the real to the textual appears to invoke Simpson's argument for a supposedly fading sense of authentic historical memory in the South impacting detrimentally on post-1960s regional and literary culture, which can mine only textbooks rather than direct memorial accounts (252). However, Kreyling's theory of the fluidity between grounded (real) and imagined (mythologized) forms of historical memory suggests that reality is not simply replaced by textuality. History may be indistinguishable from the forms of its representation, but there is nothing to suggest that this is simply a new or postregional problem, especially given the South's long-standing self-consciousness about its own mediations. The difficulty of pinpointing the historical truth in "Uncle High Lonesome" problematizes Simpson's charge that waning firsthand memory would incrementally lessen the impact of historical events on contemporary southern literature, because one generation's history cannot be accessed any more authentically than any other's. Thus, we readers also become complicit in the guilt, not for the actual crime (Uncle Peter's) but for having been seduced by its storied account. By drawing the reading audience into complicity in this way, more subtly, the metafictional *author's* true guilt is revealed to have stemmed from the recognition of his own "crime" of storytelling, a feat that has been indistinguishable from lying from its very first instance in "A Creature in the Bay," where "I even worked in the lie more" (51). Here, then, is the narrator's imagined crime—and indeed, the corruption of all writing from the metafictional perspective (Hutcheon, *Narcissistic Narrative* 49)—which stems from the narrator's self-reflexive cognizance of his story's inability to represent truthfully or mimetically.

This metafictional acknowledgment of authorial guilt sheds subtle light on some of the complexities of the story's curious ending, enriching our interpretation of the narrator's final, strange confession of inherited culpability. As a foil for Hannah's authorial self-reflexivity about his own telling about the South, this metafictional aspect of the story is integral to its value. It offers a means of mitigating a major contemporary tension between "traditional" and "new" southern studies, because the South reemerges as something that is simultaneously both material *and* discursive. Such writing is informed by a palpable sense that regional history continues to burden contemporary subjects in mysterious ways, even while it is careful to acknowledge how *southern* burden is essentially a myth. This characterizes the sophisticated duality of Hannah's writing: a story that appears to present an apparently straightforward disquisition on southern historical haunting reveals that the inherited burden, at the metafictional level, is that of the storyteller-liar's acknowledgment of his act of false performance, and of the self-reflexive performativity of (post)southern regionalism. This is the world Uncle Peter never considered possible, one where the narrator's postmodern staging of inherited sin happens at a crucial historical distance. It is precisely this imagined detachment, this removal from more rigid (foundational) understandings of southern burden, that enables performative appropriations of historical discourses, which can be vitally liberating. And this is even more remarkable when the appropriated narratives appear to articulate oppression and entrapment.

"The Agony of T. Bandini" sustains the paradox that there is scope for agency in a place where subjects self-consciously adopt a regional discourse of historical burden as part of a performative imagined southernness. The ideas about performance implicit in "Uncle High Lonesome" are much more pronounced in this story, which focuses on how southern regional identity is mythologized, constructed from texts and images that are enacted and consumed in the service of personal, social, political, or aesthetic agendas. The story scrutinizes a specific cultural narrative in which white southern masculinity is bound to a concept of stoic defeat, or what Bjerre calls "a Faulknerian ability to endure suffering" ("Heroism" 46). Bjerre's words suggest the indebtedness of contemporary masculinity to its prior textual constructions. The language of Faulknerian, romantic male defeat resounds openly throughout "The Agony of T. Bandini," with such discursive constructions as "the burden of shame and guilt" (127), "the world of pain and ruin" (128), "the defeated" and "the vanquished" (131), and of course "the burden of history," which becomes conspicuously repetitive and demands our attention (130, 131). The narrative follows a series of Tiger Bandini's drunken escapades in his newly adopted home of Oxford, Mississippi. In these theatrical episodes, Bandini displays a stoic ability to endure a succession of public, abject scandals in a manner that instills a curious kind of admiration from his audience. These are acts of enamored performance, inspired by an image of the "vanquished" South gleaned from key homosocial relationships in the story. Thus, the (Confederate) South's historic defeat is reconceptualized in the terms of a problematic mythology that contemporary white masculinity can tap into, by which it can be recovered.

Bandini, like Uncle Peter, killed someone as an adolescent and dodged punishment. He too struggles with alcoholism as an adult, and he has a pathological preoccupation with the past. These narrative parallels are explicit enough to suggest that we consider the two stories together. Yet in Bandini's case homicide was the result of notably dishonorable circumstances. Celebrating a New York Giants win in a bar, we are told bluntly, "when he left he got in his car and killed another man in a bad head-on accident" (127). This event causes little obvious remorse in its perpetrator, who continues to drink heavily and whose wealthy parents continue to bail their wayward son out of trouble, seemingly without judgment or consequence. This presents a crucial difference in each story's presentation of historical haunting: Bandini, while his crime equals the other's, feels no personal shame or guilt as far as we can tell; we cannot say that the past haunts him in the same way. This seemingly trivial distinction between these two male characters provides a vital point of contrast, a sense already that there is something fundamentally inauthentic about Bandini's self-proclaimed "agony" compared with Uncle Peter's genuine guilt. Relocating from upstate New York to the Deep South after the accident, Bandini actively performs those aspects of "southern burden" in which he discerns the best potential for personal redemption or historical absolution. The southern "world of pain and ruin" is presented as the product of a highly suspicious mythology, but nevertheless there is something to be gained from men's appropriating aspects of southern mythology. Because he is a northerner, Bandini's southernness is especially performative, which invites us to consider the extent to which Hannah's own stagy appropriation of southern-burden discourse is sincere, parodic, or indicative of something more nuanced—*if* the concept of southern burden can retain value after its discursive dependency and performative nature have been acknowledged.

In the story's opening pages, the narrator recounts Bandini's brief time at a New York college, where he idolizes two homesick "Southern boys who are crazed for the work of William Faulkner, and even more crazed as their homesickness grew" (127–28). Bandini is so "impressed by" the Southern boys because he believes that they, "like Faulkner, had elaborate reasons for doing almost anything" (128). The boys' talk of "worthy subjects [. . .] coiled up and crossed like nylon fishing line" (128) is exactly the sort of narrative Bandini would like to attach to his own pathetic history, and his infatuation with the Southern boys signals the first of Bandini's many investments in an image of southern masculinity personified in the various figures he encounters, much as the Southern boys are themselves "crazed" with the "worthy" vision of southern culture they identify in Faulkner's work.

Faulkner embodies Bandini's romantic idea of the South, where the cataclysmic fall of the so-called Lost Cause catalyzes a cultural narrative of historical determinism from which defeated and shamed white men can yet rise in feats of stoic heroism. Within this dubious version of southern mythology, it is the Southern boys' frequent talk of fate as a central aspect of Faulknerian southernness that attracts Bandini, and he ventriloquizes the boys' language with increasing fervor: "Like them, Bandini began to speak much of destiny and twists of fate. This comforted him. Much was inevitable and bound to the blind dice-thrower fate. Fishing line left overnight would coil of its own. So he thought it was in the dice and natural that he would wind up way down south in the precincts of the great author Faulkner himself" (128). Thanks to the Southern boys, Bandini is able to invest his own historical fall with a lofty Faulknerian narrative: "He felt he was in the world of pain and ruin now after the [car] wreck, but he saw there were elaborate reasons for it, and he relished this. [. . .] Ruin talked to him" (128). For Bandini, the South represents the proper place for the disgraced and shunned, an imagined community of the vanquished that Bandini sees himself as having entered after the accident: "Bandini advised himself that he could no longer exist in his own town in upper New York State under the burden of shame and guilt" (127). Bandini recognizes the potential in adopting a Faulknerian mythology of heroic defeat to redeem his own distinctly unheroic fall from grace, and this accounts for his decision to relocate to the author's former hometown, Oxford, Mississippi. Bandini's deliberate southward move ("He advised himself") is merely shrouded in a bogus language of fated historical inevitability ("it was in the dice and natural"), borrowed from the deterministic vision of the South championed by the Southern boys and indeed, at a broader level, the discourse of southern burden as something inherited or natural.

Bandini's first impression of the South is heavily mediated from the start, not only by his infatuation with the Southern boys but by the boys' own nostalgia for the image of the South presented by Faulkner. It is an act of textual parasitism that becomes even more suspect when we acknowledge the boys' proneness to quoting "long [memorized] passages from Faulkner" in the vein of a "preacher schooled on an enormous dictionary" (128). That the boys' enthusiasm for Faulkner "grew" with "their homesickness" in New York suggests that even their own seemingly more authentic identification with the Faulknerian southern-burden theme was not so much an innate part of their southernness (as Bandini imagines) but rather a nostalgic attempt to construct a sense of tangible regional identity threatened by feelings of displacement in the North. Bandini's own imagined southernness is a mediation on a mediation, a case of misappropriated regional identity that becomes doubly questionable when we are also told that the wealthy white northerner "sided with [poor] blacks, especially now that he was in disgrace and felt shunned" (128). Bandini's parroting the Southern boys is merely part of his enactment of a fictional image of the disgraced and shunned South, gleaned from the Southern boys' nostalgic and equally bogus appropriation of Faulknerian discourse.

Because Bandini's identification with the South's imagined burdens comes principally from discourse or text, we can ponder Hannah's treatment of this theme relative to "Uncle High Lonesome." While Bandini does possess an intimate experience of historical trauma accompanied, we would assume, by real guilt (compared with Uncle Peter's nephews, who only imagine they have killed someone), it is difficult to imagine what Faulknerian "worthy" or "elaborate" reasons we might attach to Bandini's irresponsible act of killing a man through his recklessness. Indeed, his earlier claim to be living "under the burden of shame and guilt" seems to refer only to the fact that "[h]is family had struggled in measures grievous to them to keep Bandini out of prison" (127) rather than to any proper sense of remorsefulness for the fact that he has killed someone. Ironically, while the northerner Bandini arguably does have an authentic claim to the "healthy" shame Wyatt-Brown espoused as an integral part of honorable southern masculinity, any conceivable honor inherent in it is promptly invalidated when Bandini's infatuation with the mythology of "the burden of shame and guilt" overtakes the real experience. It is this abstract mythology of the tragic southern "world of pain and ruin," rather than any properly informed sense of southern culture or its history, that Bandini relishes. Nor, indeed, is there any genuine sense of agony, despite the traumatic event in his past that we might expect to have generated such feelings. It is possible that "The Agony of T. Bandini" simply parodies the concept of southern burden.

Once again, however, and despite popular interpretations of Hannah's broader oeuvre (see, e.g., SOP 43; and Kreyling, "Fee, Fie" 11), the story complicates our efforts to interpret it simply as postsouthern parody, where the postsouthern text knowingly reworks or rebukes prior modernist forms. This is because Hannah posits that something vitally enabling can be gleaned from the parasitical appropriation of cultural mythology. Bandini's identification with the indicted South is parasitic on those elements of southern-burden mythology in which he discerns the best potential for *story*, for veiling private disgrace with a public narrative of heroic fated failure. Unlike the real southerner Uncle Peter, who was truly burdened and entrapped, the young northerner is at liberty to appropriate regional discourse, symbolized by his autonomous choice to perform the most drastic physical reroute possible in America, while Uncle Peter was powerless to escape his high lonesomes or to leave Mississippi. For Bandini, the process of filtering firsthand shame through a historical narrative he has no part in dulls its impact and immediacy, captured neatly by the narrator's idyllic description of Oxford as a source of comfort: "The town was *storied* and cozy, filled with shady lanes under great oaks" (128, my emphasis). While Bandini's past crime equals Uncle Peter's, he recognizes the liberating distance that textual mediations afford. Here, the contrived nature of the Southern boys' own appropriations of Faulknerian discourse suggests that it is not simply Bandini's status as a northerner that invalidates his claim to southern mythology. Instead, the story suggests that all forms of southern exceptionalism are anxiously contingent. In turn, we can appreciate the ways in which texts and images have contributed to a falsely romanticized mythology of the fallen white South, which Bandini fetishizes and consumes in his attempt to attach a profound and redemptive narrative to his own wretchedness. The onus of critiquing the terms of this sentimentalized vision of southern burden falls, subsequently, on the reader.

In the storied town of Oxford, Bandini encounters several images of the "vanquished" South with which he becomes besotted. He becomes enamored of certain men who, like the Southern boys, are preoccupied with a masculine mythology of (military) defeat, failure, abjection, and stoic endurance. The story contains a trio of male characters, social outcasts who recognize the potential for story in one another's fallenness: Bandini, Cruthers, and a character called "the town writer who specialized in the burden of history" (130), who serves as a doppelgänger for the story's narrator, whose voice suddenly changes from omniscient third-person to first-person toward the end (132). Like Bandini, these men are mindful of the value of adopting southern mythology even though—or perhaps because—their abject circumstances do not warrant it; each feeds vicariously off the others' abjection, some explicitly (the town writer, Bandini) and some less so (the story's narrator, who becomes another important male presence in the story once he is established as a witnessing "I" presence). In the homosocial world of failed masculinity that the story dramatizes, each man asks who the greater failure is and thus has the most right to a storied persona.

The town writer adopts as his chauffeur the wretched Cruthers, an alcoholic, thief, and police informant "who claimed to be a sergeant in the Vietnam conflict who carried about an M-60, his sweet big baby, and mowed down hundreds" (130–31). Cruthers is prone to (fictional) reminiscences about his most abject military experiences, but his worth to the writer lies in his symbolic status as the fallen soldier. To the writer, Cruthers evokes the defeats of not only Vietnam and Korea but also, importantly, the Civil War, subjects of the writer's latest historical novel. Cruthers affords prized writerly material in his embodiment of southern burden, to the extent that the writer "would introduce him to his cronies as the burden of history" (131). The sense of historical misappropriation is epitomized when we are told: "Late at night with enough whiskey the writer and Cruthers would listen to Sinatra and Presley" and begin "weeping over the Vietnam dead and the Confederate dead, and, *appropriate to the writer's novel,* the Korean dead. When Sinatra sang, it was the dead of World War II" (131, my emphasis). If it seems incongruous that the Black character Cruthers should join the writer in weeping for the Confederate dead, then he too is a fraudster, much as Bandini tenuously identifies with "shunned" Black people. While we know that Cruthers only "claimed" to be a sergeant who "went native" in Vietnam on a depraved mission of "independent slaughter" (130), the abject nature of this assumed identity (and indeed, the abjection inherent in the act of its assumption) signals Cruthers's unique value to both Bandini and the town writer. The writer sees echoes of both "the Korean dead" and "the Confederate dead" in the character Cruthers, not only because he claims to have shared in America's national defeat in Vietnam (prefigured in the Lost Cause) but because he symbolizes for both Bandini and the writer a man who has been doubly defeated, historically, in his Blackness.

The writer also adopts the notorious Bandini for his similar storied potential. Bandini's shameful public spectacles in Oxford, "[t]he lobsters and cat and scaling of the soldier," we are told, "were precious to the writer and Bandini was in solid at the writer's bungalow" (131). The writer creates an imaginative mythology of "Northern agony" that is appropriate to his novel's theme, which he attaches to the character Bandini. Again, this mythology is gleaned from history books and the textual mediations of others: "He [the writer] read up on Bruce Catton and could account for the Northern agony, better and better, when the topic moved over to Those Who Fell once Elvis sang his medley of 'Dixie' and 'Battle Hymn of the Republic' with the highly sincere Las Vegas band behind him" (131). In the narrator's ironic reference to the "highly sincere Las Vegas band" (if Vegas epitomizes phony simulation), the speciousness of Bandini's "agony" is revealed. Like Elvis singing "Dixie" and "Battle Hymn of the Republic," it is merely a performance of fallenness, for personal gain and public consumption, that has not been wrought from any real sense of historical contrition. This draws attention to how myths about Dixie, the Confederate States, and the Lost Cause have been "media-made" to serve certain political agendas, just as the writer consumes both Bandini and Cruthers as "appropriate" material for his well-worn literary topic "Those Who Fell."

Cruthers's war stories are equally precious to Bandini because they speak to the northern imaginary of the dark and violent South. We learn that "[i] n fact he [Bandini] rather kidnapped Cruthers from the writer" (131), insisting that the man move in with him and imploring him to repeat awful tales of "slaughter" (130), confessions of the most deplorable behavior, to which Bandini listens in an entranced state of enamored witness. That Cruthers's tales are probably tall ones is of no consequence for their audience: Bandini avidly consumes narratives of southern disgrace because they fuel his fantasy of southern men being the puppets of blind fate, bound to repeat the failings of their forefathers in an endless, shameful cycle. It is seductive, violent masculinity in the making, something intimated very early on when it is revealed of Bandini's homoerotic infatuation with football linebackers, "He worshipped the violent crush" (127).

The town writer's obsession with "the burden of history," personified, he imagines, in both Cruthers and Bandini, pertains to Bandini's own adopted southernness as arbitrated through these other male figures. Like the writer, we learn that "Bandini filled up [his] old shabby yellow house with history books" (130). It is the absence of a genuine heroic narrative that breeds Bandini's desire to appropriate one, writing himself into southern mythology while remaining only superficially invested in its terms. Bandini has uncritically appropriated the discourses of southern history, caught in the narrator's revelation: "Around the room, all over the sofa and the bed, were books of history. I noticed markers were in all of them just a few pages deep. He seemed to be reading many at once instead of one at a time" (135). Later, the narrator overhears Bandini telling Cruthers and the writer, "Nobody is really everything. Everyone is just a collision," poetic words that become immediately suspect when the narrator ventures, "I wondered where he had got that" (134). While each character can certainly be accused of acts of textual plagiarism, nevertheless their simulated "agony" provides invaluable material for creative inspiration.

The narrator recounts various scenes in which Bandini is witnessed undergoing public humiliation, including the episodes with the cat and the lobsters and his drunkenly climbing the statue of the lone Confederate soldier in Oxford's town square. In the first episode, fleeing the police after shoplifting two lobsters to feed a starving stray cat, Bandini finds a discarded bottle of liquor, and we are told: "Tiger Bandini had got new lungs and legs off the boon of drink and he was again that twisty shifting dodger who had almost made the team nine years ago. [. . .] He came out of an alley into the town square free of the police, crafty and game, rid of the pain in his hands" (130). It is a baptismal rebirth of sorts (Bandini gains new lungs and legs and becomes his lithe sporting self of nine years earlier), especially if we consider that it was the loss of Bandini's sporting career that signaled his real fall from grace, the nostalgic past or historical might-have-been that haunts him more than the dead man does: "He came from sports people but even to other hard-bitten fans he was over the line" (127). This would account for the character's alcoholism and bizarre behavior at sporting events even before the car accident, substantiating the interpretation that Bandini's alcoholism is not (like Uncle Peter's) a symptom of his remorse for killing someone. Ultimately, the language that accompanies Bandini's exploits in Oxford appears sincere more than simply parodic, for example, in the image of the fleeing Bandini being "gravely" hurt "but he staggered on" (129), or when the narrator concedes that "had they shined a light on him they would have seen a man near vomitous with joy" (130), suggesting a sort of triumph gleaned from adversity. Because the language of these scenes seems incompatible with their trivial nature, the narrative lends a sense of gravity to Bandini's otherwise pathetic exploits. In the end it is not clear whether Bandini has actually achieved the status of the stoically surviving "wretched" (129) or whether the story simply parodies the romantic image of the stoically defeated South, described as "a sad and wonderful place" (129).

The answer becomes clearer as these scenes progress. For example, in the second abovementioned scene, we are told that Bandini "saw in the cold moon before him the courthouse statue of the lone Confederate looking curiously southward. He became infatuated right off and with great conviction he emancipated the cat and lobsters, then began climbing the ten feet of pedestal and statue. [. . .] Bandini had a free wide heart for the vanquished. He scaled toward the man, all fours engaged, in an act of hunching and embracing" (130).[2] Again, it is an infatuation with a false *image* of the vanquished South, an act of veneration toward the conspicuously southward-facing defeated soldier. The statue of the lone Confederate evokes further ideas about the fraudulence of memorial cultures and the fictions they help to maintain about the Lost Cause when retrospective legends and mythologies have disguised historical reality. By drawing attention to the forms of the South's historical representation and how our apprehensions of the region become mired in narrative, Hannah's preoccupation with the issue of the false image is revealed. Initially, then, Bandini's assuming the role of the defeated Confederate with "a free wide heart for the vanquished" parodies the sentimentalized view of southern military history, underwritten by Agrarian narratives about white southerners being the stoic survivors of defeat who have become honorable in their shame.

While Bandini's self-conscious embracing of the image of southern masculinity personified in the statue is described in the scene as an explicit "act," it is one that is performed "with great conviction" nonetheless. Importantly, it requires an audience to witness it, to testify to the performance's paradoxical sincerity. Things take an interesting turn when a police officer beholding the scene describes Bandini's behavior toward the statue: "The policeman had driven up to witness this remarkable love, as Bandini reached the boots of the defeated. The policeman heard the man cry out like a thing impaled and then it was too ugly for him to watch anymore. The odor of rank sea and a low hissing brought the officer to kneel with his light" (130). The moment emphasizes the transforming effect of Bandini's theatrics on a witnessing audience, the policeman "with his light," who is literally moved to a pose of religious reverence, brought to kneel in reflection of Bandini's own worshipful pose in a moment of transference. The infatuated Bandini's staged act of veneration toward the image of the defeated South is dependent on the presence of an equally infatuated policeman, who quite literally illuminates the epiphanic significance of the act, lending a sense of authenticity that otherwise it would have lacked. The performance becomes surprisingly affecting, as if another gothic act of transference has occurred and Bandini has momentarily inhabited the persona of "the defeated"; that "[t]he policeman heard [Bandini] cry out like a thing impaled" directly evokes an image of Civil War violence (sabers). There is an integrity to Bandini's agony, however phony or theatrical, in a way that demands we rethink the town writer's spurious conceptualization of Bandini's Northern agony. Because his performance is so moving, perhaps Bandini has successfully appropriated a mythology to equal the fallen South's. By the end of this initially dubious scene, we must concede that Bandini's performative southernness has the potential to become, paradoxically, authentic.

However playful or merely parodic some of the story's scenes may appear at first glance, it is paramount that each one is described in a language of religious awe and beguiled witness. At the football game and in the bar, Bandini appears to wrest private honor from public disgrace by enduring physical violence and public humiliation. The legitimacy of Bandini's stoicism is entirely contingent upon a witnessing audience's interpretation of honor, but that does not lessen its power. In both scenes it is the onlookers' awed witness that validates actions that are ostensibly abject. The audience's retrospective testimony attests to the authenticity of Bandini's theatrics, which are undoubtedly compelling and transformative to behold. The accompanying religious diction might seem parodic, but perhaps it implies that the (Christian) performance of abjection and the stoic endurance of inherited (original) sin constitute another form of authenticity. The success of Bandini's performance, measured only in its ability to persuade an audience of sincerity where perhaps there is none, suggests that the vicarious consumption of southern burden produces a new form of authenticity, one characterized by an ethics of self-reflexivity that recognizes (at the metalevel if not at the level of Bandini's own characterization) the arbitrariness and contingency of all forms of identity, which are always performative.

The transformative potential of the staged moment of dramatic revelation is best captured when Cruthers confesses an unforgettable experience in Vietnam that is probably fabricated, to Bandini, the town writer, and the story's narrator. Bandini and Cruthers, drunk, are listening to the movie soundtrack from *Platoon* (another reference to mediation and text), and the witnessing narrator acknowledges: "The two of them were moving into something and I'll never forget it. [. . .] They listened intently to the soundtrack and I felt to say anything would be like speaking aloud in church. [. . .] Bandini raised his head and said to Cruthers softly, 'Tell it all.' The mood had gotten almost holy and eerie. Cruthers began talking" (135). In his subsequent telling Cruthers purports to recount a violent sexual encounter in Vietnam that he deems "the best I ever had" (136). Having shot five Vietnamese civilians from his vantage point in a tree (where he has been "fucking" his M-60, which he calls "my honey"), Cruthers notices that one of the injured civilians is "a teenage girl [with] just the top of her head blown back," and he shockingly "commence[s] giving it to her mouth when I hold her up by the shoulders" (136). This awful confession has a near-spiritual effect on its audience, implied by the Christian imagery that frames Cruthers's tale, after which "[t]he room was as quiet as a tomb" (136). Perhaps more important than its verifiability is the impression the story makes on those listening: first Bandini, who "was staring at the floor with a smile. His eyes were wet and he was in a hypnotic region" (136), and then the narrator, who watches Bandini's reaction and is similarly "stunned": "I looked down to Bandini [and] could see how deeply in love he was" (136). The performance might be bogus and abject, but it can awe its audience, as we can observe in this doubled witnessing effect.

At the narrative level, Bandini is "in love" with Cruthers's confession because it feeds his fantasies about violent rebel masculinity in the South, epitomized in Cruthers having been "abandoned to independent slaughter by an army who did not love it enough and did not have the hair" (131). Further, we have already been told that Bandini "sided with blacks" (128) because he believes their opportunities are stunted, presumably because of the South's racist history. Bandini imagines that poor Black men in the South are the property of an indifferent fate steering them toward an inevitable fall—just as he would like to think his own fall was inevitable. Here, Bandini explicitly states that for Cruthers, "a boy from Water Valley, Mississippi," this abject "rendezvous" in Vietnam was somehow predetermined or inevitable: "Nothing could stop it, nothing" (136). Once again this offers an interpretative window on Bandini's "being partial always to the blacks" when watching college football because "[h]e wanted to think of the boys as pure cruising crushing meat, a kind of express ham" (132); Bandini reveres this image because it symbolizes the complete lack of agency in which the potential for historical absolution resides.

But beyond this, Bandini's fascination with Cruthers's tale is also significant at the level of aesthetic merit. In keeping with the vicarious appropriation of stories that occurs across *High Lonesome,* Bandini's astonishment at Cruthers's story—"*Feel* the twistings and turnings of all that" (136)—is a direct reference to the Southern boys' infatuation with Faulkner, whose supposedly "worthy subjects" are characterized by narratives "twisted and coiled like fishing line" (128). Suggesting that degeneration and suffering may be the prerequisites for creating authentic and redemptive art, Cruthers's story approximates the intricacies of Faulknerian narrative, and Bandini, as a surrogate for the narrator, appreciates the aesthetic merit of this formal technique. Bandini's response to Cruthers's tale appears to be authentic and spontaneous, and the narrator's own awed witness confirms Bandini's ostensible sincerity—"I could see how deeply in love he was" (136)—but once again it is an infatuation with a text. Finally, the confession itself was not simply Cruthers's inevitable fate as a poor Black "boy from Water Valley," as Bandini imagines, because even aside from the suspicious politics behind Bandini's infatuation with the idea of Black fate, we cannot finally determine whether Cruthers's experience was real or not. In this case, can the epiphany be authentic?

Arguably, the problems of determining authentic from phony are subordinate to Bandini and the narrator's recognition of Cruthers's storied potential. A moment of transference occurs in which Bandini gains a new authorial voice of his own, revealed in his poetic description of Cruthers's history leading up to the epiphanic confessional moment: "*Feel* the twistings and turnings of all that, how Cruthers got there and the dispossessed without any mission but this rendezvous with a boy from Water Valley, Mississippi, and the gun he sleeps with in a tree, making love to it sixteen thousand miles from home. Nothing could stop it, nothing" (136). In turn, Bandini's awe is duplicated and transferred onto the narrator, who admits, "I was stunned by the new deep voice of Bandini, and this whole language" (136). Once again, the ersatz nature of the episode is secondary to what certain types of performance can achieve. It is the act that is important, and the peculiar nature of the performance creates a transcendent moment to recall the elevated detachment from real history enjoyed by the postmodern generation in "Uncle High Lonesome." While the subject of Cruthers's story may be grotesque, morally debauched, and probably untrue, its remarkable aesthetic expression has catalyzed a kind of creative regeneration in its audience, who find a new voice and a whole new language.

There are many levels of performative appropriation here. Bandini gains the longed-for storied persona by creatively adopting the narratives of other disgraced men, and in turn, he becomes writerly material for both the town writer and the narrator of the story itself, who has similarly collected those episodes from Bandini's life that provide the best artistic material. In an apt dramatization of southern invention and the political significance of stories, the narrator makes a textual creation of Bandini that not only is informed by but feeds the mythology of fallen southern masculinity that Bandini has actively appropriated. Tapping into an existing regional mythology of ill-fated determinism, the charlatan "southerner" Bandini escapes the burden of real historical guilt by moving to the place of imagined shame and burden. Appropriating the narrative detaches from the immediacy of the event, much as the image of the lone Confederate evokes the dubious practice of memorial cultures that cloak the violent realities of the wistfully named Lost Cause. Meanwhile, the liberating possibilities in acknowledging how a performative southernness might become, paradoxically, authentic is mirrored at the level of Hannah's metafictional writing, which is parasitical on the appropriation of historical texts by which it is invigorated and renewed.

Kreyling understands postmodern parody partly as a means of saving contemporary southern writers from Faulkner's anxious influence in such a way as to "liberate themselves from the burden of literary history" (Bone, "Neo-Confederate" 87). He thus envisions the "enabling" possibilities inherent in the concept of the postsouthern (Kreyling, *Inventing* 153–55). Bone and Romine have each taken issue with Kreyling's arguments, which suggest that parodic discourse becomes mere copy, imitating only "previous imitations" of something rather than the thing itself (Romine, "Where is" 22). While Bone is rightly concerned that postmodernist introspection and aesthetic playfulness might obscure or erase what he calls "the real and highly capitalist, geography of the *post*-South" (*SOP* 44), this concern for the loss of the referent tacitly presupposes that it existed in the first place in some sense that was realer than it is now. Insofar as Hannah parodies key aspects of modernist southern burden, he parodies a "previous imitation" of the South rather than the real thing itself.

However, because these texts so thoroughly complicate distinctions between modernist and postmodernist formulations of southern burden, we are forced to question whether the South was ever *not* postmodern or metafictional in the ways that we conceive of those terms today. This is not to reduce the material realities of southern history to mere textuality but rather (and as Woodward similarly intended) to expand the conceptual boundaries of our thinking about southernness beyond reductive discussions of the waning of cultural memory, regional distinction, and historicity itself. We can recall Woodward's own acknowledgment (amplified in significant additions to his original text in 1968 and 1993) that southern history and identity never were intended to be understood as foundational or essential concepts in his formulation of southern burden, but rather as a complex and sometimes paradoxical set of evolving interactions between stories and lived experience. If we conceive of cultural identity as a dynamic synthesis of diverse and hybrid components, real and imagined, then Woodward's theory can be brought into accordance with contemporary (and poststructuralist) explorations of what constitutes regional authenticity in a postregional moment.

Hannah's writing is not simply postregional in the way Hobson's 1991 study implies. By acknowledging the paradox of the authentically simulated South and the ways that myths combine with reality to inform our ideas of the regional, a reconfigured sense of southernness can be recovered by so-called postsouthern aesthetics. This argument is borne out by Hannah's characters' regenerative acts of performance, in this case staging one's historical entrapment as part of a self-consciously imagined regionalism. Both Bandini and Uncle Peter's nephew are postmodern characters whose appropriations of southern-burden discourse happen at an empowering critical distance, just as Hannah's postsouthern writing gains significant aesthetic power from inflecting past discourses in creative new ways. Importantly, this is only possible in the absence of foundational notions of history and place. By simultaneously dramatizing and challenging the forms of its aestheticization, southern burden endures in these stories, in some vestigial or reconfigured form at least, and it remains conducive to critical thinking about contemporary southern identity and literature after modernism, testament to the productive coexistence of regional and postmodern in postsouthern fiction. As far as Hannah's stories appear to dramatize modernist notions of southern historical entrapment, therefore, they also reconfigure them in a postmodern disquisition of the power of simulacra to create something powerfully authentic.

4

Southern Decline and the Politics of Nostalgia

"Rat-Faced Auntie"

"Rat-Faced Auntie," one of the longer and more remarkable stories of Hannah's midcareer collection *Bats Out of Hell* (1993), can be usefully interpreted as a creative disquisition on the problem of white southern nostalgia. The two central characters of "Rat-Faced Auntie," Aunt Hadley and her nephew Edgar, each reveal a desire to articulate some calamitous point of origin, a distinct moment of historical fall, against which their present predicaments might be measured. Both aunt and nephew regret having fallen from better times past: Hadley from her youth in "old Savannah," a bygone era (Georgia in the 1930s) of purported prosperity, stability, gentility, and beauty with which she observes the present culture matching up unfavorably (182); Edgar from his "privileged jazz adolescence" as a gifted trombonist in Big Thunder Hounds, a once famous band that has fallen into inexplicable obscurity, leaving him destitute, a thirty-something recovering alcoholic, returning from Chicago to his native South to live under the patronage of his wealthy but rancorous aunt (161). Because these characters are dissatisfied with their present experience in particular ways and look back to an earlier time when they feel things must have been different, the story invites us to question constructions of the imagined past that posit a return to it as a kind of Edenic restoration. The story therefore dramatizes some compelling ideas about the politics of memory in the face of southern decline, while scrutinizing nostalgia as a form of historical representation.

A further level of complexity is introduced with the story's metafictional dimension. It is about an aspiring author, Edgar, commissioned (reluctantly) to write his elderly aunt's memoirs. Memoirs, while they may commonly be understood to represent nonfictional accounts of personal histories, are highly subjective and often political narratives that can undermine any claim of authenticity where the concept of an honest memoir is a highly suspect one. The story itself is not a memoir; while it is a fictional autobiography of sorts, Edgar has not even begun writing by the time the story ends, and the anticipated memoir is not his own. As a literary form, memoir is important nevertheless, as it informs Hannah's fictional author's search for the "right" form of linguistic expression amid multifarious forms of rhetorical duplicity—his aunt's outspoken nostalgia for an older South most obviously—in a manner that reveals the difficulty of retrieving a historical account that is sufficiently credible to hold some form of ethical and political purchase. In typical Hannah fashion the story seems dedicated to undermining the notion of authentic memory, recalling David Lowenthal's contention that "it is wrong to imagine there exists some *non*-nostalgic reading of the past that is by contrast 'honest' or authentically 'true'" (30). By examining the narrative construction of history, as well as the erroneousness of thinking about southern history as a series of nostalgic turns in a trajectory of declension, "Rat-Faced Auntie" reveals how nostalgic memories can be underwritten by ideas about false historical origins that we are ethically obliged to scrutinize.

At the time of Hannah's writing, debates about the textuality of history in contemporary culture, where it is widely accepted that we cannot *know* history in any real sense outside its representations, complicate thinking about the verisimilitude of any literary account of the past. There is no access to authentic historical discourse; historicity is not possible outside the narratives that constitute it. Jameson's formulation of the postmodern condition is revealing here. While his ideas about postmodern depthlessness undermine a modernist lexicon of authenticity (within which real could at least theoretically be distinguished from fake), his pessimistic portrayal of a dystopian postmodern culture of *pure* surface ironically becomes nostalgic when it implies that postmodernism signals a break from a presimulative or precapitalist culture in which things were *not* postmodern. That the postmodern turn cannot be dated definitively and unproblematic ideas about history cannot be easily defined prompted Linda Hutcheon to refute some of Jameson's arguments for historical waning on similar grounds (*Politics* 113–14). Thinking about postmodernism, or postregionalism, in terms of some critical turning point is a mistake if each era has already been preceded by an approximate crisis point or turn.

Nostalgia and memory have become central though controversial concepts in modern historical studies, with works such as Michael Roth's *Memory, Trauma, and History* (2011), Geoffrey Cubit's *History and Memory* (2007), Susannah Radstone's *The Sexual Politics of Time* (2007), Svetlana Boym's *The Future of Nostalgia* (2001), Nancy Peterson's *Against Amnesia* (2001), and Rita Felski's *Doing Time* (2000) exploring the relationship between nostalgia, history, and politics and addressing ideas about how nostalgia can inform politicized ideas about historicity and about how historicity can have a gendered inflexion. The rise of the multidisciplinary field of memory studies from the late twentieth century onward reveals a heightened critical interest in the importance of memory as "an alternative historiographical discourse" (Cubit 3) in which nostalgia is integral to debates about the role memory plays in constructing such discourse (Radstone 116). Nostalgia (and indeed memory itself) may be a phony account of history, but it can be a revealing window on what the contemporary culture is perceived to be lacking or what it is felt to have separated from. While it is not possible to accommodate the entirety or complexity of the memory or nostalgia studies fields that might be utilized in readings of Hannah, this chapter is broadly informed by their outline, and by the question whether there ever was a time when regional culture was not embroiled in a system of signs without origin. By making a conceptual problem of the origin, Hannah's fictional enactment of white southern nostalgia troubles the notion of authentic memory, while drawing our attention to the politics underwriting this concept.

Disputes over memory and associated modes of memorializing have been especially urgent in the South, as a site of contested memory and representation where the intersection of history and place and the many competing narratives that coexist within the region is imbued with an exceptionally fraught politics. Who has the power to record the past and to publicize and commemorate it, which version will become the more widely accepted as the truth, and which audience is meant to decide? Nostalgia has been central to such disputes, where, traditionally, debates about the problem of southern memory have centered on the oppositional historical narratives of the Black and the white South. While Civil War memory remains vitally important, as David R. Goldfield maintains (298), the centrality of romanticized commemorative images of the Confederacy has come under powerful scrutiny since the late twentieth century, not only with the rise of countercommemorations of the civil rights movement but also with the violent clashes we have witnessed recently over the Confederate flag and Civil War statues, monuments, and museums.

Aside from the now frequently discussed racial inequalities in sites of southern memory, more recent debates about the exclusion of poor whites (for example) from mainstream southern cultural reproductions have exposed further divisions between the historical experiences of different groups of white southerners along socioeconomic and class lines. The rise of so-called Grit Lit since the beginning of the twenty-first century speaks to a need for more authentic ways of capturing the reality of alternative kinds of southern experience; Tom Franklin describes the Grit Lit genre (his own) as being concerned with "the dirty [or "Rough"] South seen without romanticism or the fake nostalgia of *Gone with the Wind* fans" (Carpenter and Franklin viii). Similarly, Sarah Robertson discusses the difficult politics of memorialized histories in works such as Rick Bragg's memoir trilogy of 1997, 2001, and 2008. She contends that Bragg's "gritty" writing seeks to avoid romanticizing the Depression-era South, "destabiliz[ing] the boundaries between grand and micro-narratives as he oscillates between neo-Agrarian and anti-Agrarian sentiments in a bid to reenvisage poor whites and their place in the southern community" ("Memorialization" 459). However, this bid is somewhat undercut when Robertson considers Bragg's *Southern Living* articles, whose celebration of declining authentic southern foodways in a homogenizing region reveals the reappearance of what Robertson identifies as the author's "most blatant and sepia-tinted love for the South" (*Poverty Politics* 71–72). Clearly, memory is seldom a straightforward recalling of facts or events, yet the issue of seeking out more accurate forms of historical representation remains central.

While in broad psychological terms nostalgia may be an inevitable effect of experiencing sudden or significant change,[1] we cannot ignore the highly charged politics involved in remembering southern history. Leigh Anne Duck argues that specific ways of memorializing the past prevent ethical modes of witnessing by overlaying history with fantasy (*Nation's Region* 159). W. Fitzhugh Brundage commends the value of "ongoing contests over southern memory" but cautions against the tendency of nostalgic memory to produce a monolithic vision of history by "idealiz[ing] an imagined past when a single collective memory prevailed" (*Memories Grow* 20). The special appeal of the nostalgic past to the postbellum southerner was, as Ayers explains, that it provided white inhabitants of the New South with "a way back into the national mythology of innocence [. . .] as means to national redemption" (*Promise* 372). Lisa Hinrichsen writes similarly that white southerners have reimagined the past as part of a "desire for a historically unburdened, 'clear conscience,'" giving rise to "narratives heavily invested in fantasy and the development of both national and regional imagined communities dependent on the continual displacement of history with mythology" (*Possessing* 5). James C. Cobb explores how the idea of the Old South (formerly just the South) was cemented in the post-Reconstruction imagination as a "once-upon-a-time pastoral paradise of long ago," revealing a contemporary wish to reconstruct a threatened sense of regional identity and confidence (74). Where the past is "mythologized [. . .] as a means of understanding and evaluating the present," it is a comment on the present as much as the past, as Richard Gray notes (*Literature of Memory* 38). Imagined histories can be at least as revealing as the actual past, therefore, precisely because of their historical inaccuracy.

For good or ill, the practice of returning to pivotal historical origins has informed countless analyses of the South and its postbellum literature ever since Allen Tate and the Nashville Agrarians pitted nostalgia for an imagined monolithic past against the onslaught of industrialization, urbanization, (im)migration, and the alleged weakening of southern identity in the face of sociocultural and economic change. Anxieties about the loss of southern distinction in the New South catalyzed the Agrarians' regress to the diminishing pastoral realms of the "gentleman planter" and the "good farmer" (Tunc 18), lest the modern generation forget their purportedly worthier cultural values. Of course, this historical golden age had to be actively created by the Agrarians, because it never existed in such terms, much as the post-Reconstruction ideology of the "New South"—a phrase coined by Henry Grady in 1874—was itself contingent on Grady's imagined vision of southern economic progress empowered by northern capital (Rutheiser 22). This recalls Martyn Bone's formulation of New South Atlanta as a located "nonplace" (*SOP* 39), to which I will return.

The historical practice of constructing different versions of the South also recalls John J. Su's discussion of the etymological contradiction inherent in the word *nostalgia,* which appears to evoke "homesickness" for a lost "utopia," while *utopia* itself means simultaneously both "good place" and "no place" (3). It is unsurprising that white southern nostalgia becomes especially fraught where the nostalgic past—constructed as "a prior wholeness that has been lost" (*PA* 37)—is underwritten by the atrocities of slavery. While the post-Agrarian writings of Faulkner, Welty, and others challenged idyllic constructions of the Old South by revealing its gothic flip side, they nevertheless sustained the idea of the (white) South's unique historical introspection in ways that continue to inform contemporary regional studies, as examined in chapter 3. However constructed or contingent the Agrarian vision of the past, it established a problematic foundation for modern southern studies, whose scholars appear obligated to expose the duplicity of nostalgic constructions of the Old South as a lost utopia of chivalry and order. While we can easily dispute that the Civil War represents the locus of nostalgia for all white southerners, nostalgia still plays a key role in the contemporary South's perception of itself, as McPherson and Ayers (among others) have conceded.

Where mythologies are deployed as a means of idealizing and legitimizing the past at the expense of the present (and if nostalgia is essentially a product of the present more than the past), then nostalgia can perform a curious historical reversal. Anthony D. Smith argues in this regard that nostalgic memory offers the dispossessed inhabitants of the present the possibility of "imminent [return to] former glory" (A. Smith 50–51, qtd. in Cobb 74). Modes of white southern public memorialization such as those explored by Duck reveal the national as well as local interests underwriting constructions of the backward-looking South inhabiting a similarly "anomalous relationship to time," suggesting that while such discourses may be obviously false, they have the power to authorize imagined histories by reproducing them at the expense of counternarratives (*Nation's Region* 159). With mythology supplanting history in constructed remembrances of the past, not only are imagined histories (e.g., of the Slave South, the Civil War, or the Depression-era South) revealing, but they can become problematically entrenched, for example, with the discernible perpetuation of both neo-Agrarian and neo-Confederate myths about the Old South and the Lost Cause, circulating under the guise of authentic memory but underwritten by a contrived mythology of race. Again, this underscores the importance of understanding constructed histories alongside actual historical events in the southern struggle over memory.

We can observe the practice of southern retrospection played out in critical apprehensions of the region across history. In the modern South, for example, consider first the defeated Confederacy; then the Agrarians, who were nostalgic in the 1920s and 1930s for the waning of southern distinctiveness; next the southern modernists, who anticipated the approach of postmodernity and lamented the decline of confidently mimetic languages; then the postmodernists, who perhaps unwittingly bemoaned the disappearance of the real with the 1960s linguistic turn; and finally, the New Southern Studies scholars, whose break away from "traditional" (post)southern literary studies necessitated the (attempted) abandonment of "the South" as a conceptual scale of analysis, hence Duck's clarion call for a "Southern studies without 'The South'" (329). Ironically, these historical developments recall Ayers's much earlier acknowledgment that the concept of the "disappearing" South has always been integral to a still distinctive southern identity (*All Over the Map* 69), however constructed, imagined, or self-aware. Such is the paradox of nostalgic historic regress: each point of supposed historical calamity opens itself up to ever-antecedent origins, where the same kind of problems present themselves.

I argued in my introduction that the concept of the perpetually disappearing South reveals not only the politics behind constructions of regional authenticity in different historical moments (the Old South compared with the New) but also the fundamentally spurious nature of nostalgic regress to a foundational South. It is not clear exactly when "the very beginning" of the South's alleged removal occurred (Ayers, *All Over the Map* 69), nor is it clear when such a South existed before—or whether it exists beyond—the nostalgic discourses that lament its passing. If the South has always been nostalgically retrospective, even in its earliest conceptions, then what can *southern nostalgia* even mean—a kind of regression that is infinite? The South, then, has always been "past," or "post," by its very nature, and not just in its recent formulations, for example, after the postsouthern turn, or as the NSS seeks to dismantle the critical paradigm of "the South" altogether. This invites us to question whether there can be any such rupture except in imaginative constructions of the South.

Kreyling's work on postsouthern memory and history in *The South That Wasn't There* further explores the social politics behind the images and texts that inform our sense of the region in the absence of a foundational sense of place. He argues that "myths of antebellum southern culture involved in *Gone with the Wind* have become, in some way and to some people, real 'history,' with many regarding the picture they experience in this narrative as *the truth* of history. This raises important questions of what is or is not allowed to survive as 'history' and who decides which narratives may actually reach the public" (165). Myths about southern history are consumed and often believed despite being only myths, and places that "weren't there" paradoxically become real via living cultural memories. Alice Randall's *Gone with the Wind* parody, *The Wind Done Gone* (2001), usefully reflects this fraught politics of historical representation and reproduction. Written from the perspective of an enslaved person, it is a self-conscious attempt to repossess Black southern history from the dominant white discourses that have colonized and falsely articulated it. In keeping with Bone, Ward, and Link's "creating and consuming" paradigm, ideas about history that are purely fictional or performative can come to be accepted as real, inverting the idea that stories come from history by suggesting that what we accept as real history is actually contingent on the forms of its representations.

Mcpherson's critique of nostalgia in the "imagined South" condemns the (Agrarian-informed) practice by which "a general nostalgia for an earlier time, for an imagined past lost via the Civil War, gets narrowed into a kind of white male melancholia" that "impedes a more productive kind of historical memory" (*Reconstructing* 125, 126). The NSS has accused traditional (i.e., not "new") southern literary studies of exactly this practice, suggesting that attempts (such as mine here) to formulate (if not recover) some conceptualization of the authentic South from the vicissitudes of its textual representation, partly in order to reinstate its political importance after poststructuralism, is a project that is itself nostalgic. (I would disagree.) Jon Smith, for example, warns against talking about the uniquely nostalgic South, because it perpetuates a harmful and reductive melancholia. He describes "white southern melancholy," or "the pathological, melancholy, *over*presence of the past, of the lost loved object," as the fundamental error of southern studies (*PA* 35). Talking about the simulative or constructed nature of the present South may appear to posit an earlier version that was different, but equally, attending to the storied nature of the region (in the past as well as now) can enable more nuanced understandings of memory and mythologizing that are not necessarily melancholic.

Joseph Mali points out that myths, while they are fictional constructions of history, are nevertheless "stories that are not merely told but actually lived" (6). The South cannot escape its own storied mediations, but it can make lived experience central to those representations in ways that facilitate a more productive politics of the region, akin to what the Grit Lit writers are attempting. To some extent this is in keeping with Hutcheon's warning that while ideas about "postmodern" nostalgia may be underwritten by poststructuralist ideas about historical contingency, we must not ignore the "historical and cultural specificity" of the postmodern ("Irony" 205)—it is a reaction to specific conditions of social and material culture. The "meta" dimension so commonly found in Hannah's stories amounts to an implicit acknowledgment that a lost authentic or mimetic South has always been a fiction, but its allure compels his fictional characters to pursue elusive origins both historical and aesthetic, such that history and aesthetics are inevitably entangled. My interpretations of "Rat-Faced Auntie" therefore explore an imagined past that is twofold: the once "realler" South (176) and the lost "original" southern art form, or language (161). Where the parallel tropes of historicity and mimesis begin to unravel in "Rat-Faced Auntie," so too do seemingly simple narratives of southern decline. Hannah shows how white southerners are typically nostalgic, while concurrently undermining simple ideas about what it means to be white and nostalgic in and for the South. This remarkable ability—to simultaneously enact *and* undermine the South's problematic backward glance—is testimony to Hannah's unique value at the intersection of southern and postmodern.

Hannah's narrative opens in the generic convention of the traditional bildungsroman, with a third-person omniscient narrator (a device rarely used by Hannah) declaring, "Edgar played the trombone and for eight years he was a most requested boy"; "He'd come out of Athens [Georgia] roaring [. . .] because he was such a prodigy" (157). After recounting a brief period of international renown with a pioneering "new sound" (157), "a sound such as not heard *any*where" (158), the narrator documents the abrupt turn in the band's good fortune—"Then, pop, America forgot their band almost wholesale" (162)—which marks the onset of Edgar's rapid descent into alcoholism and depression until he is deserted by both manager Lambert and wife Snooky, the band's female bassist and Edgar's first love. At a basic level, then (aided by Hannah's use of omniscient narration), Edgar's story follows a typical declension narrative, from the golden years of jazz fame, at whose heights Edgar "could make other grown trombonists cry" (161) with his prodigious talents, through several years spent studying sociology at Northwestern College, in Texas, a mature student and "a sick drunk by then," to the final lows at which he surrenders his two trombones to a homeless thief in return for a slug of port because "[h]e wanted, he thought, never to play the horns again" (165). This is the point at which the story begins anew, and Edgar must attempt to start over, reclaiming a meaningful sense of identity and artistic purpose in the South as he turns from music to writing.

While the central character of "Rat-Faced Auntie" is Edgar rather than the eponymous "rat-faced" Aunt Hadley, much of the narrative is driven by the account of how Edgar becomes the author of Hadley's memoir, the sentimentalized account of "My life. My life and times," which she believes would warrant "a discerning audience" (177). As Edgar tentatively agrees to shoulder the task of scripting Hadley's history, he embarks on his own retrospective historical excavation of what we might term the ugly truth (note the story's title), a counternarrative to refute his aunt's waxing lyrical about old Savannah. Edgar's writerly research is partly an attempt to get past the acrimonious woman's present social animosity to the true origin of her self-loathing, of which her loathing of everyone else is merely a symptom: "Auntie Hadley," Edgar asks at the story's climax, "when did you first know you were a *shit*? Was it a sudden revelation, what? When did it arrive that you were and would be, *awful*?" (190). We have here one of several pursuits of authentic origins within Hannah's text, which does arrive at a dark explanatory origin of sorts in the case of Hadley's history (if not Edgar's), but the feat and the outcome are by no means simple. Once more, the southern method of beholding the past to understand the present becomes deeply problematic in Hannah's creative adaptation of this theme.

The loss of Edgar's good fortune, both professional and marital, is posited as an elusive historical utopia augmented by its marked contrast to the character's present status as a "bum" (164) and "gutless lackey" (174), unable to play trombone because of the painful memories evoked but lacking an alternative vocation or artistic direction. Here, Edgar's historical fall becomes inextricably bound to ideas about aesthetics: it is the absence of a worthy form of *artistic* pursuit that contributes majorly to Edgar's present dystopia. Importantly, the value of Edgar's musician years comes from his claim to a truly authentic art during this era: we are told quite plainly that "[h]e felt safe in history then" because "jazz was the only original American art form" (161). Recalling the notion of pure or absolute music in chapter 1, this idea of jazz being the only aesthetic to aspire to implies that all subsequent aesthetic pursuits—including, of course, Edgar's writing—can only be viewed as less worthy copies. Edgar's "privileged jazz adolescence" signals a lost state of grace, a historical safe space to which he cannot return in the absence of his music; his nostalgia centers on his lost craft, which has rendered him suddenly perilous, dispossessed of history. This complicates simple readings of Edgar's decline by entwining history and aesthetics. (Something similar happens with Hadley, with an illusory *linguistic* origin becoming an integral part of the memorializing process, as we will see.)

Hadley's vision of southern decline also interlaces the material (history) and the aesthetic (art). In one of the story's most pointedly nostalgic statements, Hadley neatly sums up the ostensible contemporary historical and artistic crisis when she reproves her "drunkard" nephew: "When men were *realler*, they drank for good reasons. Look at Grant and Churchill with their great wars. Look at Poe and Faulkner [. . .] and their masterpieces. Now you've got a national curse of [. . .] millions of nobodies who never once had a great day or a fine thought. [. . .] It seems to me you became a drunkard just for lack of something to do" (176, my emphasis). Evoking Poe and Faulkner, Hadley transmutes the "national" curse onto expressly regional ground and implies that Edgar's declension mirrors that of southern society. Hadley envisions modernity as an era of cultural and intellectual exhaustion, incorporating the concurrent diminishment of reality ("When men were realler"), male heroism ("great wars"; "great day[s]"), subjectivity ("millions of nobodies"), philosophical and intellectual culture ("good reasons"; "fine thought[s]"), and artistic value ("masterpieces"). The alleged pathology of contemporary masculinity specifically recalls McPherson's claim that "elegiac odes to the 'honorable manhood' of the war era [. . .] fixat[e] on loss, and what emerges as the thing lost is a sense of stable, honorable white masculinity" (*Reconstructing* 125). In Hadley's nostalgic vision, the lost qualities of "realler" masculinity have disappeared in a world that encumbers both the possibilities for masculine subjective agency and the production of worthwhile *art*, both of which Edgar must contend with as he transitions from musician to writer.

By namechecking Poe and Faulkner as two forbidding local forefathers, both antebellum and modernist, Hadley emasculates her nephew as an imminent postsouthern author and a "nobody" by comparison. It seems likely that Edgar's very name is meant to evoke Edgar Allan Poe, corroborated when Edgar's new girlfriend, Emma Dean, declares of her boyfriend in a fit of exasperation, "You're *gothic*, Edgar!"; this occurs in a gothic scene of its own in which Emma partially blinds Edgar by throwing a bowl of Lysol in his face (187–88). In turn, Hannah's own postsouthern writing is pitched (alongside the fictional Edgar's) against the imposing influence of Southern Renaissance writing, in which critics have discerned southern distinctiveness at its best. Again, ideas about regional and/or historical authenticity are combined with ideas about aesthetic value; such is the nature of self-reflexive writing that calls attention to the modes of representation.

The making of fiction is indeed one of "Rat-Faced Auntie'"s "meta" concerns. As it ends, we realize that the story has been about the potential making of another story all along; the title "Rat-Faced Auntie" directly anticipates the literary project Edgar is about to embark on as the story reaches its climax: "*Rat-Face Confesses*—that would be the title of their book" (190). Hannah's subtle technique of metafictional layering therefore prompts readers to judge not only the value of Edgar's imminent writing as a fictional author but also, by extension, the efficacy of Hannah's story itself, as a product of late-twentieth-century postsouthern culture in an alleged state of artistic crisis. The parallels we can draw between "Rat-Faced Auntie" and *Yonder Stands Your Orphan* (below) imply that nostalgia for the southern past is inextricably linked to nostalgia for an accompanying artistic virtuosity that has perhaps become exhausted, epitomized in the concept of the lost *original* American art form as the antithesis of the contemporary "culture of the copy" (Hillel Schwartz's title phrase). We can view Hannah's writing as a specific creative response to nostalgic denunciations of the supposedly unenviable state of southern literature after modernism.

As noted above, nostalgic constructions of the postmodern condition turn partly on a notion of waning reality, an authentic historical origin that lies beyond text, signs, and simulacra. In fact, Hadley's expression "when men were realler" directly anticipates the remarkably similar words of Ulrich in *Yonder Stands Your Orphan,* who in an equally damning decree of the state of contemporary southern society declares of "everybody" in Eagle Lake, "They're all homesick for when they were real" (46). Ulrich initially appears as a character in Hannah's first collection, *Airships*, in the stories "Water Liars" and "All the Old Harkening Faces at the Rail" (the former first published in *Esquire* in 1970); as well as in *Bats Out of Hell*'s "High-Water Railers," suggesting the conceptual significance of these much earlier stories to interpretations of nostalgia in Hannah's last novel. Extending Su's arguments about nostalgia as a form of homesickness, Romine interprets Ulrich's predicament in *Yonder Stands Your Orphan* as emblematic of the "cultural pathology" of "homesickness for the real," and he reads the novel as an indictment of twenty-first-century global consumerism and mass-media culture ("Orphans All" 162). And yet here we can see remarkably similar conceptual groundwork having been laid in the author's much earlier writing, a sense of longing for a time when people and places were purportedly more authentic.

Hadley's pronouncement of the modern "curse of millions of nobodies" is further echoed by Ulrich when he asks rhetorically, "And who gets the highest pay? Actors. Paid to mimic life because *there is no life*" (*Yonder* 46, my emphasis). Romine reads this as "Hannah's concern with pathological mimicry," with "[t]he regime of the simulacrum, of empty performance," and with "representational systems that gravitate toward fantasy" (*RS* 193). Certainly it is possible to interpret this as a problem of contemporary culture, described by Romine as a "late southern economy that [. . .] turns everything into a fake" (*RS* 192)—especially when we consider the indebtedness of the "zombie" trope that underwrites *Yonder Stands Your Orphan* to an established tradition of "the living dead serving as a critique of 'consumer capitalism'" (Bjerre, "Southern Evil" 83),[2] symbolizing the imagined death of a more authentic (living) culture predating this distinctly contemporary socioeconomic change. However, this interpretation presupposes an implicit distinction between the real people of an earlier time and the simulative people of a later one, "nobodies" or mere "actors" who at best can only copy the more authentic cultural forms of the past. What these stories highlight, therefore, is not so much the *actual* loss of authentic history as the politics underwriting cultural *discourses* of authenticity, in which nostalgia exposes the fallacy of the alleged loss.

In "Rat-Faced Auntie," Edgar certainly appears to be suffering the ill effects of what Romine would later call "reality homesickness" or "deregulated reality" in *Yonder Stands Your Orphan* (Romine's two essay titles), further suggesting Hannah's early creative interest in the elusive historical referent *South*. Significantly, Edgar's fall from grace is dramatized in the devastation of both his geographical and his historical grounding in the wake of his ended musical career. Edgar's spatial displacement is dramatized when we learn that returning from Chicago to his southern home, Edgar "was torn between languages, even whole modes. He hadn't heard Southern spoken [. . .] in ages and it sounded dead wrong" (166). These words dually evoke the allegedly moribund nature of contemporary southern writing ("*dead* wrong"), as well as the idea that Edgar has become an exile even in his native region: "One day he stopped [. . .] and for several minutes *he had no real idea where he was*" (166, my emphasis). Added to this sense of sociospatial dispossession or groundlessness, our protagonist's temporal dislocation or weightlessness is also alluded to, for example, when Emma tells Edgar, "You look *delayed* or off track" (172). Edgar's placelessness is therefore a key part of his decline as an artist, further connecting questions of aesthetic value with the concepts of declining historical and regional authenticity, which Hannah's texts interrogate.

Jameson describes nostalgia as a symptom of the lack of "genuine historicity" in capitalist cultures that negate "our lived possibility of experiencing history in some active way" (*Postmodernism* 19, 21). Edgar's problem, being both temporally misaligned and geographically exiled or displaced, certainly seems in keeping with this, as well as with Romine's further contention that the postmodern economy of signs effaces not only time but also spatial reality in the South: it "assaults the local" (*RS* 192). It also evokes the Baudrillardian phenomenon Romine discerns in *Yonder Stands Your Orphan*, of "time-space compression" (David Harvey's coinage), occluding "coherent space" and chronological consistency in a global mass-production culture of texts, surfaces, and simulations (Romine, "Orphans All" 179). Edgar's return to a place that seems dizzying and foreign provides little in the way of the psychological anchoring we might have expected from this homeward move. Because he feels alienated in his own time and place (he no longer feels "safe in history" nor even properly "Southern"), Edgar's decline not only recalls Fred Davis's description of nostalgia as the result of "identity dislocations" (6) but is characteristically postmodern, we might say. The return to putatively safer historical and geographical origins proves expressly problematic, and the southern backward glance is not permitted in any straightforward way.

One of the most obvious ways "Rat-Faced Auntie" rejects linear temporality and thus conceptualizations of southern history as a process of decline is in the curious temporal anomalies that the story presents. Edgar's historical displacement is described in a series of incongruities, first as a "cooking infant" (161) in his band days and then as "older than everybody" at college: "He felt elderly in the classroom, the reverse of his band experience" (166, 163). Youth and age seem oddly reversed throughout, for example, when we learn that Emma Dean—who heretofore has been repeatedly characterized according to her juvenile appearance—has become Aunt Hadley's doppelgänger, adopting the daily rituals of the elder woman: "Emma sat, a Manhattan like Hadley's in her hand, at six-thirty that evening" (190); the doubling effect is evoked by our recollection of "[t]he single Manhattan she [Hadley] poured herself at six-thirty" every evening (167). In the same moment, Hadley too embodies a historical irregularity, trading places with Emma when we learn, "Here she was seventy or more [with] young legs that were an anomaly, tight in their hose" (167), looking "girlishly simple" (168). Many other Hannah texts are rife with similar historical clashes and obscurities of this kind—recall the anomalous description of the nostalgic-by-eleven population of Eagle Lake in *Yonder Stands Your Orphan* (40). We might also consider "Water Liars," in which a "new younger man, maybe sixty" (6) is later conflictingly described as an "old man" (7); or "Evening of the Yarp," whose young narrator ambiguously describes himself as occupying a liminal position as "man/boy" (91). Similarly, in the story "Get Some Young" the middle-aged character Tuck's "boys" are said to be "like old uncles, older than him, mellow and knee-slapping around a campfire" (28), and the story itself derives its drama from the gothic conflation of innocence and experience. Temporal narratives are frequently confused or reversed in Hannah's texts, challenging apprehensions of southern nostalgia as the result of tangible historical breaks or turns. The incongruous relationship Hannah's characters appear to have with temporality is echoed at the close semantic level of his distinctive mode of writing, where gothic historical anomalies and recurrences are a consistent southern feature.

When we look closer at "Rat-Faced Auntie," it refuses to be understood simply in terms of historical diminution. Following his southward return, for instance, we learn that "Edgar's sobriety did curious things to him. [. . .] He had the impression he looked suddenly older, thrown forward into his forties at thirty-four. He had intimations that he would die soon, and must hurry. He also felt exceedingly and cheerfully dumb, as a saint or a child might feel. He greatly enjoyed not knowing vast lots of things. [. . .] Going back to school now under the patronage of his aunt [. . .] he found he could barely write [nor] stutter his name" (165–66). On the one hand this suggests a distinct fissure between past and present, contrasting the safe and privileged history in which Edgar practiced an accomplished veteran talent to a vertiginous present in which the budding author struggles to articulate even his own name. The considerable array of temporal contradictions contained in this single paragraph—with Edgar inhabiting at once both a condition close to death and a rebirth of sorts, into a state of saintly grace or childish innocence, uninitiated even into language—establishes a sense of temporal displacement that seems neatly in keeping with Jameson's formulation of postmodern historical crisis. However, the way temporal opposites compete with one another here without resolution—with Edgar concurrently "thrown forward" toward death and backwards into a nascent state—also undercuts simple conceptual distinctions between the halcyon past and the fallen present. It seems that Edgar's subjectivity was already off-kilter even during his proposed golden age; we are told explicitly that "Edgar had *always* felt behind on his personality" (159, my emphasis). The Jamesonian sense of characters' inability to "place" themselves is, I would argue, not a new phenomenon at all. Here, as in the South more generally, perhaps, temporality has *always* been curiously awry, troubling the prospect that Edgar could have experienced genuine historicity in the past.

In *Yonder Stands Your Orphan,* Ulrich claims that "[p]eople are not even in the present moment. Everybody's been futurized" (40). The intrusion of the *future* on the present appears to invert the southern modernists' preoccupation with the southern backward glance, where the past intrudes on the present. This seems to attest to Guinn's claim that postsouthern writing is noticeably detached from a modernist preoccupation with the past (162). Curiously, though, the concept of "futurizing" the South's characteristic retrospection would be analogous to bringing backward-looking southerners precisely back *into* the present moment, from which nostalgic Ulrich explicitly declares they are absent—which might offer some relief. We might reformulate Ulrich's claim, then, not simply as a case of waning historical consciousness in the South but rather as a case of going *forward* to go back. It is an interesting inversion of southern modernist narratives, which go back to go forward. Hannah's playful disregard for chronology in both stories—the ambivalent temporal transpositions that refuse linear understandings of history—reflects usefully on postmodern theorizations about the demise of historicity (which have often taken the form of nostalgia) and on reductive understandings of the waning of the South.

In one of "Rat-Faced Auntie'"s most important scenes, Edgar makes the literal and figurative homesick return to visit his parents in his childhood hometown of Athens, Georgia. If we agree with Jameson that postmodernity begets the crises of time and space, then it is telling that Edgar's return to "old time" Athens is described in a lexis that initially appears to assuage his present feelings of historical vertigo and geographical exile: "When he left Athens he felt fixed and relieved" (180). It seems initially that Edgar's physical return to the old-timey place of his own beginnings renders him suddenly more real, or more distinctively *southern*. The return provides a source of nostalgic comfort: "[It] was sweet nostalgia" (180) that might be expected to recoup a sense of meaningful subjectivity absent from this contemporary culture of reality-homesick "nobodies," caught memorably in Edgar's earlier inability to name himself. When Edgar leaves Athens, there is the sense that he has been placed safely back in history in this symbolic act of homecoming. Edgar's return to Athens also reveals, however, the futility of returning to a foundational past. It is likely that the name Athens represents the paradigmatic place of origin, the keystone of Western civilization itself, but in fact Edgar's literal arrival at this archetypal historical origin denies the secure return to a lost utopia we might have imagined. Rather, his return generates a sequence of problems that work to undermine surface readings of Edgar's homecoming as reparative. Edgar's perception that "[a]ll this dereliction was unlike his father in the old times" and the fact that "he hadn't remembered his house as this unprosperous" (180), for example, initially imply that these are somehow new, or modern, problems, but in fact it is not clear whether old-time Athens ever *was* so prosperous or whether Edgar has simply imagined it to have been so retrospectively, misremembering "the old times" (when men like his father were "realler") in a sweetened version of history, as Hannah's word choice above ("sweet nostalgia") suggests.

Further problematically, coming home fosters representational crisis rather than the relief of verisimilitude, the illusory "plainer language" ("Uncle High Lonesome" 222); we have already been forewarned of this in the revelation that his indigenous southern language sounds wrong to Edgar upon his return from the North. Edgar's ancestral visit generates communicative failure between old and young: "His dad didn't understand: why couldn't Edgar just recover it all?" (180). This results in a sense of interpretative unease between the generations rather than the comfort of mutual comprehension, redolent of the similar clash between old and new lexicons in "The Ice Storm" (191). Expressions of interpretative collapse are certainly endemic to "Rat-Faced Auntie," with refrains such as "What does it . . . mean?" (175) and "What was the truth?" (177) circulating widely. But crucially, the postmodern collapse of meaning happens *after* Edgar's nostalgic southward return, thereby radically upsetting the narrator's pronouncement that Edgar should have left Athens with a more secure sense of his southernness. Indeed, the notion of old-time Athens embodying the last vestiges of regional authenticity has already been undermined by the lexis of performance that accompanies the family reunion—"For his advent, Edgar's folks [. . .] had *dressed up*"; "Edgar *played* her [Hadley] as a more minor crank than she was" (180, my emphases)—and this upsets any simple binary between performance and authenticity in the transition from old to new. If acting is not simply antithetical to authenticity in this context, this paradox neatly anticipates the narrator's description in "The Ice Storm" of his *"true* old-timey" mother being "in the *act* of dying" (190, my emphases); for the "true" older generations as much as for contemporary ones, even death is not exempt from simulacra. The old places of the past may be no realer than those of the present, therefore, but this can be a helpful warning against nostalgic recourse to the past.

To summarize my arguments thus far: the deliberate and persistent temporal slippages in Hannah's narratives create an intriguing sense of the impossibility of linear historical excavations. While they offer no simple resolution of the conundrums of southern history and nostalgic memory, these implicit paradoxes and contradictions certainly encourage new reflections on long-established tropes of southern regress. In Hannah, nostalgia for the declining real is problematized in ways that counter conventional understandings of southern history (and distinctive regional identity) as a narrative of cultural waning during which the designation *South* has also become critically defunct. Likewise, the polarized distinctions between utopic past and dystopic present the story initially appeared to posit are also undercut. This contention is vital to my upcoming interpretations of the two putative historical utopias "Rat-Faced Auntie" presents: Edgar's "privileged jazz adolescence" and Hadley's memorialized "old Savannah." By further challenging the concept of deferral to more authentic origins, Hannah confounds the very concept of historicity, at least insofar as it can be represented in writing. This is complicated when we appreciate that it is the absence of worthwhile *art* that is at the core of Edgar's current predicament, and it is in the potential *writing* of the book *Rat-Face Confesses* that the possible remedy lies. Thus, we might expect the recovery of some lost original art form to be integral to nostalgic narratives of historical recuperation.

Alongside the rebuked authentic historical origin, the "realler" South, "Rat-Faced Auntie" simultaneously begins to trouble the concomitant concept of the authentic *linguistic* origin—such as would be contained within the logos (or God's Word) as a form of pure mimesis that cuts through the noise of textual mediation to true meaning. In an apt description of Derrida's formulation of *logos* (*Grammatology* 73) applied, importantly, to *music*, we are told in "Rat-Faced Auntie" that "[w]hat that permanent silence gave [deaf people]" was that "some claimed to hear music from heaven, or right from the brain" (178). Since Hannah's narrator has already proffered jazz music as the *only* worthy art form (161), it is curious that Hadley defers to southern writers (Poe and Faulkner) rather than to southern musicians in her nostalgic description of a true earlier time. This deference reveals that the aesthetic element of Hadley's nostalgia for the southern past is specifically concerned with *writing*, as we might expect from a metafictional text such as this. If we understand it as the story of Edgar's transition from musician to writer, then the initial implication here is that writing is a secondary art form because it relies on the mediation of language. The question of Edgar's relative proficiency as a former musician and potential writer is integral to ideas about aesthetic value underpinning the story. However, logocentric ideas about language are, if not exactly parodied, then certainly challenged in "Rat-Faced Auntie" via its self-reflexive interrogation of the practice of writing and of its own forms of production as a text to be consumed. Much as the story appears to pursue this idea of true art (be that music or writing), the very prospect of some pure, original, or singular form of aesthetic expression, unsullied by forms of simulation or copy, proves increasingly troublesome.

First of all, it is never clear why Hadley intends Edgar to transcribe her memoirs in the first place. Hadley tells Edgar, "You can write" (177), but we have already been told that in fact he can barely stutter his own name let alone write, which he does "with his tongue out, counting letters and misspelling" like a child new to language (165). Likewise, Edgar's professor characterizes his pupil's writing as a pained "grunt-talk," a "primitive getting-there" (183). While he ascribes a quality of aesthetic innovation to Edgar's writing that initially recalls the pioneering new sound of Edgar's music, his one true talent—"Your prose style. Your writing. We don't see that kind much. [. . .] Now I am a Hemingway fan, a Raymond Carver *zealot*, but are you trying something *new*, dimensional . . . ?" (183)—it is of course ironic that the professor should evoke an existing writer (Carver) to describe the novelty of Edgar's own style, which is only a belated copy. The concept of Edgar's originality as a writer seems further irreconcilable with the vicarious nature of his sociological project itself. His master's thesis appropriates the tales of the "Chicago bums" (186): "Guilty, [Edgar] began making notes on the bums. [. . .] Some of the bums were long and vibrant narrators. Two of them spoke to Edgar in Russian. He kept scrawling on the page. As payment for their stories he would buy them drinks" (165). Crucially, there is little that is authentic here: the stories Edgar barters are the property of others. Some are literally foreign to him (Russian), far removed from their author, who, "guilty," is cognizant of this fact. Edgar's penchant for the vicarious appropriation and marketing of others' stories appears to have been inherited from his own journalist father, who writes "timid" and "innocuous historical features" for the local newspaper, described as "reprinted," secondhand versions of other people's "obscure" histories (166). It is also echoed when Emma submits and "[t]hrows herself into long rituals of [sexual] defilement" in exchange for the currency of Edgar's tales: "what stories he could tell about [the bums]!" (187); and, finally, when we recall how Edgar "capture[d]" his ex-wife, Snooky, "with his new vocabulary stolen from" the poetry of "Ms. [Anne] Sexton," which "he liked especially and reread" (160). Once again, ideas about newness are inextricable from the concept of the secondary copy.

The sense of parasitical storytelling is extended most explicitly when we learn how, at Northwestern College, Edgar "would *retell* the story of how he'd had all the clubs going with his '*new*' sound, [. . .] the spitty and flat noise *duplicating* him" (164, my emphases). This focus on forms of mimicry (rereading, retelling, duplicating) that are opposed to ideas about originality implies that writing is parasitical on reality in a way that it at best can only simulate it, by appropriating and rehashing the real events of history. This notion of mendacious literary borrowing, so integral to thinking about the status of contemporary southern writing in a state of anxious influence, is augmented when we learn that "[s]omebody gave Edgar books by Kerouac, Bukowski, Brautigan, Hemingway and Burroughs" (160). Because Edgar is enthralled by this American literary tradition of transient male loners, it seems that even his own status as a "bum" (164) can be viewed as the product of aesthetic performance (whether conscious or not), a role "stolen" both from his sociological research on the homeless Chicago population of male "*renuncios*"—who have "given up the regular world on purpose, and could explain why in long and wonderful stories" (187)—and from this adopted literary culture of male "hobo" outsiders.

Edgar's writing in its various guises is mere "research" (182), to be collected and commodified, rather than something authentically from Edgar himself. Similarly, the subject of Edgar's imminent book *Rat-Face Confesses,* or rather *"their* book," is his aunt's "life and times" rather than his own. This raises problematic questions of authorship that might serve to undermine the putative authenticity not only of *Rat-Face Confesses* but also, of course, of the very story we are reading. Frank Hart characterizes some distinctions between the literary genres of the confessional novel and the memoir, which Radstone has also explored according to their respective "modernity" and "postmodernity" (Radstone 192–93). Hart argues that "'confession' is personal history that seeks to communicate or express the essential nature, the truth, or the self," while "'memoir' is personal history that seeks to articulate or repossess the historicity of the self [by] plac[ing] the self relative to time" (491). There are obvious problems when such placing should be done by someone else, if Edgar is the intended author of Hadley's personal history and, as we will see, the *essential* or authentic confessional core of said text is also deeply problematic. This metafictional dimension introduces a level of complexity whereby all forms of storytelling become complicit in the problems of authenticity (regional, historical, aesthetic) that Hannah's texts explore.

While it may seem that writing is postulated as a lesser art than music, in fact the story frustrates our attempts to conceive of the two in any simple hierarchy, to determine which is the more authentic; finally, it seems unlikely that the designation *authentic* can be ascribed in any foundational way. Here, the idea that jazz was Edgar's "natural God-given ticket" (187) is directly undercut when our omniscient narrator also divulges that just as Edgar could "barely write," neither in fact could the musical "prodigy" (157) "read music, if truth be known," and "he wasn't any good at song-writing" (162). Likewise, the moment when Edgar finally takes up the horn again is deeply anticlimactic: "Edgar asked for his valved Bach trombone [and] practiced it awhile. Blind men had come forth beautifully in jazz" (188). His identifying with the worn-out cliché of the blind jazz player (having been partially blinded by Emma) augments the demonstrable phoniness of the moment, with which the scene's legitimacy and the story's resolution are concurrently threatened. We cannot simply understand the story in terms of nostalgia for some pure or perfect aesthetic origin, then, because the concept of its very existence is pushed to the point of collapse. If there *was* no singular original American art form, then this offers a playful rebuke of those criticisms that have established, intentionally or not, a hierarchical relationship between Renaissance and postsouthern literary cultures.

If music was *not* in fact Edgar's true talent, then this would explain why the story's epiphany—a revelation in which Edgar decides he will write *Rat-Face Confesses* and instantly becomes "so happy, profoundly, almost, delirious" (190)—should come in the form of writing and not music. Is writing, then, the more authentic art? This denouement comes only in the form of a series of rhetorical questions (signaling things that are beyond knowing), confounding the sense of resolution we might traditionally expect: "*Why* was [Edgar] so happy?" the narrator asks (190, my emphasis). Indeed, the language of this climactic scene seems intent on thoroughly blurring distinctions between music and writing—"Loud and bright and full of jazz, *Rat-Face Confesses*—that would be the title of their book" (190)—thereby denying any full or final separation on our part. Extending this circular sense of irresolution, the ending of "Rat-Faced Auntie" signals only the implied beginning of another story, *Rat-Face Confesses*. The genesis of Edgar's creative talent as a writer thus establishes a kind of baptismal rebirth, a *new* point of historical origin that finally subverts reductive understandings of history (Edgar's, the South's) following a linear path of declension.

When we return to Edgar's "privileged jazz adolescence," we see that it is fraught with issues of performance and the phony image. Recalling the Athens scene above, Edgar's characterization during this putative golden age deploys a language of hackneyed performance that is pointedly averse to nostalgic constructions of the period's authenticity: "He *affected* [. . .] an old Harley Davidson motorcycle and a pet weasel that clung to his neck when he dashed around Chicago"; "He had *the necessary headband* [and] tattoo of an upside-down American flag right at the bottom of his throat where a tie-knot would have been. [. . .] It was near the end of the Vietnam War, so *he had to get in fast on his outrage*" (159, my emphases). Edgar's alcoholism too is largely the result of his playing up to the culture of jazz "hipsters" he observes: "this was a grand society to him. He loved it, lived it, inhaled it. Immediately he began cigarettes [. . .] and staying out late with the guys" (157). The word *society* evokes ideas about social performance and audience that reflect usefully on Edgar's costar bandmate, a heroin-addicted young Texan named Parton Peavey. Because Peavey is described as "so good, or so wanted (guitars owned the world)" (158), this further complicates the idea of *true* talent, if being good may simply equate to being *wanted,* or to playing up to an audience. Edgar's tutor implies something similar when he declares "[t]here are outside readers" when attempting to cultivate Edgar's "unique"

writerly style (183). This subverts surface readings of Peavey's own originality, for example, that "[h]e was an imitation of nobody [and] had his own
cult" (159): it is entirely possible that this "cult" was already just the effect of
a compelling act or *imitation* of originality. If neither authentic art nor the
romance of masculine individualism was ever in fact present, then the bandmates' golden years were not so privileged after all.

This notion is augmented when we appreciate that it was the men's adolescent exposure to a clichéd hipster lifestyle that engendered their addic-
tion and downfall in the first place. Their loss of innocence was the result
of their musical success rather than of the abruptness of its historical withdrawal, as the story initially seemed to posit. This is confirmed when the
narrator divulges that Edgar had "been on the horn so thoroughly since age
ten that he'd never been to a scout camp or church camp or had even played
in a high school band, having bypassed them for the Atlanta Symphony at
age fourteen" (157). This statement establishes two further antecedent historical origins, Edgar at ages ten and fourteen, both of which upset simple
understandings of Edgar's life having been worsened by the ill-fated *demise*
of his musical career. On the contrary, it was Edgar's young proficiency on
the horn that not only facilitated his fame (and therefore his downfall, implicit within it) but compromised his childish innocence even *before* he was
famous, caught, perhaps, in the mature masculine sexual connotations of
horn. The serpent was already in Eden, it seems, and there is no going back
to a lost point of origin because such origins are already corrupt.

The idea that authenticity is a product of social performance is vital to
Aunt Hadley's characterization. While she rebukes contemporary society as
"a world of society cows looking for an audience everywhere" (171), in fact
Hadley, the product of the supposedly more genuine past, is characterized
as a performer seeking an audience throughout: "She wanted an ear, she demanded an audience" (167). In an act of phony contrivance to equal Edgar's
"rockstar" affectations above, Hadley affects the persona of an elite social-
ite "with a certain sneering polish," dressing in stylish designer clothes and
even fooling one of Edgar's female peers into thinking "she looked stamped
by Vassar or Smith" despite her humble college background (168). Similarly,
Emma observes the spectacle of Hadley at a party and declares, "She dresses
so well. Must be somebody. An older Jackie Kennedy, except for the hump
and the dog-ugly face" (170). The concept of Hadley's *being somebody*—
opposed to the "nobodies" she condemns in contemporary culture (176)—is

ironic, of course, because it is Hadley's contrived appearance, her simu-lation of real people like Jackie Kennedy, that causes Emma to call her a "somebody"—another compelling inversion of conventional notions of be-ing and performing. The sense of theater here, of costume, drama, and im-personation (like Uncle Peter in "Uncle High Lonesome," Aunt Hadley looks like other characters, but who is she really?), implies that what appears to be authentic in the story is often just an act.

While my arguments so far may seem to diverge from the politics of white southern nostalgia, they have been necessary to establish the conceptual grounds on which the following claims rest. Because we cannot interpret Edgar's predicaments as simply *contemporary* ones, Hadley's own nostalgic reminiscences of her life as a younger woman become subject to the same sort of postmodern inquiry. The idea of vanishing historical origins, which disappear vertiginously beyond the horizon of our understanding, is a very useful one for interpreting Hadley's nostalgia, which extols "old Savannah" (182) as the elusive historical utopia. While the object of Hadley's nostal-gia is the interwar, modernist South of the 1930s, her affectionate designa-tion *old* seems deliberately to evoke the prewar Old South. This is confirmed when Hadley makes two important intertextual allusions when reminisc-ing about the past, to Margaret Mitchell's *Gone with the Wind* (1936) and William Alexander Percy's *Lanterns on the Levee: Recollections of a Planter's Son* (1941). Both texts have been accused of eulogizing the Old South as a departed cultural nirvana lost irrevocably in the war, spurring widespread criticism of the tendency of white southern memorial cultures to paint a misleading picture of history. In Hannah's text, nostalgia for the past in fact reveals a complex conceptual paradigm of regressive historical origins that demands we rethink white southern nostalgia as simply symptomatic of cul-tural decline. Thus, "Rat-Faced Auntie" poses a direct challenge to nostalgic textual reproductions of the Old South by scrutinizing the legitimacy of a series of speculative historical epochs to which characters have attached a "romance of authenticity," to borrow Jeff Karem's title phrase. Where nos-talgic narratives begin to unravel and become radically self-subverting, the politics surrounding southern-decline narratives are exposed.

The story reveals two conflicting images of the South in the 1930s ex-pressed by Hadley, one voiced in the present and the other in the past. As modes of memorializing, they are very different aesthetically. As these discourses compete with each other, our test is to determine which (if either) offers the more truthful account. The first is the romanticized version of the memoir Hadley intends Edgar to write. It is a public narrative, meant for an audience (which can be contrasted to the private account of the same historical moment, to which we become privy only later): "In Savannah, old Savannah!, there were gay times. Homosexuals *won't* steal that term! There were lanterns on the levee indeed. I was good with horses. *What a picture,* I on my roan Sweetheart on the way to third grade in the city! Horses were thought elegant, a whole culture gone with the wind! Stephen Crane wrote *The Red Badge of Courage* in ten days I believe" (182, second emphasis mine). Importantly, this tainted *picture* of history marks part of an attempt to repair the perceived fissures in contemporary subjective identity and the symbolic order of the present. This is implied when Hadley voices her disdain for the signifiers of homosexuality she discerns in the contemporary moment, and her dissatisfaction with the present is expressed in the language of unwelcomed linguistic change ("Homosexuals *won't* steal that term [*gay]!*"). Hadley's aversion to modern southern lexicons—specifically in relation to sexuality—directly anticipates the aging mother's aversion to her son's gender-bending language in "The Ice Storm," when mother implores son, "Don't use that word [*bitch*]" to refer to a man (191). The discourse of southern decline is bound once again to the problem of postsouthern language.

Hadley's above reference to Crane's 1895 Civil War novel is important in this respect. While it seems simply to be part of Hadley's condemnation of Edgar's generation of lesser writers (Crane produced his masterpiece in only ten days, Hadley points out), in fact Hadley's using Crane's novel to devaluate the present literary culture is problematic because of the issue of authorial legitimacy it raises. *The Red Badge of Courage* has generally come to be accepted as one of the most influential and realistic accounts of war, yet Crane had never seen battle himself; rather, as with Edgar's research, Crane's subject was gleaned from the stories of the real veterans he interviewed. Like Mitchell's, Crane's novel was furthermore adapted for the screen, released (unsuccessfully) in 1951, during a period of mounting cynicism about the Korean War, preempting the much more ambiguous American attitudes toward Vietnam. By challenging received attitudes toward war and the image of the mythic warrior hero, *The Red Badge of Courage* subtly contests Hadley's invocation of that text in deference to an image of lost authentic (southern) manhood. This not only dampens Hadley's conceit that the present generation of writers should aspire to their more authentic forefathers. More importantly, it also recalls Michael Kreyling's understanding of Hannah's writing as "postsouthern parody" that pokes fun at neo-Confederate discourses that extol the Old South and its Lost Cause. While Bone, Kreyling, and Weston have each identified Hannah's Civil War stories as being parodic of Lost Cause mythology, I think we can see something very similar going on in this story despite its not being directly about the war. The above rhetoric of preindustrial bliss used by Hadley directly evokes Agrarian-influenced, neo-Confederate discourses that glorify the South's heroic efforts to protect its threatened agrarian culture from the unwelcome encroachments of northern industrial capitalism. As an audience-driven performance, instantly this picture of the past becomes suspect.

The indistinguishability of memory from performance is amplified by Hadley's direct citation of *Gone with the Wind* and *Lanterns on the Levee*. In fact, Hannah's satirical reference extends a parody from a similar scene in his *Hey Jack!* where a female character gets "a silly *Gone with the Wind* voice" and declares "I want to be admired from afahhhr" (99), intensifying the conceptual relationship between the South and its mediations. Nostalgic reproductions are capable of reordering history into an attractive image by eclipsing or altering the (often problematic) complexities of material reality, recalling David Anderson's description of nostalgia in plantation memoirs: "the nostalgically remembered past [. . .] is made into a spectacle that was beautiful, bearing little or no relation to the ugly latter" (107). We know that since the 1930s southern mythmaking has been greatly abetted by the rise of new technologies and "media-made Dixie," as Allison Graham's *Framing the South* (2001), Tara McPherson's *Reconstructing Dixie* (2003), and Karen Cox's *Dreaming of Dixie* (2011) have discovered. The relationship between American popular culture, the "nostalgia industry," and what McPherson calls the "imagined South" reveals how mediatized images—note Hadley's explicit use of the term *picture* above—do not so much record as construct southern history in a highly charged process of imagineering.

Here, Hadley's own memoir, a historicized picture itself, is doubly problematic. This is because, as I have intimated, it comes from other texts: Hannah's own earlier writing (*Hey Jack!*) alongside Mitchell's and Percy's, as well as David Selznick and Victor Fleming's 1939 film adaptation of *Gone with the Wind*, which played an instrumental role in perpetuating cultural misrepresentations of the Old South and the Civil War. Hadley's memoir, then, is several times removed from the increasingly elusive real thing (1930s Savannah), borrowing not only from literature but also from Hollywood, the epicenter of faking it. In its indebtedness to existing simulations or reproductions of Old Southern culture, Hadley's memorial account is not the true vision of a lost authentic history but rather an image of an image, a Baudrillardian simulacrum without an original. Romine's memorable articulation of how "the fake South [. . .] becomes the real South through the intervention of narrative" (RS 9) is helpful here. Romine argues that images can come to serve in place of the reality, the simulation overtaking reality or perhaps even constituting it. While it may be obvious that the romantic pictures portrayed in texts like *Gone with the Wind* are not faithful to reality, nonetheless fictional versions of history can gain a paradoxical authenticity and political power from the continued reproduction of images. And it is precisely these sorts of processes—Hinrichsen calls these the "earnest misrepresentations" ("I can't believe" 236) that obscure authentic historical understanding with political fictions—that Hannah's narratives illuminate when we pay his writing the sustained close attention it warrants.

The notion of duplicitous or fictitious Souths posing as authentic history—Bone uses the term *nonplace* to articulate a similar phenomenon (*SOP* 139)—has already been captured in "Rat-Faced Auntie," when the narrator reveals that "[f]or Emma he [Edgar] improved *his* history, sometimes believing it" (178). The fiction becomes believable, testimony to the power of "earnest misrepresentations" (Hinrichsen) to become paradoxically real. While images become believable even if they have no authentic basis, however, it remains imperative to acknowledge how our human apprehensions of history are inevitably party to this process of creation (mythmaking) and consumption, hence the characters' difficulties in understanding one another in Hannah's story. With this sense of historical commodification embodied in fictional representations of an imaginary past, historicity becomes a fundamentally slippery concept both in the story and *by* the story (its metafictionality). This raises important questions about the ethics of historical representation, or how we can ever truly know history beyond the modes of its audience-driven reproductions.

It is worth briefly pausing on Bone's analysis of Mitchell's representation of Atlanta in *Gone with the Wind*. In Mitchell's novel, much of Scarlett O'Hara's drama comes from the push-pull dynamic she experiences between

Old and New Souths, caught between Agrarian-informed reminiscences of a dying plantation culture (Tara is captured in its final moments of grandeur before the war) and the distinctly anti-Agrarian, forward-looking bent of Scarlett's New South philosophy. Indeed, it was Atlanta's self-promoted globality, its imagineering of itself as a true "international city," that caused Charles Rutheiser to criticize the city's effacement of "local cultural historical context" and designate it "the apotheosis of [the New South's] generic urbanism and sense of placelessness" (Rutheiser 161, 163, qtd. in *SOP* 162). Yet this is the place Mitchell appears to favor, despite the romanticized Agrarian vision of antebellum culture underwriting her narrative (and brought conspicuously to the fore in its cinematic adaptation). The point, perhaps, is that both sites (Tara and Atlanta) are essentially constructed and imagineered; neither is fully authenticated or "placed." While there is not space here to explore the differences between Atlanta and Savannah (pertaining to the fictional Tara) in terms of ideas about modernity versus nostalgia, it is certainly worth noting how both old *and* new constructions of southernness are equally reliant upon the forms of "cultural reproduction" (*RS* 59).

In "Rat-Faced Auntie," one of the most telling features of Hadley's mourning the decline of old Savannah is that her nostalgic historical origin should be situated in the 1930s specifically. The 1930s and 1940s witnessed an upsurge in nostalgic investments in reproducing Old Southern cultures, described by Brundage as "a watershed in the self-conscious commercialization of the southern past" (*Southern Past* 184). Savannah and Charleston, for example (the latter deemed "America's Most Historic City," with the Old and Historic Charleston District being established in 1931), embarked on projects of historic preservation that became inextricable from the growing heritage tourism industry in contemporary Georgia and Mississippi (Savannah, Natchez, Vicksburg). Brundage uses the example of heritage tourism in Natchez, whose still thriving "pilgrimage tours" have since their 1931 inception "unapologetically marketed Old South 'romance,'" with nostalgia being key to the attraction, whose visitors "expec[t] *Gone with the Wind*" and "to step into an earlier time and place" (*Southern Past* 322). The word *pilgrimage* denotes a disturbing spiritualization of the Old South, not only commercializing but sanctifying an image of white southern heritage and colonial gentility, reattaching a narrative of American innocence to the white South by inflecting cultural memory with a harmful political bent. Brundage's identification of the *self-consciousness* accompanying the white South's historical representation—he quotes one of the Natchez Pilgrimage hostesses saying, "It's kind of like a play" (*Southern Past* 322)—is further revealing because it suggests that white southern memory is dependent (in this context) on forms of aesthetic staginess.

Romine's essay "TARA! TARA! TARA! *Gone with the Wind* and the Work of Cultural Reproduction" discusses the commodification of the Old South as an image to be reproduced, bought, and sold on an active contemporary cultural-nostalgia market whose workings we might observe in the manifold successes of Mitchell's novel and film (*RS* 30). Jameson attributes the national popularity of the "nostalgia film" genre to the fact that it recaptures a sense of "privileged" American historicity that was lost after modernism (*Postmodernism* xvii, 19), recalling Leon Jr.'s roadhouse diner in *Yonder Stands Your Orphan*, which "harked back to the fifties" and constitutes a "must-visit" for the local nostalgic population (1, 2). Romine claims that nostalgic cultural reproductions like these carry such a high market premium because they are "located in special places discontinuous with incoherent modernity." They offer "an implicit alternative history, a located might-have-been" ("Orphans All" 168). A key word here, however, is *discontinuous;* that is, the nostalgic appeal of said "special" places (a word also used by Davis) lies precisely in their imagined difference from the present, if postmodernity represents a narrative of "history gone wrong" ("Orphans All" 168). Establishing this sense of incongruity between past and present relies on constructing a mythology of past coherence (and present incoherence), which becomes in this sense entirely contingent.

When we return to Hadley's memorialized Savannah an obvious disparity emerges between Hadley's wistful spectacle and what we know of the turbulent social realities of the 1930s American South, including sexual oppression and inequality, segregation, so-called race riots, war, and the Great Depression (which had hit Georgia's agricultural economy especially hard in the 1920s and 1930s). The romantic picture Hadley paints is precisely that: a closed, selective, and contrived representation *of* history rather than some authentically mimetic window *on* living history. It is a spectacle that has become beautiful only in retrospect, or only after the totalizing, unifying, and ordering properties of the static image—the monolith—have been applied. Ironically, this has already been captured effectively when Hadley bemoans the "*whole* culture, gone with the wind": the very idea of some monolithic, whole or *wholly* idyllic culture that could have existed having been lost is exposed as a fallacy. Romine argues something similar of Tara's construction in *Gone with the Wind*: "Tara isn't what it was, but Tara's was *never* what it was: that is its constitutive condition" (*RS* 59). Nostalgic retrospection reveals the *nonexistence* of the putative real. The proposed authentic origin evaporates, giving rise to a concept of (regional) authenticity that has simulation as its constitutive condition.

Reading Hannah in this way foregrounds how nostalgic constructions of authentic origins have lent themselves historically to practices of exclusion, whereupon "ugly" historical reality becomes more conspicuous by way of its absence from the memorialized spectacle. Jameson has advanced (via Walter Benjamin's dialectical principle) a concept of self-aware nostalgia, arguing that "if nostalgia as a political motivation is most frequently associated with fascism, there is no reason why a nostalgia conscious of itself, *a lucid and remorseless dissatisfaction with the present on the grounds of some remembered plenitude,* cannot furnish as adequate a revolutionary stimulus as any other" (*Marxism* 82, my emphasis). When thinking about the Old South, the worry is that those dissatisfied with the present on the grounds of "some remembered plenitude" are likely to be precisely the kind of "fascists" Jameson identifies as potential nostalgics, whose formulation of the declining white South obscures the antithetical progress narrative of the Black South. White nostalgia feeds parasitically on a misremembered past plenitude, or perhaps more aptly, one that demands that a significant number of people be excluded from it. I should note that it is not my contention that southern nostalgia simply or only performs a negative, conservative political function, though my focus here is on the "Gone with the Wind" mode of white memorialization embodied in the public version of Hadley's memoir. I am reminded again of E. Patrick Johnson's work on the relationship between performance and authenticity, where authenticity is a trope that can be manipulated for cultural gain, but this can cut both ways: "authenticating discourse enables marginalized people to counter oppressive representations of themselves" (3). Again, the premise that some monolithic Old culture ever existed in the first place is radically called into question.

This recalls my idea of the vanishing point of nostalgic reference. Davis identified the 1960s as the crisis point of "rude transitions rendered by [Western] history" (6). The 1960s certainly signaled a tumultuous era in Western cultures in general, and in America and its southern states perhaps uniquely. The culmination of the civil rights movement in the Acts of

1964, 1965, and 1968 (for example) was of particular consequence to a place in which forms of Black oppression, while of course they were not limited to the South, were regionally specific in the case of Jim Crow laws, or when we appreciate that the majority of Black lynchings from 1882–1968 took place in the (Deep) South. It is certainly revealing that Hadley (along with other characters, including the narrator of "Uncle High Lonesome") should locate the nostalgic past in a specifically pre-1960s moment. However, if the 1930s was itself characterized by a sudden outpouring of cultural nostalgia, as Brundage notes above, then this too was a period of change, uncertainty, and anxiety, qualities that are perfectly antithetical to the stability and comfort Hadley purports to remember from this era. It is worth pointing out the irony here that Hadley is nostalgic for the 1930s as her historical safe space or "home" even though this era was already characterized by nostalgia. Because Hadley is nostalgic *for* the 1930s from a later moment, when Mitchell and Percy were nostalgic *in* the 1930s and 1940s for an earlier time, then once again we appreciate the infinitely regressive element of southern nostalgia. At the time of Hadley's old Savannah, Mitchell and Percy were themselves already characterized by nostalgia for prior historical moments, suggesting that the "modern" problems of the present were already in the past. Historicity recedes vertiginously: the more we seek the nostalgic origin, the more elusive it becomes.

I mentioned earlier that there are two competing discourses at work in Hadley's problematic memoir: the rosy image painted above and its "ugly truth" counternarrative. Ugliness is at the heart of Hadley's characterization, a poisonous woman twice divorced whose "typical expression was the scowl, her typical comment, derision" (166). The "rat-faced" aunt admits that she has never been "the prettiest thing on the block" (177), directly undermining the elegant self-portrait above. Implicit in the story's pursuit of historical origins is the elusive explanation for Hadley's present meanspiritedness and social animosity. Throughout most of the story Edgar remains unable "to drill at the truth about [. . .] Hadley" nor to fathom even "the matter of his aunt's patronage, which he had never quite understood" (166). However, in fact the story does appear to arrive at the origin of Hadley's awfulness when Edgar unearths a seemingly authentic historical document while gathering his research: Hadley's own diaries, written, crucially, in 1931.

Hadley's sentimental reproduction of 1930s Savannah contrasts pointedly with the image conveyed in the diary. In what appears to be an intimate act of spontaneous communication, a unique confessional moment, we are suddenly in touch with something emotionally real, distinct from the many layers of performance and simulation that otherwise envelop the text. Is this the true memory, the explanatory historical origin, the dark, female confessional core in which authenticity resides? The diary possesses a shocking frankness of expression at marked odds with its author's public rhetoric: "I . . . am . . . made . . . all . . . different . . . I . . . can't . . . enjoy . . . anything . . . God . . . you . . . my . . . husband . . . pokes . . . at . . . me . . . I . . . am . . . angry . . . feel . . . there . . . is . . . a . . . dangerous . . . snake . . . down . . . there . . . not . . . him . . . me . . . before . . . he . . . got . . . there" (189). Images of alienation ("I am made all different"), sexual violence ("my husband pokes at me"), existential crisis ("I can't enjoy anything"), anger, sinfulness, and shame all combine in a picture that is radically antithetical to the sepia-tinted one above. If we think of nostalgia as an experience that includes both pleasure and regret, what is more, then certainly any sense of the former is absent from this raw and anguished account. The standout aesthetic qualities of the extract—ellipses signaling absent grammar, staccato lexis, fraught expression, and semantic indeterminacy—render the utterance curiously pre- or extralinguistic, appropriate, perhaps, to its diary form. Spontaneity is emphasized over contrivance, the qualities of speech over writing, perhaps, with the sense that these words have emerged impromptu from a moment of heightened emotion in which we might expect more rehearsed forms of narrative to break down, and this can appear more authentic.

Eric Savoy's work on how language can be made to approach the absent Real in American Gothic (a genre to which Hannah is clearly indebted) is useful here. Savoy writes, "It is the very struggle to give the Real a language that singularly shapes the [genre]" that "gives rise to gothic verbal figures, their urgent straining toward meaning, and their constant strains upon the limits of language" (169). These aesthetic conventions make the genre "entirely congruent with the notion of 'the Real'" in the Lacanian sense, that is, "the myriad things and amorphous physicality beyond representations [that] haunt our subjectivity" that "demand our attention [and] compel us to explanatory language but resist the strategies of that language"; the Real is that which structures "cannot structure" (Savoy 169). It is possible that in the realest moments of experience, those that resist incorporation into a linguistic system in which meaning is essentially *not present,* the capabilities of language are bound to fail, tested or strained to their limits.

By evoking the biblical image of the serpent in Eden, Hadley's confession becomes one of inherent female sinfulness, owning that the "dangerous snake down there" is "not him but *me before he got there.*" And while there is not space to pursue this fully here, there is the distinct sense that authenticity resides in certain female semiotics, with the struggle for expression causing language to break down in moments of heightened feminine emotion and thus (as Savoy argued) it becomes paradoxically more real. Something remarkably similar happens to Emma's language during the Lysol-blinding scene: "you don't have . . . *moxie,* moxie—that's it! [. . .] You ungrateful *bitch!* You're *gothic,* Edgar!" (187). The scene covers two substantial paragraphs in which Emma struggles for the right words, cutting sentences short, rephrasing them, and using incongruous words to describe Edgar, such as *gothic* or *bitch.* This recalls Hadley's pained expression ("God . . . you . . . me") and similarly dissonant language (describing herself in the phallic image of the "dangerous snake," for example). Coupled with each scene's heavy use of ellipsis is the impression that aesthetics that operate at the limits of linguistic reference can lay claim to (or at least approximate) a representational veracity that might be absent elsewhere, or in male discourse.

Hadley's and Emma's expressions of female sinfulness resist what I have elsewhere termed the fall into representation. They also resist incorporation into patriarchal systems of analysis, symbolized when Emma partially blinds Edgar with the Lysol just after her speech above, literally nullifying one of his interpretative capacities, vision also signifying mimetic understanding, our window on the world. In turn, Edgar's visual impairment means that he is further prevented from fully comprehending his aunt's diary, because he literally cannot read it properly. This is in keeping with Lacan's sense that the linguistically initiated subject enters (falls) into a Symbolic world of social discourse that is the "absent" realm of the patriarchal as opposed to the "present" matriarchal (Dosse 117; see also E. Wright 321). Indeed, both Hadley's and Emma's enigmatic, dense, and idiosyncratic language proves curiously poetic, compelling and allusive but interpretatively opaque: Emma's distinctly Joycean "I saw the nowhere, the awful never of you all" (187); Hadley's evoking the ancient and powerful image of the serpent in Eden. There is the suggestion, then, that this gendered language remains alien to men, as exhibited in Edgar's inability to understand both women: "There was something in her [Emma] that he couldn't touch" (179). It is possible that a female confessional core exists, expressed in a distinctive lexicon and owning a unique style that acts as guarantor of sincerity and is suddenly unearthed in moments like these. It is also possible, of course, that the private female lexicon caught in Hadley's diary signals an implicit revocation of her public nostalgic discourse, a discourse that feeds a narrative of white southern melancholia that is essentially male. Hadley's present animosity might be partially understood as stemming from the discordance between an inward experience of one's true (female) self, and an outward need to appear to subscribe to an image of southern nostalgia that is predicated on forms of prevalent male cultural discourse. There is a real that exists in the language of women, perhaps, but cannot be known by men such as Edgar (and Hannah).[3]

It is conceivable, then, that Hadley's diary represents an epiphany of authentic meaning, furthered by its allusion to the Bible's seminal parable of *original* sin, the first story, the authentic linguistic origin to which confused contemporary lexicons may refer in moments of hermeneutic crisis. Such a language might, it seems, give rise to the truth about Hadley that has eluded her nephew thus far. However, already a problem has emerged when we realize that the stylistic properties that lend Hadley's diary entry its unique sense of urgency and sincerity—the qualities of a spontaneous, confessional, *female* speech act (but of course it is writing)—become further problematic when they may in fact be the effect of the diary's reader, the visually impaired Edgar, rather than its writer, Hadley. The ostensibly authentic or original text has already been mediated by its audience, therefore, even if it was not initially intended for one. Again the issue of authorship is raised, which begs the question who the true author of "their book," *Rat-Face Confesses,* will be. Is the diary the product of its fictional author, Hadley, or its audience, Edgar?

This problem is compounded when the diarist herself, who has already confessed her own ineptitude (like her nephew's) at writing, explains why she is commissioning Edgar to write on her behalf: "I was no mean student, nephew, but in composition I couldn't quite express myself, though I was excellent in elocution" (182). Even if we try to uphold the speech-writing hierarchy, the very fact that Hadley's diary *is* written and not spoken is ironic. As a written text it is unreliable, subject to the same sorts of challenges as both Edgar's writing and the story itself (when considered metafictionally). This invites comparison with Derrida's assertion that *all* forms of language can be conceived as forms of writing, troubling traditional (structuralist) Western mythologies that have debased the written word and valorized speech as a "pure" conduit with "a direct and natural relationship with meaning" (Culler 92). In "Rat-Faced Auntie," our difficulty in determining to what extent Hadley's diary pertains to the qualities of speech rather than writing implies that it is a logocentric fallacy to regard speech as some ideal form of authentic expression that is somehow closer to its living subject (more self-present) than writing. While our diarist's shocking confession appears to epitomize authorial legitimacy—a good aesthetic basis for *Rat-Face Confesses,* surely, as the implied ugly truth—its integrity does not withstand scrutiny.

Original sin is a trope that resounds in much of Hannah's fiction, and it is instrumental in dramatizing the problematic nature of any nostalgic expedition that presupposes the return to authenticity in the past. Because Hadley's diary places sinfulness—the snake in the garden—at the heart of the historical image it presents, the image of the prelapsarian past loses its luster. Humankind's fall in Eden also symbolizes the first historical "rupture" or "identity dislocation" from which nostalgic discourse comes, but if even in Eden the danger was *already* there (we might say the "dangerous snake" was present "before [w]e got there"), then even the Fall will not be historicized as the first or *singular* catalytic event in human history. As a textual point of origin, the Bible represents a definitive beginning, the original authoritative text. If we agree, then this means that even the most definitive of historical origins in Western Christianity is simply another form of textuality or mediation. The Bible contains the Gospels, quite literally the words of *others,* rendering it just as secondary or imitative as any other form of historical retelling. While we might conceive of the Gospels as a conduit for God's Word, given the issues raised here the Bible becomes instead another textual origin, writing about speaking. Thus, the story's putative confessional heart defers indefinitely to textual precursors. Like Edgar's sociological research, his father's historical journalism, or Hadley's intertextual allusions, even biblical allegories were already "borrowed" from the beginning, and this resonates strongly with ideas about the South's heavily storied status.

When *was* there a plainer language, then, if not in the Bible? In the end, the very notion of a once "realler" or mimetic South is revealed to be a suspicious nostalgic construction that has never been as straightforward nor as simple as such phrases imply. Hannah's characters can never fully imagine a return to the lost utopia because such days never existed. By establishing a southern decline narrative in order then to parody and undermine this,

"Rat-Faced Auntie" implies that it is neither desirable nor possible to return to some mythologized historical origin. Once again, we find that on close inspection the stories of Hannah have the potential to outrun the kinds of critical paradigm that we might bring to them; this is partly why sustained close readings are so important. By dismantling linear trajectories of southern history by creating slippage between the conventional conceptual binaries of past/present, old/new, original/copy, "Rat-Faced Auntie" presents a critique of the very idea of a return to authenticity in the past. History becomes inseparable from narrative, not only in our postmodern moment but when we look closely, from the very beginning, however elusive such a beginning may be. Of course history and place exist outside the forms of their textual mediations, akin to Althusser's "absent cause" or Lacan's Real. Patricia Waugh corroborates this in her study of metafiction: "history is *not* a text," so "it is fundamentally non-narrative and non-representative" (89). However, Hannah's writing derives significant energy from dramatizing something both Waugh and Jameson have expressed, namely, that while "'reality' exists *beyond* 'text,' [it] may only be reached *through* 'text'" (Waugh 89); because "history is inaccessible to us except in textual form," it can only be appropriated "through its prior textualization [and] narrativization" (Jameson, *Political Unconscious* 35). By showing how nostalgic pursuits of authentic origins can always be deferred to prior narrativizations, "Rat-Faced Auntie" compels us to interrogate the politics behind historical representations.

The ugly realities that nostalgic discourse can serve to obscure are a reminder that history is by no means *purely* textual. Thus, conceiving of southern history as discourse-contingent does not simply encourage political relativism or apathy, as Jon Smith, McPherson, Duck, and others have recently argued. Rather, it is only *after* Hannah's postmodern dismantling of the distinctions between reality and simulacra (the real South and its textually constitutive forms) that the nostalgic past is exposed as a fantasy. It is precisely when the discursive nature of *constructions* of southern history is emphasized that the mendacity of certain kinds of nostalgic discourse, establishing points of false origin that are infinitely regressive, is exposed. While the elusiveness of true historical "referents" is certainly in line with postmodern theories of the post-region, nonetheless these remain deeply political in Hannah's work—because if the South and the nostalgic past are not what they seem, then the agendas behind romantic constructions of the region are exhumed. Thus, we are free to imagine counterversions of the past that might offer a more meaningful dialogue with the present. Where historicity and the possibilities for mimesis recede and perhaps even disappear as we approach them, Hannah shows that it is not that the "pure" or "real" South is declining or disappearing; rather, it is these very concepts themselves.

5

Authenticity and Textuality in the Postsouthern Folktale

"Evening of the Yarp: A Report by Roonswent Dover"

Barry Hannah's short story "Evening of the Yarp: A Report by Roonswent Dover," from *Bats Out of Hell* (1993), is usefully contextualized among contemporary debates about the viability of regional studies in a postmodern culture that would appear to question the very concept of the region as a means of understanding southern fiction. Hannah's story reads as distinctly regional, on one hand, while it is instilled with a markedly postmodern flavor, on the other. Because it is quintessentially southern even while it problematizes the perniciously mediated ways in which the South is understood, it offers a creative response to the impasse that a simple opposition between the regional and the postmodern appears to posit. It is a subtle metafictional inquiry into the complex operation of various forms of mediation that salvages an important vestigial idea of the real that is compelling and persuasive even while it is mired in a preoccupation with the issue of the phony image.

A contemporary folktale set in an unspecified mountain range in the upland South of the Ozarks, "Evening of the Yarp" is Hannah's only story written entirely in phonetic language, in what can be identified as "Southern Mountain" dialect (Blanton 83). It establishes a persuasive sense of regionalism at this most basic rhetorical level, intensified when its young and barely literate narrator, Roonswent Dover, gains the sudden ability to "spi[n] a yarn worthy of the oldest Ozark folktale" (*BH* 90) in "hillbilly" (mountain) vernacular, a word used directly throughout (96). It is a counternarrative of sorts, from a micro-South that can be considered as specifically Ozarkian rather than simply southern, and so it destabilizes the notion of a monolithic white South as a product of a unified or homogenous region. As such, perhaps the story becomes more authentic.

Since it is also a ghostly tall tale, "Evening of the Yarp" evokes both Southern and Appalachian Gothic, while also recalling the history of literary mythologizing about American "hill" culture by folklorists, local colorists, and travel writers (often from outside the region), who, as Brooks Blevins argues, have created and perpetuated conflicting and misleading images of the Upland or Mountain South. As if in response, Hannah's ambitious adolescent narrator delights in presenting to us aspects of the unimaginable in the tradition of the creative wit exemplified in the tall tale and the yarns of Old Southwest humor. Something similar might be said of Hannah's *Never Die*, an obvious complement as a postsouthern tall tale that, like Tom Franklin's 2006 novel, *Smonk* (which Franklin dedicated to Hannah), conflates postmodern theory, southern grotesque, and frontier mythology, revealing the South's relationship to Old West myths as influenced by Mark Twain's tall tales.[1] Hannah's relation to the southwestern humorists has been frequently overlooked, as Ruth D. Weston acknowledges in her contribution to Edward Piacentino's *The Enduring Legacy of Old Southwest Humor*. Dover's tale certainly begs some explicit comparison with Thomas Bangs Thorpe's "The Big Bear of Arkansas," for example, which exemplifies some of the dynamics subsequently discussed here, between speech and writing and between cultural insiders and outsiders. In its reference to the themes of historical imposition and geographical entrapment, the story also marks its indebtedness to southern modernist literary traditions that emphasize the significance of history and place, as Martyn Bone and others have argued.

With its self-conscious allusion to the twin southern genres of the gothic and the tall tale as well as Southern Renaissance writing, Hannah's story is firmly contextualized among regional literary cultures, both written and oral. The art of storytelling (or "legending," as the story calls it) is key, as different types of aesthetic strategy compete for efficacy and credence as they are ventriloquized through Dover's narrative. Meanwhile, the story distinguishes itself as something new or other by inflecting existing storytelling traditions with a distinctly postmodern and Ozarkian twist. Which is to say, while the idiomatic style of Dover's narrative is an apparent display of insider language, a guarantee of authentic Ozarkian discourse, of course what is local or authentic here is principally a matter of aesthetic style— especially when we consider the Mississippian author's own outsider (i.e., non-Ozarkian) status. Intertextuality and metafictionality are therefore integral to the reconfigured sense of regionalism dramatized here.

Because the tall tale is characteristically made up of narratives that challenge the audience's credulity, Hannah's indebtedness to the genre suggests already that what is authentic or believable here is a function of a textual performance whose merit readers are called upon to determine. As a tall tale, a genre characterized by its dynamic, playful nature, as well as the connection between speaker and audience in terms of an established contract of suspended disbelief, "Evening of the Yarp" pushes away questions of validity. Since tall tales do not simply involve *either* truth telling or lying, this aspect of the genre reflects usefully on Hannah's own self-reflexive writing style and on late-twentieth-century metafictional theory, as well as facilitating an understanding of American regions as a complex mix of reality and fiction. The story becomes an ingenious proposal for having it both ways, acknowledging the region as an image, while discovering something authentic in images.

The hermeneutic challenges of Hannah's fiction historicize it specifically in its late-twentieth-century moment, when critics such as Brian McHale and Hutcheon were disputing the nature of mimetic historical representation and emphasizing the textual nature of reality, having inherited Fredric Jameson's theoretical legacy. Charles Taylor's *The Ethics of Authenticity* (1991), Hillel Schwartz's *The Culture of the Copy* (1996), and Philip E. Simmons's *Deep Surfaces* (1997) are good examples of early efforts to scrutinize the problematic relation between authenticity, identity, and originality in a contemporary culture of simulacra, anticipating twenty-first-century works such as David Chidester's *Authentic Fakes* (2005) and Abigail Cheever's *Real Phonies* (2010). Meanwhile, other late-twentieth-century scholars such as Roland Robertson, Robert Brinkmeyer, Edward Ayers, and Arjun Appadurai were emphasizing the concomitant infirmity of a foundational sense of place in a newly globalized culture of shifting boundaries, in which the very idea of regional authenticity was merely a simulated one.

The metafictional genre arose partly as a cultural response to this contemporary sense of textual contingency, in which language is incapable of mimetic reflection. Here, our very idea of reality is a fictional, semantic, or linguistic one that can only gesture toward some idea of the real but without representing it. Linda Hutcheon emphasizes the consequent fraudulence of any fiction that claims to "aspire to tell the truth" or to "associate truth with claims to empirical validation," arguing instead that a contemporary sense of textual authenticity resides only in works that can be seen to "contest the ground of any claim to such" (*Poetics* 122). Consequently, fiction that "most freely acknowledges its fictionality" may be, paradoxically, the "most authentic and honest" kind (Hutcheon, *Narcissistic Narrative* 49). "Evening of the Yarp" certainly demands our interrogation of the concepts of the real, the surreal, and the hyperreal, in which the distinctly Baudrillardian possibility emerges that conceptions of the real are simply a function of compelling aesthetic or textual practices. At the same time, its narrator swears vehemently upon his mimetic legitimacy: "I swear [. . .] only the truth alone" (92). When properly acknowledged, this tension within Hannah's work produces some remarkable conceptual subtleties regarding region and real.

What Roland Robertson terms *glocalization* (28), according to which the global is appropriated locally or the global culture is itself some form of bastardized local culture gone large, is a process that can also be usefully considered in the South with the rise of "media-made Dixie" (Jack Kirby's title). Richard Gray describes this as the "particular kind of commodification that turns the South itself—or, to be more exact, an idea or image of the South—into a product, a function of the marketplace" (*Southern Aberrations* 356). We might recall Homer's declaration in Hannah's *Hey Jack!* that "the South has been pickled in the juice of its own image" (20). Appadurai explains that contemporary global processes of cultural reproduction can create falsely localized "communities" that in fact contain "no [inherent] sense of place" (29). It is with this anxiety that Michael O'Brien introduces *Placing the South* (2007), stating that the "regional historian" of the past forty years was "likely to be oppressed by a sense of his unimportance" in view of the possible redundancy of the very concept of a "grounded" (foundational) South (3), of the fundamental duplicity residing in a sense of place and in the concept of regionalism itself. Some aspects of postmodern theory seemed to have rendered regional studies antiquated, even obsolete.

Hannah writes at a critical juncture in our contemporary revisions of regionalism in which a key tension emerges between writing about the South and a growing sense that the concept of the region in contemporary America is part of an increasingly dispersed and transnational culture. While the South remained (and remains) a region, late-twentieth-century ideas about postmodernity were closely associated with material changes in global culture and economics, summarized by Jameson: "regionalism is ineffectual against late capitalism, which makes it difficult to decide whether it is authentic any longer (and indeed whether that term still means anything) [. . .] since now the regional as such becomes the business of global American Disneyland-related corporations" (*Postmodernism* 204). In a contemporary cultural economy that circulates commoditized and essentially ersatz images and reproductions of real places like the South, the very concept of a region as a distinct geographical reality proves itself to be the constituent product of cultural processes that in themselves oppose more traditional understandings of the terms.

Terms such as *postsouthern,* which were gaining critical purchase at the time of Hannah's writing, continue to inform and complicate current critical thinking about the postregional or "transnational" South (Jay 1). From the late twentieth century onward it has been common for academic southernists to emphasize the constructed nature of the terms *South* and *southern,* and this particular aspect of postregional theory has provoked a potential standoff between the real South and the imaginary, constructed, or "fake" South. Members of the New Southern Studies cohort who advocate a move away from the problem of authenticity include Melanie Benson Taylor, Leigh Anne Duck, Kathryn McKee, Annette Trefzer, Grace Hale, Debora Barker, and Tara McPherson, and we can certainly observe these critics' impatience to move beyond emphasizing the constructedness of "the South" in recent years. The whole question of what makes our conception of places real, our representations of them authentic, had come under radical scrutiny even while authors such as Hannah were writing about the region in ways that seemed compellingly authentic.

While many of the recent problems surrounding the concept of regional authenticity were in fact already presaged in earlier historical moments, certainly the period of Hannah's writing marks an important one in which critical attention to these issues became far more endemic and entrenched both in postmodern fiction and criticism and in contemporary studies of the South and West alike, perhaps because these two American regions have become historically associated with mythologies that set them apart from the national imaginary, however arbitrary such distinctions may be. In *The Real South* (2008), Romine explains how from the 1950s onward the South underwent rapid and profound changes in which the region radically shifted both as a social reality and as an aesthetic subject. Romine emphasizes the aesthetic implications of this (socioeconomic) shift "from a production-based economy to one based on consumption and the flexible accumulation of culture" (30), and his critical study of the region centers on a textual paradigm of "cultural reproduction" in which a sense of place exists in a "constitutive condition" (59) achieved through the power of the text. We can observe analogous developments in studies of the postregional West, such as William Handley and Nathaniel Lewis's *True West: Authenticity and the American West* (2004), a critical examination of the elusive "true" West that closely anticipates Romine's interrogation of the "real" South. Lewis's *Unsettling the Literary West: Authenticity and Authorship* (2003) and Jeff Karem's *The Romance of Authenticity* (2004) further trouble the concept of an authentic region by revealing the limits of historical verisimilitude in literary representations of the West. Echoing Jameson's suspicion of the terms *regionalism* and *authenticity*, Romine sums up the contemporary problem of postregionalism when he argues that *South* is "another of these words" that "mean nothing much without the quotes" (*RS* 3).

Romine's argument that a language of authenticity "cannot properly refer to anything: once something is called 'authentic,' it already isn't" (*RS* 4) is key to understanding Hannah's metafiction, both as writing about "the real South" and as writing about *writing*, an aesthetic practice that is fundamentally concerned with the politics (and elusiveness) of textual reference. At the historical moment of Hannah's writing, the terms *authenticity, history,* and *place* appeared to have revealed their bankruptcy in a postindustrial economy of signs mediated constantly by simulacra standing in for reality. Hannah's postsouthern writing thus contends with the possible placelessness of a late-capitalist post-South, where the correspondent idea of determining the southernness of his writing, of fixing the region-as-referent in a verifiably southern lexicon, becomes equally problematic.

Compounding these issues, the self-reflexivity of Hannah's fiction, its focus on the contrivances of storytelling and performance, necessitates its own inherent suspicion of *all* writing's ability to refer authentically. Paradoxically, late-twentieth-century fiction was preoccupied with questions of aesthetic value based on a conceptual lexicon of authenticity that it acknowledged to be deeply spurious. If postmodern culture had finally exposed authenticity as nothing more than the effect of the various aesthetic practices by which the concept is constituted, then in what way, if any, could a metaphysics of authenticity survive in a contemporary American South? How could new southern writers claim to speak authentically of the regions they depict, and what sort of aesthetic should new writers strive for as the most authentic, if they are ethically obliged to acknowledge the fundamental fraudulence of their medium and of precisely these terms?

The exhaustion of a foundational sense of place is the topic of much postsouthern scholarship, with some identifying a turn in contemporary southern writing that marks a radical departure from an earlier, regionally distinctive sense of place. Bone contends that "it is a truth universally acknowledged among Southern literary scholars that 'the South' and 'Southern literature' have [until now] been characterized by a 'sense of place'" (*SOP* vii) but says that this modernist "model of Southern fiction [. . .] rooted in fixed ideas of place, community and history" has now become exhausted ("Southern Fiction" 164). Similarly, contemporary studies of the postregional American West explore how our "transnational, global, media age" (from Neil Campbell's subtitle) constantly repudiates the concept of the region, testimony to the broader transformation of American regional studies. Historicizing the predicament of placelessness in the late twentieth century and emphasizing the challenges that this phenomenon poses to contemporary aesthetic practices introduces an implicit politics of nostalgia redolent of the paradox whereupon the South has always been nostalgic for its own demise.

Matthew Guinn argues that the "new challenge" facing contemporary southern writers was "no longer how to present the region to the larger world" but "how to bring that larger world into the demesne of southern letters" to create "a fully realized postmodern version of the South" (184, 103). Hannah walks this line between writing about specific aspects of regionalism, valorizing the concept of an authentic and distinctive place critics were beginning to suspect, reconfigure, or even abandon at the time of his writing, and yet doing so with a shrewd awareness that contemporary American regions are part of a larger world that changes them. "Evening of the Yarp" dramatizes some extraordinarily sophisticated ideas that problematize the very concept of regional authenticity, while locating these ideas in a region whose fervently localized representation seems both particularly southern and particularly authentic. It is self-consciously "rooted" in ideas about place, community, and history, contrary to Bone's arguments above. Meanwhile, Hannah appears to contest the contention that the "death of the region" (Henninger 10) is only a recent problem, for example, when "Evening of the Yarp" blurs the boundaries between insiders and outsiders as well as between fiction and reality in its construction of an Ozarkian sense of place. This begs important questions about how regional fiction might hope to withstand the pressures of a profoundly evolving social, literary, and philosophical culture at the end of the century. What is it to be southern, Ozarkian or otherwise, in a world that suggests that regional identities have lost meaning, being constituted from textual processes that are the very antitheses of authentic in its traditional (modernist) sense? To situate Hannah's fiction in this way is to recognize the important contribution that it makes to contemporary debates about the distinctions between southern and postsouthern, authentic and textual, and even to understanding the possibilities it suggests for having it both ways.

"Or give it another try, like a hot Hollywood novelist." Weston chose this opening line from Hannah's "Upstairs, Mona Bayed for Dong" (265) to evince a classic case of metafiction, or writing that pointedly draws attention to its own status as such (*BH* 205). *Hey Jack!* is one of countless Hannah narratives that contain a remarkably similar narrative interjection: "I must say I was stunned by the voracious range of a woman who seemed made for light civility and patter. *Say it again:* the hungry dark beneath our bright and serene veneers can cause a man to reestimate the whole town" (74, my emphasis). Despite these texts being among the few in Hannah's canon whose direct subject is not writers and writing (and despite Hannah's eschewal of the metafictional label), they are brought firmly into the realm of late-twentieth-century metafiction when, as Weston argues, such self-reflexive remarks convey the narrator's anxious "inability to tell a true story despite his best efforts" (*BH* 205). Here, Weston accentuates a link between storytelling, in its oral traditions as well as its self-reflexive metafiction, and "lying" (*BH* 91) that is integral to understanding "Evening of the Yarp," a story that conflates traditionally antithetical ideas about truth and fiction, authenticity and textuality.

David Thoreen argues that Hannah's earlier story "Water Liars" presents instead a situation where "the truth can be known; in fact, the story [despite its ironies] may be said to 'begin' with the narrator's discovery of the truth" (227). Robert Klevay agrees, observing of the same story that while the truth may be "painful," it is undoubtedly "present" (133). "Water Liars" certainly appears to sustain a distinction between truth and untruth at its narrative level that might usefully set it off against "Evening of the Yarp." In the former story, the fanciful tales of a group of "old liars" are unashamedly false (3), while the intermittent confessions of the narrator, his wife, and a truth-telling stranger are confirmed, by contrast, to be true. The story concludes with the narrator and his new "kindred" (the stranger) being "crucified by the truth" that each man has told (7). Thus "Water Liars" is an important textual precursor to "Evening of the Yarp," a story in which it becomes increasingly difficult to sustain any ontological determinacy between truth, lies, the real, and the supernatural, with which to ground our interpretations or even to invest these categories themselves with interpretive expediency.

In "Evening of the Yarp," the possibility raised in "Water Liars" that "true tale[s]" ("Yarp" 99) exist somewhere outside the falsehoods that otherwise flood the narrative has already been undermined by the obvious fact that the subject matter of Dover's report is brazenly surreal. The Yarp is a supernatural figure, seemingly human but with "hot yellow eyes," scaled "bird" legs, and, beneath its coat, a visible digestive system containing its latest victims' live remains (95). Our young storyteller possesses, as do the water liars, a flagrantly unbelievable ghost story (driving down an Arkansas mountain to the store in a rare snowstorm, he picks up a hitchhiking Yarp), yet all the while he *swears* to be telling the truth. Thus, the story becomes a subtly metafictional disquisition on what constitutes authentic storytelling. For example, the Yarp, who is not only the very stuff of legends but also a storyteller himself, berates the tale-teller Dover for exhibiting a regional proclivity for "legending" (93) that directly recalls the old water liars' preferred pastime: "I dont want to hear none of your tales, boy, [. . .] too many tales come out of these mountains and everwhere. There shouldn't be any tales" (92). The Yarp's charge "You lie!" (93) directly associates legending with the work of the storyteller's imagination, and as such (as Weston argues) with lying. Weston points out how the name Yarp conflates two terms for narrative: the "yarn" of the oral-storytelling tradition and the "barbaric yawp" that Walt Whitman called his "Song of Myself" (*BH* 91), and I would add that Roonswent possibly derives his name partly from *rune*, a symbol with secret or mysterious significance. Dover's opening line, "Darn it were boring, wisht I were a hawk or crab" (91), becomes suspect as it preempts the Yarp's subsequent rebuke: "You got to lie to stay halfway interested in yourself, don't you?" (93). Although Dover and his Yarp are in conflict, the two characters exist in significant dramatic correspondence.

In many of Hannah's stories, male coming of age centers upon entry into an adult world of masculine tall tale–telling. "High-Water Railers," a sequel of sorts to "Water Liars," implies this when it is the entrance of the female in the form of Melanie Wooten that causes the old liars to finally begin speaking the "truth" (10–11). The curious gender politics of Hannah's texts certainly warrant attention, not least because they interweave ideas about the inheritance of (original) sin, sexuality, and language in provocative ways. The suggestion here, perhaps, is that original sin inheres not in the feminine, as traditional Christian mythology would have it, but in the emergence of the masculine creative imagination, where male fall from grace accompanies his fiction making. Something remarkably similar occurs in "A Creature in the Bay of St. Louis," whose young narrator gains a coveted "Big Fish" tale of his own, true to the Southern Gothic tradition, by fabricating a near-fatal watery battle with a "giant stingaree" (49)—but not without retrospective recognition of the fall that attends his admittance into a southern world of lies, which continues to haunt the mature narrator of the story: "I would return and return to it the rest of my life" (51). It is a fall into story, or representation.

In "Evening of the Yarp," this prospect is confirmed when, voicing his distaste for the local tall tale–telling tradition, the Yarp claims: "The imagination is what ruins it. They shouldn't never imagined heaven nor hell. [. . .] You already know the more you think of something aforehand it isn't anything like that at all. They'll be legending though [. . .]. They shoulder just taken their years and practiced being dumb, over and over" (93). In telling his tale, Dover has contested the Yarp's recommendation to remain "dumb," the word evoking not only the silence of not telling ("If you tell anybody this you will die, Roonswent" [101]) but also the innocence that is lost in the "doomed" moment of telling (102), a distinctly biblical allegory. It is this recognition that constitutes the real fall from grace, Dover's fall into story, and the original-sin analogy resounds both in the Yarp's later decreeing Dover's "eternal curse" (101) and in Dover's rather opaque ruminations on his own sinfulness, "The evil things of Roonswent Dover" (91). Ultimately, the very existence of Dover's story coincides with the young man's loss of innocence, his successful ordination (despite the Yarp's threats) into a mature storytelling community with a tale to match or even exceed the others'. Given the nature and circumstances of its production, this is no mean feat. The irony, however, is that Dover's factual "report" is a paradigmatic instance of this male legending tradition that the Yarp so ardently contests, and thus we must suspect the very premise upon which it is founded, to tell "only the truth alone" (92).

Augmenting a sense of regional specificity, Dover's propensity for legending is posited as somehow native, natural, and inevitable. His account is clearly situated among a rich oral culture of "hillbilly" tale-telling, of "witches," "haints," and "supernaturals" (97). He tells us that "[m]y grandpa knewn a family of Yarps" and that "one woman saw [a Yarp's] stomach and inside were a human brain" (95); he says that his teacher, Deacon Charles, "seen exactly one Yarp and [he has] been searching all [his] life" (97). This tradition typically extends to gothic hyperbole, caught when Dover, with the Yarp as his traveling companion, describes his claustrophobia, as the narrow mountain road seems to close in on him, in the language of the supernatural: "I aint ner liked them and now, getting on dark, the mountains I feel they live and squeeze in on you to a narrow lane when nobody's around. I nere give up that feeling sinct I was a kid" (92). Despite using this language, redolent of the gothic yarns of Old Southwest humor, in whose tradition he writes, in fact Dover is also explicit in sounding his agreement with the Yarp's *antipathy* to legending: "Everything since he got in my truck was mocking me, minding back. Xcept maybe that speech on legends, hell and heaven" (95). This implicit sympathy with the Yarp's aversion to Ozarkian legending suggests Dover's complicity in the local "curse," because of which, with "tales piling up in every holler and cove" (97), imagination simply "ruins" or obscures the truth.

To complicate this reading, however, the integrity of both Dover's and the Yarp's ostensibly unbelievable tales is authenticated at the story's gothic climax, when the Yarp really does "open his coat" (101) to reveal "Miz Skatt's head in his belly, cooking and hollering" (102). Astonishingly, this verifies Dover's earlier insistence that "sudden [a Yarp] will lift his coat and you can see all his digestion, [. . .] Thered be a baby's foot or a human brain" (95). By the same token, the Yarp's own "true tale," grotesque, misogynistic, and seemingly absurd—"the crimes of murder and theft in the nights, all them I tell you now done by [Ms Skatt's] womens and girls" (100)—is also substantiated toward the end of the story by Deacon Charles and Chief Nini, who find Skatt dead, surrounded by the spoils of her criminal female protégés: "There was just, *you couldn't believe it,* piles of jewelry, watches, radios, knives and ribbons, deputies badges and wigs. Missus Skatt [. . .]

with a old head and a young body, all laid out" (102, my emphasis). More-over, this unlikely "fact" serves in turn to validate Dover's earlier and equally improbable assertion that "[a]ll the [local] killing and stealing" is done by "womens, womens and girls" (93). Here, it is ironic that the Yarp should be so averse to the local legending tradition, because in this case it seems that the perpetrators spoke true all along. Similarly, Dover's early claims to have "knewn he was the Yarp in a way already" are legitimized by the Yarp's later owning that "I aint half the Yarp (he said it!) I used to be" (95, 101). As tex-tual doppelgängers of sorts, Dover and his Yarp depend on each other for authentication, and their tales work to vindicate each other in subtle and intriguing ways.

While we must of course suspect the veracity of Dover's account, in these moments when it seems we are given factual evidence of the story's most outrageously unbelievable aspects, we cannot help but suspend our disbe-lief. Our interpretation of Dover's reliability as a historiographer has come full circle: first his status as a truth teller is established, and then it is under-mined, only to be reestablished here again. This subtly but thoroughly blurs the distinctions between true stories and lies upon which the interpretative framework of "Water Liars" was seemingly founded. In keeping with the tall-tale tradition, it seriously complicates any attempt on the reader's part to separate fact from fabrication. It is thus unequivocally dedicated to chal-lenging our credulity.

Despite its seeming integrity as a piece of spontaneous local speech, the picture Dover paints of his local territory, which he calls "our county" (93), is informed by dubious historical anecdotes about the frontier, the Civil War, and the Great Depression that become subtly indistinguishable from more overtly uncanny or supernatural reports: "In Deep Ression times [. . .] Some [mountain folk] went to California and messed it up terrible. [. . .] In Cali-fornia they have science grow eggs on a tree, and them hillbillies so sloppy and shuffling, they dont know how to harvest them down and walk crack-ing them with their stupid Arkansas feet" (97). Not only are distinctions be-tween fiction and reality fluid here but perhaps (as Romine's *The Real South* hypothesizes) one constitutes the other, a phenomenon captured when the "lying" school bus driver "Indian Don Suchi Nini sings to us [hillbillies] these stories and believes he is the one who will change them back to real" (94). Such narratives are consumed by their audiences, and they constitute rather than describe real places, like Dover's story depending for their survival and credence on the audience's persuasion. When we believe them, stories or even lies can become effectively real.

Dover's seeming digression about "Deep Re[ce]ssion times" emphasizes Hannah's blurring of the line between fiction and reality in another important way. Dover's focus on the Depression as the pivotal event of local history not only confirms the argument that for poor whites the Depression subsumes the Civil War in historical importance, thereby further troubling the notion of a monolithic South characterized by shared historical experience. Further, it seems that Hannah is referring directly here to the Federal Writers' Project (hereafter FWP), one of the New Deal programs of the late 1930s through which local oral culture was recorded and transcribed to document ("report") the cultural identity of regional groups throughout the country amid the popular rise of so-called social realism in Depression-era America. Sara Rutkowski explores this well in her first full-length study of the impact of the FWP on accepted understandings of cultural groups, *Literary Legacies of the Federal Writers' Project* (2017). Here, the Yarp's "You got to lie to stay halfway interested in yourself" (93) mirrors Dover's understanding of the FWP as a case of "folks often [telling] a tale [to] get the government interested in you as interesting, as workable or feedable" (97). This seemingly direct evocation of the real-world power of stories (or lies) pertains to Patrick Gerster and Nicholas Cords's exploration of the interrelation of history and myth in the ideological construction of the New South. They claim that because many cultural myths have become "psychologically true" despite their duplicity, myth and reality are "complementary elements in the [South's] historical record"; thus their scholarship represents "as much a commentary on southern historiography as it is on the viability of myth in the historical process" (xv).

While Hannah (or at least Deacon Charles) treats official attempts to compile authentic regional voices with something ranging from bemusement to derision, the allusion to the FWP certainly alerts us to the problematic politics of translating oral testimony into literature, as a form of historical representation. The story simultaneously dramatizes and interrogates southern mythologizing, where history and story are almost indistinguishable, perhaps as a key feature of "hillbilly" storytelling in the realms of folklore, literature, and historiography alike; hence the incongruous title of Dover's tall tale, "A Report." Dover's outlandish report places the concept of authenticity under extreme pressure by persistently undermining any interpretative distinction between what is true and what is false, and this constitutes an integral feature of Hannah's metafictional inquiry into the nature of authenticity in the postregional South.

As noted, the paradox of what might be termed the textually constitutive South has been a standard concern of contemporary western as well as southern studies, observable in Jeff Karem, Krista Comer, and Lee Mitchell's scholarship on the interrelation of authenticity and aesthetics in conceptualizations of American regions. Mitchell's review of Handley and Lewis's *True West* concludes that in the absence of the *true* West, "aestheticization itself is the authenticating gesture that lends life meaning," where "authenticity is never simply given once and for all but negotiated through the duplicitous documents we preserve" (93). Like the selective texts chosen (by whom?) for inclusion in the FWP, Dover's report is one such document. In keeping with Hannah's metafictional bent as well as with the idea that the South (like the West) represents an exceptionally storied or represented place, Dover's narrative is powerfully conscious of its own place in a long history of southern aestheticization that has served as an "authenticating gesture." Consequently, if authenticity is only attainable as a function of aesthetic practice, we must remain alert to the ethical and political consequences of which a "duplicitous" *version* of authenticity is preserved as real history; hence Hannah's interest in the FWP.

E. Patrick Johnson's discussion of performative authenticity is especially pertinent here. Without abandoning the concept or suggesting that it is used solely as a tool for cultural oppression (as Jon Smith and others in the NSS have argued), Johnson simply advances the political imperative "to be cognizant of the arbitrariness of authenticity, the ways in which it carries with it the dangers of foreclosing the possibility of cultural exchange and understanding" (3). Karem warns that "criticism grounded in tacit or explicit privileging of authenticity all too often reifies essentialist paradigms of identity and literary production" (15), and McPherson is one of several NSS scholars who have repeatedly called for the abandonment of the "authenticity" paradigm when writing about the South ("Afterword" 312–20). This pertains again to recent warnings (from Smith and others) against talking about the constructed South for fear of reifying the implied antithetical real South. However, to continue talking about authenticity in relation to American regional culture is not tantamount to an implicit desire for essentialism. Conversely, understanding how "performative authenticity" functions in Hannah's texts is to advance the continued political and ethical usefulness of the concept of (regional) authenticity as a window on how it is deployed and to what ends—provided we remain suspicious of the concept's inherent contingency as a function of aesthetics, or performance.

This idea is manifested in "Evening of the Yarp" in the tension that exists between the narrative (at the metalevel), which is dedicated to undermining the virtuosity of the putative claims it makes about authentic documentation, and its narrator, who explicitly acknowledges his audience's suspicion (*"you couldn't believe it"*) and works hard to establish a compelling sense of earnest credibility. If the metafictional dimension of the text implies that a true tale is one whose conceptual basis resides in the pragmatic effects of aesthetic strategies upon an audience, rather than in some metaphysical or ontological sense, then the issue of how performances are executed becomes vital. Deacon Charles, for example, the textual father against whom Dover defines himself and a man who is well versed in the art of storytelling, reveals the potential for narrative credibility to reside in certain aesthetic styles when he advises Dover to retain his colloquialisms and grammatical inaccuracy and "go a head and write like this dont change. He wants to see it quick cause I seen the Yarp" (91). Where truth and authenticity undergo a conceptual transformation, questions of style are integral to the new sense of postsouthern authenticity offered here.

The "illiterate" style of Dover's story is vital to the impression of urgency it conveys, with which the claims of the eyewitness account might be authenticated. Aside from the sense of "local color" evoked, the idiomatic nature of Dover's hurried and unpolished narrative imbues it with the qualities of a spontaneous speech act or confession: "I werent going to adventure, Nat Hidey, no I werent" (95). When we look closely, however, it seems that Dover (like Deacon Charles) recognizes the respective rhetorical effects of speech and writing ("I had a true *tale* and would be the center of the lunch *talkings*") as distinct aesthetic forms, while the problems of determining the truth in his story undermine any conclusive effort on our part to distinguish the different styles explored according to traditional conceptualizations of referential veracity. In the end, Dover's having written rather than spoken his tale is ultimately of no consequence: "So I havent said it, Ive written it and I hope this might make a difference. But I think it wont, not at all. Im got, Im doomed" (102). This final blurring of speech and writing reveals how Dover's semiliterate idiom cloaks its own rhetorical contrivance, when really this idiomatic language is itself an example of aesthetic construction (of a spontaneous oral folktale) manufactured in the style of a specific literary tradition.

Like Deacon Charles, Dover is acutely conscious of the formal properties of his narrative and its status as a piece of language in which his own ability as a storyteller to bear honest witness is simultaneously challenged. This tension is dramatized throughout, in moments of discord between such self-contradictory proclamations as "This Im getting xactly I think" (101) and "I cant hope to repeat [it]" (100) or "I seen the Yarp. *Or somebody like him*" (91, my emphasis). At the heart of the story is Dover's attempt to ventriloquize the Yarp's own tale, the "true" revelation of "what is wrong around here" (101), the metanarrative to explain the predicaments of the present in historical terms: "I am going to tell you of [Mrs. Skatt's] children and her charming history which will explain why you are sitting here poor, ignorant and stupid with bad backs" (99). However, Dover announces his awareness of the failure that is probably inherent in the prospect of "getting it [e]xactly": "he [Yarp] told a long weirded thing such as *I cant hope to repeat* only relying on my memory with my simular attempt" (100, my emphasis). Evoking notions of counterfeit simulation integral to contemporary discussions of a global, postindustrial economy of signs—the hyperreal "age of simulation" that "substitute[s] signs of the real for the real itself" (Baudrillard, *Simulations* 14)—Dover confesses the merely simulative ("simular") nature of his purportedly mimetic report in what is, ironically, his most honest utterance. At best, the "Report by Roonswent Dover" relies on a memory that is probably unreliable. At worst, it is a work of pure fantasy. All the while, it relies on the duplicitous representational medium of written language, however simulative it may be of natural speech.

Perhaps the Yarp's own eloquent lexis is meant to contrast with elements of Dover's pained, misspelt, and grammatically incorrect narrative: "Before this night is over I will be with her" (98); "Roonswent Dover, son of Grady and Miriam" (93); "It is over for her now. One last night of pleasure and it will be done" (101). However, immediately after Dover hears the Yarp's strange tale, the creature's characteristic archaism and linguistic command resounds temporarily in Dover's authorial voice: "Before no man could commence his tongue" (99). Similarly, at times Dover conjures a different sort of aesthetic, one that is not only more literate but more *literary:* the eerie evocation of the young mountain girl with "a dreadsome ancient sneer on her face" (94) or the snow that "made my truck ghosted" (97); the haunting image of the Indian pianist "playing something ghostly like what were wrote by a man with a long beard in a Asian castle and sung by his beautiful grand-daughter" (100); the slowed, gothic narrative hyperconsciousness (such as we might find in Edgar Allen Poe's writing) observable in his "lights flickering at the snow that were like gray scales, I finally got it, like gray fish scales aflapping on the glass" (96). Ultimately, Dover does triumph insofar as he manages to "repeat" the Yarp's "weirded," unknowable, and untellable tale, despite having confessed he is unable: it is the story that we are reading.

Unlike the articulate Yarp, Dover tells his story "quick," mistakes and all, as if to circumvent the charge of authorial mendacity. Yet these moments in the text where our narrator betrays an awareness of the artificiality of his language (and, we would assume, his supernatural subject) destabilize the author's truth telling at the very level of the story's language itself. By acknowledging that tall tales depend on linguistic contrivances to test their audience's credulity, "Evening of the Yarp" gives rise to considerations about the fraught nature of language, and specifically southern language. This recalls Hannah's *Black Butterfly* (1982), subsequently renamed "It Spoke of Exactly the Things" in *Captain Maximus* (1985), which provides a useful complement here. Anticipating the character Royce in Hannah's later "Through Sunset into the Racoon Night," an aspiring writer who laments the fallen condition of his "loser's language" or "jabber" (123–24), the self-reflexive narrator of *Black Butterfly* rebukes himself at various points, calling himself an explicit liar. For example, when describing a seascape with the metaphor "the rocks which are drunk hags with their time," he checks his hyperbolic poetic impulse with "No are not, liar. Remember, they are just it, themselves" (3). When we recall Dover's atmospheric description of the snow-flakes on his windshield "like gray fish scales" (96), the implication, perhaps, is that the more poetic and contrived, the falser or more fallen the language.

In keeping with the Yarp's aversion to legending as well as Homer's suspicion of the overrepresented, or "pickled," South in *Hey Jack!* (20), the narrator of *Black Butterfly* explicitly scorns the South's compulsion to tell stories about itself, preempting Royce's use of the word *jabber* as the antithesis of self-present or unmediated language that could speak of "exactly the things." Invoking a nonsouthern and non-American textual authority, Shakespeare, the *Black Butterfly* narrator chastises "the stinking chicken South [with] All this nimble jabber [. . .] to the point that you are scaring us shitless, good folks not worthy of shoveling Shakespeare's house of nightsoil" (3). This authorial anxiety over the constructedness of rhetorical language—ironically, necessary deployments of the tall tale–teller to persuade his audience—would certainly explain Dover's interest in retaining the qualities of spontaneous speech, which counters, at times, his increasing rhetorical confidence and lyrical proficiency as a raconteur. Despite asking us to "Xcuse me please for not correct" (89), our amateur yarn spinner retains an implicit cognizance of the aesthetic properties of stories to equal that of Hannah's other, more openly self-reflexive narrators.

The notion of the performative and constructed nature of regions underwriting "Evening of the Yarp" is integral to its value as a postregional text that dramatizes the fruitful coexistence of regional and postmodern. This is encapsulated when the sense of surrealism evoked by Dover's narrative, even while it appears to be dedicated to valorizing an idea of the true story (almost as a foil to the generic conventions of the tall tale), culminates in Dover's intimation of his local habitat as the very antithesis of the regionally placed or authentic: "It aint Arkansas or no real place" (92). Despite acknowledging his own Ozarkian ancestry and explicitly placing his Yarp "here in Arkansas" (95–96), Dover also claims that "[w]e must be higher, higher than all Arkansas and Missouri [i]n our county" (93), and his tale remains conspicuously displaced throughout. Dover's sentiments when he refuses to place his tale firmly or unequivocally (it *is* Arkansas, and it is *not*) appear to echo those of the previous story's narrator, who says in "Allons, Mes Enfants," "You could call my city Atlanta, although it's not. It hardly matters, but some approximations of Atlanta I find apt" (81). The passage epitomizes a sense of the geographically transplantable nature of place in a contemporary economy that reproduces images or "approximations" of local cultures and circulates these to national and transnational audiences, to the extent that it hardly matters, perhaps, where the original really is. "Through Sunset into the Raccoon Night" parodies this notion succinctly when one of its characters declares, "I never traveled. I never intend to travel. [. . .] We've got the big-screen TV and all the good stations. What more is there to see?" (113). The possibility here is that the image becomes the reality. Consumed by their audiences in place of the real thing, cultural reproductions gain a paradoxical authenticity.

Ostensibly, these arguments recall the phenomena of media-made Dixie and glocalization, regional identities becoming not only subsumed by but constituted from global cultural processes that might seem incompatible with the concept of the region. The reference to Atlanta above is further significant here if we agree that Atlanta symbolizes a self-conscious departure from Agrarian constructions of the supposedly more grounded premodern, precapitalist Old South, as well as being a city that has successfully constructed itself in the image of northern commercial hubs like New York, as Bone argues (*SOP* 159). However, in "Evening of the Yarp" the process of recognizing the textual contingency of a true story with an authentic sense of place happens even while a sense of place is poignantly upheld, even to the extent of the historical or geographical entrapment we might expect to find in the modernist fiction of Faulkner or Welty. Which is to say, Dover may emphasize the unreal aspects of a region that feels like "no real place" (92). But this directly follows the scene in which, driving in the mountains, he feels the peculiar oppressiveness of his home landscape as a burden, the arrangement of the local topography quite literally "squeezing in" on him (92). It seems that the postsouthern sense of place remains even while its constructed nature is acknowledged.

This notion of historical imposition, of the strong significance of place even or especially for the dis-placed outsider, is useful when thinking about the putative disappearance of contemporary American regions. Hutcheon points out a paradox of historical metafiction that is valuable in this respect. She writes that because the metafictional text actively foregrounds the storied nature of history, it "re-introduces historical context" even while (or I would suggest, because) it paradoxically "problematize[s] the entire question of historical knowledge" (*Poetics* 285–86). Michael Kreyling writes, similarly, that a critical paradigm of a South that has become historically "post"—in which authenticity and reality emerge as central concepts, at least insofar as they are problematic ones—does not completely deconstruct the past and meaning; rather, it "interrogate[s] the systems by which those entities have been [traditionally] known" (*Inventing* 155). In a language pertaining to Hutcheon's, Kreyling writes: "To put quotation marks around the real is not to efface the real; rather, it is to put it into a condition of multiple codes rather than the traditional realistic mimetic system. History still exists; [but] we now acknowledge that we know it through a system of representations rather than in an unmediated, direct way" (155). Conceptualizations of places become more authentic when they incorporate self-reflexivity about the "multiple codes" underwriting our understandings of the regional.

The region Dover depicts is both placed and placeless. It acknowledges its own fictionality ("It aint [. . .] no real place") at the same time that it is grounded in an awareness that "our county" is distinct from other places, within the South as much as within the broader United States, and of how the South's sociocultural shifts have impacted the inhabitants of different regions differently. The self-reflexive nature of Dover's narrative, which is highly self-conscious about the process of its own telling and the status of the story as a text, may well render distinctions based on metaphysical notions of authenticity and what Comer calls "an ethics of place" ("Exceptionalism" 160) severely problematic. However, Dover's fraught preoccupation with the very prospect of creating an authentic mountain tale that is related to an established local tradition signals Hannah's continued investment in precisely these concepts. By subverting the argument that postsouthern fiction has simply detached from a sense of tangible regional identity and cultural specificity, Hannah's story maintains a vestigial sense of regional authenticity even while apparently eschewing that authenticity in favor of postmodern textuality.

In *Rooting Memory, Rooting Place: Regionalism in the Twenty-First Century American South* (2015), Christopher Lloyd explores Cormac McCarthy's *The Road* (2006) as a similarly complicated mix of regional and postregional. Lloyd challenges Gray's interpretation of the novel, which argues that while it contains echoes of "perhaps East Tennessee, the author's Appalachian birthplace," as a text it is not regional but "postregional," or "postsouthern" (Gray, *After the Fall* 41, qtd. in Lloyd, *Rooting* 130). In support of his argument, Gray describes a scene from *The Road* not dissimilar to Dover's depiction of the surreal feeling of the Ozarks, concluding that the fact that "the journey down from the mountains occurs in a broader territory, between substantial fact and surreal dream" (Lloyd, *Rooting* 130) denies McCarthy's fictional setting any proper claim to regional specificity. Lloyd contends, however, that Gray's partial interpretation overlooks the "so many Southern signs and references littered across [McCarthy's work]" (131). I would agree that Gray posits an exclusivity between regional and postregional that Hannah also destabilizes, for example, by writing (as does McCarthy) very closely and persuasively on the local landscape as well as its idioms and traditions, however typically surreal its subjects. Much of these texts' energy comes, in fact, from this interplay of fiction and reality, place and displacement, and insider and outsider discourse (below), where neither is permitted finally to reign supreme.

It is useful to explore how tensions between real and "unreal" places have been articulated in the critical reception of postsouthern literature, and here Hannah's writing encourages a revision of Gray's arguments for what constitutes postregionalism in contemporary writing. If the implications for a foundational sense of place are that while in some respects "it hardly matters" where a place *really* is, or where regional distinctions are blurred or confused, then Hannah proposes that places continue to exert pressure on their inhabitants in ways that pertain distinctly to the regional while transcending rigid or metaphysical apprehensions of the real. In "Evening of the Yarp," Deacon Charles's accounts of his travels in California compress this dual sense of the slipperiness and persistence of the concept of American regionalism: "You say I went West to go East, how? Well, friends, there is a line in the ocean all stormy where everything gets backwards, that's how" (97). Geographical markers remain, but they are not as we have known them. If regional culture (the South, the Ozarks) cannot be fully known or represented except with a sense of anxious contingency, then a (performative) sense of authenticity can yet reside in our textual simulations of places.

This issue is integral to Hannah's metafictional aesthetic, where the artificiality of *writing* about the South as a referent is an active concern. By acknowledging the contingent and provisional nature of all storied compositions of historical reality, thinking about the South in terms of "the pragmatics (as opposed to the metaphysics) of authenticity" (*RS* 106) renders it no less real precisely for being in this condition. An important aspect of this paradox is that no legender's tale, in any historical moment, can finally be deemed the most truthful or sincere; distinctions based on a lexicon of authenticity and mimetic verisimilitude that claim a monopoly on these qualities are already dismantled at the core of the tall-tale tradition and not simply in a new postregional moment (where the monolithic South has disappeared). Kreyling may claim that there is "no escape from a world mediated through representations, no recourse to the totalizing and totally authoritative referent: [. . .] the South" (*Inventing* 155), but the South is not simply textualized out of existence in what Hutcheon calls "some infinite regress into textuality" (*Politics* 95). Instead, a new kind of regional authenticity is constructed in the interplay between authenticity and textuality and in recognizing the former's contingency on the latter. As with the implicit agreement between the tall tale–teller and his audience, *convincing* textual representations signal a crucial means by which the region can reemerge. The South might be preserved, or "pickled," in its own representations insofar as it can be authenticated with the making of fiction, which, equally paradoxically, acknowledges its own fictionality. Self-reflexive fiction makes its contribution to the real while drawing attention to its own textuality or phoniness.

Dover and the Yarp have a complex relationship to history and place because both are characterized, literally and figuratively, as outsiders. Dover occupies a liminal position on the threshold of adulthood, "a mountain man/boy nineteen first that day" (91). He is in literal transit with the hitchhiking Yarp, an eloquent, old-worldly shapeshifter who is physically other— "You never seen that brand nigh nowhere round here" (98)—and equally displaced—"A Yarp really belong in Europe or Asia [. . .], he dont like it here in Arkansas" (95–96). At the story's climax, the Yarp forecasts Dover's enduring masculine alienation: "Youre of the age where a woman has already touched you and touched you deeply"; "You are going to know whats wrong [with women] around here but you cant do nothing about it and that is your eternal curse" (101). At the same time, the creature confesses his own affinity with the boy: "Youd think not, but I tell you, even Ive been womaned" (101). Similarly, Dover's initial, disaffected musings foreshadow his later affiliation with the socially outcast other's philosophy, further solidifying the pair's important dramatic correspondence: "The sin of the old people I wondert what it was cause I dint feel it. The evil things of Roonswent Dover which is me werent felt by me like the others cause I had no feltedness of their kind of sin. I found out the Yarp did too" (91). Both Dover and his Yarp are detached from old tradition by way of their liminality.

Again, the Ozark setting is significant if we consider, for example, that Dover's alienation is not simply part of his adolescence (as Harry Monroe's was in *Geronimo Rex*); rather, it has what Bone terms a "sociospatial basis" (*SOP* 154). While Bone's term relates specifically to the urban space of Atlanta, Dover's socioeconomic prospects, as well as his "spatial" possibilities for escape, are severely limited by his being a member of poor white mountain culture, whose denizens are kept "sitting here [in the mountains], poor, ignorant and stupid with bad backs" (99). While Dover may be satirizing "hillbilly" stereotypes, the sociospatial basis of these characteristics is important because it offers a counter to Guinn's and others' claims for Hannah's allegedly resolute departure from modernist ideas about the (Faulknerian) inevitability of history and place.[2] Here, the local history Dover inherits—tainted with poverty, poor education, illness and disability, and crime—burdens its inhabitants with an analogous inability to move forward or escape.

It may be tempting to attribute this to the "backwardness" of southern mountain demographics, which perhaps have not yet become conceptually "post" in the way that less marginalized groups and their literatures have owing to the relatively late homogenization of America's mountain regions. Zackary Vernon, for example, in his article "Toward a Post-Appalachian Sense of Place" (2015) analyzes the seeming persistence of history in recent Appalachian writing by Ron Rash, Terry Roberts, and Charles Frazier, and he anticipates such fiction following the trajectory of postsouthern writing by commodifying and/or parodying outmoded notions of Appalachian exceptionalism. Whether or not we can attribute this to its "postness" or lack thereof, Hannah's story certainly dramatizes an imposing sense of history and place, both topographically, and in terms of material opportunities for individual agency and progress in a place where historical narratives appear to stifle new voices in a peculiarly indigenous way. Dover's inability to understand the sins of his community—notably, the sins of its *old* people (91)—is important, therefore, because it is expressive of contemporary cultural conditions from which both he and his Yarp feel themselves estranged. In this historical moment, modern southern mountain culture may have undergone irrevocable change, but old traditions still bear heavily on contemporary inhabitants, heirs to the "eternal curse" of an explicitly regional problem with a spatial basis: "what is wrong around *here*" (101, my emphasis). In a place steeped not just in old "sin" (for which Dover professes to have no "feltedness") but also in "old stories" (91), the present spatial landscape is mediated by an oppressive cultural mythology that can "make your back clammier, your head colder, your heart miserabler" (96). By transposing the old modernist southern-burden trope to a new socioeconomic and spatial realm (the poor white South of the Ozarks), Dover's postsouthern folktale dramatizes how a tangible sense of place is built and sustained by its storied representations.

Here (as in Hannah's "Even Greenland"), existing narratives stand as obstacles in the way of contemporary legenders as they attempt to make themselves heard or to lay claim to original or untold stories. Dover's story must contend with the Yarp tales of his grandfather, peers, neighbors, Don Nini, Gene James, and, crucially, Deacon Charles, as well as with the many other voices and anecdotes that are co-opted into his narrative. His belated position as an anxious new tale-teller acts as a surrogate for Hannah's post-southern generation of writers, where the new enters a fraught, Bloomian dialogue and must establish its value against the overbearing voices of the past. The question of contemporary aesthetic enervation is certainly a burning one in Hannah's writing, as it is in the South more broadly. Bone argues that in Fred Hobson's formulation of influence, literary "'latecomers' have forever fought futile, oedipal battles to overcome their poetic antecedents" (Bone, "Neo-Confederate" 85), and Axel Knoenagel stresses similarly that contemporary southern writers must "write in conscious relationship to tradition" (96), a tradition that Guinn argues "menaces, rather than informs" (103).

The nuance here is that Hannah's Ozarkian narrator takes on a tradition of outsider misrepresentations of local culture ("our country") at the same time that he must contend with stifling insider discourse, which remains very much alive. Thus, the recognizable trope above, with new (white) authors entering an overpopulated field from an anxiously belated standpoint, is ironic when we acknowledge the conspicuous *absence* of upland and poor white voices from the high southern modernist moment—such as we would find in the recent Appalachian fiction of Rick Bragg, Chris Offutt, and Ron Rash. W. Fitzhugh Brundage argues that this trend "draws attention to the [. . .] forgotten [and] misrepresented in southern history and memory" (*Memories Grow* 3), and Hannah's choice of fictional setting becomes further symbolic here as a means of destabilizing the concept of a South historically united in its (Confederate) cause, since the Ozarks were the site of "borderland rebellion" during the Civil War (Ingenthron and Van Buskirk's title). While it is tempting to view the Ozarkian fondness for legending as pertaining simply to the modernist compulsion to tell about the South, therefore, of course the Ozarks (like Appalachia) remained until relatively recently a distinctly underrepresented micro-South. Dover's upland South represents, as Appalachia does, a socioeconomically disenfranchised region typically excluded from fictional reconstructions of the South. Consequently, Hannah's fictional Ozarkian protagonist reclaims the agency of a self-constructed regional identity, one that challenges American popular myths about the impoverishment of "hillbilly" culture such as have been "documented" by the selective publications of the FWP.

The concept of southern literary "belatedness" being lent further political significance in the Mountain South is best dramatized when Dover self-consciously admits, "Now someways out of my fear [. . .] I thought I had evened with Deacon Charles. I had a true tale and would be the center of the lunch talkings for a long time. Gene James was only a fifth or eighth on what he'd seen true, at eighty or more" (99). Dover ends his tale with a direct and urgent appeal to the reader, among the story's most significant "meta" moments: "That makes me even or better than Deacon Charles, remember" (102). While he may exhibit the classic anxieties of the literary latecomer, it is crucial that Dover believes that his story not only equals (is "even" with) but probably trumps (is "better than") that of his literary forebear, Deacon Charles. The fact that this remarkable coup of outdoing the old stories is achieved in "hillbilly" vernacular is vital. Coming from a (fictional) micro-South typically excluded from mainstream southern literature, it indicates an anti-intellectualism to counter criticisms that bemoan the creative impoverishment of postsouthern aesthetics and charge southern literature after modernism with lacking the force of Southern Renaissance writing, Faulkner's most prominently (Hobson, *Southern Writer* 2, 10, 34). Such elitism has already been parodied, of course, by Dover's satiric reference to the "stupid" Arkansas mountainfolk (97, 99). While telling his tale signifies Dover's fall in some ways, in others it marks the successful resolution of the oedipal conflict (which is not simply futile) by creating a contemporary gothic yarn that more than stands up to its venerable literary inheritance.

Ayers declared that "from its very beginning, people have believed that the South was not only disappearing but also declining, defined against an earlier South that was somehow more authentic, real, more unified and distinct" (*All Over the Map* 69). By problematizing the whole concept of telling honestly about the South, "Evening of the Yarp" implies similarly that if this feat is not possible now, then it probably never was, as the region's long-running oral traditions suggest. Crucially, Dover designates "liar" Don Nini as the inheritor of an *ancient* Indian tradition of narrative treachery that predates not only the origins of white southern storying but also the "Great Modernisms," which supposedly were more attached to history and place and could therefore lay claim to the qualities of "originality, authenticity, and aesthetic value" now supposedly "depleted" (Jameson, *Postmod-*

ernism 198, 192). With this reference to a Native American tradition that predates even the very beginnings of modern American history itself, the likelihood is that a "truer" language of the South has never been operative.

If we agree that the perpetually disappearing South has always been "past" by its very nature and not just in recent formulations of post-place, then history and regionalism remain just as conceptually integral to post-southern aesthetics. They are simply figured differently, or in ways that have only recently gained a critical language to articulate their contingency, as focus shifts from historicity and a foundational sense of place to the coded processes (and political functions) of their representations. A storied sense of place is no less authentic, confirming Matthew Shipe's argument that, despite a popular critical vocabulary of regional displacement that can be attached to Hannah's texts, their metafictional aspect does not in fact "negate the value of place and region" in any simple way (109). If metafiction paradoxically reintroduces historical context while problematizing the very concept of historicity, then Hannah's postsouthern fiction can preserve a sense of the region in a postsouthern "artistic vision" that, in questioning the ethics of place and the very concept of the South therefore "need not leave the South behind" (Guinn 178).

Interrogating the systems by which the South has traditionally been known as real or authentic does not simply make regionalism obsolete. On the contrary, nonmonolithic conceptions of American regions, comprising multiple and often competing "codes," can be reconstructed according to a contemporary interpretative paradigm of textual contingency that becomes, paradoxically more honest. This earns the metafictional storyteller a claim to authenticity and a renewed sense or ethics of place. Recalling Wallace Stevens's proposal that "the exquisite truth is to know that it is a fiction and that you believe in it willingly" (163), Romine argues that the South may now be conceived of as "the fake South" but that it "becomes the real South through the intervention of narrative" (9). The push-pull dynamic surrounding the question of Dover's integrity as a reporter dramatizes this prospect well, prompting us to read for an authenticity that is simply not permitted by the genre even as the performance is legitimized by advertising its fakeness.

Henry Louis Gates declared that in a culture of simulations "authenticity remains essential: once you can fake that, you've got it made." Like the wish of the young author-narrator in Hannah's *Boomerang* to "make something happen in vacant air [that is] a sweet revenge on reality" (17), Dover's fantastical report of the "Evening of the Yarp" intends to parade the artificial ways in which it enacts *and therefore constitutes* a sense of its own (regional) integrity. The narrative continually draws the reader's attention to the contrivances of the story and the reasons that it is not really to be believed, prosecuting his aesthetic to the limit and challenging the reader's credulity at the same time. Meanwhile, its narrator goes to great lengths to make his a remarkably believable story, the perfect aesthetic simulation or lie. Because we readers are its audience, we are the final arbiters and guarantors of regional authenticity in the performance we have witnessed. If we believe it, our narrator becomes a convincing liar who has not only "seen the Yarp" but discovered Stevens's "exquisite truth." Or something like it.

6

Narcissistic Narrative and the New Language of the Post-South

"Get Some Young"

"Get Some Young," the lead story of *High Lonesome* (1996), Barry Hannah's last collection published during his lifetime, is unique in Hannah's canon. It is longer, fuller, and denser than the other stories in the collection (and in much of Hannah's broader oeuvre). Stylistically, the story is extraordinary. In a relatively static tale spanning just a few short days, the drama resides as much in the language deployed to tell it as it does in the narrative events themselves. "Get Some Young" also occupies a unique position in relation to the structure of *High Lonesome*. If "A Creature in the Bay of St. Louis" and "Uncle High Lonesome" provide the collection's two bookends (the latter ends by making the imaginative return to the old Bay St. Louis that the former promised), then "Get Some Young" stands apart as a precursor to the collection at large, as if to demand that we abandon our preconceptions of what southern writing is capable of or what it will perform in this particular set of stories. "Get Some Young" is different in ways that present a series of specific hermeneutic challenges, and Hannah's creative interpretation of the metafictional aesthetic makes "Get Some Young" the culmination of some of the key elements of his fiction, and of my arguments about its value.

While in many respects "Get Some Young" provides the most striking instance of the new kind of self-reflexive southern lexicon that Hannah is forming, this story is not obviously metafictional in the same way that most other Hannah texts are. It contains no central artist figure to suggest that storytelling or the writing of fiction is a principal concern. The more obviously metafictional stories I have discussed have a ready critical language to invoke when writing about them, while "Get Some Young" requires readers to unpack its subtleties to discern the ways that it can be considered metafictional. What is "meta" in this story happens at such a minutely close semantic level (even down to individual word choice) that it cannot be called metafictional in the traditional sense, but it is nevertheless deeply self-conscious about itself as the product of a new kind of aesthetic in the making. I interpret "Get Some Young" as an internalization of the metafictional strategies that are more apparent in Hannah's other works, and in the other *High Lonesome* stories especially. Whether consciously or not, Hannah's interrogation of the character and value of southern writing at the end of the twentieth century seems to have been woven into the very fabric and linguistic patterns of this text. It signals an extraordinarily innovative literary form, but one that has been created from its author's questioning the ways we would attribute aesthetic value (and have done historically).

"Get Some Young" is a story about south-central Mississippi in a particular historical moment. It asks what it means to write that South historically without making writing or the South obvious thematic concerns. It is a cautionary tale about what is wrong with the society of southern Mississippi, where adults (and especially men) are pathologically nostalgic, preying vicariously on the young to reverse the passage of time and reclaim an imagined grace period predating the dysfunctions of the present. As one middle-aged male character (Tuck) aptly confesses of his predacious behavior toward adolescent boys, "I am a vampire I am a vampire" (13). These words also resonate at the parallel level of aesthetic (if not metafictional) inquiry, where "Get Some Young" signals a parasitical literary excavation of multiple historical discourses. This offers a means of not only questioning but *affirming* the text's own contemporary cultural value as the product of a postsouthern literary culture. While anxiously postmodern as far as it is heavily preoccupied with discourse and texts, the story also has its origins in a distinct material history among the "Civil War ghoulments" (25) that lie beneath the Mississippi river Strong, which acts as the locus of events and which the story references directly throughout. This chapter examines how the issues raised by the story's social inquiry speak to broader conceptualizations of what it means to tell about the South at this time.

To pursue this story's unique value as a product of postsouthern culture, we must contemplate what political comment its internalized metafictional strategies seem to make on the contemporary status of the South as a social reality and literary subject. Can writing that is both acutely introspective regarding its own contrivances of style (Hutcheon coined the term *narcissistic narrative* in 1980 to describe this) and also aware that *South* is (and always has been) in many ways an arbitrary term still be called authentically southern? "Get Some Young" resolves this paradox by creating persuasive, new southern writing from its own self-reference; it ties up the various threads of my inquiry so far in regard to how we might go about determining regional authenticity in terms of language and performance, masculinity, history and nostalgia, and postsouthern literary aesthetics. I also expand on some existing interpretations of Hannah's story to show how its significance far exceeds what has been attended to so far in its critical reception, as if fresh interpretative paradigms ought to be created if we are to come close to articulating what "Get Some Young" represents as a text.

William Caverlee describes "Get Some Young" as "Barry Hannah's late love song to Mississippi," in which the author's linguistic inventions, closer to poetry or music than to prose in Caverlee's view, reach their peak. In my first chapter, on *Geronimo Rex*, I argued that Harry Monroe's *Künstlerroman* involves contemplating the possibility of an authentic articulation of subjectivity in writing. Harry finds at least partial resolution in creating a "musical" writerly tone, as Hannah described in an early interview with Robert Vanarsdall. The tone of "Get Some Young," however, is distinctly linguistic: language, not music, is its chief concern. Yet this is not a postmodern kind of linguistic play that obscures the historical referent beneath; as noted, Hannah has repeatedly shunned both the labels "southern" and "postmodern" (Vice 17) and even declared himself an "elder modernist" in a late (2010) interview with Wells Tower. Unlike *Geronimo Rex*, in which language was made to appear to transcend the confines of its linguistic medium (becoming more musical, epiphanic, more curiously self-present), "Get Some Young" does not shy away from language seen for what it is, as something tricky, contingent, socially and politically inflected, and historically mutable.

As a text, "Get Some Young" is an account of multiple historical languages that have been collected together in a particular moment in history, the voices of the past ventriloquized through the narrative in a series of intertextual citations and speech acts brought into conversation with the present. We might characterize its linguistic strategy as a pastiche of cultural discourses in which fragments of past cultures are wrenched from their "high" cultural contexts and presented alongside the languages of popular and mass consumer culture, a Baudrillardian "playing with the pieces" of art forms already produced, perhaps (Baudrillard, *Baudrillard Live* 95). In Hannah's text, however, these past languages are not simply featured as "dead" (or even *past*) cultural artifacts, because they are successfully reanimated by their contemporary inflections. Just as metafictional writing interrogates the forms and processes of its own composition, "Get Some Young" provides a compelling dramatic disquisition on the nature and value of postsouthern literary aesthetics in relation to a history of antecedent southern cultural forms with which the new is in dialogue. The story therefore lends itself especially well to analysis in the context of Bakhtin's theory of dialogism in *The Dialogic Imagination,* where the "dialogic" work exists with other literary works in an ongoing process of "re-accentuation" (421) that is mutually informative rather than indicative of nostalgic cultural decay.[1] It is a process of going back in order to go forward, in classic southern fashion, but with this distinctly antinostalgic or dialogic bent Hannah's text departs from the Agrarian origins of this practice.

Hannah's use of Sophocles's *Oedipus Rex* parable, inflected in the much later contexts of Freudian psychoanalysis and Jungian individuation theory (below), provides a neat example of this concept of history experienced in continual dialogue. The polyphonic fusion of languages in "Get Some Young" has been wrested from Christian religious discourse; from oral cultures, including Greek mythology and Southern Gothic folklore; from literary quotations from British and European modernism; from the lexis of psychoanalytical and feminist studies; as well as from the voices of high and low culture, Hollywood and the media, popular music, and the contemporary southern vernacular. "Get Some Young" also seems to anticipate the various interpretative paradigms we might bring to bear on it, only to dismantle or outrun them. Ultimately, none of the established cultural myths or historical metanarratives that Hannah so self-consciously proffers to his readership prove sufficient to extricate the complexities of the story's characters and events. The competing play of discourses alongside shifting and multiple perspectives renders "Get Some Young" a far cry from the mythical "plainer language" that might have offered a simpler window on the world (Hannah, "Uncle High Lonesome" 222). Instead, we have a kind of pressure cooker of intensified language in use across history—Bakhtin emphasizes the importance of "speech acts," "utterances," and "parole" when discussing language as a reflection of different sociohistorical circumstances (*Dialogic* xxi)—that instantaneously incorporates a freeze-framed picture of late-twentieth-century southern Mississippi, while placing this in relation to a much wider-reaching matrix of antecedent cultures and (inter)texts that have informed it, and that *it* can inform, even retrospectively.

In his insightful discussion of Hannah's "anti-myth method," James B. Potts draws on Philip D. Beidler's claim that Hannah's "protean" and often "ungraspable" narratives seem intent "on befuddling academic critics" (Beidler, qtd. in Potts, "Anti-Myth" 237) by invoking established cultural mythologies only to complicate or surpass them. I would agree that "Get Some Young" certainly unsettles familiar literary conventions and philosophical theories, to the extent that they do not aid our critical understandings in any simple way. The simultaneity with which Hannah's text consumes the critical discourses of history, while challenging us to apply them to it, foregrounds the difficult politics of historical representation (writing) and interpretation (reading) in any given moment. To properly understand *this* story, we must mine the repository of existing critical languages to show how it is considerably new or different, how the narrative itself cannibalizes the cultural discourses of different historical moments for aesthetic effect—the revival of what we might call dead languages is a crucial part of Hannah's formal strategy here—to create a radically innovative form of postsouthern writing.

Several Hannah critics have variously accentuated the linguistic allusiveness and density of Hannah's late writing, but without pursuing its cultural significance much beyond verifying its kinship with typically late-twentieth-century forms of aesthetic experimentation and linguistic play. Similarly, if Hannah seems to be parodying something with "Get Some Young," it is hard to determine exactly what, or why. Cormac McCarthy, a southerner himself, has acknowledged his debt to his literary antecedents and has been famously quoted as saying that "the ugly fact is books are made out of books" and that writing "depends for its life" on the writing that precedes it (R. Woodward, "Venomous Fiction").[2] This idea that literature is a Frankenstein's monster of all the books that have come before it is of heightened political significance in the context of the South's anxious literary influence, as we have seen in Hannah's dramatic enactments of the problem of originality in "Even Greenland," "Evening of the Yarp," and "A Creature in the Bay." This concept of new writing being pieced together from past works is especially useful here, for it evokes nostalgic ideas about mediatization (Baudrillard) and pastiche (Jameson), compared with more positive critical theorizations of heteroglossia (Bakhtin) and parody (Hutcheon). It also speaks to a concept imagined by T. S. Eliot in *The Waste Land*, of amassing the "fragments" (430) of past cultures and making art from them, renewing the (sterile) present by mining the resources of the past in creative new ways.

This notion of ventriloquism—to which Eliot's early working title, "He Do the Police in Different Voices" (itself ventriloquizing Dickens), alludes—invites initial comparison with Jameson's formulation of pastiche as a contemptible genre that has replaced (political) parody in the postmodern age: "Pastiche is [. . .] the imitation of a peculiar or unique, idiosyncratic style, the wearing of a linguistic mask, speech in a dead language" (*Postmodernism* 17). Jameson sees this as a downward turn from modernism, where individual authors (Faulkner is mentioned specifically in Jameson's study) could be characterized by their individual, "inimitable" styles (16), styles that the lesser postmodernists can only imitate in the absence of any true originality of their own. In Jameson's view of pastiche, "modernist styles [. . .] become postmodernist codes," leaving nothing but "a field of stylistic and discursive heterogeneity without a norm" (17). Heterogeneity—and heteroglossia, to use Bakhtin's term—are certainly prevalent features of "Get Some Young" that might initially be thought to support Jameson's contention that postmodern cultural productions amount merely to "the cannibalization of all the styles of the past, the play of random stylistic allusion" (18). In Jameson's view of pastiche our connection to history is lost, turned into a series of "random" signs, simulacra, and "codes," a repository of the *images* of the past to be mined and commodified without properly understanding it: "all that is left is to imitate dead styles, to speak through the masks and with the voices and styles in the imaginary museum" (*Postmodernism* 18).

"Get Some Young" in fact directly rebukes these arguments, even while it appears to be dramatizing itself as a form of postmodern pastiche that cannibalizes the voices and styles of a historical repository of texts, images, or "ghoulments" (25). This model is instructive when applied to conceptualizations of the South, a cultural identity that has traditionally imagined the past being an integral part of the present; it is not even "dead" in the same way that Jameson imagines it here. With its staged presentation of historical discourses, it is crucial that the story retains at both the thematic *and* *linguistic* levels a distinctly regionalized interest in history. Many of the stories discussed so far seem to interrogate the tricky nature of contemporary language, and they question whether an insurmountable impasse between regional and global, southern and postmodern, has emerged. By integrating these tensions into its own language, "Get Some Young" not only stands as a remarkable affirmation of the South—authenticating the relevance of its regional history, its contemporary literary productions; it is testimony even to the value of its languages *for their own sake*—but is one of the most remarkable narratives of late-twentieth-century (southern) fiction.

"Get Some Young" is the coming-of-age tale of five white southern boys—Swanly, Walthall, Bean, Arden Pal, and Lester Silk. The teens travel from Jackson, Mississippi, to the Strong River as they do every year, a retreat to an adult-free camp where they drink homemade peach wine, play music, and tell stories "reminiscent of serious acts never acted, women never had" (23). This time, however, on the threshold of adulthood, something is different: "It was their fourth trip to the Strong and something was urgent now [. . .]. They were not at peace and were hungry for an act before the age of school job money and wife" (10). This early sense of time running out resonates much more ominously as the story unfolds, and as Hannah puns with increasing gravity on the concept of "the act," referring ultimately to the act of sex (*BH* 62). The sense of urgency is caught in Hannah's title, an idiomatic amalgamation of the boys' juvenile wish to get some sex while they are young and the story's nostalgic adult characters' aberrant longing to get some sex *from* someone young, as if to "get" young again themselves. More than simply a teenage coming-of-age tale, then, "Get Some Young" acts as a social inquiry of unchecked southern nostalgia, a motif that resonates strongly with Edward Ayers's contemporaneous (1995) contention that nostalgia has always been an integral part of the southern imaginary (*All Over the Map* 69).

Of all the boys, Swanly is especially beautiful, with a wraithlike purity about him, "like a Dutch angel" (5), "a piece of [. . .] Attic statuary" (24), or "the avatar on the bow of a ship" (27). Because of Swanly's otherworldly allure, the teenagers' "sanctuary" is soon "ruined" (26) by three adult intruders: Tuck, a bitter, middle-aged veteran of Korea, who runs the local store, with his attractive younger wife, Bernadette, and a river-dwelling hermit called Sunballs (Tuck's nemesis). The three voyeurs cannot help but spy on and lust after Swanly ("They're watching you, Swanly!" [25]), transfixed by his beauty because it provokes a profound (gendered) nostalgia in them for lost youth. Swanly's chief predator is Tuck, who succeeds in luring the boy to his house to drug and seduce him into enacting a disturbing version of a ménage a trois with Bernadette, a quasi-spiritual "rite" (35) that in the story's gothic climax causes extensive collateral damage to participants and witnesses alike. Tuck bemoans his own aging as well as his wife's, but while the couple despise each other with "silent equal fatigue" (3), they find a shared renewed passion in Swanly. Thus, (the) youth becomes the sacrificial lamb, the means by which the elder couple might invert their own botched historical narratives in their quest for lost (American) innocence, a feat described in a worrying coalescence of religious language, childish naïveté, and illicit sex: "The boy savior, child, and paramour at once" (33).

Earlier, as the boys journey downriver "from the large city some miles North," talking dirty and making fun of the locals in the small towns they pass through (4), their initial cocksure obliviousness to the threat awaiting them "out in the river boonies" (32) lends Hannah's narrative a sense of impending danger, which Caverlee suggests is redolent of Faulkner's *Sanctuary* or Poe's "The Tell-Tale Heart." Potts further identifies the correspondence between the hidden adult perversity lurking in remote rural Mississippi and James Dickey's 1970 novel, *Deliverance* ("Anti-Myth" 243). Yet despite the boys having taunted Sunballs with "You been wantin' it, [. . .] Been beggin' for it, [. . .] Come get some!" (12), in Hannah's story it is not the backwoods hermit the youths should have been wary of but rather Tuck and Bernadette, who prove themselves to be far more sinister than the boys' early perceptions of the pair as overfamiliar but harmless "Busybod[s]" (26) foretold. A sense of unease, of something menacing lurking beneath the surface, is initially corroborated by the opening descriptions of Tuck as a hateful man who "felt clever in his beard and believed that his true expressions were hidden" (3). It is sustained in the marked discrepancies between the couple's innocuous outward speech ("I'm just a friendly man in a friendly store" [5]) and their tormented and often violent inward thoughts before finally coming to full fruition when the pair succeed in "getting some young," after which none of the story's characters will ever be the same.

Swanly's sexual initiation at the hands of Tuck and Bernadette is witnessed by Sunballs, who spies through a window "bewitched like a pole-axed angel" in equal disgust and desire: "he commenced to rutting on the scabbard of his knife grabbed desperately to his loins but immediately also to call out scolding as somebody who had walked up on murder" (36). The language of sex, violence, and death extends to Swanly's depiction thereafter: in a poignant evocation of the Fall, the boy's "nudity was then like one dead, cut down from joy," and "overcome by grief and nausea," his horrified peers "could not bear to see him. He was not the bright shadow of their childhoods anymore" (36, 39). Finally, the narrative proceeds with an act of doubled retrospection to project this unbearable historical scene into the future. The story ends when, "Some fourteen years later," then adult Walthall is suddenly "struck by a nostalgia he could not account for," and he makes an impromptu diversion from his planned trip to Florida to return to Tuck's old store. He is met with the chilling apparition of Bernadette (Tuck has since died), a now "almost unrecognizable and clearly mad old woman" wearing the decayed remains of Swanly's old football jersey, who, when confronted about Swanly's whereabouts, "began to scream without pause" (41). Transplanted back to that same unwelcome spectacle those fourteen years prior that Walthall "couldn't forgive he was ever obliged to see" (34), we are told finally that "[t]he vision was so awful he fled almost immediately and was not right in Boca Raton nor much better when he came back home" (41). Closing the story with this unwelcome visitation of trauma, Hannah's tale of historical repetition, characterized by cycles of loss, regret, and violence, is inflected with a distinct regional specificity at both the thematic and formal levels.

In "Get Some Young," the gothic way that adults anxious about their own aging prey on the young in an attempt to reverse history is captured in Tuck's fantasy of shape-shifting renewal by "getting" Swanly: "All execrable minutes, all time regained. I would live backwards until I took the shape of the boy myself" (29). Tuck's similarly rapacious behavior toward adolescent boys when he was a Scout leader establishes a motif of youth being ingested by the "old" that underwrites "Get Some Young": "It was not clear whether he wished to ingest them or exterminate them or yet again, wear their bodies as a younger self, all former prospects delivered to him again" (4). Hannah's earlier story "Revealed: Rock Swoon Has No Past" offers a directly equivalent image with its (repeated) refrain, "Pa. Is it true the old eat their young?" (261). The narrative drama concerns cannibalism, therefore, while the story's language cannibalizes.

Ruth D. Weston argues that "Get Some Young" is a dramatization of "the modern psyche which succumbs to the contemporary cult of youth, in a postmodern parable of the dysfunctional family, whose obsessions drive them into more and more aberrant behavior" (*BH* 61). Potts agrees that "Hannah twists the paradigm of individuation in Freud's [oedipal] theory: instead of the formative child modeling upon the adult Ego Ideal, the adult becomes obsessed with the child" ("Anti-Myth" 243). These interpretations of oedipal failure relate directly to misplaced and unfettered adult nostalgia. Tuck's wish to possess Swanly is therefore part of a narcissistic project of reclaiming his own younger self, "my dead little boyhood" (16), believing that the child's history, unlike the adult's, has not yet been determined. It is the youth's preoedipal state—"He was all boy but between genders" (29)—that so enamors Tuck, who perceives himself, by contrast, as "the final waste product of all maturity [. . .], a creature fired-out full molded by the world, the completed grown-up" (17). Notably, however, Tuck covets Swanly's boyhood because of his belief that "[m]y own boyself was eat up by the gooks and then this strolling wench" (29). These two points of historical calamity directly associate Tuck's coming of age with martial (his enlistment in Korea) and marital (his marriage to Bernadette) duty. Thus, the boyhood that Tuck mourns has been devoured, he imagines, by these external social factors, lending Tuck's nostalgia a historical specificity unacknowledged in Weston's broader attribution of the postmodern "cult of youth" being responsible for the contemporary failure of the family.

Both Weston's disquisition on postmodernism and Potts's application of Greek mythology and Freudian theories of subjectivity suggest that the social problems of "Get Some Young" are both a spinoff of postmodern culture and part of a much more timeless model of human sexual development. However, I would argue that the issues Potts and Weston identify as part of a global postmodern culture can be placed into much sharper regional focus. While oedipal dysfunction is certainly a central aspect of the social malady Hannah dramatizes, we can situate it amid regionally specific understandings of what has gone so awry in (recent?) southern history that southern white men mourn the loss of their youth in a way that not only prevents them from maturing properly or aging gracefully but manifests in abusive predatory behavior toward those who have not yet matured themselves. Here, neither the concept of some universalized wistfulness for lost childhood nor that of a postmodern culture that fetishizes youth in the absence of historical referents supports the idea of Tuck's nostalgia being the direct result of the limited opportunities for working-class white men in this culture.

This latter prospect is amplified significantly when we learn that Walthall, a creative boy whose "impressions were quicker and deeper than those of the others" (11), is destined to follow in Tuck's military footsteps because of his family's restrictive socioeconomic circumstances. In a moment of pathos the narrator reveals, "But he would go in the navy. There was no money for college right away" (11).[3] This sense of the future being radically curtailed is dramatically enacted when, while Swanly is being "instructed in ways of the adult world" by Tuck and Bernadette (7), the other boys, drunk, project with morbid historical foresight the course of their adult futures in miniature, in "great parlor anguish swooning like people in berets near death" (23). Their tales uniformly end in tragedy and loss, with the boys "sore in gloom" and "defeated" (31) and, crucially, nostalgic as adults. Lester Silk, for instance, envisages a doomed romance, ending with, "Forever afterward I will whup my lap mournfully in her memory" (23). Somehow, the distant defeated future is already urgently present.

Because of the dismal prospects envisioned for men in this culture, Potts suggests of Tuck's social aberrance that "part of the scenario hints at *Huckleberry Finn* and *Tom Sawyer*" ("Anti-Myth" 243), two novels that recall Leslie A. Fiedler's description in *An End to Innocence* (1955) of an American tradition of fiction about men escaping domesticity (144). This interpretation would certainly account for Tuck's vehemently despising the figure of the hermit as a man who has exempted himself from male social and domestic responsibilities: "Sunballs was not that old either. [Tuck] was suddenly angry at the man. Above the fray, absent, out, was he? Well" (12). By contrast, Tuck remains trapped not only by his marriage and his experience of war, the former having suffered as a result of the latter ("Since he had returned from Korea he and his wife lived in mutual disregard" [3]), but also by his participation in capitalist consumer culture, where, as Sunballs puts it, "Nothing ain't a tenth its value and a man's soul knows it's true" (20). In an apt conveyance of the concept of Marxist alienation, the aisles of Tuck's own store are made to seem in Swanly's presence "a fantastic dump of road offal brought in by a stranger" (22). Resultantly, and paralleling both the teenagers' boyish withdrawal to "a river pirates playhouse" outside the imminent realm of adult responsibility (26) and Sunballs's willful abstention from civilization and domesticity, Tuck despises (and envies) the hermit and fetishizes Swanly's boyishness for each one's exemption from the entrapments (patriotic, domestic, mercenary) of the adult male "fray."

Because Swanly offers a "double" for Tuck's character in key ways, our impressions of dysfunctional nostalgia as a distinctly *southern* malady are strengthened. Possessed of an astute historical consciousness akin to Tuck's, and mindful of the implacable advancement of time, Swanly is described as "a prescient boy" who "hated that their youth might end" and who "had felt his own beauty drawn from him in the first eruption of sperm, an accident in the bed of an aunt by marriage whose smell of gardenia remained wild and deep in the pillow" (5, 6). Swanly's crippling forward precognition of his own aging—"He saw the foul gloom of job and woman ahead, [. . .] the counting of diminished joys like sheep with plague" (6); "[he] felt ahead of him the awful tenure in which a man shuffles up and down the lanes of a great morgue" (10)—mirrors Tuck's retrospective perception of the "horrible millions of minutes collected and evident" behind him (28), such that the two characters become curiously interchangeable. On the cusp of adulthood, Swanly knows that to retain his boyhood is impossible, which both frightens and saddens him and gains tragic import when we realize that by the end of the story Swanly's "boy ways" will be a thing of the past (7). The retrospection of the adult meets the foresight of the child, such that neither character inhabits a coherent present, and a perverse transposition of youth and age has occurred.

As noted, "Get Some Young" is a doubly retrospective narrative, further implying the unique significance of southern history to narratives about historical circularity, or how history is experienced as a process of recurrence in the local imaginary. The grotesque "vision" at the end of the tale of the screaming Bernadette—who has aged disproportionately (another instance of temporal anachronism: the "nearly toothless" and "old woman" [41] or "Hag" [40] was an attractive woman in her thirties only fourteen years earlier) but is yet suspended in the historical moment of her tryst with Swanly—signals an aesthetic staging of the gothic phenomenon in which the past is not dead or even past. Just as Bernadette is reminded of her historical loss in the image of Walthall, so too is Walthall momentarily transplanted back to the same unwelcome spectacle that befell him as an adolescent those fourteen years prior. The aesthetic strategy of doubled retrospection captures the sense of history repeating: both Walthall and Bernadette fall prey to the sudden reanimation of a pivotal event from the past that prevails upon the present but without offering any solace or reparation. Weston argues that Bernadette's closing scream is an aesthetic device typical of experimental postmodernism that is meant to signal "a darkly ambiguous ending [that] withholds a final revelation" (*BH* 41), but I would contend instead that its real significance lies in the sense of (southern) circularity that this final act of temporal slippage lends Hannah's story. Repeating its historical traumas beyond the temporal confines of the present, the story's formal strategies significantly reinforce its self-staged southernness, in which characters are trapped in histories whose events are not only burdensome but recurring. Not only is a sense of historical regression part of the story's nostalgia theme, therefore, but the temporal inversions become a key feature of the story's regional aesthetic, even while it is conspicuously pieced together from historical discourses (classical, biblical, Freudian) that are much more wide-ranging.

Hannah's southern take on a postmodern problem of historicity is intensified at the level of the story's intertextuality. The story presents a series of staged narratives of historical defeat: the oedipal myth, with the sins of fathers vested onto sons; the Christian parable of original sin, with the Fall inevitable; the Christ sacrifice; Korea (certainly not an American victory, if not a defeat), a precursor to the nation's pivotal military failure, Vietnam. In chapter 2 I discussed the Vietnam War as a means of southernizing a national narrative of defeat, or of retrospectively northernizing the South's imagined uniqueness as a defeated region. Here, once again, Vietnam marks an important event in rethinking the distinctions between regional and national, with northerners forced to recognize the contingency of the triumphalist and American-innocence mythologies with which they had separated themselves from their southern counterparts. The memory of white southern defeat (discussed in chapter 3) might be brought most violently back into the contemporary southern consciousness with the national defeat of the Vietnam War, whose outbreak Tuck would have witnessed just two years after returning from Korea in 1953. Each war narrative is offered as a means of understanding historical failure as a specifically southern problem, because it evokes the cultural myth of the Lost Cause; the story's "Civil War ghoulments" (25) might be read as a reminder of the (white) South's primal defeat, of which Korea or Vietnam are mere repetitions. The historical origins that the loss-of-innocence metanarrative posits—preadulthood, prewar, premodernity—are each related directly back to the question of what has gone wrong not only in contemporary Mississippian culture but perhaps with the South's, and America's, own formative histories more broadly conceived, where the concept of breaking cycles of violence and loss is truncated when the ills of the past are repeated as if inexorably.

The problem of cultural stasis in the South is caught neatly in Tuck's conception of marriage. In an image that invokes Robert Brinkmeyer's arguments about southerners being excluded from American fantasies about freedom of movement, or "going West" (14–15), Tuck broods, "Fore you know it you got her spread around you like a tree and fat kids. You [. . .] ain't going nowhere even in an automobile on some rare break to Florida, no you just a rolling tree" (14). Similarly, when spying on Swanly bathing naked in the Strong, Tuck (rightly) imagines: "Already Tuck knew the boy had no good father, his home would stink of distress. He had known his type in the Scouts, always something deep-warped at home with them, beauty thrown up out of manure like" (12–13). This idea of common and identifiable "types" in the poor white South suggests the tragedy of this recurrent historical narrative ("*always* something deep-warped at home").[4] It is this "stock" character's want of paternal care that makes him the easy victim of sexual abuse, revealed when Hannah's omniscient third-person narration takes a sudden disturbing turn into second-person free indirect discourse (Tuck's): "A boy like that you had to take it slow but not that much was needed to replace the pa, in his dim criminal weakness. You had to show them strength then wait until [. . .] that hazy fog of moment when thought required act, the kind hand of Tuck in an instant of transfer to all nexus below the navel, no more to be denied than those rapids they're hollering down, nice lips on the boy too" (13). Again, the corruption of the oedipal narrative in this culture—Tuck's reassuring Swanly that "[o]lder ones are here to teach and guide the young" just before having sex with him is especially sinister here (33)—speaks to the southern historical predicament at the heart of the story, the sense of historical paralysis in which dysfunctional cultural narratives repeat themselves indefinitely.

This idea is protracted when each of the five boys has a father who is either "dead" (30) or "a failure" (10), to the extent that Swanly is "a full orphan" in Bean's view (30). This anticipates Scott Romine's 2007 article "Orphans All: Reality Homesickness in *Yonder Stands Your Orphan*," which interprets the orphan trope in Hannah's last novel as a metaphor for cultural and familial degeneration in the (postmodern) South, ideas that we can clearly see played out in Hannah's earlier text. Again these notions are encapsulated in both titles, "Get Some Young" and *Yonder Stands Your Orphan* (the latter taken from Bob Dylan's "It's All Over Now, Baby Blue"), seemingly trivial colloquialisms or references to contemporary pop culture that in fact are expressive of these much graver social failures in the South. The failure of the symbolic father in these narratives further invokes Michael Kimmel and Michael Kaufman's argument that in a culture where there is no essential masculinity (recall chapter 2) the male yearning for the illusive "deep masculine" constitutes "a search for lost boyhood, that homosocial innocence of preadolescence" (281). The poet Robert Bly, one of the main promotors of the so-called mythopoetic or new men's movement of the 1980s and 1990s (the focus of Kimmel and Kaufman's criticism), contentiously pioneered a return to the concept of "essential" rather than patriarchal masculinity. Directly recalling Tuck's distaste for the "consumption" of his own innocence by patriarchal expectations (military service, marriage, and work), Bly's idiosyncratic conception views patriarchy as having a "destructive essence" that "moves to kill the young masculine" (qtd. in Kimmel, *Politics* 272). The idea is that some return to an essential(ist) masculinity might be possible outside the social structures of modern patriarchal society, described by Kimmel and Kaufman as "an effort to turn back the clock to that time before work and family responsibilities yanked men away from their buddies" (281). But of course it is precisely the nostalgic pursuit of this erroneous original masculine innocence that drives the tragedy of Hannah's story.

Judith Gardiner argues that the mythopoetic men's movement encourages adult men to conceive of themselves as fatherless sons rather than responsible fathers (102), aptly analogous to the "motherless [and fatherless] pirates" trope in "Get Some Young" (24), in which the boys' flight from work and responsibility to family and women, or as Swanly conceives it, "school job money whore" (10), is encapsulated. This interpretation would explain Tuck's implicit "envy of the hermit [Sunballs]" (12): Tuck imagines that in shirking the responsibilities of husbands and fathers, Sunballs has somehow managed to turn back the clock, captured in Tuck's descriptions of the man as "ageless" (10) and "a scot-free thief of time" (14). Therefore, while "Get Some Young" is not a critique of nostalgia for an alleged authentic South in the same way that I argued "Rat-Faced Auntie" was, the social aberration of its characters' nostalgia for lost boyhood is a distinct part of being white, working class, and male in this culture, "courtesy of the Southern regions," as Walthall neatly puts it (26).

I mentioned earlier the gendered nostalgia of Hannah's protagonists. Bernadette's own inappropriate infatuation with Swanly stems from an equally tormenting inability to come to terms with her own gendered history and loss as a mother with grown-up sons: "Her own boys were hammy and homely and she wandered in a moment of conception, giving birth to Swanly all over again as he stood there, a pained ecstasy in the walls of her womb. He was what she had intended by everything female about her" (21). The vision of Swanly's boyish beauty allows Bernadette to make an imaginative regress back to conception and birth, like Tuck's fantasy of living backwards to "renew his person" (22). In the (incestuous) fantasy of "giving birth to Swanly all over again," the boy morphs into a surrogate for the woman's grown sons. On several occasions when she beholds Swanly, birth and death, fear and desire paradoxically coexist in Bernadette: "she felt away on palisades over a sea of *sweetening terror*"; "a wave of *terrible exhilaration* overcame her" (21, 25, my emphases). At the moment of their tryst, when Tuck invites Swanly "to examine their lovely Bernadette since he had never seen a woman," the boy is "pulled inward through love and death and constant birth gleefully repeated by the universe" (35). Similarly, Tuck's idea of "the act" merges sex, conception, birth, and death: "It ain't pondering or chatting or wishing it's only the act, from dog to man to star all nature either exploding or getting ready to" (15). Hannah's representation of female nostalgia (however problematic) is something defined by a woman's relationship to maternity and, specifically, to bearing male sons. Tuck is nostalgic for his own lost boyhood, while Bernadette is nostalgic for her sons', but ultimately the maternal desire to possess (the) youth is as corrupted as the paternal, "somewhere between mother love and bald lechery" (21).

These juxtapositions of life and death, terror and exhilaration, ecstasy and pain, are explored by William Patrick Day in his study of gothic fantasy, *In the Circles of Fear and Desire,* which argues that gothic (like Freudian) systems of thought, in which dreams, nightmares, Eros, and Thanatos collide, are a direct response to "the problems of selfhood and identity, sexuality and pleasure, fear and anxiety" (181). We can see these ideas clearly enacted in Hannah's earlier story "Coming Close to Donna" (first published in *Esquire* in 1977), which merges sex and death in four dramatic pages reducing the oedipal fable to darkly comic absurdity. The culmination of "Get Some Young" also provides a grotesque parody of the Oedipus myth. The imminent violent showdown between Tuck and Sunballs sees the hermit blinded by Tuck as punishment for his unwelcome witness ("I can't see, moaned Sunballs. He never stopped hitting my eyes" [39]), a modern King Oedipus, who blinded himself in an abortive attempt to erase the horror of historical vision. However, this comic playfulness is notably absent from Hannah's portrayal of Bernadette's feminine nostalgia ("everything female about her"), which, in addition to catalyzing her own descent into gothic madness in the story's final scene, manifests in Swanly's tragic downfall, encompassed in a distinctly Joycean moment of linguistic compression worthy of the experimental opening line of *Finnegans Wake:* "Eden in the bed of Eros, all Edenwide all lost" (39).[5]

Here, besides drawing on classical, Freudian, and gothic conceptualizations of human sexuality inflected with a southern twist, "Get Some Young" also acts as both a parable of original sin (as noted) and a corruption of the Christ narrative. It is Sunballs's voyeuristic witness that illuminates the fallen reality of Swanly's sexual awakening, cloaked previously in a language of religious transcendence and a recaptured lost Eden, "as if in the garden before the fall" or "as those ignorant animals amongst the fruit of Eden just hours before the thunder" (35). The trio of Tuck, Bernadette, and Swanly are shamed in their nakedness by the watchful "fiend outside [Sunballs]" (36), and the Christian Fall analogy is crystalized in Tuck's final fatalistic decree, an expression of original sin (where "the fall" and "the thunder" were prewritten in the Garden of Eden parable): "Damn us, damn it all" (40). The narrative morphs subsequently into a grotesque transposal of the Christ story with a sick Swanly looking as if "[h]e might well be dying" (36), lying across Bernadette's lap "in a condition of the Pietà" (38), "her breasts over his twisted face" (39). It is an intertextual compression of weighty cultural narratives, none of which alone offers an adequate means of interpreting events.

Hannah's strategic deployment of these distinct cultural mythologies not only speaks to the tragedy brought on by Hannah's adult characters' vain and destructive fantasy of vicarious historical reversal by "getting some young." It also evokes much broader (regional) concerns about southern historical burden and the gothic impingement of past ills on the present. Just as wider myths are both invoked and parodied by Hannah at the level of intertextual citation, simultaneously aiding and complicating our readings, so too at the narrative level is the adults' hunger for historical reversal a myth that cannot hold. If we agree with Weston that "Get Some Young" represents "a quest for eternal youth and lost innocence, in which the protagonist [Tuck] tries to create an innocent self" (*BH* 62), then this is a fantasy bound to end, as the boys' tales are, in a putatively southern sense of defeat and failure analogous to the concept of original sin. Persistently, Hannah's broader cultural analogies are brought back from the realms of the timeless or universal to a series of historically and regionally specific concerns.

The seeming inevitability of southern historical circuitousness is conveyed in the last image we are given of fallen Swanly, who "thenceforward [. . .] was wolfish in his glare and often dirty" (40). It is an abrupt transition from a "cowlicked and blithe" (7) boyish innocence to full adult sexual maturity, prey turned predator, with no proper process of coming of age in between: "He was neither child, boy, nor man, and he was dreadful" (39–40). Swanly's radical transition from innocence to experience is a problem directly redolent of that described by Hannah's earlier narrator Bobby Smith in both "Midnight and I'm Not Famous Yet" and *The Tennis Handsome*, who resents that his service in Vietnam has made him transition straight "from teen-age giggling to horror" ("Midnight" 108–9; *Tennis* 47) in a course of rude subjective becoming. In "Get Some Young," Tuck also has suffered the violence of masculine coming of age as a soldier in Korea, suggesting that this vicious cycle of predatory male behavior results at least partially from the failure of the national father to protect its sons, a failure that southerners of course were privy to long before Korea and Vietnam. In this tale of unchecked nostalgia, it is the adults' maladjusted regret for lost youth (their own, their grown-up sons') that renders Swanly the victim of his own untimely loss of innocence, in a sense that is established as something both inevitable (especially if we identify Dickey's *Deliverance* as a textual precursor) and tragically avoidable. While in many ways the story's nostalgia motif turns on a concept of modernity—"I seen what it come down to in your modern world," Sunballs tells Tuck in explanation for his social reclusiveness (20)—the sense of temporal circularity established by the story's drama resists any simple attribution of its social problems to "modern" or recent southern history. Given what Ayers argued of late-twentieth-century southern culture, that southerners have *always* been diagnostically nostalgic (*All Over the Map* 69), we might question whether this is a recent problem, the result of modernity (or modern warfare), or whether it is an inevitable consequence of being white and male in the South.

These are important questions raised, if not answered, by "Get Some Young," whose narrative invites interpretation according to this series of significant social issues and historical events, challenging us to declare it historically detached or politically disinterested. This contrasts strongly with the concept of narcissistic narrative as a solipsistic and politically ineffectual genre. In the next section I explore how Hannah's social inquiry gains ground (and his writing, value) as an interrogation and enactment of post-southern *aesthetic* value. What makes "Get Some Young" metafictional and "narcissistic," and how does its language encourage some revision of the metafictional genre as a sterile aesthetic form, emblematic of cultural, artistic, and linguistic degeneration?

Earlier I claimed that "Get Some Young" is significant beyond plot and theme, and that it outruns the various conceptual frameworks within which it has been critically evaluated. The notion discussed so far, of "getting some young" as a form of parasitical revival, is redoubled at the level of the story's language, and this is testimony to the significance of Hannah's writing. The concept of historical vampirism, cannibalizing the past to renew the present, is lent further dramatic expression in the distinctive aesthetic form that Hannah achieves, one that self-consciously stages its own processes of historical excavation, its assembling of protean and manifold linguistic styles and registers that are regional, national, and global. Here, we can explore how the concept of southern historical regress, going back to go forward, is also fundamental to Hannah's implicit metafictional agenda, which interrogates its own retroactive methods of historical recuperation. In fact, this textual approach becomes vitally regenerative, such that Hannah's aesthetic inquiry acts as a conceptual foil to his story's social diagnosis of a culture characterized by stasis and entrapment.

Tom Wolfe infamously indicted the metafictional genre as one comprising "merely decadent forms of self-absorption which deprive [its texts] of significant energy" (qtd. in Currie 17). This indictment invites comparison with Hobson's formulation of (Hannah's) postsouthern writing as "lacking the tragic sense, devoid of Faulkner's high seriousness and social consciousness" (34) and exhibiting "a relative want of *power*" (*Southern Writer* 10). Wolfe's words are perfectly redolent of Hannah's fictional character the aspiring writer Royce's depiction of human language. Drawing on the Christian creation story and the prefect self-presence of God's Word, Royce confesses that his own writing is "lost like a two-headed snake in jabber at itself" ("Through Sunset" 123–24). This is an echo of Tuck's similar view of female sexuality in "Get Some Young," as "two lips forever kissing each other down there and they got no other subject" (30). His (misogynistic) perception of female bodies as "always with themselves having sex with themselves" (30) provides an apposite metaphor for the allegedly solipsistic and sterile nature of postmodern art in views such as Baudrillard's playing-with-the-pieces analogy, to which Jameson's contemporary formulation of postmodern pastiche as a creatively moribund genre is directly indebted.

Before proceeding with this section, it is worth briefly pausing on the scene in "Get Some Young" from which these words come. Amid the ménage-a-trois of Tuck, Bernadette, and Swanly, the story's most rhetorically distinctive passage, announced by a section break in the text, reads: "Whosoever you are, be that person with all your might. Time goes by faster than we thought. It is a thief and so quiet. You must let yourself be loved and you must love, parts of you that never loved must open and love. You must announce yourself in all particulars so you can have yourself" (35). The words demand attention as a staged moment of linguistic epiphany, a formal idiosyncrasy whose archaism and enigmatic opacity suggests its rhetorical significance. In a sudden shift from Tuck's broken internal narrative, which makes up most of the text, and in marked contrast to the man's few outward expressions, an eloquent, transcendent second-person pedagogic voice appears to have been ventriloquized through the conduit Tuck, directly addressing "we" audience (as well as the story's fictional one), as if to bridge the gap between Tuck's external speech and his hidden "true expressions" (3).

However, while the overtones of the speech accord with a biblical and humanistic sense of social communion ("love" and "be loved"), itself at radical odds with what is transpiring in this scene, implicitly the rhetoric retains the fallen condition of a contemporary culture based on narcissistic individualism: its aim is simply to "announce yourself" so that "you can have yourself." Further (and opposing the essentialist formulation of being oneself, which we might have expected here), both the sexualized connotations of having and the verbal ones of announcing oneself evoke Tuck's earlier use of the "self-absorbed conversation" analogy to convey his perception of the feminine. The femininity of Bernadette, as a surrogate for Eve, is expressly associated with "the fall" imminent in the scene (35), but when we appreciate the correspondence with Royce's impression of postlapsarian linguistic reference, we can infer a version of what I have elsewhere termed the fall into representation. We can read these scenes as a metaphor for the purported sterility of both postsouthern social and literary cultures—sustained when the nonproductive sexual implications of "having" oneself are continued in the subsequent masturbatory image of Sunballs "rutting" on the knife "grabbed desperately to his loins" (36). Therefore, the absence of the (Christian) concept of the creative "act" resonates in each scene, in the dual realms of sexual and artistic impotency, recalling the concept of the Imaginary in Lacanian psychoanalysis, which posits that all forms of representation are just inadequate attempts to fill a lack, to use the words of Faulkner's Addie Bundren (*As I Lay Dying* 172).

This juxtaposition between the remarkable and indeed, transcendent language of this scene and the ideas about cultural exhaustion (both sexual and linguistic) implicit within it perfectly demonstrates how Hannah succeeds in making powerful art from his own anxious disquisition on the potential enervation of postsouthern languages. In the previous section I argued for the prevalence of the "southern self-consciousness" whose absence Hobson lamented in postsouthern writing (*Southern Writer* 10). In this section, I argue for the significant "power" (Hobson) and "energy" (Wolfe) of "Get Some Young" as a piece of postsouthern writing, qualities Hobson, Wolfe, Jameson, and others have declared wanting in contemporary art.

Because the discourses that make up "Get Some Young" incorporate intertextual references that range far beyond the temporal and geographical confines of its late-twentieth-century Mississippian setting, it is much more difficult to place the story's discourses as firmly as we could Roonswent Dover's Ozarkian gothic folktale in Hannah's earlier "Evening of the Yarp." The drama of Dover's first-person narrative comes largely from its narrator's explicit awareness of the act of telling his story, which becomes obviously metafictional as a result. "Get Some Young," though similarly self-reflexive, is radically different aesthetically. Notably, it lacks a single first-person narrator. Even the distinction between speech and thought is not marked by punctuation, and it is often difficult to ascertain who is speaking at any one time. Tuck's internal first-person dialogue (occasionally morphing into a rare second-person "you") merges with the boys' speech and with the voice of an intermittent omniscient third-person narrator, whose own voice slips frequently into free indirect discourse. The language of the story's characters is disjointed and provides frequent moments of narrative prolepsis and analepsis, just as the language of the narrative at large jumps back and forth to offer "snapshots" of different historical moments across time. The problems of interpretation inherent in Dover's anxious narrative are assimilated into the very language and style of "Get Some Young," suggesting that Hannah's metafictional aesthetic has collapsed in on itself, or rather, that the author's metafictional strategies have become thoroughly internalized. This formal shift adds significant complexity to Hannah's late writing, which seems to

excavate the history of the story's languages as part of the author's (metafictional) critiquing of the story's own production, in which interpretation becomes something of a formal challenge in itself.

On one hand, the language of "Get Some Young" can be recognized as an
apt portrayal of the kind of narcissistic aesthetic condemned by Wolfe, one
that feeds off itself to sustain itself. This language, having ingested its own
aesthetic strategies, offers an alternative interpretation of Tuck's confessed
vampirism (13), which can be reconceived as a fitting characterization of the
kind of internalized self-reflexivity dramatized by this peculiar kind of narrative. *Yonder Stands Your Orphan* contains a distinctly similar image, the
character Egan parodying the commodification of the South and declaring
that "we have fed on the blood of our own" (148). The critically self-aware
"meta" voice of "Get Some Young," which not only is mindful of its own
vampiric processes but also co-opts the very critical paradigms according
to which it might be interpreted, also feeds off the past, consuming the reanimated historical narratives from which it derives its own contemporary
aesthetic identity—much as the voices, past and present, that emerge from
the Mississippi river Strong provide the creative lifeblood of the story.

On the other hand, "Get Some Young" (as with its social inquiry) is anything but solipsistic. The self-reflexivity of its language, which has ingested
the "pieces" (Baudrillard) or "fragments" (Eliot) of the past, renders the text
part of a distinct historical dialogue. It is a dialogue acutely aware of its
own postsouthern historical moment, while extending exponentially outward to a cultural and linguistic history that far exceeds its fiercely localized
placing in south-central Mississippi. The sweeping discursive registers contained within "Get Some Young"—incorporating classical works of global
high culture, often directly cited, including Hemingway, Dylan Thomas,
Poe (6), Shakespeare and Nabokov (14, 39), Tennessee Williams (whose *Orpheus Descending* contains characters memorably bemoaning lost youth), as
well as the popular contemporary cultural discourses of Nat King Cole and
Johnny Mathis (7), Peter Gunn (4), Leslie Caron (23), and *Esquire* magazine
(8), in which Hannah published widely in the early years of his career—are
persistently contrasted to its tenacious locality, with its references to real
towns and places like Jackson, Mendenhall, Rodney, Whitfield, and the
river Strong. Thus, while the story's language feasts on a number of important wider intertexts to which it is knowingly indebted, and that we readers
can place specifically in nonsouthern contexts, we have already seen how it

stages "southern" themes of nostalgia and trauma, historical recurrence, and cultural stagnation. These themes speak to the story's geographical placing on identifiably southern territory, and this meeting of theme and topography pays homage to the peculiar regional conditions of the story's making (real or imagined), in which it is knowingly rooted.[6]

This marriage of regional and global is caught most effectively in the previously mentioned image of "the ancient river dead roused from their Civil War ghoulments" (25). The Civil War has defined southern masculinity in such a way that contemporary subjects continue to be menaced by the ghouls of the past; we have seen this evinced when each of the boys' severely restricted futures imply the continuance of the southern legacy of defeat and failure. Concurrently however, the phrase "*ancient* river dead" reveals that the river harbors the ghosts of men long preceding the war whose polyphony of voices prelude the white South's supposedly pivotal fall from grace. The Strong predates America's geographical and political divisions and the southern mythologies established in the wake of the war, suggested by the image of the boys sitting on a "sunken petrified log like an immense crocodile forced up by saurian times, in the first rush of small rapids of the pool" (22). This line is distinctly reminiscent of the ending of Norman Maclean's short story "A River Runs Through It" (1976), whose closing lines read: "Eventually, all things merge into one, and a river runs through it. The river was cut by the world's great flood and runs over rocks from the basement of time. On some of the rocks are timeless raindrops. Under the rocks are the words, and some of the words are theirs. I am haunted by waters" (119).

As a focal point of "Get Some Young," the river Strong provides a similar sense of historical merging. It is both a beginning and an ending (cue the story's numerous references to the acts of conception and death); it is a vehicle through which ideas about transience, endurance, and historical continuity play out. The river has witnessed the Civil War, (perhaps) the most monumental event in southern history, but even this pales into significance in the historical scope of geology and topography, whose historic witness, "from the first rush of small rapids" (or in Maclean's words, "from the basement of time"), extends far beyond the confines of the South, such that "[t]he river in this place transported them to Germany or the Rockies or New England, anywhere but here" ("Get Some Young" 22–23). The story is full of extraordinary images that transport the reader's imagination well beyond Mississippi, while these are juxtaposed to the story's local backdrop, which forms a sense of topographical witness. Coupled with Hannah's many references to what Weston calls "the mythic (timeless) realm" (*BH* 62), historicity and (linear) temporality are concepts to be reconsidered here, along with the notion that a series of neat historical ruptures (e.g., the South before and after the Civil War) could have taken place. The material events of local history witnessed by these rivers are integral to conceptualizations of the regional, while also placing that region in a much wider realm of historical witness.

The concept of historical witness is conveyed at the level of Hannah's language. For instance, while not its direct subject, the specter of the Civil War is never far from "Get Some Young": Tuck imagines the American welfare state as an "army, the biggest thing ever invaded the USA, [. . .] worse than Sherman's march" (14). Swanly is said to aspire to the old masculine "ideal" of the warrior hero "with saber in hand" (8), and Arden Pal is said to have "held up his flute like a saber" (23), the saber being commonly associated with Confederate officers in Hannah's work. With similar regional specificity, the narrative is underwritten with descriptions of minute locality, of flora and fauna—"the south Mississippi fifth-grown pine, the rabbitweed, the smaller oaks and hickories, the white clay and the coon-toed bracken" (21)—along with descriptions of the Strong which appear suddenly at various points, slowing the narrative and bringing its focus sharply back to the present from the temporal and spatial wanderings of characters and narrator alike—"The little river rushed between the milky bluffs like cola" (8); "The water moved past them into a deep pit of sand under the bridge [. . .] terra-cotta besieged by black roots" (10); "on both sides of the washboard gravel was the erosion where the ditches of white limesoil had been clawed into deep small canyons by heavy rains, then swerved into bogs in wild fingers" (24). Meanwhile, the close detail of the story's natural topography is paralleled in the enumerated lists of "legitimate country food" (4) items bought by the boys from Tuck's grocery store, including Pall Malls, Roi-Tans, hoop and rat cheese, Nehi, Orange Crush, Beech-Nut, and Moon Pies (5).

Staged dramatic moments stand out in "Get Some Young" as part of its textual documenting of the late-twentieth-century South. Throughout, instances of condensed contemporary southern American discourse bring the focus back to how acts of language (and especially speech) can frame particular moments in history—just as Maclean described the haunting *words* beneath the rocks underlying the Blackfoot River in Montana. In "Get Some Young," examples of this freeze-framed historical discourse include the boys singing "Uh found your high school ring in muh baby's twat" (7), Sunballs recounting having witnessed "two smoky old queers availing theyselve," getting "one last 'bomination in" aboard a falling plane (19–20), Tuck's "Why my wife, she's a right holy wonder, she is" (21), and Walthall classifying Bernadette as a typical "Big Mama Busybod" (26). Meanwhile, the idiosyncratic similes deployed throughout the narrative—Walthall's ancient Jaguar sedan "smelling like Britain on the skids or the glove of a soiled duke" (6), Swanly being "graceful as a tennis player from the era of Woodrow Wilson" (5), or Bernadette "like a jazz siren between the great wars" (21); as well as the story's metaphoric allusions to "pilgrims" or "some pagan cavalry" (38)—evoke times and places stretched far and wide, reawakened or revivified in their contemporary verbal usage much in the way Hannah's unusual metaphors demand that we see things afresh.

Even Walthall's viola and Pal's bass flute are described as "two instruments unrecognized by anybody in [their] school [or] city," and the boys "played them passing strange" in a "baroque" and "alien strain" (23). Bernadette views the spectacle of Swanly naked in the shallows "through a haze of inept but solemn chamber music" (24–25). After being spied by Sunballs bathing naked in the Strong, Swanly "was evilly shaken like a maiden thing out of the last century" (29). Such is the story's unique oratory style that even so commonplace a description as the hermit's filthy footwear is profoundly evocative of past eons and foreign places: "You would not see such annealed textures at the ankles of a farmer, not this color of city gutters back long past" (17); similarly, citizens on welfare are imagined (by Tuck) as "Old Testament specters with birds all over them eating honey out of roadkill" (12). Thus, the kaleidoscopic nature of the story's narrative, focusing in and out on different scenes and moments, proves as grounding as it is dizzying, despite illuminating a series of static images and scenes of spectacle, voyeurism, and witness.

This idea of old voices being ventriloquized through new ones is observable throughout "Get Some Young," and it lends the text extraordinary creative energy. Introducing this chapter, I argued for the significance of individual word choice in Hannah's writing, and here examples include Tuck's rhetorical musing on Swanly's beauty: "who dared give a south Mississippi pissant youth such powerful flow and comeliness" (12). The word *comeliness*, from sixteenth-century Latin, is traceable back to Old English, and it carries connotations of Old World British elite culture, a far cry from the social realities of this boy's home life, despite his incongruous appearance. The conflation of the contemporary southern American idiom with older European discourse is further evident in the word *pissant,* a possible corruption of *puissant,* from Old French, meaning having great power or influence ("Puissant"). This sense of the youth's imagined power over the adult recalls the "Particular Scouts" in "Get Some Young," who "seemed to know their charms very well and worked him [Tuck] like a gasping servant in their behalf" (4)—an image that evokes in turn the figure of the nymph in Greek and Latin mythology, a cultural reference deployed also by Nabokov in *Lolita* to describe the same theme. Similarly, Tuck's archaic lament for his lost boyhood, "oh wrath of loss, fair gone sprite" (11), carries similar echoes of Old French ("Sprite").

The resurrection of historical texts is key to Hannah's story, then, recalling the (nostalgic) "fragments" Eliot assembled in *The Waste Land* to renew an enervated present. If history is an ongoing process whose "ghoulments" are reaccentuated and transformed in new contexts across time, then new acts of historical appropriation do not signal a (nostalgic) fissure between past and present, just as the history of the river Strong provides a useful means of conceptualizing this notion of history as a continuum, a course of back-and-forth between old and new. I would propose that in these ways Hannah's writing, rather than marking a sense of historical rupture such as Jameson identified, establishes a strong sense of continuity between past and present, a sense of history in process and dialogue, its discourses intertwined. Again, this is exhibited in the boys' distinctive language. It is saturated with intertextual references to American and European, classical and colloquial discourses, in which past and present voices collide. For example, the boys' "AM teenage castrati" voices sing along to the car radio with "You are muh cuntshine, muh only cuntshine" (7), a corruption of the 1930s song "You Are My Sunshine." In a single utterance, Walthall irreverently misquotes the classics of both Hemingway and Dylan Thomas: "Send not to ask for when the bell tolls. I refuse to mourn the death by fire of a child's Christmas on Fern Hill. Do not go gently in my sullen craft, up yours" (23). Similarly, Lester Silk's retired Army veteran father is described as "going to seed through smoke and ceaseless hoisting on his own petard of Falstaff beers" (8), the Shakespearean idiom an allusion to the play *Hamlet* conjured by the brand name "Falstaff," and possibly a corrupt literary reference, because the character Falstaff does not appear in that play.

Potts has discerned the "markedly uneven value" of Hannah's intertextual allusions ("Anti-Myth" 243), a claim that resonates with Philip E. Simmons's argument that a postmodern "culture glutted with mass-cultural artifacts" renders contemporary discourses "fragmented and scrambled without regard for hierarchies of cultural position or status" (16). Indeed, because high and low cultural artifacts are placed side by side in Hannah's text, we may infer a process of the contemporary devaluing of once high art in a culture of surface and commodity over real value. It is therefore possible to interpret the examples above as part of Hannah's documenting a series of linguistic corruptions, with the vestiges of past cultures debased by the boys' present distortions ("up yours"; "cuntshine"), as if to suggest the sullying of more valuable past cultural artifacts by their contemporary inflections. On closer inspection, however, the boys' exploitation of existing art forms ("You Are My Sunshine" to "You Are Muh Cuntshine") becomes a creative reworking rather than a simple corruption or act of plagiarism, especially when we consider the problems of determining authorship or the purity of the original. Interestingly, and whether Hannah was aware of it or not, even this seemingly throwaway reference is important when we consider the popular song's history. First recorded by Jimmie Davis and Charles Mitchell in 1939 and declared one of the state songs of Louisiana because of its association with Davis, although Davis was never known to actually claim authorship, having originally bought the song and rights from Paul Rice and then subsequently been credited as songwriter. If not intentional on Hannah's part, then it is certainly a pertinent coincidence that this cultural remnant from the Deep South should come with such profound issues of authorship and appropriation. At every level of Hannah's writing, the concept of an authentic historical or textual origin is a serious problem.

Elsewhere I have suggested that a deliberate conceptual slippage occurs in Hannah's texts between the concepts modern and postmodern, original and copy. This is further significant when we consider that the title *High Lonesome* evokes the bluegrass musical aesthetic, notably a modern reworking of "old-time" southern mountainfolk music that emerged in the mid to late 1930s (see, e.g., Tichi). Hannah's reference to bluegrass is important because it recalls a local aesthetic that was radially innovative for its time, while simultaneously revealing the genre's indebtedness to the previously established art forms upon which this purportedly new form was already parasitic. We might recall the concept of the Southern Renaissance itself as a form of aesthetic revival (of dead cultures) and thus parasitism. This issue of originality versus parasitical indebtedness to prior historical moments has been part of the metafictional considerations of Hannah's texts as explored thus far. But in "Get Some Young" these problems are ingrained into the very material of the text, just as they provide something of a unifying theme for the more obviously metafictional concerns of the other *High Lonesome* stories.

Hutcheon's formulation of postmodern parody (as a counter to Jameson's pastiche) can help to elucidate these ideas. In her influential *The Politics of Postmodernism*, a complement to her *Poetics of Postmodernism*, Hutcheon takes direct issue with allegations of postmodern intertextual parody or pastiche as forms of aesthetic narcissism, symptomatic of an age of surfaces that has lost connection to the past (and to effective political critique). Hutcheon argues that for artists, the postmodern involves a process of historical textual excavation that we can apply directly to a text like "Get Some Young": "a rummaging through the image reserves of the past in such a way as to show the history of the representations their parody calls to our attention" (*Politics* 93). Compared with the nostalgia of Eliot or Jameson, Hutcheon's view of postmodern parody is of a "parodic reprise of the past of art" that is not nostalgic or melancholic but critically engaged, because it interrogates the very notion of originality: "With parody—as with any form of representation—the notion of the original as rare single, and valuable (in aesthetic or commercial terms) is called into question" (93–94). In a similar way, the intertextuality of "Get Some Young" is neither nostalgic nor ahistorical or apolitical. Its parody (when read alongside Hutcheon's arguments) simply signals "how present representations come from past ones and what ideological consequences derive from both continuity and difference" (93). In Hannah's postsouthern writing, this dialogic interchange between past and present has resonance not only at the aesthetic level but at the thematic level too, sustaining my contention that the past is still conceived of as present in the southern literary imaginary after modernism.

In "Get Some Young," the sheer variety of parodied texts present, even if we are not exactly sure what is being parodied or why, suggests a richly intertextual tapestry not simply indicative of academic play or some infinite regress to textuality (as with the high postmodernism of Coover, Pynchon, or Barthelme, for example). Nor does Hannah's "rummaging through the image reserves of the past" (in Hutcheon's words) demark a process of cultural decline from old to new. Instead, Hannah calls to our attention the very process of representation, both historical and literary, and how such image reserves are produced. Here, the impossibility of finding any totalizing model to resolve the contradictions and interpretative difficulties of "Get Some Young" can be attributed to this deliberately anxious problematization of the (exclusive) concepts of original and copy. In the context of the South and southern identity especially, Hannah's writing alerts us to the (political) ways in which *South* and *southern* have been constructed historically and how past representations come to inform present constructions of southern social and literary identity. In "Get Some Young," the images of the past are woven into Hannah's stagy appropriation of historical discourse as a way to move forward by reinventing them in a new creative context.

Again, close attention to the story's language fosters these arguments. The five boys recognize the creative value inherent in the adoption of different linguistic styles and in dramatic acts of linguistic play such as "I claim this land for the Queen of Spain" (37), "Something stinketh, I tell you," "Teenage suckface. Dark night of the suck," or "Having a bit of a transversion, them old boy and girl" (34). In this last example, the neologism *transversion* seems fitting to describe the historical transference of the old getting some young; it depicts social transgression or perversion as well as historical regression, reversal, or transition. It offers a microcosm for the feat of language performed by Hannah's narrative at large, of renewing the present by creatively inflecting past languages. This is captured when Tuck, furious with "moocher" Sunballs for browsing through and reprimanding the cost of the items in his store (17), conjures an image distinctly redolent of Eliot's *The Waste Land* and its "crowd [that] flowed over London Bridge, so many," to the static watcher's dismay (62): "Hordes of them [. . .] pouring across the borders of the realm from bumland" ("Get Some Young" 18). Similarly, Tuck must invent a new vocabulary of what Potts terms "bizarre compounds" ("Anti-Myth" 248) in order to articulate the depth of his repugnance for the hermit, which exceeds the referential capacities of existing language: "mouthbroom" (18); "Pissmouth" (21). Again, this provides a fitting analogy for Hannah's language itself, which stitches old languages together in new ways, changing their meaning and rhetorical effect. Tuck's projected loathing of Sunballs as a version of himself thus denotes how Hannah's language is always significant far beyond what we might expect it to be conveying.

Both the language of Hannah's characters and that of the omniscient narrator (when present) convey aspects of this discursive play, this cobbling together of different languages to create something radically new. Bakhtin identifies an important power inherent in the "clashes" between different discourses within the text (*Problems* 196), and certainly the energy of "Get Some Young" and its aesthetic uniqueness derives largely from the conflict between these many voices contained in a single authorial performance or language. Recalling the paradox in which authenticity in Hannah's stories is a quality contingent on the interaction between performance and audience, often with a third level of interpretative witness present, Jacqueline Howard argues that in resisting resolution or unity, literary polyphony establishes a third level of dynamic interpretative "openness" between author, text, and reader (4). Gary Saul Morson describes this phenomenon in "Parody, History and Metaparody," which explains that Bakhtin's "stylization" is "best described not simply as an interaction of two speech acts, but as an interaction designed to be heard and interpreted by a third person (or second 'second person'), whose own process of active reception is anticipated and directed" (Morson 65). In the above examples of unique linguistic constructions in "Get Some Young," new meanings are generated alongside established ones, traversing different contexts and acts of reinterpretation. This is a process reliant upon an audience's identifying the cultural reference being parodied, just as "Get Some Young" itself involves the mindful appropriation of others' utterances to create a new literary language of its own.

Romine reproves Kreyling's vision of postsouthern parody for conveying a sense of literary decline that "move[s] in an exclusively deconstructive direction" (Romine, *Narrative Forms* 207). I have argued variously that Hannah poses a significant challenge to ideas about the supposedly diminished value of postmodern art and postsouthern writing—a feat even more remarkable in those stories that make such a spectacle of their own cannibalistic indebtedness to precedent styles and genres. While many of its ventriloquized voices are markedly borrowed from other texts and eras—Kenneth Millard calls this "the parasitical feeding on southern history," which "ha[s] a strongly textual dimension in which the past is devoured to keep the future alive" ("Cultural Value" 24)—and while at the narrative and thematic levels southern decline is a key concern, as a dramatic disquisition on the nature of contemporary southern *languages* "Get Some Young" is distinctly not nostalgic. Its myriad intertexts and voices lend it vigor, rather than signaling contemporary creative enervation, literary "exhaustion" (Barth's term), or linguistic decay.

The five boys' resourcefulness in ventriloquizing the adopted languages of different historical personae not only enables them to temporarily exceed the confines of an otherwise historically determined region and the concomitantly limited possibilities for masculinity that place affords. It also enables them to invest the various roles they play with the semblance of authenticity. This supports Millard's argument that the stories of *High Lonesome* "often seek to redeem, by art, characters who in life seemed worthless" ("Cultural Value" 17), and it pertains to Abigail Cheever's concept of the "real phony," the paradox whereby authenticity is reinstated through acts of performative agency that have the capacity to transcend their own phoniness (Cheever 21). For Hannah's "actors," the possibility of any redemption lies in the creative agency by which the future might be imagined or performed differently, thereby to "outrun the conditions of its emergence," as Cheever writes (21). And this suggests that Hannah's heightened interest in performance is not simply part of a literary enactment of postmodern image culture, even though the entire story is steeped in the language of spectacle and performance.

"Get Some Young" is made up almost entirely of a succession of static scenes of voyeurism and witness. Throughout the narrative, images and acts draw on both their fictional audience and an implied reading audience to interpret them. Initially, the prevalent lexis of theater appears to point to the pathologically inauthentic nature of this contemporary southern culture, which comes across in the languages that document it. Which is to say, the text's social critique, the failure of adult responsibility and what Bone calls "the grim historical continuities" between post–Civil War and post-Vietnam trauma ("Neo-Confederate" 96), finds expression in Hannah's aesthetic preoccupation with the phony image. For example, Swanly imagines that "there was no real such thing as maturity, no, people simply began acting like grownups, the world a farce of playing house" (10). Tuck is described as "like something in a storekeeper's costume activated by a pullstring and thrust into a playhouse by a child" (198). Sunballs demands of Swanly, "Is it real? Has this boy escaped out of a theatre somewheres?" (21), and even the boy's own mother "would say he would at any moment be kidnapped by Hollywood"

(11). It is possible that this language reveals Hannah's depiction of a hyper-real culture in which reality is indistinguishable from its simulations.

Potts draws on the work of William Simon, who argues (via Julia Kristeva) that Hannah's writing fractures the illusory unity of myth, because the idea of subjectivity in Hannah's stories reflects a broadening range of options for self-definition (Simon 8; Potts, "Anti-Myth" 248). In "Get Some Young," the boys' theatrical personae certainly appear to reflect multiple identities. We are told, for example, that Swanly "would practice with a monocle and cigarette and swagger stick" (7) while imagining himself as the Nordic warrior horseman-hero "in silver spurs with saber in hand" (8), a role not only derived from a vision of (Confederate) southern culture but also encompassing an image of northern Europe, quite literally the global North. Likewise, Walthall is "an actor" and "a connoisseur" who wears a beret and a goatee and (indiscriminately?) impersonates both the high art of Edgar Allan Poe and the popular movies of Leslie Gunn. Weston contends that the boys' peculiar language conveys a sense of schizophrenic and confused identity (*BH* 62–64), pertaining to Simmons's description of how "[g]lobal electronic mass culture" has "saturated [. . .] the contemporary psyche with images and newly imperil[led] the distinctions between image and reality, self and world" (9). Potts claims similarly that the boys are in the process of creating and re-creating themselves according to the images they have imbibed from a dizzying array of proffered cultural "choices" ("Anti-Myth" 250).

I would extend the above claims to argue that the boys' postmodern performativity implies, as does Hutcheon's theory of historiographic metafiction, that history is a complex mix of image and reality, and this is especially pertinent to understandings of the self-reflexive South. Like Hannah's narrative itself, the five boys glean a series of performative roles from a pastiche of the different images produced by cultural representations. The significance of this in a postregional context, however, is that this is a story deeply mindful of the fact that southern identity is (and always has been) a performance and how subjectivities are forged from and written into a long-established history of stories and texts. More than simply denoting the fractured or "schizophrenic" nature of contemporary identity, then, our five boys role-play a series of appropriated cultural narratives, regional and global, to suggest a sense of remedial promise inherent in the creative appropriation of texts.

Ironically, the narratives the boys choose to appropriate and stage speak of tragedy and defeat, recalling the sense of creative promise in forms of the abject articulated in "Through Sunset into the Raccoon Night." In that story, the narrator, Royce, perceives a curiously transformative power in the Radiohead song "Creep," whose "defeated tenor" cries "I don't belong here!" and prompts Royce to confess, "God, what freedom in that statement. I just adore it" (109). In "Get Some Young," we are told that Walthall writes poems about a woman in Nashville "in the manner of E. A. Poe at his least in bonging rhymes. In every poem he expired in some way and he wanted the 'woman' to watch this" (6). While Walthall's craft is bogus insofar as it is parasitical on Poe's, it is effective nonetheless, perhaps because of the abjection inherent within it, which, as we have seen elsewhere, often carries the potential for masculine agency in Hannah's stories, with male becoming frequently associated with points of crisis. The actor Walthall epitomizes the self-consciousness of performance by which identity can be achieved by weighting it in substantial narrative, here writing himself into an *alternative* southern narrative of defeat, that of the romantic artist-hero who is characterized by his stoic endurance. Walthall's imagined suffering demands a watching audience to testify to the significance of the narrative he has constructed (he wants the woman to *watch* him "expiring"), and it offers creative inspiration for his own audience in turn: Lester Silk, a boy "who never made anything but fun of poetry and acted the fairy whenever it occurred at school" (23), is inspired by Walthall's performance to compose his own haunting tale of anguish and lost love. In turn, even Bean, the "sternest" and meanest "of them all" (23), is moved to rather poetically designate Swanly as "a full orphan," and we are told that in the wake of this act of creative linguistic performance Bean "intended to loom there in his acuity for a moment" (30), cognizant of his own rhetorical faculty. The self-conscious performance can be both enabling and authenticating, just as Walthall performs his acts "with high seriousness" (6)—words that, coincidentally, evoke verbatim Hobson's claim that Hannah's writing lacks Faulkner's "high seriousness" (*Southern Writer* 34).

Finally, the concept of performativity is integral to the implicit metafictional nuance of "Get Some Young." The text is profoundly aware of itself as a performance, even while its principal characters are depicted in the language of performance, and as a self-reflexive (narcissistic) text it also demands an audience to testify to its worth. As noted, "Get Some Young" is composed of several key, staged acts of drama, rhetorically distinct, in which the story's language self-consciously advertises its own theatricality. This is revealed playfully when the image offered of Walthall, with raised viola and arms spread out "like a crucified musician," is described by the narrator as a piece of theater "evoking God knows what" (30). Acts are central not only to the story's dramatization of (white male) southern identity as a performance, therefore, but also to the aesthetic theory Hannah formulates, of fiction that self-reflexively acknowledges the acts of both writing and reading. The sense of creative promise underwriting the successful execution of certain types of (borrowed) aesthetic staginess suggests a sense of the transformative—and *transporting*—power of art (recall the image of the Strong transporting the boys to "anywhere but here"). The restorative power of the boys' creative language is mirrored in the language of the story at large, which creates a new kind of postsouthern metafiction that gains significant aesthetic purchase from its imaginative excavations of history, from its peculiar conflation of regional and global, old and new. Hannah's subtle inquiry into the nature of postsouthern aesthetics affirms that the past—and the South—can be renewed.

Hannah's devouring of historical languages is not simply part of his dramatization of the vertiginous experience of contemporary existence, in which "roles" are readily available to be cannibalized in a pastiche of multiple texts, eras, and discourses, as we might observe in the pathology of Hannah's eponymous Ray. It is also testimony to how we can mine history while lending its discourses a contemporary twist, suggesting again that the polyphonic array of historical discourses that are "still alive" (*Ray* 41) in "Get Some Young" are not simply part of an experimental literary postmodernism, nor merely the depiction of a postmodern fragmented psyche in which contemporary selves are lost in a deafening cacophony of historical discourse. Instead, we can view "Get Some Young" as a Bakhtinian plural form, one that "draws on and recontextualizes or transforms prior discursive structures, fragments of 'the already said,' both literary and non-literary" (Howard 16). Hannah's eccentric linguistic ventriloquism perfectly evinces the aesthetic style Bakhtin applauded in Dostoevsky's novels, where "a plurality of voices [. . .] is not meant to be eliminated [. . .] but in fact is meant to triumph" (Bakhtin, *Problems* 204). The remarkable use of language in the story, the dynamic synthesis of a triumphant plethora of historical narratives both regional and global, unequivocally confirms Mark Currie's defense of contemporary metafictional aesthetic practices against Wolfe (Currie 17). And because the text, like its "Civil War ghoulments," is made up directly of the (unvanquished) voices of material history, or what Howard calls "historically concrete situations of social interaction" (16), Hannah challenges us to declare his story politically or ethically disengaged. Instead, it interrogates the nature and value of late-twentieth-century postsouthern languages by giving a performative account of the linguistic history, the fragments of the already-said to which its own contemporary regionality is indebted.

Foregrounding its own parasitism on the cultural relics of the past while advertising itself as something significantly different results in a radically innovative linguistic aesthetic that, while it exceeds any unified conceptual framework by which we might fully or finally interpret it as southern, postsouthern, or otherwise, is testimony to Hannah's affirmation of the value of (post)southern languages for their own sake. "Get Some Young" proves that metafictional strategies need not equate to forms of self-absorption or creative drought, and this is what lends Hannah's writing its vital place in contemporary debates about the possibilities for authenticity in a postregional moment. The formal circularity achieved by narcissistic narratives that feed off their own appropriated languages and the remembered scenes from the past to which they refer interminably aptly denotes a classically *southern* case of the historical restatement of established cultural narratives, formulated in the past, which continue to inform the narratives of the present. In these ways the story is both southern and postmodern, while resisting neat classification as either. That Hannah can achieve this feat while persistently acknowledging the contrived *act* of his own writing about the authentic South is remarkable. All the while that it advertises its own performative strategies, "Get Some Young" stages its own literary parasitism on the historical narratives to which its contemporary cultural identity remains indebted, as integral to its southernness as the Mississippi river Strong.

Imagined Lacks and Literal Losses

The Post-postregional South?

In chapter 4 I quoted the character Ulrich in Hannah's *Yonder Stands Your Orphan*, a nostalgic old-timer who regrets that the people of Eagle Lake, Mississippi, "don't love each other as much as we used to. [. . .] You look at everybody and maybe they're a little sad, some of 'em. They're all homesick for when they were real" (46). Informed by Scott Romine's earlier readings, Thomas Bjerre interprets *Yonder Stands Your Orphan* as Hannah's lament for the waning of the South, a condemnation of what Henry Giroux calls "casino capitalism" in contemporary consumerist culture (Giroux 2, qtd. in Bjerre, "Southern Evil" 83), as a trope for a nationwide epidemic threatening regional difference via "the increasing lack of unique southern traits and the continuous homogenization of the South that Hannah seems to lament" (Bjerre, "Southern Evil" 83). Recalling recent disputes about whether believing the South exists as a viable area of study is to subscribe to the (Agrarian) conservatism that accompanied its first nostalgic rise, Eagle Lake's apparent compulsion to "har[k] back" (1) to the past seems to presume an implicit historical alternative, a true earlier time when people and places *were* real. Thus, Bjerre infers that the collapse of the distinctive South "is partly rooted in a nostalgia that affects the characters of [Hannah's] novel" ("Southern Evil" 83), such that Ulrich's words might indeed be expressive of Hannah's own mourning of the death of the region.

This reading seems convincing enough. Hannah's last novel certainly features his most openly nostalgic assemblage, and the "nostalgia industry" that allures characters dispossessed of time and space with its simulations of a truer past (*RS* 168) is central to the text's social critique. In this culture, it seems that simulations have besieged not only reality—where "images, roles, scripts, codes, and themed spaces threaten to colonize and eradicate the real"

(Romine, "Orphans All" 162)—but also an attendant realm of ethical human action, captured in the figure of the story's antihero, a serial killer aptly named Man Mortimer. Romine's tentative conclusion argues that the antidote to this deathly "regime of the simulacrum, of empty performance, and of deadening consumption" is "a countercurrent of redemption in a minor key," a quiet sort of humanism comprising "human decency" and "manners" ("Orphans All" 162) with which to offset the life-sucking properties of a self-consuming cyberspace South. The presence of animals and music in the novel—communicating in pre- or nonlinguistic forms that contrast poignantly with the novel's wider enactments of language's failure to signify—can support the claim that Hannah's final novel should be read as an indictment of the textuality of the postmodern South.

Yonder Stands Your Orphan certainly invites interpretation according to ideas about the collapse of the historical referent and the erasure of the original. Eagle Lake's thriving nostalgia industry suggests that history has become part of this culture's relentless consumerism. Just another piece of capital, reality is consumed by its own mediations or even "pickled in the juice of its own image" (Hannah, Hey Jack! 20). This is neatly captured in a poem from the character Byron Egan that contains the lines "The Best Southern Art On-Screen is Stupid and / Heartwarming. But you do not know what is beyond the window / of your own home" (Yonder 148). In Egan's concise parody of media-made Dixie, the South has "fed on" (148) its own image and thereby obscured itself, such that its people can know only the insipid simulations of their homeplace rather than what is truly there.

Jameson's conception of postmodern pastiche defines the genre by its moribund imitations of already "dead styles" (Postmodernism 18) rather than by anything properly creative or original. This is directly analogous to the zombies in Yonder Stands Your Orphan, who, worse than the actors who at least "mimic life," are completely detached from their referent, merely "imitating one another, mimicking the next mimicker in no time, no space, no place, no history" (48, 175–76). This recalls Michael Kreyling's vision of postsouthern parody, which has rightly caused concern for both Romine and Martyn Bone, who worry that such literature can imitate only previous texts or imitations of place (mimicking the next mimicker) rather than the increasingly elusive and removed real thing. Initially at least, this all seems an apt description of the postmodern, postfamilial, and hyperreal culture that

Yonder Stands Your Orphan depicts, a historyless "no place" of textual deferment or signs without their original referents.

Bjerre's inference above, however, that Hannah's own lamenting of the loss of the South is rooted in his characters' nostalgia, is an obvious matter of contention, especially when Hannah's other writing seems almost uniformly dedicated to removing the mythological authentic origin from nostalgic constructions of the past. If we believe that Hannah's last novel signals its author's obituary for an earlier "placed" or not-post South, this would complicate many of my arguments herein. Of course, it is possible that Hannah took a regressive nostalgic turn in his last novel in view of the unique circumstances of its writing. It was the only novel he produced while "sober," and its publication date comes just one year after the author almost died of pneumonia while receiving chemotherapy for the lymphoma that would eventually kill him. When interviewed by Ellen Kanner in 2001 about his latest novel, Hannah declared, "It's a pretty new direction for me. I have become more spiritually aware this year. I think anyone who was facing his death would be" (Hannah, "Barry Hannah"). Accordingly, Romine identifies a spiritual-redemption narrative in *Yonder Stands Your Orphan* that is absent from Hannah's earlier work, one made up of "small acts of kindness" that comprise "almost all of life that's beautiful" (*Yonder* 94). Perhaps, then, Hannah's self-professed new direction did consist of a renewed lament for the passing of the distinctive South and of Old Southern (Christian) community values and manners ("We don't love each other as much as we used to") and the avowal of an older humanistic ideology at odds with the antifoundationalist leanings of postmodern philosophy discussed here.

There are several problems with this reading, which can be complicated by using Romine's arguments about the nostalgia industry. To say that the present South is beset by themed space instead of authentic place, by nostalgic simulations of imagined pasts instead of real histories, is to suggest implicit recourse to a more authentic prior or alternative version of reality, a move radically discordant with Hannah's powerful affirmation of postsouthern languages and the strongly antinostalgic bent of his narratives. Recalling the heritage tourism industry that valorizes the (white) Old South and glosses over the ugly realities of slavery and segregation, Patricia Yaeger's *The Geography of Identity* (1996) argues that we consume themed space to feed our desire for homogenized, coherent space (18–19). But of course the creation of this product for consumption happens in the same way that nostalgic memory serves to order the past into an image that bears little relation to the reality. This feeds rather anxiously into Romine's argument for the preservation of Old World gentlemanly "manners" in *Yonder Stands Your Orphan*, itself redolent of more suspicious mythologies of the Old Southern way, as the antidote to the present posthuman culture.[1] Because Hannah's texts expose the inherently bogus nature of the southern-nostalgia industry, it is difficult to concur with Bjerre's conjecture that Hannah himself is nostalgic for the passing of a distinct and realer South.

Many of Hannah's characters appear to have inherited a distinctly southern nostalgia, further complicating the idea that *Yonder Stands Your Orphan* signals a radical departure from the author's earlier work. Indeed, Ulrich and his cohort of elderly nostalgics appear in Hannah's *Esquire* stories as early as 1970. The nostalgic past is a space that is coded as authentic and desirable, as Romine rightly points out, but ironically, it is precisely its *being* coded as authentic that renders it fundamentally obscurantist (to recall Edwin Yoder's uneasy foreword to Reed's *The Enduring South* [xv]) or inauthentic. This has been the nature not only of the vanishing authentic origin in the stories discussed but also of the metafictional ways that these texts draw our attention to how said "codes" are artificially constructed and enacted. When we recall John's predicament in Hannah's "Even Greenland," where mediations appear to have "used up" what is there until the possibility of authentic vision is lost (32), it becomes much harder to distinguish *Yonder Stands Your Orphan* from Hannah's earlier interrogations of regionality. Thus, while it is certainly compelling and important (not least as one of the few rigorous scholarly analyses of Hannah), in ways it is difficult to reconcile Romine's reading of the post-real South of *Yonder Stands Your Orphan* with Hannah's persistent breaking down of binarized conceptions of place and post-place elsewhere, in which contested ideas about historical rupture are foregrounded. Romine's diagnosis of the novel as the "culmination of Hannah's concern with pathological mimicry" (162) invites us then to question what previous or alternative realities these textual mediations might be mimicking and erasing in the first place.

It is telling here that some of the most direct (and the most questionable) statements of nostalgia for the Old (antebellum) South should come from the story's textual villain, Mortimer. In one key scene, Mortimer and his nemesis-doppelgänger, Frank Booth, contemplate the memorial site of the Battle of Vicksburg, a place that has signaled the conceptual turning point of the Confederacy's fortunes in the Lost Cause imaginary. As Hannah's first novel, *Geronimo Rex,* suggested (218), the site is also symbolic of what Romine identifies as the classic Faulknerian scenario, where every "southern boy fourteen years old" can imagine an alternative historical discourse in the South (Faulkner, *Intruder* 125–26, qtd. in Romine, "Orphans All" 168–69). The pivotal moment when the Confederate South lost the Civil War has been conceived of as crucial to contemporary constructions of defeated white southern masculinity, and it has invited the retrospective creation of a redemption narrative seen most obviously in Lost Cause mythology and what has more recently been termed neo-Confederate discourse.[2]

In *Yonder Stands Your Orphan,* Mortimer's and Booth's fantasies of the South that might have been lend insight into how alternative histories are imagined and turned into discursive mythologies: "They agreed that one expert Navy SEAL could have won the war that month. [. . .] It was common wisdom that the South would have given the slaves their freedom the instant they kicked the North's ass, but the slaves would have chosen to remain. [. . .] The South was so good. Why was this never discussed? [. . .] [Y]ou couldn't [discuss] it now, [with] all this correctness" (62). Becoming conspicuously more parodic as white southern discourse, as Romine notes ("Orphans All" 169), the men's fantasy reveals that nostalgic thinking about some alternative utopian present occluded by the failed realization of an imagined alternative past (the freed slaves would have *chosen* to remain had the Confederacy not fallen) is a fallacy precisely because it depends on a mythical version of history that never was. Just as media-made Dixie is vulnerable to its sentimentalized, Hollywood versions, so too is the region susceptible to what Romine calls "the grotesque historiography that here waxes rhapsodic over bizarre Lost Cause terrain" ("Orphans All" 169).

Mortimer's own nostalgia is parodied throughout. When thrashed "nearly to ectoplasm" he is "nostalgic for himself" (298), and the final "picture" he imagines, of himself making local history and "shaking hands with the law," is also parodic, and crucially, it contains a direct parody of nostalgic practice in itself: "Get nostalgic about when times were colorful and wilder and better" (277). I would argue here that southern nostalgia itself is the subject of Hannah's critique, more so than the postmodern culture that has lost touch with the nostalgic Real. It is an industry that has its dubious origins in Vicksburg, in "the instant" that the Confederate Cause was lost, as much or even more so than in today's postmodern culture, which feeds off the "lost" South's belated simulations. Hannah's novel cannot simply be nostalgic for some phantasmal older or alternative South, therefore, because this is a fiction that his writing challenges, thus eschewing reductive understandings of postsouthern cultures as being simply synonymous with the removal of the region.

This idea of the South being simultaneously real and unreal is furthered in the Vicksburg scene above, where the bloody reality of the South's unique history persists at the same time that the historical referent is erased by its subsequent memorializing and mythologizing ("The South was so good"). Crucially, the region's history joins the contemporary moment in a continuum of violent recurrence that is neatly in keeping both with gothic ideas about past ills resurfacing and with my arguments for continued (post) southern burden as a form of white cultural guilt. *Yonder Stands Your Orphan* begins with a sinkhole that drains the water from the bayou in which Mortimer has been dumping his victims' bodies. This prompts the narrator's historical introspection, rooted in the local topography, which catalogues a violent history: "Scores of corpses rested below the lakes, oxbows, river ways and bayous of these parts, not counting the skeletons of Grant's infantry. The country was built to hide those dead by foul deed, it sucked at them. Back to the flood of 1927, lynchings, gun and knife duels were common stories here. Muddy water made a fine lost tomb" (20–21). Recalling the "Civil War ghoulments" beneath the Strong River of Hannah's "Get Some Young" (25), Bjerre notes that "violence is inherent in the landscape; a common theme in southern fiction" ("Southern Evil" 84). In classic Faulknerian fashion, the landscape refuses to bury the region's ills, however mute a witness to history it might appear to be. The gruesome reality of the South's history, one that becomes gothically present in the actions of Mortimer (as well as in Hannah's grotesque inflection of pastoral in this scene), persists as a still tangible referent, while the nostalgic past, an imagined utopian fantasy, disappears.[3]

In *The Real South*, Romine cites Vladimir Nabokov's conjecture that "reality is one of those words that mean nothing without the quotes," and he suggests that *South* is another of these words (3). "The South is full of fakes" (2), Romine writes, but he concludes that this "fake" South becomes the "Real South" through "the intervention of narrative" (33). In Hannah's stories, mediations do not simply consume, obscure, or constitute reality in the way of hyperrealism or an inability to distinguish reality from fiction. Rather, his writing seems to refute the idea that the South exists in a purely constitutive condition by recognizing that material history persists while it is inextricably bound to the discursive politics of its representations. The voices of the past are kept alive by the tales we tell about them, the "common stories" of those dead by homicide, war, accidents, lynchings, and duels in the example above. Local history leaves traces in the ways we attempt to articulate it retrospectively.

Evoking Bone's self-professedly ongoing "historical-geographical materialist" approach, Tara McPherson has recently implored contemporary cultural studies to "be more materialist and less southern" by "pushing beyond representation and narrative" in our understandings of regional cultures ("Afterword" 320). Conversely, Handley and Lewis have argued that "the relation between history and representation, and between history and *its* representations, is the most crucial subject for critics of the region to engage" (3). My interpretations of Hannah's fiction have argued instead for something of a middle ground, a lessening of this imagined standoff between real and represented Souths, between southern and postmodern. This offers a means of reconciling some of the tensions in contemporary regional studies, where understandings of the region as discourse-predicated have been criticized for intentionally overlooking what Jon Smith calls the "real bodies" of history and the real violence that has been wrought upon them ("Toward" 75). I began this book by acknowledging that the South has always been a storied place, without suggesting that narrative is simply incompatible with material reality; certainly, the figure of Mortimer dumping newly murdered corpses on an already disfigured landscape emphasizes the enduring corporeality of southern history and the real lives that constitute it. Understanding southernness as a product of historical representation as much as material reality is not to deny the dynamic living history that unfolds within any physical region, which exists both within and beyond its storied representations.

Southernness endures in Hannah's postsouthern fiction, but the problems of postregionalism are integral to it, reformulating "South" into a postmodern framework within which history is inextricable from memory and memory is inextricable from myth, stories, and performance. All stories have a politics that demands proper critical attention; hence the interest in staging and audience-response in the stories discussed. *Yonder Stands Your*

Orphan cannot be finally understood as Hannah's eulogy for a once realer South nor as a representation of a *purely* simulated, mediated, or storied culture; history and story were already entwined in a manner that annuls any imagined fracture between South and post-South in terms of the relative authenticity of different historical moments. Romine argues that in *Yonder Stands Your Orphan* a nostalgic desire (or homesickness) for reality signals an attempt to recover the real as an antidote. In *The Plague of Fantasies,* Slavoj Žižek explains a corresponding paradox, that a narrative paradigm of "historical break does not simply designate the 'regressive' loss [. . .] of something, but *the shift in the very grid which enables us to measure losses and gains.*" Or more simply, that "when a certain historical moment is (mis) perceived as the moment of loss of some quality, upon closer inspection it becomes clear that the lost quality only emerged at this very moment of its alleged loss" (12–13). Again, Homer's formulation of the "pickled" South in *Hey Jack!* is helpful, pertaining to the preservation of regional difference, of a duplicitous vision of the waning South, through processes of mythologizing and cultural reproduction that have come about only in retrospect.

Jon Smith has also deployed Žižek to suggest the unhelpfulness of the prefix *post* in contemporary American cultural studies. Smith argues that as with the "historical break" paradigm above, in Žižek's formulation of melancholy the (Lacanian) desire for the lost object creates a paradox in which the elusive South is made possible again, harmfully so in Smith's view. Hence the call for a new southern studies without the South, a practice Smith imagines would cease perpetuating what he calls "White Southern Melancholy" or "the crisis fantasy" about "forgetting" the "traditional" South (*PA* 34, 4). Smith believes that this crisis fantasy—wherein white southerners have misconceived an imagined lack as the literal loss of a South from which they have departed or become "post" (34)—has been responsible for reinforcing Agrarian ideology about a "Grand Old sense of place" (J. Smith, Review 373), however progressive the rhetoric one uses to disguise it (*PA* 30).

Hannah's postsouthern fiction becomes curiously authentic (and authentically *southern*) at the precise moments when it shatters the illusion of the mimetic South. But in preserving some vestigial sense of the region, should writing that refuses to abandon the South altogether be simply accused of believing the literal loss of the literal South, thence preserving an outdated and nontransgressive (white, male, Christian, Agrarian) image of the South in place of properly engaged historicism? Of course Smith is right to be apprehensive about how postsouthern studies might unwittingly preserve older narratives about the loss of the South (declension narratives concerned only with an imagined lack rather than a literal loss) and suspicious of how the Agrarian roots of white southern melancholy or nostalgia for a mythical singular South have sometimes bled worryingly into subsequent thinking. While on many counts Hannah's writing accentuates the "postness" of its referent, it also quite radically eschews rigid or reactionary formulations of place and cultural identity. This is precisely the sort of rhetoric that Hannah's writing curtails: simple oppositions (real/fake, southern/postsouthern, old/new, better/worse) simply are not permitted in mutual exclusivity in his stories. Suzanne Jones and Sharon Monteith claim that "in a postmodern world, premodern and modern conceptions of place are inevitably insufficiently fluid" (4), and Hannah's fiction certainly demands a much less linear comprehension of the South's transition from regional to global. A more flexible approach to the distinction between southern and postsouthern is needed to rethink what we mean by southern exceptionalism.

Smith accuses the "old" southern studies of indulging in "narcissistic fantasies," and he wants the new southern studies to learn to look beyond these at "the real world" (*PA* 4). With McPherson, he rejects discourse-oriented studies of postmodernity and cultural reproduction such as Romine's, Ladd's, Kreyling's, and to a lesser extent Bone's. But as Hannah's characters Homer (in *Hey Jack!*) and John the pilot (in "Even Greenland") implied, to truly *see* the South beyond its mediations is itself an impossible fantasy: where *is* the real world outside our human (and thus narrative) perceptions of it? The "postmodern relativism" Smith discerns in scholarship centered on forms of narrative production—Smith invokes Jodi Dean's conception of the "postpolitical" as an "inherently conservative effect of postmodernism that forecloses real political activity on the left" (J. Smith, "Toward" 84)—does not do proper justice to the political and ethical bent of writing about a region that has always been self-consciously textual, metafictional, or *post*. Such an argument fails to acknowledge the ways that postregional criticism, like Hannah's fiction, complicates the prospect that the South ever was unified or distinct, that it ever did enjoy a Grand Old sense of place.

As with the problematic nostalgia industry above, efforts to locate culture often have the opposite effect of dislocating it from the here and now by "deferring its imagined 'true' or 'authentic' existence to some nostalgic past or utopian future" (*RS* 3), a false origin. Ulrich claims that "[p]eople are not even in the present moment" in *Yonder Stands Your Orphan* (46), in line with Romine's proposal that "culture has a habit of not being where and when we are presently" (*RS* 3). If the South and cultural identity more broadly have always been essentially not-present by their very nature, then postregional critical discourse cannot simply imply the *actual* loss of the South nor, by extension, a conservative attempt to preserve it. Rather, such discourse implies that the South has never been perfectly present in any cultural moment. If we agree, we can cease deferring the existence of the authentic South to a false nostalgic image, and in so doing reauthenticate a contemporary sense of the region.

What southern scholars should be asking, perhaps, is which *versions* of the South will take precedence in its contemporary narrative constructions; what sorts of imagined cultures will be preserved in the future by the multiplying critical discourses that accompany our ideas about the region. The real world inheres precisely in those artificial fantasies that Smith believes are proof of the South's nonexistence, and the real-world effects of political fantasies carry a similarly tangible (and often deadly) influence: recall the abused bodies in the bayou scene from *Yonder Stands Your Orphan*. Recent eschewals of *all* the South's distinctions can be just as potentially damaging in terms of denying the South's violent racial history, which does remain unique and specific in many ways. This can be observed in the far-reaching consequences of Reconstruction on the southern states, for example, or in the regional significance of so-called race riots and the (ongoing) struggle for civil rights when considered in relation to the South's century-long Jim Crow laws and their belated removal. The New Southern Studies movement first emerged from Baker and Nelson's call for a removal of ideological constructions of the region that cloak the corporeal wounds beneath, but perhaps the radical break from tradition its followers have endorsed (in the form of denying the South's specificity) has not helped this early imperative to be met. It is my contention that reality is discernible in our representations of reality, which are always political, and that the politics of narrative can be actively illuminated by the poststructuralist theory underwriting such postregional criticisms as Smith and others have rejected.

Discussing "the problem of place" in contemporary Western studies, Stephen Tatum and Nathaniel Lewis ask "what themes, forms, images, and rhetorical figures begin to define what we might call a postregional cultural style, one that nevertheless bears the traces of an older regional iconography and mythology about so-called 'western' places with their specific histories" (538). Hannah's postregional cultural style, his literary version of the modern South, certainly bears more than the traces of older regional mythology and a distinctly local history, while these are reconfigured in new ways. His stories are aesthetic products that cannibalize an existing tradition *of* aesthetic products as a key part of the new postregional aesthetic in the making. A sophisticated convergence of regional and postregional results in the dramatic interplay or symbiosis between textuality and authenticity and in the constant dynamic flux between stories and reality. Performances are integral to this style, one that becomes new while retaining a critical awareness of older southern ideologies and its own indebtedness to them.

Earlier I cited Giovanna Summerfield and Lisa Downward's twenty-first-century reconfiguration of the classical bildungsroman, arguing that the presence of narrative retrospection in a mostly future-oriented genre may be read not simply as an indicator of a closed future as per its usual understanding (Franco Moretti's [68]) but rather as a crucial means of opening the future by readdressing the past (Summerfield and Downward 107). Something similar emerges in Kelly Oliver's study of historical witness, which posits "a reverse causality whereby the future affects the past. The image of a better future affects the past that makes it (the future) possible. In a sense, we revisit the past for the sake of a better future" (136). This evokes Rick Bragg's method of "dreaming backwards" in his 1997 memoir of growing up in poor white Alabama hill culture, *All Over but the Shoutin'* (xiii), as well as Jesmyn Ward's reverse-time, etiological study of racism in Mississippi in her own memoir, *Men We Reaped* (2013). Oliver argues that we should be vigilant in ensuring that the past be never "closed" or dead, because "the future opens onto otherness only insofar as the past does too" (136). She draws on Derrida's *Archive Fever*, which claims that history, the archive, is more about the future than the past, such that meaning remains open. If history "is a question of the future [and] of a response, of a promise and of a responsibility for tomorrow" (Derrida, *Archive* 36, qtd. in Oliver 136), then the still useful southern modernist trope of the undead past is a question that persistently requires a response from the present. In this way the dialogue is kept open, and so too the question of what the South's future will hold.

In a fraught and crowded field, we might view the NSS's posited break from existing tradition as evidence of an implicit desire to transcend the potential paralysis of contemporary southern scholarship, whose belatedness necessitates the continual renegotiation of past ground. However, to deny or cease talking about this past ground is a mistake, because it establishes a historical fissure of its own that denies the possibility of reimagining the past to imagine the future, and the future is only open insofar as the past remains so. The roots of the South's retrospection lie in highly tendentious ground, but in view of the region's distinctly dystopian past, to continue to look back is to continue critically to revisit the past for the sake of a more positive future. Our contemporary compulsions to constantly remap the South can transcend their nostalgic origins for a South that was once better, realer, or not-post, while retaining an awareness of the South's turbulent beginnings as a reminder of the rhetorical doctoring that can underwrite regional criticisms and the construction of regional differences. To return to Žižek's "lack" paradox (the lost thing emerges in the moment of its imagined disappearance), I would argue, therefore, that the version of the South that emerges in a postregional moment is not simply a recovery of the problematic exceptional South that the Agrarians first envisioned in the 1930s.

The "marriage of postmodernity and the southern literary imagination" (Guinn 178) was bound to be an interesting one. The question of the South's preservation or disappearance occurs during the collision between a culture that has fetishized its own distinction since before the Civil War and a contemporary recognition of the frailty of historicity and region. Because the problems of postregionalism are so integral to Hannah's oeuvre, his writing forms an important response to the quandaries of a specific historical moment. And precisely *because* such postsouthern writing is attentive to the problems of history, place, and aesthetic authenticity, its place in evolving negotiations of what the South was, is, or will be is ensured. As Susan Van D'Elden Donaldson suggests, "There is still too much to be said about the seemingly endless capacity of the American South to generate stories about itself, and nowhere more so than in a time when master narratives and the places they purport to represent and defend have splintered into a multitude of micronarratives and microplaces" (133). In a postregional moment, to be suspicious of master narratives and a foundational "hermeneutics of place" (Janz 4) while recognizing the region's persistent propensity for story is not simply to leave the South behind.

Jones and Monteith do not deny the significance of place altogether but rather promote a "traveling theory" of place from which "new coordinates of southern identity" can come, "read[ing] region as a site of exchange" amid contemporary debates that question not only the meaning but the very *existence* of "South" (9, 10). Christopher Lloyd agrees that "a global perspective on southern literature therefore does not necessarily disregard regionalism (though many critics push toward that anyway), but locates it within a larger network of forces, places, and cultures" ("Contemporary" 14). Barbara Ladd argues similarly that as a product of transnational culture, the South "needs to be constructed not as a stable site of tradition and history" (39) but as something more "dramatic and fleeting, produced by encounter, contingent" (40). Hannah's fiction makes a vital contribution to such arguments by revealing the fleeting contingency of the very region (and the plurality of its inhabitants and their encounters) that his writing appears at first to valorize. Problematizing the South as a fixed and stable entity with its roots in a single authentic origin, but not abandoning its specificity completely, allows a more open approach to regional studies to emerge. The absence of the true or foundational South is not something to be lamented but rather to be celebrated, for the interpretative inclusivity that the concept of the post-region facilitates.

As changing interpretative parameters shift our conceptualizations of regional identity to new realms, the problem of southern postregionalism is far from over. Not least as new voices, as well as previously unheard or silenced ones, emerge within the ever-expanding parameters of southern literature. While there has not been space to accommodate them here, such voices might come from the Native South; from African or Asian Americans; from poor white "hillbilly" or "backwoods" cultures; from homosexual or transgendered writers of different ethnicities; and so on. Similarly, Hannah's fiction invites analysis in terms of several further important areas of critical inquiry that lie beyond the scope of this book. These include but are not limited to economic issues of social class and migration; gendered nostalgia or female referentiality; feminine subjugation in Western Fall mythology; the relationships between Catholic guilt (original sin) and white guilt in the South and between (evangelist) shame-honor culture and white southern narcissism. Finally, the ongoing complexities of southern race relations, where the paradoxical issue of performative authenticity discussed here might be productively extended to discussions of Blackness as well as whiteness or to indigenous studies and the concept of "playing Indian."

Thinking about a literary post-South that exists somewhere between an old southern distinctiveness tradition and a new one that at its most ex-treme denies the existence of the exceptional South altogether offers a pro-ductive middle ground upon which I have situated Hannah's fiction. Because he writes at so crucial a moment in our rethinking of regions, Hannah's intense self-reflexivity reveals how contemporary creative writing that fo-rensically cross-examines its own aesthetic methods might still be called authentically southern, and no less engaged with the political and socio-cultural contexts in which all writing is inevitably situated. Krista Comer argues that "self-reflexivity needs to play a critical role in negotiating in-sider and outsider discourses" ("Exceptionalism" 170), and there is no ques-tion that self-reflexivity is a key feature of the postsouthern aesthetic imag-ined by Hannah, one that acknowledges its own complicity in negotiating the changing terrain upon which it writes, while inflecting established re-gional discourses in new ways that question and challenge them. This sort of writing invites critical attention to the interactions between texts and their audiences at the dynamic intersection of history and story. To under-stand Hannah's fiction properly, we need to move beyond the problem of whether the South *exists*, a misnomer in my view, in favor of a complex un-derstanding of a regional (literary) culture that is simultaneously as authen-tic and distinctive as it is performative and contrived and acutely aware of this tension.

In terms of opening up postregional debates, the period of Hannah's lit-erary success spans an instrumental period of critical inquiry into the con-structedness of authenticity, history, identity, and region. His fiction shows how local cultures and places emerge through the material and the discur-sive simultaneously, and this is vital to thinking about the South as a meet-ing of these two elements. If the South has always been in a process of be-coming, as Edward Ayers suggested, then the region can never be simply "dead," because it will never truly be *finished*. It is in a constant process of emerging, such that I would argue that poststructuralist contemplations of regional identity that emphasize the textuality of history and culture and resist the finality of interpretation have not yet had their day.

Writing against Jameson's conjecture of the postmodern "enfeeblement of history" ("Magic Realism" 303), Hutcheon contends that postmodernist art "is, if anything, obsessed with history and with how we can know the past today" (Hutcheon, *Politics* 114). It is the putative loss of something (his-tory) that makes its presence more palpably felt, paradoxically, in its imagined absence. I think something similar can be said of the South. The myriad attempts to articulate what the South is or is not in a culture that not only recently radically eschewed its existence but has from its earliest conception been characterized by a sense of its own suspected enfeeblement are tantamount to a recognition not of the South's enervation but of its endurance. The fact that we keep telling about the South in what Jon Smith called an already "overdetermined" field (*PA* 6) is testimony to the region's tenacity as a material reality, a literary subject, and a viable avenue of critical inquiry. As long as it remains in our critical vocabulary, the South will continue to be real insofar as it has the power to create narratives and fantasies that will affect real actions in the world, good and bad, on the left and on the right. And the more self-reflexive these narratives become, however paralyzing that can seem in a field of inquiry whose subject has been anxiously metafictional from the start, the less its scholars will reiterate harmful old ideologies, knowingly or otherwise.

In her discussion of exceptionalism and the American West, Comer ponders whether the concept of the post-region must simply dismantle the guarantors of regional authenticity. She asks, "Can a critical field that began by way of oppositional identity and an ethics of place retain that ethics as one important genealogy while evolving beyond it?" ("Exceptionalism" 160). Hannah's fiction offers deeply valuable ways of rethinking southern history and identity, from the very beginnings of critical thinking about the region and what it means to write about it. Approaching his writing in this mode is a vital way of reconceptualizing our approaches to modern southern studies, not only in the contemporary global moment but also in ways that are useful retrospectively, complicating earlier ideas about regional identity and reopening a dialogue between old and new. It is my contention that Hannah's writing will retain its critical currency as we explore the ongoing quandaries of postsouthern cultures and their literatures, while we are in the imminent process of articulating a new lexicon of what might be termed *post-postregionalism,* one that is evolving beyond discussions of the (post-) region and an ethics of place. Can contemporary southern writing retain a sense of regional authenticity after it has been obliged to acknowledge the death of its own referent? Hannah's extraordinary fiction shows us unequivocally that it can.

Notes

Introduction

1. Herein, bracketed ellipses are my own, whereas unbracketed ellipses are present in the original quoted text.

2. See Coski; McPherson, *Reconstructing Dixie* 33–36, 264; and Thornton.

3. Similar charges have been leveled at Hannah's own writing, whose politically incendiary and often violent and grotesque humor has its roots in some specific American literary traditions, as Weston notes (*BH* 106); and it showcases, I would argue, some of the discourses that circulate in contemporary southern culture but are not simply indicative of the author's personal political beliefs.

4. Early attempts to articulate the white South's stigmatization as uniquely "un-American," antithetical to the nation at large, where national racist practices can be contained and localized, include C. Vann Woodward's *The Burden of Southern History,* Killian's *White Southerners,* and Reed's *The Enduring South.* Such texts continue to inform apprehensions of southern otherness and white southern burden in the twenty-first century; see, e.g., L. Griffin's "Southern Distinctiveness, Yet Again"; Duck's *The Nation's Region;* or *The Ongoing Burden of Southern History,* by Maxwell et al.

5. Brinkmeyer distinguishes Hannah from a number of his contemporaries (Doris Betts, Cormac McCarthy, Madison Smartt Bell, Richard Ford, Rick Bass, Barbara Kingsolver, Chris Offutt, Frederick Barthelme, Clyde Edgerton) who have exceeded the geographical confines of the South by "going West" in their choice of fictional setting (2).

6. For a rebuttal of Hobson's inference of the negation of place, region, and historical consciousness in Hannah's fiction, see Shipe 111.

7. I have chosen herein to capitalize *Black* but not *white,* following university press preference in view of some recent calls (at the time of writing) for this stylistic change.

8. See *SOP* 44; and G. Wright 16.

Chapter One

1. Barth's skepticism of the mimetic fallacy is outlined in "The Literature of Exhaustion." Hannah's now out-of-print second novel, *Nightwatchmen* (1973), covers remarkably similar conceptual terrain, as Lee argues in his "Off with Their Heads!," his contribution to Bone's *Perspectives on Barry Hannah.*

2. Boes identifies the 1980s as an "end of an era" period in which "new conceptual approaches to the novel of formation were radically transforming the discipline" (233). Millard explores recent disputes over the generic conventions of bildungsromane, where critics have questioned the continued application of a late-eighteenth-century European concept to recent American texts that are "removed both historically and culturally from the term's origin" (*Coming of Age* 3). See Ellmann 192 for further discussion of the bildungsroman genre's historical transformation.

3. Like Joyce's *Portrait*, D. H. Lawrence's *Sons and Lovers* offers another useful comparator as a modernist bildungsroman. And while space prevents this here, the issues of authenticity and subjectivity explored in Harry's epiphanies might be usefully compared to the aesthetic device of epiphany in other modernist literature (e.g., Virginia Woolf's "moments of being").

4. See Joyce, *Critical Writings* 145 and *Stephen Hero* 211–13, 218. If the modernists' call to "make it new" can be understood as a response to a profoundly shifting culture after World War I, we can observe something similar occurring in the post-1960s South. For example, when the cultural transitions accompanying belatedly wrought civil rights in the region (the success of which remains deeply problematic, and not just in the South) necessitated a radical reappraisal of the white South's literary perception of itself.

5. See Bucknell 26–32 for an overview of modernist scholarship in the tradition of the "absolute music" paradigm Chua writes against.

6. Hannah's unique writerly style has earned him an entry under "*H*" in the southerner Nicholas Rombes's *A Cultural Dictionary of Punk: 1974–1982.* Remarkably, Rombes claims that despite its anachronistic position in relation to the American punk era and, indeed, the parameters of his own study, "in many ways, Hannah's 1970 [*sic*] novel *Geronimo Rex* is responsible for the book you are reading." By way of explanation, Rombes gives examples of Hannah's dazzling prose style, and he coins a new aesthetic category to describe it: "southern gothic punk" (116).

7. Bone argues that the adolescent estrangement of the character Blackie Pride in Windham's *The Dog Star* (1950) has a similar sociospatial basis because of Pride's inhabiting Atlanta's impoverished white urban underclass in the 1930s Depression-era South (*SOP* 152).

8. See D. Schwarz's edited collection of essays, *Naming and Referring,* or Q. Smith 179 for a comprehensive bibliography of key scholars in the field.

Chapter Two

1. *The Guardian* obituary for Giap contains several useful comparisons with Hannah's fictional character: www.theguardian.com/world/2013/oct/04/general-vo-nguyen-giap.

2. For sociological studies of hegemonic masculinity and sport, see Bryson; Young and Smith; Messner; and Boyle and Haynes. Messenger's *Sport and the Spirit of Play in American Fiction* charts different "types" of masculine sports hero in American fiction over time. While space prevents this here, it would be useful to consider the South's relationship to an American mythology of sporting victory, for example, in relation to the Old Southwestern humorists (frequent contributors to men's or sports magazines) and their humorous treatment of sport in southern "gentleman" society; see Messenger 119.

3. "Midnight and I'm Not Famous Yet" and "Return to Return" appear almost verbatim as two chapters of *The Tennis Handsome,* where John Whitelaw is latterly renamed French Edward and golf is replaced with tennis.

4. While beyond my scope here, Smith's word choice (specifically, *brave* and *mighty*) could offer a contrary means of problematizing the alterity, or "hybridity," of Whitelaw's masculinity, because it blurs my purported distinction between "traditional" and "modern" ideas about what makes a real man.

Chapter Three

1. Much recent critical anxiety surrounds the political implications of the concept of white guilt; see, e.g., Steele's *White Guilt* or McKee's "Globalization and Southern Literature."

2. Bandini's "hunching" is both a comic nod to the Southern boys' (homoerotic) infatuation with Faulkner and a word for masturbation that Hannah uses to parody the notion of new southern writers working under Faulkner's anxious influence (see, e.g., *Hey Jack!* 122, when the character called Foot masturbates over Faulkner's grave).

Chapter Four

1. See Davis 6; and Langer 263. If space permitted, it would be interesting to explore whether indigenous American cultures would experience nostalgia in the same way if their conception of history were of something living and continuous, that is, if it did not include imagined points of rupture or even a sense of *past* as Western cultures would conceive of the term.

2. See also Boluk and Lenz 11. In *Undead Souths* (2–15), Ellis explores alternative meanings behind the prevalence of "zombie" narratives in southern culture and literature, from their earliest conceptions in 1929 through to their continued relevance to the new global southern studies.

3. Radstone's *The Sexual Politics of Time* and Greene's *Changing the Story,* which explore how narratives can be gendered and have "different meanings for men and women" (Radstone 295–96), might prove useful when pursuing this idea.

Chapter Five

1. We can observe Twain's influence also in the contemporary southern fiction of Charles Portis, Richard Ford, Ishmael Reed, and Cormac McCarthy (Graybill 120–21).

2. See *BH* 33, 53, 84; Guinn xii, 163–64; Kreyling, *Inventing* 156–57; and Kreyling, "Fee, Fie, Faux Faulkner" 11–12.

Chapter Six

1. Bakhtin reserves his theory of dialogism for discussions of the novel and novelistic discourse as a uniquely open-ended genre, but I would argue that it can certainly be extended to a short story like "Get Some Young," if not to the short-story genre more broadly.

2. McCarthy's words lend Crews's recent critical study of McCarthy, *Books Are Made Out of Books*, its title.

3. Fry documents the high numbers of poor southern whites who enlisted for the Vietnam War, attributing this to the lack of college prospects for this socioeconomic group (along with poor southern Blacks) and to their hope that the military offered "a way up and out" (157).

4. While space does not permit this here, the idea of literary representations of character "types" in the South would be an interesting area for further inquiry, such as Robertson has explored in "Poor Whites in Recent Southern Fiction."

5. The line in Joyce reads, "riverrun past Eve and Adam's, from swerve of shore to bend of bay" (*Finnegans Wake* 3).

6. For an instructive breakdown of the story's intertextual references, see *BH* 63. Caverlee has extended the Tuck–Humbert Humbert parallel to the characters Jason Compson in Faulkner's *The Sound and the Fury* and Travis Bickle in Martin Scorsese's *Taxi Driver*. Pagan's postmodern approach to Williams's *Orpheus Descending* is interesting here, as it points out parallels between Orphic music and contemporary southern blues, both of which are associated with loss and what Pagan calls "lonesomeness." This directly pertains to the title of Hannah's collection, and it is a term recurrent both in blues music (Pagan invokes the Mississippian musician Robert Johnson's popular 1930s lyrics) and in Williams's play alike (Pagan 54–57).

Conclusion

1. J. Smith's "Toward a Post-postpolitical Southern Studies" censures Romine's focus on the simulative South as being inherently conservative, contending that Romine's claim "better a cyber-Confederacy than a real one" (*RS* 236) problematically "cuts both ways," to the end that it can equally imply "better a cyber–civil rights movement than a real one" (J. Smith, "Toward" 86).

2. See Bone, "Neo-Confederate"; and Loewen and Sebesta.

3. Cormac McCarthy's *Child of God* (1973), Mark Richard's *Fishboy: A Ghost's Story* (1993), William Gay's *Provinces of Night* (2000), and Charles Frazier's *Nightwoods* (2011) provide good further examples of contemporary Southern Gothic. See Bjerre, "Southern Gothic Literature" 16, for further discussion of the "undead" trope in both traditional and recent Southern Gothic literature.

Works Cited

"About Us." *Southern Living*, 18 Feb. 2016, www.southernliving.com/general/about-us
-page. Accessed 4 Oct. 2020.

Allison, Dorothy. *Bastard Out of Carolina*. Flamingo, 1993.

Anderson, Benedict. *Imagined Communities: Reflections on the Origins and Spread of Nationalism*. Verso, 1983.

Anderson, David. "Down Memory Lane: Nostalgia for the Old South in Post–Civil War Plantation Reminiscences." *The Journal of Southern History*, vol. 71, no. 1, Feb. 2005, pp. 105–36.

Anderson, Eric Gary. "Rethinking Indigenous Southern Communities." *American Literature*, vol. 78, no. 4, Dec. 2006, pp. 730–32.

Appadurai, Arjun. *Modernity at Large: Cultural Dimensions of Globalization*. U of Minnesota P, 1996.

Attridge, Derek. "Language, Sexuality and the Remainder in *A Portrait of the Artist as a Young Man*." *James Joyce and the Difference of Language*, edited by Laurent Milesi, Cambridge UP, 2003, pp. 128–41.

"Authentic." *Oxford Dictionary of English*, 3rd ed., 2010.

Ayers, Edward. *All Over the Map: Rethinking American Regions*. Johns Hopkins UP, 1996.

———. *The Promise of the New South: Life After Reconstruction*. Oxford UP, 2007.

Baker, Houston, and Dana Nelson. "Preface: Violence, the Body and 'The South.'" *American Literature*, vol. 73, no. 2, June 2001, pp. 231–44.

Bakhtin, Mikhail. *The Dialogic Imagination: Four Essays*. Edited by Michael Holquist, translated by Caryl Emerson, U of Texas P, 2008, pp. 41–83.

———. *Problems of Dostoevsky's Poetics*. Edited and translated by Caryl Emerson, U of Minnesota P, 2009.

Barker, Deborah, and Kathryn McKee, editors. *American Cinema and the Southern Imaginary*. U of Georgia P, 2011.

Barth, John. *The End of the Road*. Dalkey Archive Press, 2017.

———. "The Literature of Exhaustion." 1967. *The Friday Book: Essays and Other Non-Fiction*, Johns Hopkins UP, 1984, pp. 62–76.

Baudrillard, *Baudrillard Live: Selected Interviews.* Edited by Mike Gane, Routledge, 1993.

———. *Simulations.* Translated by Paul Foss et al., Semiotext(e), 1983.

Bederman, Gail. *Manliness and Civilization: A Cultural History of Gender and Race in the United States, 1880–1917.* U of Chicago P, 1996.

Beidler, Philip D. Review of *Barry Hannah: Postmodern Romantic,* by Ruth D. Weston. *Southern Literary Journal,* vol. 33, Fall 2000, p. 154.

Beja, Morris. *Epiphany in the Modern Novel.* U of Washington P, 1971.

Benson Taylor, Melanie. *Reconstructing the Native South: American Indian Literature and the Lost Cause.* U of Georgia P, 2012.

———. "Southern and Western Native Americans in Barry Hannah's Fiction." Bone, *Perspectives on Barry Hannah,* pp. 139–60.

The Bible: Authorized King James Version. Edited by Robert Carroll and Stephen Prickett, Oxford UP, 1998.

Bibler, Michael P. "Introduction: Smash the Mason-Dixie! or, Manifesting the Southern United States." *PMLA,* vol. 131, no. 1, Jan. 2016, pp. 153–56.

Bidney, Martin. *Patterns of Epiphany: From Wordsworth to Tolstoy, Pater, and Barrett Browning.* Southern Illinois UP, 1997.

Bjerre, Thomas. "Heroism and the Changing Face of American Manhood in Barry Hannah's Fiction." Bone, *Perspectives on Barry Hannah,* pp. 46–64.

———. "Southern Evil, Southern Violence: Gothic Residues in the Works of William Gay, Barry Hannah, and Cormac McCarthy." *The Scourges of the South? Essays on "The Sickly South" in History, Literature, and Popular Culture,* edited by Thomas Bjerre and Beata Zawadka, Cambridge Scholars, 2014, pp. 77–92.

———. "Southern Gothic Literature." *Oxford Research Encyclopedia of Literature,* June 2017, pp. 1–27, doi: 10.1093/acrefore/9780190201098.013.304.

Blanton, Linda. "Southern Appalachia: Social Considerations of Speech." *Toward a Social History of American English,* edited by Joey Dillard, Mouton, 1985, pp. 73–90.

Blight, David. *Race and Reunion: The Civil War in American Memory.* Harvard UP, 2001.

Blevins, Brooks. *Ghosts of the Ozarks: Murder and Memory in the Upland South.* U of Illinois P, 2012.

———. *Hill Folks: A History of Arkansas Ozarkers and Their Image.* U of North Carolina P, 2002.

Bloom, Harold, editor. *Thomas Pynchon.* Chelsea House, 2003.

Bly, Robert. *Iron John: Men and Masculinity.* Element, 2001.

Boes, Tobias. "Modernist Studies and the *Bildungsroman:* A Historical Survey of Critical Trends." *Literature Compass,* vol. 3, no. 2, Feb. 2006, pp. 230–43, *Wiley Online Library,* doi:10.1111/j.1741–4113.2006.00303.

Boluk, Stephanie, and Wylie Lenz. "Introduction: Generation Z, the Age of Apocalypse." *Generation Zombie: Essays on the Living Dead in Modern Culture,* McFarland, 2011, pp. 1–14.

Bone, Martyn. Introduction. Bone, *Perspectives on Barry Hannah,* pp. ix–xvii.

———. "Neo-Confederate Narrative and Postsouthern Parody: Hannah and Faulkner." Bone, *Perspectives on Barry Hannah,* pp. 85–101.

———, editor. *Perspectives on Barry Hannah.* 2007. UP of Mississippi, 2010.

———. *The Postsouthern Sense of Place in Contemporary Fiction.* Louisiana State UP, 2005.

———. "Southern Fiction." *The Cambridge Companion to American Fiction After 1945,* edited by John Duvall, Cambridge UP, 2012, pp. 154–66.

———. *Where the New World Is: Literature about the U.S. South at Global Scales.* U of Georgia P, 2018.

Bone, Martyn, et al., editors. *Creating and Consuming the American South.* UP of Florida, 2015.

Boyle, Raymond, and Richard Haynes. *Power Play: Sport, the Media and Popular Culture.* Edinburgh UP, 2012.

Boym, Svetlana. *The Future of Nostalgia.* Basic Books, 2008.

Bragg, Rick. *All Over but the Shoutin'.* Vintage, 1997.

———. *Ava's Man.* Knopf, 2001.

———. *Prince of Frogtown.* Knopf, 2008.

Bridges, Tristan, and Cheri Pascoe. "Hybrid Masculinities: New Directions in the Sociology of Men and Masculinities." *Sociology Compass,* vol. 8, no. 3, Mar. 2014, pp. 246–58.

Brinkmeyer, Robert. *Remapping Southern Literature: Contemporary Southern Writers and the West.* U of Georgia P, 2000.

Brooks, Cleanth. "History and the Sense of the Tragic." *William Faulkner's* Absalom, Absalom!: *A Casebook,* edited by Fred Hobson, Oxford UP, 2013, pp. 17–46.

Brundage, W. Fitzhugh. "From Appalachian Folk to Southern Foodways: Why Americans Look to the South for Authentic Culture." Bone et al., pp. 27–48.

———. *The Southern Past: A Clash of Race and Memory.* Belknap Press of Harvard UP, 2005.

———, editor. *Where These Memories Grow: History, Memory, and Southern Identity.* U of North Carolina P, 2000.

Bryson, Lois. "Sport and the Maintenance of Masculine Hegemony." *Women's Studies International Forum,* vol. 10, no. 4, 1987, pp. 349–60.

Bucknell, Brad. *Literary Modernism and Musical Aesthetics: Pater, Pound, Joyce and Stein.* Cambridge UP, 2001.

Butler, Judith. *Gender Trouble: Feminism and the Subversion of Identity.* Routledge, 1990.

———. "Performative Acts and Gender Constitution: An Essay in Phenomenology and Feminist Theory." *Theatre Journal,* vol. 40, no. 1, 1988, pp. 519–21.

Campbell, Neil. *The Rhizomatic West: Representing the American West in a Transnational, Global, Media Age*. U of Nebraska P, 2008.

Carlton, David L., and Peter A. Coclanis. *The South, The Nation, and The World: Perspectives on Southern Economic Development*. U of Virginia P, 2003.

Carpenter, Brian, and Tom Franklin, editors. *Grit Lit: A Rough South Reader*. U of South Carolina P, 2012.

Caruth, Cathy. *Unclaimed Experience: Trauma, Narrative, and History*. Johns Hopkins UP, 2016.

Casey, Edward. *The Fate of Place: A Philosophical History*. U of California P, 1997.

Cash, W. J. *The Mind of the South*. Knopf, 1962.

Caverlee, William. "Barry Hannah's Late Love Song to Mississippi: 'Get Some Young.'" *Literary Traveler*, 23 Mar. 2015, www.literarytraveler.com/articles/barry-hannahs-late-love-song-to-mississippi-get-some-young/.

Chapman, Mary, and Glenn Hendler, editors. Introduction. *Sentimental Men: The Politics of Affect in American Culture*, U of California P, 1999.

Charney, Mark J. *Barry Hannah*. Twayne, 1992.

Cheever, Abigail. *Real Phonies: Cultures of Authenticity in Post–World War II America*. U of Georgia P, 2010.

Chidester, David. *Authentic Fakes: Religion and American Popular Culture*. U of California P, 2005.

Chua, Daniel. *Absolute Music and the Construction of Meaning*. Cambridge UP, 1999.

Clarkson, Carol. "'By Any Other Name': Kripke, Derrida and an Ethics of Naming." *Journal of Literary Semantics*, vol. 32, no. 1, Feb. 2003, pp. 37–47.

Cobb, James C. *Away Down South: A History of Southern Identity*. Oxford UP, 2005.

Cobb, James C., and William Stueck, editors. *Globalization and the American South*. U of Georgia P, 2005.

Cohn, David L. *Where I Was Born and Raised*. Houghton Mifflin, 1948.

Cohn, Deborah. *History and Memory in the Two Souths: Recent Southern and Spanish American Fiction*. Vanderbilt UP, 1999.

Comer, Krista. "Exceptionalism, Other Wests, Critical Regionalism." *American Literary History*, vol. 23, no. 1, Spring 2011, pp. 159–73.

———. *Landscapes of the New West: Gender and Geography in Contemporary Women's Writing*. U of North Carolina P, 1999.

Connell, R. W. *Gender and Power: Society, the Person and Sexual Politics*. Stanford UP, 1987.

Cooke, Deryck. *The Language of Music*. Oxford UP, 1989.

Coski, John. *The Confederate Battle Flag: America's Most Embattled Emblem*. Harvard UP, 2006.

Cox, Karen. *Dreaming of Dixie: How the South Was Created in American Popular Culture*. U of North Carolina P, 2011.

Crane, Stephen. *The Red Badge of Courage.* Ignatius Press, 2012.

Crews, Michael. *Books Are Made Out of Books: A Guide to Cormac McCarthy's Literary Influences.* U of Texas P, 2017.

Cubit, Geoffrey. *History and Memory.* Manchester UP, 2007.

Culler, Jonathan. *On Deconstruction: Theory and Criticism after Structuralism.* Routledge, 1982.

Currie, Mark, editor. *Metafiction.* Longman, 1995.

Davis, Fred. *Yearning for Yesterday: A Sociology of Nostalgia.* Free Press, 1979.

Day, William Patrick. *In the Circles of Fear and Desire: A Study of Gothic Fantasy.* U of Chicago P, 1985.

Dean, Jodi. *Democracy and Other Liberal Fantasies: Communicative Capitalism and Left Politics.* Duke UP, 2009.

Deloria, Philip J. *Playing Indian.* Yale UP, 1998.

Derrida, Jacques. *Archive Fever: A Freudian Impression.* Translated by Eric Prenowitz, U of Chicago P, 1996.

———. *Of Grammatology.* Translated by Gayatri Chakravorty Spivak, Johns Hopkins UP, 1974.

Dickey, James. *Deliverance.* Houghton Mifflin, 1970.

Didion, Joan. *South and West: From a Notebook.* 4th Estate, 2017.

Dissanayake, Wimal, and Rob Wilson, editors. *Global/Local: Cultural Production and the Transnational Imaginary.* Duke UP, 1996.

Dosse, François. *History of Structuralism: Volume 1, The Rising Sign, 1945–1966.* Translated by Debora Glassman, U of Minnesota P, 1997.

Du Bois, W. E. B. "The African Roots of War." *The Atlantic Monthly,* vol. 115, no. 1, May 1915, pp. 707–14.

Duck, Leigh Anne. *The Nation's Region: Southern Modernism, Segregation, and U.S. Nationalism.* U of Georgia P, 2006.

———. "Southern Nonidentity." *Safundi: The Journal of South African and American Studies,* vol. 9, no. 3, July 2008, pp. 319–30.

Duvall, John, and Ann Abadie, editors. *Faulkner and Postmodernism.* U of Mississippi P, 1999.

Eagle, Christopher. *Cratylism and Its Discontents: Modernist Theories of the Perfect Language.* BiblioBazaar, 2011.

Eastman, Jason T. "Rebel Manhood: The Hegemonic Masculinity of the Southern Rock Music Revival." *The Journal of Contemporary Ethnography,* vol. 42, no. 1, Nov. 2011, pp. 189–219, doi:10.1177/0891241611426430.

Eliot, T. S. "The Love Song of J. Alfred Prufrock." *The Waste Land and Other Poems,* edited by Joseph Black et al., Broadview Press, 2011, pp. 17–22.

———. *The Waste Land. The Waste Land and Other Poems,* edited by Joseph Black et al., Broadview Press, 2011, pp. 63–83.

Ellis, Jay. *Undead Souths: The Gothic and Beyond in Southern Literature and Culture.* Louisiana State UP, 2015.

Ellmann, Maud. "Disremembering Dedalus: *A Portrait of the Artist as a Young Man.*" *Untying the Text: A Post-Structuralist Reader,* edited by Robert Young, Routledge, 1981, pp. 189–206.

Epstein, Helen. *Children of the Holocaust: Conversations with Sons and Daughters of Survivors.* Bantam Books, 1980.

Faulkner, William. *Absalom, Absalom!* Vintage, 1990.

———. *As I Lay Dying.* Vintage, 2007.

———. *"Go Down, Moses" and Other Stories.* Vintage, 2013.

———. *Intruder in the Dust.* Random House, 1948.

———. *Requiem for a Nun.* Vintage, 2013.

———. *Sanctuary.* Knopf Doubleday, 2011.

———. *Sartoris.* Penguin, 1953.

———. *The Unvanquished.* HarperCollins, 2013.

Federman, Raymond. *Surfiction: Fiction Now . . . and Tomorrow.* Swallow Press, 1975.

Felski, Rita. *Doing Time: Feminist Theory and Postmodern Culture.* New York UP, 2000.

Fiedler, Leslie A. *An End to Innocence: Essays on Culture and Politics.* Beacon Press, 1955.

Franklin, Tom. *Smonk, or Widow Town.* Harper, 2006.

Frazier, Charles. *Nightwoods.* Sceptre, 2011.

Friend, Craig Thompson, editor. *Southern Masculinity: Perspectives on Manhood in the South since Reconstruction.* U of Georgia P, 2009.

Friend, Craig Thompson, and Lorri Glover, editors. *Southern Manhood: Perspectives on Masculinity in the Old South.* U of Georgia P, 2004.

Fry, Joseph. *The American South and the Vietnam War: Belligerence, Protest, and Agony in Dixie.* UP of Kentucky, 2013.

Gardiner, Judith, editor. *Masculinity Studies and Feminist Theory: New Directions.* Columbia UP, 2002.

Gates, Henry Louis. "'Authenticity,' or the Lesson of Little Tree." *New York Times Book Review,* 24 Nov. 1991, p. 30.

Gay, William. *Provinces of Night.* Doubleday, 2000.

Gerster, Patrick. "Religion and Mythology." *The New Encyclopedia of Southern Culture: Volume 4, Myth, Manners, and Memory,* edited by Charles Raegan Wilson, U of North Carolina P, 2006, pp. 158–62.

Gerster, Patrick, and Nicholas Cords, editors. *Myth and Southern History: Volume 2, The New South.* U of Illinois P, 1989.

Gerzon, Mark. *A Choice of Heroes: The Changing Face of American Manhood.* Houghton Mifflin, 1982.

Gilbert, James. *Men in the Middle: Searching for Masculinity in the 1950s.* U of Chicago P, 2005.

Giles, Paul. *The Global Remapping of American Literature*. Princeton UP, 2011.

Gilman, Owen W., Jr. "Regenerative Violence; Or, Grab Your Saber, Ray." *Vietnam and the Southern Imagination*, UP of Mississippi, 1992, pp. 77–93.

Gilmore, David. *Manhood in the Making: Cultural Concepts of Masculinity*. Yale UP, 1990.

Gilmore, Glenda. *Gender and Jim Crow: Women and the Politics of White Supremacy in North Carolina, 1896–1920*. U of North Carolina P, 2013.

Giroux, Henry. *Zombie Politics and Culture in the Age of Casino Capitalism*. Peter Lang, 2011.

Goldfield, David R. *Still Fighting the Civil War: The American South and Southern History*. Louisiana State UP, 2013.

Gordon, Avery. *Ghostly Matters: Haunting and the Sociological Imagination*. Minnesota UP, 2004.

Graham, Allison. *Framing the South: Hollywood, Television, and Race during the Civil Rights Struggle*. Johns Hopkins UP, 2003.

Grant, Richard. *Dispatches from Pluto: Lost and Found in the Mississippi Delta*. Simon & Schuster, 2015.

Gray, Richard. *After the Fall: American Literature Since 9/11*. Wiley-Blackwell, 2011.

———. "Afterword: Negotiating Differences: Southern Culture(s) Now." *Dixie Debates*, edited by Richard King and Helen Taylor, New York UP, 1996, pp. 218–26.

———. *The Literature of Memory: Modern Writers of the American South*. Johns Hopkins UP, 1977.

———. *Southern Aberrations: Writers of the American South and the Problems of Regionalism*. Louisiana State UP, 2000.

Graybill, Mark. "'I Am, Personally, the Fall of the West': Postmodernism and the Critical Reception (and Legacy) of Barry Hannah's Fiction." *Literature Compass*, vol. 8, no. 10, Oct. 2011, pp. 677–89.

———. "'Peeping Toms on History': *Never Die* as Postmodern Western." Bone, *Perspectives on Barry Hannah*, pp. 120–38.

Greene, Gayle. *Changing the Story: Feminist Fiction and the Tradition*. Indiana UP, 1992.

Greeson, Jennifer Rae. "The Figure of the South and the Nationalizing Imperatives of Early United States Literature." *The Yale Journal of Criticism*, vol. 12, no. 2, Fall 1999, pp. 209–39.

———. *Our South: Geographic Fantasy and the Rise of National Literature*. Harvard UP, 2010.

Griffin, Christopher. "Bad Faith and the Ethic of Existential Action: Kierkegaard, Sartre, and a Boy Named Harry." *Mississippi Quarterly*, vol. 54, no. 2, Spring 2001, pp. 173–96.

Griffin, Larry J. "The American South and the Self." *Southern Cultures*, vol. 12, no. 3, Fall 2006, pp. 6–28.

———. "Southern Distinctiveness, Yet Again, or, Why America Still Needs the South." *Southern Cultures,* vol. 6, no. 3, Fall 2000, pp. 47–72.

Grimes, William. "Barry Hannah, Darkly Comic Writer, Dies at 67." *New York Times,* 3 Mar. 2010, www.nytimes.com/2010/03/03/books/03hannah.html.

Grimwood, Marita. *Holocaust Literature of the Second Generation.* Palgrave Macmillan, 2007.

Griswold, Robert. *Fatherhood in America: A History.* Basic Books, 1993.

Guinn, Matthew. *After Southern Modernism: Fiction of the Contemporary South.* UP of Mississippi, 2000.

Gwin, Minrose. "Nonfelicitous Space and Survivor Discourse: Reading the Incest Story in Southern Women's Fiction." *Haunted Bodies: Gender and Southern Texts,* edited by Anne Goodwyn Jones and Susan Van D'Elden Donaldson, UP of Virginia, 1997, pp. 416–40.

Haddox, Thomas F. "Elizabeth Spencer, the White Civil Rights Novel, and the Postsouthern." *Modern Language Quarterly,* vol. 65, Dec. 2004, pp. 561–81.

Hale, Grace. *Making Whiteness: The Culture of Segregation in the South, 1890–1940.* Vintage, 1999.

Handley, William, and Nathaniel Lewis, editors. *True West: Authenticity and the American West.* Nebraska UP, 2004.

Hannah, Barry. "The Agony of T. Bandini." Hannah, *High Lonesome,* pp. 125–36.

———. *Airships.* Grove Press, 1978.

———. "Allons, Mes Enfants." Hannah, *Bats Out of Hell,* pp. 79–87.

———. "All the Old Harkening Faces at the Rail." Hannah, *Airships,* pp. 139–42.

———. "Barry Hannah: Murder and Madness in Mississippi." BookPage interview by Ellen Kanner, July 2001, bookpage.com/interviews/8102-barry-hannah.

———. *Bats Out of Hell.* Grove Press, 1993.

———. "Bats Out of Hell Division." Hannah, *Bats Out of Hell,* pp. 43–50.

———. *Black Butterfly.* Palaemon Press, 1982.

———. *Boomerang. Boomerang and Never Die: Two Novels by Barry Hannah,* UP of Mississippi, 1993, pp. 1–150.

———. *Captain Maximus.* Knopf, 1985.

———. "Coming Close to Donna." Hannah, *Airships,* pp. 45–48.

———. "A Conversation with Barry Hannah." By Rob Trucks, *Conversations with Barry Hannah,* edited by James Thomas, UP of Mississippi, 2015, pp. 113–35.

———. *Conversations with Barry Hannah.* Edited by James Thomas, UP of Mississippi, 2015.

———. "A Creature in the Bay of St. Louis." Hannah, *High Lonesome,* pp. 43–52.

———. "Dragged Fighting from His Tomb." Hannah, *Airships,* pp. 49–60.

———. "Even Greenland." Hannah, *Captain Maximus,* pp. 31–34.

———. "Evening of the Yarp: A Report by Roonswent Dover." Hannah, *Bats Out of Hell,* pp. 89–102.

———. *Geronimo Rex.* Grove Press, 1998.

———. "Get Some Young." Hannah, *High Lonesome,* pp. 1–51.

———. *Hey Jack!* Penguin, 1988.

———. *High Lonesome.* Grove Press, 1996.

———. "High-Water Railers." Hannah, *Bats Out of Hell,* pp. 1–11.

———. "The Ice Storm." Hannah, *High Lonesome,* pp. 185–92.

———. "An Interview with Barry Hannah." By Wells Tower, *Believer,* 1 Oct. 2010, www.believermag.com/an-interview-with-barry-hannah.

———. "Interview with Barry Hannah." By Daniel E. Williams, *Perspectives on Barry Hannah,* edited by Martyn Bone, UP of Mississippi, 2010, pp. 183–90.

———. "It Spoke of Exactly the Things." Hannah, *Captain Maximus,* pp. 45–53.

———. *Long, Last, Happy: New and Selected Stories.* Grove Press, 2010.

———. "Midnight and I'm Not Famous Yet." Hannah, *Airships,* pp. 105–18.

———. *Never Die. Boomerang and Never Die: Two Novels by Barry Hannah,* UP of Mississippi, 1993, pp. 1–152.

———. "Nicodemus Bluff." Hannah, *Bats Out of Hell,* pp. 361–82.

———. *Nightwatchmen.* Viking, 1973.

———. "Rat-Faced Auntie." Hannah, *Bats Out of Hell,* pp. 155–90.

———. *Ray.* Penguin, 1981.

———. "Return to Return." Hannah, *Airships,* pp. 67–96.

———. "Revealed: Rock Swoon Has No Past." Hannah, *Bats Out of Hell,* pp. 259–61.

———. "'The Spirits Will Win Through': An Interview with Barry Hannah." By Robert Vanarsdall, *The Southern Review,* vol. 19, no. 2, Apr. 1983, pp. 317–41.

———. *The Tennis Handsome.* Knopf, 1983.

———. "Testimony of Pilot." *Airships and Ray,* Vintage, 1991, pp. 13–41.

———. "Through Sunset into the Raccoon Night." Hannah, *High Lonesome,* pp. 97–124.

———. "Two Gone Over." Hannah, *High Lonesome,* pp. 167–84.

———. "Uncle High Lonesome." Hannah, *High Lonesome,* pp. 211–30.

———. "Upstairs, Mona Bayed for Dong." Hannah, *Bats Out of Hell,* pp. 263–82.

———. "Water Liars." Hannah, *Airships,* pp. 3–8.

———. *Yonder Stands Your Orphan.* Grove Atlantic, 2001.

Hart, Frank. "Notes for an Anatomy of Modern Autobiography." *New Literary History,* vol. 3, no. 1, Spring, 1970, pp. 485–511, doi:10.2307/468268.

Hartmann, Geoffrey. *A Scholar's Tale: Intellectual Journey of a Displaced Child of Europe.* Fordham UP, 2007.

Harvey, David. *The Condition of Postmodernity.* Blackwell, 1989.

Henninger, Katherine. *Ordering the Facade: Photography and Contemporary Southern Women's Writing.* U of North Carolina P, 2007.

Hinrichsen, Lisa. "'I can't believe it was really real': Violence, Vietnam, and Bringing War Home in Bobbie Ann Mason's *In Country.*" *Southern Literary Journal,* vol. 40, no. 2, Sept. 2008, pp. 232–48.

———. *Possessing the Past: Trauma, Imagination, and Memory in Post-Plantation Southern Literature.* Louisiana State UP, 2015.

———. "Trauma Studies and the U.S. South." *Literature Compass,* vol. 10, no. 8, Aug. 2013, pp. 605–17, *Wiley Online Library,* doi:10.1111/lic3.12079.

Hobson, Fred. *A Southern Enigma: Essays on the U.S. South.* Universitat de Valencia, 2008.

———. *The Southern Writer in the Postmodern World.* U of Georgia P, 1991.

Holman, Hugh. "No More Monoliths, Please: Continuities in the Multi-Souths." *Southern Literature in Transition: Heritage and Promise,* edited by Philip Castille and William Osborne, Memphis State UP, 1983, pp. xiii–xxiv.

hooks, bell. "Eating the Other: Desire and Resistance." *Black Looks: Race and Representation,* South End Press, 1992, pp. 21–39.

Horrocks, Roger. *Masculinity in Crisis: Myths, Fantasies, and Realities.* Palgrave, 1994.

Howard, Jacqueline. *Reading Gothic Fiction: A Bakhtinian Approach.* Clarendon Press, 1994.

Howard, John. *Men Like That: A Southern Queer History.* U of Chicago P, 1999.

Humphries, Jefferson, editor. *Southern Literature and Theory.* U of Georgia P, 1990.

Hutcheon, Linda. "Irony, Nostalgia, and the Postmodern." *Methods for the Study of Literature as Cultural Memory,* edited by Raymond Vervliet and Annemarie Estor, Rodopi, 2000, pp. 189–207.

———. *Narcissistic Narrative: The Metafictional Paradox.* Methuen, 1984.

———. *A Poetics of Postmodernism: History, Theory, Fiction.* Routledge, 1988.

———. *The Politics of Postmodernism.* Routledge, 1989.

———. *A Theory of Parody: The Teachings of Twentieth-Century Art Forms.* U of Illinois P, 2000.

Ingenthon, Elmo, and Kathleen Van Buskirk, editors. *Borderland Rebellion: A History of the Civil War on the Missouri-Arkansas Border.* U of Wisconsin P, 1980.

Jameson, Fredric. *Marxism and Form: Twentieth-Century Dialectical Theories of Literature.* Princeton UP, 1974.

———. "On Magic Realism in Film." *Critical Inquiry,* vol. 12, no. 2, Winter 1986, pp. 301–25.

———. *The Political Unconscious: Narrative as a Socially Symbolic Act.* Cornell UP, 1981.

———. *Postmodernism, or, The Cultural Logic of Late Capitalism.* Duke UP, 1991.

———. *The Seeds of Time.* Columbia UP, 1994.

Janz, Bruce, editor. *Place, Space and Hermeneutics.* Springer, 2017.

Jay, Paul. *Global Matters: The Transnational Turn in Literary Studies.* Cornell UP, 2010.

Johnson, Alison M. "Sam Hughes as Second Generation Trauma Victim in Bobbie Ann Mason's *In Country." War, Literature & The Arts,* vol. 26, Jan. 2014, pp. 1–15.

Johnson, E. Patrick. *Appropriating Blackness: Performance and the Politics of Authenticity.* Duke UP, 2003.

Jones, Anne Goodwyn, and Susan Van D'Elden Donaldson, editors. *Haunted Bodies: Gender and Southern Texts.* UP of Virginia, 1997.

Jones, Suzanne, and Sharon Monteith, editors. *South to a New Place: Region, Literature, Culture.* Louisiana State UP, 2002.

Joyce, James. "Araby." *Dubliners,* Penguin, 2000, pp. 21–28.

———. *The Critical Writings of James Joyce.* Viking Press, 1964.

———. *Dubliners.* Penguin, 2000.

———. *Finnegans Wake.* Faber & Faber, 1971.

———. *A Portrait of the Artist as a Young Man.* Penguin, 1969.

———. *Stephen Hero.* Jonathan Cape, 1956.

———. *Ulysses.* Dover, 2002.

Kantrowitz, Stephen. *Ben Tillman and the Reconstruction of White Supremacy.* U of North Carolina P, 2000.

Kaplan, David. "Demonstratives: An Essay on the Semantics, Logic, Metaphysics, and Epistemology of Demonstratives and Other Indexicals." *Themes from Kaplan,* edited by Joseph Almog et al., Oxford UP, 1989, pp. 481–564.

Karem, Jeff. *The Romance of Authenticity: The Cultural Politics of Regional and Ethnic Literatures.* U of Virginia P, 2004.

Killian, Lewis. *White Southerners.* U of Massachusetts P, 1985.

Kimmel, Michael. *Manhood in America: A Cultural History.* Oxford UP, 2017.

———, editor. *The Politics of Manhood: Profeminist Men Respond to the Mythopoetic Men's Movement (And the Mythopoetic Leaders Answer).* Temple UP, 1995.

Kimmel, Michael, and Michael Kaufman. "Weekend Warriors: The New Men's Movement." *Theorizing Masculinities,* edited by Harry Brod and Kaufman, Sage, 1994, pp. 259–88.

Kirby, Jack. *Media-Made Dixie: The South in the American Imagination.* U of Georgia P, 1986.

Klevay, Robert. "'He tossed his line out grimly': Barry Hannah's Literary Parables." *Mississippi Quarterly,* vol. 64, no. 1–2, Winter–Spring 2011, pp. 129–47.

Knoenagel, Axel. Review of *After Southern Modernism: Fiction of the Contemporary South,* by Matthew Guinn. *International Fiction Review,* vol. 30, no. 1, Jan. 2003, pp. 95–97.

Kornegay, Jamie. "The Evolution of Southern Gothic." *HuffPost,* 6 Dec. 2017, www.huffpost.com/entry/the-evolution-of-southern-gothic_b_6987510.

Kreyling, Michael. "Fee, Fie, Faux Faulkner: Parody and Postmodernism in Southern Literature." *The Southern Review,* Winter 1999, pp. 1–15.

———. *Figures of the Hero in Southern Narrative.* Louisiana State UP, 1987.

———. *Inventing Southern Literature.* UP of Mississippi, 1998.

———. *The South That Wasn't There: Postsouthern Memory and History.* Louisiana State UP, 2010.

———. "Toward 'A New Southern Studies.'" *South Central Review,* vol. 22, no. 1, Spring 2005, pp. 4–18.

Kripke, Saul. *Naming and Necessity.* Harvard UP, 1980.

LaCapra, Dominick. *Writing History, Writing Trauma.* Johns Hopkins UP, 2014.

Ladd, Barbara. "Dismantling the Monolith: Southern Places—Past, Present, and Future." *Critical Survey,* vol. 12, no. 1, 2000, pp. 28–42.

Langer, Susanne K. *Feeling and Form: A Theory of Art Developed from Philosophy in a New Key.* Scribner, 1953.

Lassiter, Matthew D., and Joseph Crespino, editors. *The Myth of Southern Exceptionalism.* Oxford UP, 2010.

Lawrence, D. H. *Sons and Lovers.* Penguin, 1994.

Lee, Richard. "Off with Their Heads! *Nightwatchmen,* Campus Novels, and the Problem of Representation." Bone, *Perspectives on Barry Hannah,* pp. 26–45.

Lewis, Nathaniel. *Unsettling the Literary West: Authenticity and Authorship.* U of Nebraska P, 2003.

Leys, Ruth. *Trauma: A Genealogy.* U of Chicago P, 2000.

Lloyd, Christopher. "Contemporary Southern Literature." *Oxford Research Encyclopedia: Literature,* edited by Paula Rabinowitcz. Oxford UP, 2017, doi:10.1093/acrefore/9780190201098.013.300.

———. *Rooting Memory, Rooting Place: Regionalism in the Twenty-First Century American South.* Palgrave Macmillan, 2015.

Loewen, James, and Edward Sebesta, editors. *The Confederate and Neo-Confederate Reader: The "Great Truth" about the "Lost Cause."* UP of Mississippi, 2010.

Loomba, Ania. *Colonialism/Postcolonialism.* Routledge, 2000.

Lowenthal, David. *The Past is a Foreign Country.* Cambridge UP, 1985.

MacLean, Nancy. *Behind the Mask of Chivalry: The Making of the Second Ku Klux Klan.* Oxford UP, 1994.

Maclean, Norman. *A River Runs Through It, and Other Stories.* U of Chicago P, 2017.

Madden, David. "Barry Hannah's *Geronimo Rex* in Retrospect." *The Southern Review,* vol. 19, no. 2, 1983, pp. 309–16.

Mali, Joseph. *Mythistory: The Making of a Modern Historiography.* U of Chicago P, 2003.

Mason, Bobbie Ann. *In Country.* Harper & Row, 1993.

Maxwell, Angie. *The Indicted South: Public Criticism, Southern Inferiority, and the Politics of Whiteness.* U of North Carolina P, 2014.

———. "Introduction: Impact of C. Vann Woodward's *The Burden of Southern History*." *American Review of Politics*, vol. 32, Summer 2011, pp. 79–81.

Maxwell, Angie, et al., editors. *The Ongoing Burden of Southern History: Politics and Identity in the Twenty-First-Century South.* Louisiana State UP, 2012.

McCarthy, Cormac. *Child of God.* Picador, 2010.

———. *The Road.* Knopf, 2006.

McHale, Brian. *Postmodernist Fiction.* Routledge, 2004.

McKee, Kathryn. "Globalization and Southern Literature." *The New Encyclopedia of Southern Culture: Volume 9, Literature,* edited by Thomas Inge, U of North Carolina P, 2008, pp. 82–85.

McKee, Kathryn, and Annette Trefzer. "Preface: Global Contexts, Local Literatures: The New Southern Studies." *Global Contexts, Local Literatures: The New Southern Studies,* edited by McKee et al., Duke UP, 2006, pp. 677–90.

McPherson, Tara. "Afterword: After Authenticity." Bone et al., pp. 309–23.

———. *Reconstructing Dixie: Race, Gender, and Nostalgia in the Imagined South.* Duke UP, 2003.

Messenger, Christian. *Sport and the Spirit of Play in American Fiction: Hawthorne to Faulkner.* Columbia UP, 2012.

Messner, Michael. "When Bodies are Weapons: Masculinity and Violence in Sport." *International Review for the Sociology of Sport,* vol. 25, no. 3, Sept. 1990, pp. 203–20.

Milesi, Laurent, editor. *James Joyce and the Difference of Language.* Cambridge UP, 2003.

Millard, Kenneth. *Coming of Age in Contemporary American Fiction.* Edinburgh UP, 2007.

———. *Contemporary American Fiction.* Oxford UP, 2000.

———. "The Cultural Value of Metafiction: *Geronimo Rex* and *High Lonesome*." Bone, *Perspectives on Barry Hannah,* pp. 2–25.

Mitchell, Lee. "Authenticity, the West, and Literature." *Western American Literature,* vol. 40, no. 1, Spring 2005, pp. 88–97.

Mitchell, Margaret. *Gone with the Wind.* Pan Macmillan, 2008.

Moretti, Franco. *The Way of the World: The Bildungsroman in European Culture.* Verso, 1987.

Morrison, Toni. *Beloved.* Vintage, 1987.

Morson, Gary Saul. "Parody, History and Metaparody." *Rethinking Bakhtin: Extensions and Challenges,* edited by Morson and Caryl Emerson, Illinois UP, 1989, pp. 63–86.

Nabokov, Vladimir. *Lolita.* Penguin, 2000.

Nachmanovitch, Stephen. *Free Play: Improvisation in Life and Art.* Penguin, 1990.

Noble, Donald. "'Tragic and Meaningful to an Insane Degree': Barry Hannah." *Southern Literary Journal,* vol. 15, no. 1, Fall 1982, pp. 37–44.

Norris, Christopher. "Deconstruction, Naming and Necessity: Some Logical Options." *Journal of Literary Semantics,* vol. 13, no. 3, 1984, pp. 159–80.

O'Brien, Michael. *The Idea of the American South, 1920–1941.* Johns Hopkins UP, 1990.

———. *Placing the South.* U of Mississippi P, 2007.

Oliver, Kelly. *Witnessing: Beyond Recognition.* U of Minnesota P, 2001.

Pagan, Nicholas. *Rethinking Literary Biography: A Postmodern Approach to Tennessee Williams.* Fairleigh Dickinson UP, 1993.

Peacock, James L., et al., editors. *The American South in a Global World.* U of North Carolina P, 2005.

Percy, William Alexander. *Lanterns on the Levee: Recollections of a Planter's Son.* Louisiana State UP, 1973.

Peterson, Nancy. *Against Amnesia: Contemporary Women Writers and the Crises of Historical Memory.* U of Pennsylvania P, 2001.

Pilkington, John. "The Memory of the War." *The History of Southern Literature,* edited by Louis D. Rubin Jr. et al., Louisiana State UP, 1985, pp. 356–62.

Plantinga, Alvin. *The Nature of Necessity.* Oxford UP, 1974.

Plath, Lydia, and Sergio Lussana, editors. *Black and White Masculinity in the American South, 1800–2000.* Cambridge Scholars, 2009.

Pleck, Joseph. *The Myth of Masculinity.* MIT Press, 1981.

Poe, Edgar Allan. "The Tell-Tale Heart." *The Collected Tales and Poems of Edgar Allan Poe,* Modern Library, 1992, pp. 303–6.

Polk, Noel. "Even Mississippi: Legending in Barry Hannah's *Bats Out of Hell*." *Texas Review,* vol. 30, no. 1/2, 2009, pp. 75–88.

Potter, David. *The South and Sectional Conflict.* Louisiana State UP, 1968, p. 4.

Potts, James B. "Barry Hannah's Anti-Myth Method: Anti-Freudian Plots and Fractured Fairy Tales." *Mississippi Quarterly,* vol. 54, no. 2, Spring 2001, pp, 237–50.

———. "The Shade of Faulkner's Horse: Cavalier Heroism and Archetypal Immortality in Barry Hannah's Postmodern South." Bone, *Perspectives on Barry Hannah,* pp. 65–84.

"Puissant." *Oxford English Dictionary,* 3rd ed., 2010.

Pynchon, Thomas. *V.* Vintage, 2000.

Radstone, Susannah. *The Sexual Politics of Time: Confession, Nostalgia, Memory.* Routledge, 2007.

Randall, Alice. *The Wind Done Gone: A Novel.* Houghton Mifflin, 2001.

Reed, John Shelton. *The Enduring South: Subcultural Persistence in Mass Society.* U of North Carolina P, 1986.

Reeser, Todd. *Masculinities in Theory: An Introduction.* Wiley-Blackwell, 2010.

Richard, Mark. *Fishboy: A Ghost's Story.* Doubleday, 1993.

Ricoeur, Paul. *History and Truth.* Northwestern UP, 1965.

Riesman, David, et al. *The Lonely Crowd: A Study of the Changing American Character.* Yale UP, 1961.

Robertson, Roland. "Glocalization: Time-Space and Homogeneity-Heterogeneity." *Global Modernities,* edited by Mike Featherstone et al., Sage, 1995, pp. 25–44.

Robertson, Sarah. "The Memorialization of Poor White Men's Labor in Rick Bragg's Memoir Trilogy." *Journal of American Studies,* vol. 47, no. 2, Aug. 2012, pp. 459–74.

———. "Poor Whites in Recent American Fiction." *Literature Compass,* vol. 9, no. 10, Oct. 2012, pp. 631–41, *Wiley Online Library,* doi:10.1111/j.1741–4113.2012.00920.

———. *Poverty Politics: Poor Whites in Contemporary Southern Writing.* UP of Mississippi, 2019.

Rombes, Nicholas. "H." *A Cultural Dictionary of Punk: 1974–1982,* Bloomsbury, 2009, p. 116.

Romine, Scott. "God and the MoonPie: Consumption, Disenchantment, and the Reliably Lost Cause." Bone et al., pp. 49–71.

———. *The Narrative Forms of Southern Community.* Louisiana State UP, 1999.

———. "Orphans All: Reality Homesickness in *Yonder Stands Your Orphan.*" Bone, *Perspectives on Barry Hannah,* pp. 161–82.

———. *The Real South: Southern Narrative in the Age of Cultural Reproduction.* Louisiana State UP, 2008.

———. "Southern Homes After the Family: Deregulated Reality in Barry Hannah and Josephine Humphries." Romine, *The Real South,* pp. 192–225.

———. "TARA! TARA! TARA! *Gone With the Wind* and the Work of Cultural Reproduction." Romine, *The Real South,* pp. 27–59.

———. "Where is Southern Literature? The Practice of Place in a Postsouthern Age." *Critical Survey,* vol. 12, no. 1, 2000, pp. 5–27.

Romine, Scott, and Jennifer Rae Greeson, editors. *Keywords for Southern Studies.* U of Georgia P, 2016.

Rorty, Richard, editor. *The Linguistic Turn: Recent Essays in Philosophical Method.* U of Chicago P, 1967.

Roth, Michael. *Memory, Trauma, and History: Essays on Living with the Past.* Columbia UP, 2012.

Rubin, Louis D., Jr. *Southern Renascence: The Literature of the Modern South.* Johns Hopkins UP, 1953.

Rutheiser, Charles. *Imagineering Atlanta: The Politics of Place in the City of Dreams.* Verso, 1996.

Rutkowski, Sara. *Literary Legacies of the Federal Writers' Project: Voices of the Depression in the American Postwar Era.* Palgrave Macmillan, 2017.

Salmon, Nathan. *Reference and Essence.* Princeton UP, 1981.

Sampson, Curt. *Golf, Money, and Power in Augusta, Georgia.* Random House, 2010.

Saussure, Ferdinand de. *Course in General Linguistics*. Translated by Wade Baskin, McGraw Hill, 1966.

Savoy, Eric. "The Rise of American Gothic." *The Cambridge Companion to Gothic Fiction*, edited by Jerrold Hogle, Cambridge UP, 2001, pp. 167–88.

Schalkwyk, David. *Literature and the Touch of the Real*. Rosemont, 2004.

Schwartz, Hillel. *The Culture of the Copy*. MIT Press, 1996.

Schwartz, Stephen, editor. *Naming, Necessity, and Natural Kinds*. Cornell UP, 1977.

Schwarz, Benjamin. "The Idea of the South." *The Atlantic*, Dec. 1997, www.theatlantic .com/magazine/archive/1997/12/the-idea-of-the-south/377028/.

Schwarz, David S. *Naming and Referring: The Semantics and Pragmatics of Singular Terms*, de Gruyter, 1979.

Schwenger, Peter. *Phallic Critiques: Masculinity and Twentieth-Century Literature*. Routledge & Kegan Paul, 1984.

Seib, Kenneth. "'Sabers, Gentlemen, Sabers': The J. E. B. Stuart Stories of Barry Hannah." *Mississippi Quarterly*, vol. 45, no. 1, Winter 1991, pp. 41–52.

Shipe, Matthew. "Accountability, Community and Redemption in *Hey Jack!* and *Boomerang*." Bone, *Perspectives on Barry Hannah*, pp. 102–19.

Simmons, Philip E. *Deep Surfaces: Mass Culture & History in Postmodern American Fiction*. U of Georgia P, 1997.

Simon, William. *Postmodern Sexualities*. Routledge, 1996.

Simpson, Lewis P. "The Closure of History in a Postsouthern America." *The Brazen Face of History: Studies in the Literary Consciousness of America*, Louisiana State UP, 1980, pp. 268–69.

Smith, Anthony D. "The 'Golden Age' and National Renewal." *Myths & Nationhood*, edited by Geoffrey Hosking and George Schopflin, Hurst, 1997, pp. 36–59.

Smith, Jon. *Finding Purple America: The South and the Future of American Cultural Studies*. U of Georgia P, 2013.

———. "Response to the Emerging Scholars Roundtable." *Mississippi Quarterly*, vol. 68, no. 1, Spring 2015, pp. 43–57.

———. Review of *The Postsouthern Sense of Place in Contemporary Fiction*, by Martyn Bone. *Mississippi Quarterly*, vol. 59, no. 1–2, Winter–Spring 2006, pp. 369–73.

———. "Toward a Post-postpolitical Southern Studies: On the Limits of the 'Creating and Consuming' Paradigm." Bone et al., pp. 72–96.

———. "What the New Southern Studies Does Now." *Journal of American Studies*, vol. 49, no. 4, Nov. 2015, pp. 861–70.

Smith, Jon, and Deborah Cohn, editors. *Look Away! The U.S. South in New World Studies*. Duke UP, 2004.

Smith, Quentin. "Marcus, Kripke, and the Origin of the New Theory of Reference." *Synthese*, vol. 104, no. 2, 1995, pp. 179–89.

Spikes, Michael P. "Lee Durkee's *Rides of the Midway* and Barry Hannah's *Geronimo Rex*." *Mississippi Quarterly,* vol. 53, no. 3, Summer 2002, pp. 408–18.

———. "Saul Kripke and Poststructuralism: A Revaluation." *Philosophy and Literature,* vol. 511, no. 2, 1987, pp. 301–6.

———. "What's in a Name? A Reading of Barry Hannah's 'Ray.'" *Mississippi Quarterly,* vol. 42, no. 1, Winter 1988, pp. 69–82.

"Sprite." *Oxford English Dictionary,* 3rd ed., 2010.

Squint, Kirstin. *LeAnne Howe at the Intersections of Southern and Native American Literature.* Louisiana State UP, 2018.

Steele, Shelby. *White Guilt: How Blacks and Whites Together Destroyed the Promise of the Civil Rights Era.* HarperCollins, 2006.

Stevens, Wallace. *Opus Posthumous: Poems, Plays, Prose.* Alfred Knopf, 1957.

Su, John J. *Ethics and Nostalgia in the Contemporary Novel.* Cambridge UP, 2005.

Summerfield, Giovanna, and Lisa Downward. *New Perspectives on European Bildungsroman.* Continuum, 2010.

Tate, Allen. *Essays of Four Decades.* Swallow Press, 1969.

Tate, Allen, et al. *I'll Take My Stand: The South and the Agrarian Tradition.* Louisiana State UP, 2006.

Tatum, Stephen, and Nathaniel Lewis. "Tumbling Dice: The Problem of Las Vegas." *A Companion to the Literature and Culture of the American West,* edited by Nicholas Witschi, Wiley-Blackwell, 2011, pp. 528–47.

Taylor, Charles. *The Ethics of Authenticity.* Harvard UP, 1991.

Taylor, Helen. *Circling Dixie: Contemporary Southern Culture through a Transatlantic Lens.* Rutgers UP, 2001.

"Testimony." *Oxford English Dictionary,* 3rd ed., 2010.

Thompson, Graham. "Roundtable." *Journal of American Studies,* vol. 48, no. 4, Nov. 2014, pp. 1082–86.

Thoreen, David. "The Narrative Structure of Barry Hannah's 'Water Liars.'" *Mississippi Quarterly,* vol. 54, no. 2, Spring 2001, pp. 223–36.

Thornton, Kevin. "The Confederate Flag and the Meaning of Southern History." *Southern Cultures,* vol. 2, no. 2, Winter 1996, pp. 233–45.

Thorpe, Thomas Bangs. "The Big Bear of Arkansas." 1841. *The Norton Anthology of American Literature,* vol. 1, edited by Robert S. Levine and Nina Baym, 2nd ed., Norton, 1985, pp. 1535–45.

Tichi, Cecelia. *High Lonesome: The American Culture of Country Music.* U of North Carolina P, 1994.

Trefzer, Annette. *Disturbing Indians: The Archaeology of Southern Fiction.* U of Alabama P, 2006.

Tunc, Tanfer Emin. "'We're what we are because of the past': History, Memory, Nostalgia, and Identity in Walter Sullivan's *The Long, Long Love.*" *American Studies in Scandinavia,* vol. 46, no. 2, Sept. 2014, pp. 17–36.

Twain, Mark. *Adventures of Huckleberry Finn.* Houghton Mifflin, 1996.

Ulin, David. Review of *Long, Last, Happy: New and Selected Stories,* by Barry Hannah. *Los Angeles Times,* 2 Jan. 2011, www.articles.latimes.com/2011/jan/02/entertainment /la-ca-barry-hannah-20110102.

Updike, John. "From Dyna Domes to Turkey-Ping." *New Yorker,* 9 Sept. 1972, p. 124.

Van D'Elden Donaldson, Susan. Review of *South to a New Place: Region, Literature, Culture,* edited by Suzanne Jones and Sharon Monteith. *South Central Review,* vol. 22, no. 1, Spring 2005, pp. 132–35.

Vernon, Zackary. "Toward a Post-Appalachian Sense of Place." *Journal of American Studies,* vol. 50, no. 3, Aug. 2016, pp. 639–58.

Vice, Brad. "Barry Hannah: In the Academy but Not of It." *Moravian Journal of Literature and Film,* vol. 3, no. 2, Spring 2012, pp. 17–36.

Ward, Brian. "Forum: What's New in Southern Studies—And Why Should We Care?" *Journal of American Studies,* vol. 48, no. 3, August 2014, pp. 691–733.

Ward, Jesmyn. *Men We Reaped: A Memoir.* Bloomsbury, 2015.

Warren, Kenneth. *So Black and So Blue: Ralph Ellison and the Occasion of Criticism.* U of Chicago P, 2003.

Watts, Trent. *White Masculinity in the Recent South.* Louisiana State UP, 2008.

Waugh, Patricia. *Metafiction: The Theory and Practice of Self-Conscious Fiction.* Methuen, 1984.

Weston, Ruth D. *Barry Hannah: Postmodern Romantic.* Louisiana State UP, 1998.

———. "Barry Hannah's 'High Lonesome' Humor: New Voices for Old Grotesqueries." *The Enduring Legacy of Old Southwest Humor,* edited by Edward Piacentino, Louisiana State UP, 2006, pp. 174–89.

———. "Debunking the Unitary Self and Story in the War Stories of Barry Hannah." *Southern Literary Journal,* vol. 27, no. 1, Spring 1995, pp. 96–106.

Whaley, Preston. *Blows Like a Horn: Beat Writing, Jazz, Style, and Markets in the Transformation of U.S. Culture.* Harvard UP, 2004.

Wheeler, Kathleen. "Constructions of Identity in Post-1970 Experimental Fiction." *An Introduction to Contemporary Fiction: International Writing in English since 1970,* edited by Rod Mengham, Polity Press, 1999, pp. 15–31.

Widiss, Benjamin. "They Endured: The Faulknerian Novel and Post-45 American Fiction." *The New Cambridge Companion to William Faulkner,* edited by John Matthews, Cambridge UP, 2015, pp. 148–63.

Williams, David. *Rich Man's War: Class, Caste, and Confederate Defeat in the Lower Chattahoochee Valley.* U of Georgia P, 1998.

Williams, Tennessee. *Orpheus Descending, and Other Plays.* Penguin, 1961.

Williamson, Joel. *The Crucible of Race.* Oxford UP, 1984.

Wilson, Charles Raegan, editor. *The New Encyclopedia of Southern Culture: Volume 4, Myth, Manners, and Memory,* U of North Carolina P, 2006.

Windham, Donald. *The Dog Star.* Hill Street Press, 1998.

"Witness." *Oxford English Dictionary,* 3rd ed., 2010.

Woodward, C. Vann. *The Burden of Southern History.* 3rd ed., Louisiana State UP, 1993.

———. "The Search for Southern Identity." 1958. Woodward, *The Burden of Southern History,* pp. 3–26.

Woodward, Richard. "Cormac McCarthy's Venomous Fiction." *New York Times Magazine,* 19 Apr. 1992, pp. 28–31.

Wolfe, Tom, and E. W. Johnson, editors. *The New Journalism.* Harper & Row, 1973.

Wright, Elizabeth, editor. *Feminism and Psychoanalysis: A Critical Dictionary.* Blackwell, 1992.

Wright, Gavin. *Old South, New South: Revolutions in the Southern Economy since the Civil War.* Louisiana State UP, 1997.

Wyatt-Brown, Bertram. *Honor and Violence in the Old South.* Oxford UP, 1986.

Yaeger, Patricia. *Dirt and Desire: Reconstructing Southern Women's Writing, 1930–1990.* Chicago UP, 2000.

———. *The Geography of Identity.* U of Michigan P, 1996.

Young, Kevin, and Michael Smith. "Mass Media Treatment of Violence in Sports and its Effects." *Current Psychology,* vol. 7, no. 4, Dec. 1988, pp. 298–311.

Young, Thomas Daniel. *The Past in the Present: A Thematic Study of Modern Southern Fiction.* Louisiana State UP, 1981.

Žižek, Slavoj. *Living in the End Times.* Verso, 2000.

———. "Melancholy and the Act." *Critical Inquiry,* vol. 26, no. 4, Summer 2000, pp. 657–81.

———. *The Plague of Fantasies.* Verso, 1997.

Index

abjection (southern), 13, 32–33, 86; as re-demptive, 100, 131–33, 136, 238

Absolute Music (Chua), 48–49

adolescence, 45, 53, 200. *See also* bildungs-roman; coming of age

Adventures of Huckleberry Finn, The (Twain), 216

After Southern Modernism (Guinn), 14, 88, 91, 92–93, 97, 106, 109, 111, 120, 157, 185, 202, 204, 252

Agrarians, 6, 10, 13–14, 16, 17–18, 19, 25–26, 28–29, 107, 113, 136, 145–47, 149, 167, 169, 248–49, 252

All Over but the Shoutin' (Bragg), 251

All Over the Map (Ayers), 3, 148, 203, 212, 223

Allison, Dorothy, 19

Althusser, Louis, 177

American innocence, 6, 43, 83, 145–46, 169, 213, 216, 218; and American exceptional-ism, 10; and American triumphalism, 83; the South's exclusion from/relationship to, 9, 83

American South in a Global World, The (Peacock et al.), 21

Anderson, Benedict, 6

Anderson, David, 167

Anderson, Eric Gary, 20, 65

Antebellum/Slave South: and masculinity in the South, 80–83, 94–95; mythology of, 147–48; and white guilt/shame, 121, 145–46; and white (male) nostalgia, 145–46, 169–71, 244; slavery, 30, 110, 146–47.

See also colonialism; Old South; race and racism

anxiety of influence, 2, 14, 202, 210–11

Apache. *See* Native Americans

Appadurai, Arjun, 181–82

Appalachia, 180, 198, 201–3; and place/(post)regionalism, 201–3. *See also* Southern Gothic (Appalachian Gothic)

Appropriating Blackness (E. Johnson), 79

Archive Fever (Derrida), 251

Asian Americans in the South, 19, 253

Atlanta, GA: in *Gone with the Wind,* 146, 170; and "imagineering" (Rutheiser), 169; as an "international"/"northern" city, 168–69; as a located "non-place" (Bone), 146; and the transition from Old to New South, 196–97

Augusta, GA, 89; Augusta National Golf Club, 89

Authentic Fakes (Chidester), 181

authenticity: definition, 54; in art, 36–37, 46–47, 73–74, 145, 162, 181–82, 184–85, 191–92; constructed from culture stories, 24, 27; constructed from oral histories, 79–80; faking/performing authenticity, 36–38, 123–26, 141, 187, 192–93, 204–5, 253; and language/mimesis, 44–47, 67–72, 158–60, 184–85; and masculinity, 77–80; and nostalgia, 24–25, 154, 170–72, 242–44; and place/(post)regionalism, 25–27, 37–38, 41, 73, 159–60, 182–86, 192, 197–98, 203–4, 246–49; and postmodernism, 24, 126–27, 182–85. *See also* postregionalism

Away Down South (Cobb), 7

Ayers, Edward, 3, 25, 29, 145, 147, 148, 181, 203, 212, 223, 254

backward glance (southern), 7, 19, 30, 43–44, 109, 111, 114, 116, 125, 147–48, 150, 155, 157
Baker, Houston, 18, 19, 21, 109, 250
Bakhtin, Mikhail, 209–11, 235, 239
Barker, Deborah, 183
Barry Hannah (Charney), 4, 35, 63
Barry Hannah (Weston), 35, 43, 89–90, 94, 115, 117, 186, 214–15, 217, 222, 229, 237
Barth, John, 5, 37, 40
Barthelme, Donald, 5, 233
Barthelme, Frederick, 109, 257n5
Bass, Rick, 257n5
Bastard Out of Carolina (Allison), 19
Battle of Vicksburg, 52–53, 244–45
Baudrillard, Jean, 37, 54, 73, 155, 168, 182, 194, 208, 210, 224, 227
Beat culture, 49
Bederman, Gail, 78
Beidler, Philip D., 210
Beja, Morris, 52, 101
Benjamin, Walter, 171
Benson Taylor, Melanie, 20, 63–65, 68, 112, 183
Betts, Doris, 257n5
Bibler, Michael P., 19
Bidney, Martin, 101–2
"Big Bear of Arkansas, The" (Thorpe), 180
bildungsroman, 40–41, 43–44, 45, 251; and Joyce, 46, 57; in postsouthern literature, 43, 53, 57, 73, 258n2 (chap. 1)
Bjerre, Thomas, 81, 83, 88, 99
Blanton, Linda, 179
Blevins, Brooks, 180
Bloom, Harold, 2, 57, 202
bluegrass. *See* music
Bly, Robert, 220
Boes, Tobias, 46
Bolero (Ravel), 98, 104
Bone, Martyn, 2, 3, 4, 5, 11–12, 13–15, 16, 17, 18, 19, 23–24, 26–28, 64, 80, 83, 92, 112, 113,

140, 146, 149, 167, 168–69, 180, 185, 197, 200, 202, 236, 242, 247
borderland rebellion, 202–3
Boym, Svetlana, 144
"boys' own" fiction, 88
Bragg, Rick, 19, 145, 202, 251
Bridges, Tristan, 90
Brinkmeyer, Robert, 13, 17, 108, 109, 181, 218, 257n5
Brooks, Cleanth, 111
Brundage, W. Fitzhugh, 4, 145, 202
Bucknell, Brad, 48, 50
burden of southern history, 106–8, 113–14; as "defeated" white masculinity, 113, 131–32, 136, 145–46, 245; and NSS/postregional theory, 126–27, 140–41; as a performance, 123–25, 140; as southern mythology, 129–30, 132
Burden of Southern History, The (C. Vann Woodward), 107
Butler, Judith, 78, 92

Campbell, Neil, 185
capitalism, 23, 154, 167, 182–83; casino capitalism, 241; effect on regionalism, 182–83
Carlton, David L., 30
Carpenter, Brian, 145
Caruth, Cathy, 114, 121
Casey, Edward, 12
Cash, W. J., 6
Caverlee, William, 208, 213
Chapman, Mary, 80
Charleston, SC, 169
Charney, Mark J., 4, 35, 63
Cheever, Abigail, 24, 36, 75, 92, 77, 105, 181, 236
Chidester, David, 181
Choctaw. *See* Native Americans
Choice of Heroes, A (Gerzon), 78
Christianity and the Bible: Catholic guilt, 253; and "fallen" language, 48, 195; and female sinfulness/subjugation, 173–75, 253; and logos/logocentrism, 159–60, 175–76, 224; original sin/Fall narratives, 176, 188,

218, 222; in southern community, 243, 248

Chua, Daniel, 48–49

Circling Dixie (H. Taylor), 17

civil rights movement, 78, 109, 110, 144, 171–72

Civil War, 7–8, 19, 33, 88, 108–10, 112–13, 144–45, 147, 149, 166–67, 191, 202, 218, 228–29, 236, 245. *See also* Confederacy/neo-Confederacy

Clarkson, Carol, 62

"Closure of History in a Postsouthern America, The" (Simpson), 12, 109

Cobb, James C., 7, 21, 22, 146, 147

Coclanis, Peter A., 30

Cohn, David L., 8

Cohn, Deborah, 17, 18, 21, 24

colonialism, 20, 23, 29–30, 64, 169–70

Comer, Krista, 12, 192, 198, 254, 255

coming of age, 42, 43, 100, 115–16, 121, 142, 151, 159, 188, 212–13, 215, 220, 223

Confederacy/neo-Confederacy: "culture wars" fought over, 8; Lost Cause mythology, 7, 14, 53–54, 81–83, 88, 91–93, 113, 129–30, 133–34, 136, 140, 147, 167, 218, 244–45; the politics of memorialization, 8, 136, 140, 144–45; as "rebel" masculinity, 80, 83, 89. *See also* Civil War

confession, 85–87, 138–39, 162, 173; and femininity, 174–75, 188; and original sin, 176

Connell, R. W., 81, 83, 88

Cooke, Deryck, 48–49

Coover, Robert, 5

Cords, Nicholas, 191

Cox, Karen, 167

Crane, Stephen, 166

Creating and Consuming the American South (Bone et al.), 3, 4, 19, 25, 26–27

"creating and consuming" paradigm, 3, 4, 19, 26–27, 39, 76, 79–80, 105, 149

Crespino, Joseph, 21

Crews, Harry, 14

Crucible of Race, The (Williamson), 82

Cubit, Geoffrey, 144

Culler, Jonathan, 176

cultural reproduction, 7, 17, 145, 169–70, 182–84, 196, 248, 249

cultural stasis in the South, 108, 111, 218–19, 224

Culture of the Copy, The (H. Schwartz), 181

Currie, Mark, 5, 224, 239–40

Davis, Fred, 155, 170, 171

Day, William Patrick, 221

Dean, Jodi, 249

Deep South, 9, 30, 31, 114–15, 129, 232

Deep Surfaces (Simmons), 181

DeLillo, Don, 5

Deliverance (Dickey), 213, 223

Deloria, Philip J., 63

Denney, Reuel, 78

Derrida, Jacques, 159–60, 175–76, 251

descriptivist theory, 61

determinate reference, 60–61

diacritical principle (Saussure), 44, 60, 71

Dialogic Imagination, The (Bakhtin), 209

dialogism (Bakhtin), 209

Dickey, James, 213, 223

Didion, Joan, 9, 33

Dirt and Desire (Yaeger), 114

Dispatches from Pluto (Grant), 8

Dissanayake, Wimal, 27

Dog Star, The (Windham), 258n7

Dosse, François, 174

Dostoevsky, 239

Downward, Lisa, 44, 251

Du Bois, W. E. B., 29–30

Duck, Leigh Anne, 22, 23, 145, 147, 148, 177, 183

Dylan, Bob, 219

Eagle, Christopher, 69

Eastman, Jason T., 80

Edgerton, Clyde, 257n5

Eliot, T. S., 45, 46, 211, 227, 231, 233, 234

End of the Road, The (Barth), 40

End to Innocence, An (Fiedler), 216

Enduring South, The (Reed), 244

epiphany, 50–59

Epstein, Helen, 121–22

Esquire, 83, 153, 221, 227, 244

Ethics of Authenticity, The (C. Taylor), 181

Fate of Place, The (Casey), 12

Faulkner, William, 2, 14, 88, 109, 110–11, 112, 128, 129–31, 139, 140, 147, 152, 197, 203, 211, 224, 238; *Absalom, Absalom!*, 13; *As I Lay Dying*, 226; *Go Down, Moses*, 116; *Intruder in the Dust*, 245; *Requiem for a Nun*, 33, 107; *Sanctuary*, 213; *Sartoris*, 2

Federal Writers' Project (FWP), 191–92, 203

Federman, Raymond, 4

Felski, Rita, 144

Fiedler, Leslie A, 216

Finding Purple America (J. Smith), 16–17, 18, 22, 147, 149, 248–49, 255

Fitzgerald, F. Scott, 88

folklore (southern), 180, 189–92, 209

Ford, Richard, 257n5

Franklin, Tom, 145, 180

Frazier, Charles, 201

Frege, Gottlob, 61

Friend, Craig Thompson, 81

frontier mythology, 88, 180

Gaddis, William, 5

Gardiner, Judith, 220

Gates, Henry Louis, 204–5

Geronimo, 62–64, 68

Gerster, Patrick, 191

Gerzon, Mark 78, 83

Giap, General Vo Nguyen, 85, 91–93, 97

Gilbert, James, 78, 80

Giles, Paul, 23, 27

Gilman, Owen W., Jr., 83

Gilmore, David, 78

Gilmore, Glenda, 82

Giroux, Henry, 241

Glazer, Nathan, 78

Global Contexts, Local Literatures (McKee and Trefzer), 21

Global Matters (Jay), 20

Global Remapping of American Literature, The (Giles), 23, 27

Global South, The, 20, 22

Globalization and the American South (Cobb and Stueck), 21

globalization, 9–12, 18–19, 20–21, 23–24, 27–28, 29–30, 155, 169, 182–83, 185, 194, 253

glocalization, 182, 196

Glover, Lorri, 81

golf, 87–88, 89–91

Gone with the Wind (film, Selznick and Fleming), 148, 167–71

Gone with the Wind (novel, Mitchell), 148, 165, 167–71

Goodwyn Jones, Anne, 19, 114

gothic. *See* Southern Gothic

Graham, Allison, 167

Grant, Richard, 8

Gray, Richard, 19, 110, 119, 146, 182, 198–99

Graybill, Mark, 31, 62

Great Depression, 19, 145, 147, 170, 190–91

Greeson, Jennifer Rae, 11, 18, 22

Griffin, Christopher, 49

Griffin, Larry J., 9, 113

Grimes, William, 32–33

Grimwood, Marita, 121–22

Griswold, Robert, 78

Grit Lit about the "Rough South," 19, 145, 149–50

Guinn, Matthew, 11, 14, 64, 75, 88, 91–93, 97, 106, 109, 111, 113, 120, 157, 185, 201, 202, 204, 252

Gwin, Minrose, 32

Haddox, Thomas F., 14–15

Hale, Grace, 183

Handley, William, 11–12, 30, 184, 192, 247

Hannah, Barry: "The Agony of T. Bandini," 128–41; *Airships*, 75–105, 153; "All the Old Harkening Faces at the Rail," 153; "Allons, Mes Enfants," 196; *Bats Out of Hell*, 142–178; 179–205; "Bats Out of Hell Division," 14; *Black Butterfly*, 195–96; *Boo-*

merang, 2, 204–5; *Captain Maximus,* 1, 4,
195; "A Creature in the Bay," 111–12, 127,
188, 206, 210; "Coming Close to Donna,"
221; "Even Greenland," 1–3, 15, 25, 33, 37,
42, 85, 201, 210, 244, 249; "Evening of the
Yarp," 2, 5, 156, 179–205, 210, 226; *Geronimo Rex,* 2, 40–74, 75, 77, 84, 200, 208, 245;
"Get Some Young," 116, 156, 206–40, 246;
Hey Jack!, 3, 44, 167, 182, 186, 195, 242,
248, 249; *High Lonesome,* 38, 48, 69, 106
–41, 206–40; "High-Water Railers," 153,
188; "The Ice Storm," 9, 36, 94, 118, 158–59,
166; "It Spoke of Exactly the Things," 195;
Long, Last, Happy, 10; *Never Die,* 31, 63,
180; "Midnight and I'm Not Famous Yet,"
75–76, 83–98, 223; "Nicodemus Bluff," 1,
13, 32; *Nightwatchmen,* 257n1 (chap. 1);
"Rat-Faced Auntie," 25, 142–78, 220; *Ray,*
33, 60, 63, 66–67, 83–84, 112–13, 239; "Return to Return," 259n3 (chap. 2); "Revealed: Rock Swoon Has No Past," 214; *The
Tennis Handsome,* 89, 223, 259n3 (chap.
2); "Testimony of Pilot," 75–76, 84, 86–87,
98–105; "Through Sunset into the Raccoon
Night," 32–33, 195, 196, 238; "Uncle High
Lonesome," 4, 25, 114–28; "Upstairs, Mona
Bayed for Dong," 186; "Water Liars," 85–
86, 89, 103, 112, 153, 156, 186–88, 190; *Yon-
der Stands Your Orphan,* 25, 69, 74, 153–57,
170, 219, 227, 241–48, 250
Hart, Frank, 162
Hartmann, Geoffrey, 44–45
Harvey, David, 23, 155
Haunted Bodies (Jones and Van D'Elden
Donaldson), 114
haunted South, 13, 107, 109–10, 111–14,
122
hegemonic masculinity. *See* masculinity
Hemingway, Ernest, 88, 227
Hendler, Glenn, 80
Henninger, Katherine, 20, 185
heritage tourism, 169–70, 243; in Charleston,
SC, 169; in Natchez, MS, 169; in Savannah,
GA, 169; in Vicksburg, MS, 169

heteroglossia (Bakhtin), 211
"hillbilly" culture, 179–80, 189, 191–2, 200–3,
253
Hinrichsen, Lisa, 114, 119, 146, 168
historical circularity in the South, 111–12,
217–18, 223, 240
"hobo" subculture, 161
Hobson, Fred, 11, 12–14, 110, 111, 141, 202,
203, 224, 226, 238
Holman, Hugh, 12
Holocaust, 121–22
hooks, bell, 82
Horrocks, Roger, 78
Howard, Jacqueline, 235
Howard, John, 79
Humphries, Jefferson, 7, 109–11
Hutcheon, Linda, 4, 14, 15, 127, 143, 150, 181–
82, 197, 199, 207, 210, 233, 237, 254
hybrid masculinity. *See* masculinity

I'll Take My Stand (Tate), 6
imagined community, 6, 8–9, 130, 146
"imagineering" (Rutheiser), 43, 167, 169
imperialism, 23, 29, 63, 68
In Country (Mason), 119, 123
In the Circles of Fear and Desire (Day), 221
Indian removal. *See* Native Americans
indicted South, 131
Indicted South, The (Maxwell), 81–83
Inferno (Dante), 48
Ingenthon, Elmo, 202
intertextuality, 14, 45–46, 176, 180–81, 208–
9, 218, 222, 226–7, 231–34
Inventing Southern Literature (Kreyling), 17,
22, 45, 140, 197, 199

Jameson, Fredric, 3, 16, 69, 143, 155, 157, 170,
171, 177, 181, 182–83, 184, 203, 210–11, 225,
231, 233, 242, 254
Jay, Paul, 20, 183
jazz. *See* music
Jim Crow laws. *See* race and racism
Johnson, Alison M., 119
Johnson, E. Patrick, 79, 171, 192

Jones, Suzanne, 11, 19
Joyce, James: "Araby," 70; *Dubliners*, 70; *Finnegans Wake*, 222; Joycean epiphany, 46, 50–51, 54, 56; *A Portrait of the Artist as a Young Man*, 42, 46; *Stephen Hero*, 53; *Ulysses*, 53

Kanner, Ellen, 243
Kantrowitz, Stephen, 82
Kaplan, David, 62
Kaufman, Michael, 219–20
Kimmel, Michael, 78, 87, 219–20
Kingsolver, Barbara, 257n5
Kirby, Jack, 3, 182
Klevay, Robert, 85, 186
Knoenagel, Axel, 202
Kornegay, Jamie, 33
Kreyling, Michael, 9, 11, 13–15, 17, 18, 22, 45, 64, 90, 92, 126–27, 131, 140, 148–49, 167, 197, 199, 235, 242, 249
Kripke, Saul, 60–62, 66–67, 71–72
Kristeva, Julia, 237
Künstlerroman, 40, 42

Lacan, Jacques, 173–74, 177, 226, 248
LaCapra, Dominick, 114
Ladd, Barbara, 12, 22, 30, 249, 253
Language of Music, The (Cooke), 48–49
Lanterns on the Levee (Percy), 165
Lardner, Ring, 88
Lassiter, Matthew D., 21
Lewis, Nathaniel, 11–12, 184, 250
Leys, Ruth, 114
Literature of Memory, The (Gray), 110, 146
Living in the End Times (Žižek), 23
Lloyd, Christopher, 9, 17, 198, 253
local color, 180, 193
Lolita (Nabokov), 70, 231
Lonely Crowd, The (Reisman et al.), 78
Look Away! (Smith and Cohn), 17–18
Loomba, Ania, 9, 16
Lost Cause. *See* Confederacy
"Love Song of J. Alfred Prufrock, The" (Eliot), 45

Lowenthal, David, 143
Lussana, Sergio, 81

MacLean, Nancy, 82
Maclean, Norman, 228, 229
Madden, David, 63
Mali, Joseph, 149
Mallarmé, Stéphane, 48, 49
Manhood in the Making (Gilmore), 78
masculinity (white southern), 53, 76–77, 80–81, 86, 93–95; crisis of, 78–79; "deep masculine," 220; defined against racial others: Black, 79–80, 81–83; Native American, 63–65; "hegemonic" versus "hybrid," 83, 88–90, 93; hypermasculinity: in Sport, 88, 134; in War, 81, 87–88, 90–91, 134; as a performance, 78–80, 94–95; "rebel" masculinity 80–81, 83, 89, 134, 138. *See also* mythopoetic men's movement; shame-honor culture in the South; white southern melancholy
Mason, Bobbie Ann, 119–20
Maxwell, Angie, 81–83, 86, 113
McCarthy, Cormac, 198, 210, 257n5
McHale, Brian, 181
McKee, Kathryn, 21, 23, 28, 29, 183
McPherson, Tara, 11, 23, 24, 25, 147, 149, 152, 167, 177, 183, 192, 247, 249
Media-Made Dixie (Kirby), 3, 182
media-made Dixie, 3, 134, 167–68, 182, 185, 196–97, 242–43, 245–46
memory (southern), 7–9, 126–27; of the Civil War, 7–8, 108–13; (global) memory studies, 10, 144; the politics of memorialization, 8, 144–47; second-generation memory as historical transference, 121–22. *See also* nostalgia
Men in the Middle (Gilbert), 78, 80
Men Like That (E. Johnson), 79
Men We Reaped (J. Ward), 251
Meridian, MS, 9, 31
Metafiction (Currie), 5, 224, 239–40
Metafiction (Waugh), 4–5, 177
metafiction, 4–5, 23, 42–43, 127, 177, 181–82, 186, 197, 204, 206–8, 223–24, 239–40

micro-Souths, 10, 19, 27, 31, 81, 113–14, 179–80, 202–3, 252
Milesi, Laurent, 46, 52
Millard, Kenneth, 36–37, 119, 235, 236
Mind of the South, The (Cash), 6
Mitchell, Lee, 192
Mitchell, Margaret, 31, 165, 167, 168–69, 170, 172
Monteith, Sharon, 11, 19, 249, 252–53
Moretti, Franco, 43–44, 251
Morson, Gary Saul, 235
Mountain/Upland South, 19, 180, 200–3; Mountain dialect/vernacular, 179, 203
music: "absolute" music, 48–49; bluegrass, 69, 232; compared with writing, 48, 52, 74, 208; "high lonesome" musical aesthetic, 232; jazz, 49–52
Myth of Masculinity, The (Pleck), 78
Myth of Southern Exceptionalism, The (Lassiter and Crespino), 21
mythopoetic men's movement, 83, 90, 220

Nabokov, Vladimir, 70, 227, 231, 246
names and naming, 60–62, 65–67, 71–72. *See also* rigid designation
Naming and Necessity (Kripke), 60–62, 71
Napoleon, 85, 92–93, 97, 117
Narcissistic Narrative (Hutcheon), 4, 127, 182, 207–8
Narrative Forms of Southern Community, The (Romine), 18, 235
Natchez Pilgrimage, MS, 169–70
Nation's Region (Duck), 145, 147
Native Americans: Apache, 62–64; Choctaw, 64–66; Indian removal, 68; the Native South, 20, 65, 68, 253
Nelson, Dana, 18, 19, 21, 109, 250
"Neo-Confederate Narrative and Postsouthern Parody" (Bone), 2, 140, 202, 236
neoliberalism, 16–17
New Deal, 191
new men's movement, 220
New South, 28–29, 81–82, 145–46, 168–69, 191
New Southern Studies (NSS), 16–19, 21–28,

37, 38, 73, 109, 126, 148, 149, 183, 192, 248–50, 251–52. *See also* white southern melancholy
Noble, Donald, 31, 33, 63, 111
Nordan, Lewis, 33
Norris, Christopher, 60–62
northernization/Americanization of the South, 29, 82, 218
nostalgia, 22–23, 24–26, 28–29, 31, 110, 142–50, 154–56, 165, 167, 169–72, 212, 215–16, 220–21, 241–46. *See also* heritage tourism; white southern melancholy

O'Brien, Michael, 23, 182
Offutt, Chris, 202, 257n5
Old South, 28–30, 83, 110, 146–48, 165, 167–71, 243–44
Old Southwest humor, 180, 189
Oliver, Kelly, 251
Ongoing Burden of Southern History, The (Maxwell et al.), 113
original sin. *See* Christianity and the Bible
"Orphans All" (Romine), 25, 69, 154, 155, 170, 219, 242, 245
Orpheus Descending (T. Williams), 227
Our South (Greeson), 11, 22
Ozarks, 179–81, 185–86, 189–92, 196, 198–203, 226; and place/(post)regionalism, 184–86, 197–204

Paradise Lost (Milton), 48
parody. *See* postmodernism; postsouthern parody
Pascoe, Cheri, 90
pastiche. *See* postmodernism
Pater, Walter, 49
Peacock, James L., 21
Pendarvis, Jack, 33
Percy, William Alexander, 167, 172
performance theory, 78–79
Perspectives on Barry Hannah (Bone et al.), 35, 83
Peterson, Nancy, 144
Phallic Critiques (Schwenger), 99
Phillips, U. B., 81

Piacentino, Edward, 180

Pilkington, John, 7

place. *See* postregionalism

Plague of Fantasies, The (Žižek), 248

Plantinga, Alvin, 62

Plath, Lydia, 81

Playing Indian (Deloria), 63, 253

Pleck, Joseph, 78

Poe, Edgar Allan, 152, 195, 213

Poetics of Postmodernism, The (Hutcheon), 233

Politics of Postmodernism, The (Hutcheon), 233

polyphony, 209, 211, 228, 235, 239

poor whites in the South, 19, 145, 191

Portis, Charles, 33

Possessing the Past (Hinrichsen), 114, 146

postmodernism, 2–3, 4–6, 45–46, 69, 72–73, 112, 143, 150, 155, 157, 182–85, 215, 232, 242–43, 254–55; hyperreality, 15, 26, 119, 182, 194; the linguistic turn, 2, 28, 40, 44–45, 60, 148; mediation/simulation, 3, 15, 54, 126, 153–54, 167–68, 177, 184, 211, 242; pastiche, 210–11, 224–25, 233, 242; postmodern parody, 14–15, 140, 233; post-modern relativism, 17, 23, 177, 249. *See also* metafiction; postregionalism; postsouthern parody

Postmodernism, or, The Cultural Logic of Late Capitalism (Jameson), 2–3, 155, 170, 182–83, 211, 242

postregionalism, 11–17, 23, 26, 28–30, 183–85; in Appalachia, 201; the authenticity problem, 11–12, 24–25, 198–99, 250–51; the declining/disappearing South, 3, 20, 185, 241; an ethics of place, 3, 198, 204, 255; homogenization/hybridization of American regions, 11–13, 19, 201; immigration/migration in the South, 10, 20, 28, 253; and postmodernism, 26, 181–86, 254; the postsouthern "closure of history" (Simpson), 7, 12, 33, 109; in postsouthern literature, 12–15, 32–34, 110–12, 204, 224–25; the postsouthern turn, 12–13, 148; a "sense of

place," 12–14, 15–16, 19, 23, 26, 28, 34, 111, 148, 169, 181–85, 204, 248–49; southern studies without "The South," 22, 148, 248; a "traveling theory" of place (Jones and Monteith), 252–53; and the (American) West, 11–12, 24, 30, 184, 192, 255. *See also* globalization; New Southern Studies; post-southern parody; transnationalism

postsouthern parody, 14–15, 131, 167, 235, 242

Postsouthern Sense of Place in Contemporary Fiction, The (Bone), 12, 14, 15–16, 17, 140, 146, 168, 185, 197, 200

postsouthern. *See* postregionalism

post–World War II America, 78, 79

Potter, David, 10

Potts, James B., 83, 112, 113, 210, 213, 214, 215, 216, 232, 234, 237

Poverty Politics (S. Robertson), 19–20, 145

Powers, Richard, 5

Price, Reynolds, 14

Pynchon, Thomas, 5, 40, 57, 233

queer South, 19, 79–80

race and racism: appropriating Blackness, 79, 82; Black cultural trauma, 122; Jim Crow laws/segregation, 81–82, 170, 172, 243, 250; white cultural guilt, 113, 121, 246, 253; white supremacy, 22, 63, 64–65, 81–83, 113. *See also* civil rights movement

Radstone, Susannah, 144, 162

Randall, Alice, 149

Rash, Ron, 201

Real Phonies (Cheever), 75, 181

Real South, The (Romine), 3, 10, 11, 24, 92, 154, 155, 168, 169, 170–71, 184, 199, 241–42, 250

reality homesickness (Romine), 154, 219

rebel masculinity. *See* masculinity

Reconstructing Dixie (McPherson), 11, 167

Reconstruction, 6, 7, 81, 146, 250

Red Badge of Courage, The (Crane), 166

Reed, John Shelton, 11

Reeser, Todd, 79

regionalism. *See* postregionalism

Remapping Southern Literature (Brinkmeyer), 17

Richard, Mark, 33

Riesman, David, 78

rigid designation, 61–62, 66–68

"River Runs Through It, A" (Maclean), 228

Road, The (McCarthy), 198

Roberts, Terry, 201

Robertson, Roland, 181, 182

Robertson, Sarah, 19, 145

Romine, Scott, 3, 11, 15–16, 18, 22, 23, 24, 25, 26, 69, 74, 140, 153–54, 155, 168, 170–71, 183–84, 204, 219, 235, 241–42, 243–44, 245, 246–47, 249, 250

Rooting Memory, Rooting Place (Lloyd), 9, 198

Rorty, Richard, 62

Roth, Michael, 114, 144

Roth, Philip, 5

Rough South. *See* Grit Lit

Rubin generation, 12–13, 17, 109

Rumi, 73

Russell, Bertrand, 61

Rutheiser, Charles, 43, 146, 169

Rutkowski, Sara, 191

Salmon, Nathan, 68

Sampson, Curt, 89

Saussure, Ferdinand de, 44, 46, 60–61, 62, 71

Savannah, GA, 25, 165–66, 169–71

Savoy, Eric, 173–74

Schalkwyk, David, 44

Schwartz, Hillel, 153, 181

Schwarz, Benjamin, 10, 29

Schwenger, Peter, 99

Searle, John, 61

second-generation trauma, 114

Seib, Kenneth, 92

sexual abuse, 214–15, 219, 221–23

Sexual Politics of Time, The (Radstone), 144, 162

shame-honor culture in the South, 88, 115–16, 118, 131, 136–37, 152, 253

Shields, Todd, 113

Shipe, Matthew, 204

Simmons, Philip E., 181, 232, 237

Simon, William, 237

Simpson, Lewis P., 7, 12–13, 33, 109, 110, 111, 126–27

Simulations (Baudrillard), 54

Singleton, George, 33

Slave South. *See* Antebellum South

Smartt Bell, Madison, 257n5

Smith, Anthony D., 147

Smith, Jon, 16–18, 21, 22–24, 26, 27, 149, 177, 192, 247, 248–50, 255

Smonk (Franklin), 180

social class, 7, 8, 10, 19–20, 81, 82–83, 89, 145, 200–1, 215–16, 219–20, 253

social realism in Depression-era America, 191

South That Wasn't There, The (Kreyling), 9, 17, 126, 148

South, The Nation, and The World, The (Carlton and Coclanis), 30

South to a New Place (Jones and Monteith), 11

Southern Aberrations (Gray), 119, 182

southern distinctiveness/exceptionalism, 6–10, 11–12, 16–19, 20–23, 107–8, 113–14, 146

southern gentleman, 77, 81–82, 88, 244

Southern Gothic, 33, 100, 180, 188, 209, 260n3 (concl.); American Gothic, 173, 203; Appalachian Gothic, 180; gothic conventions in southern literature, 121, 152–53, 156, 189, 195, 217, 221–22

Southern Living, 7, 32, 145

Southern Modernism. *See* Southern Renaissance

Southern Past, The (Brundage), 169–70

Southern Renaissance, 2, 7, 13–14, 107, 110–11, 119, 203, 232–33

Southern Spaces, 20

Southern Strategy, 8

Southern Writer in the Postmodern World, The (Hobson), 12–13, 110–11, 203, 224, 226, 238

Spikes, Michael P., 43, 60, 62, 66, 72
Squint, Kirstin, 20, 65
Stevens, Wallace, 204
Stuart, J. E. B., 92–93, 95, 97
Stueck, William, 21
Su, John J., 146
Summerfield, Giovanna, 44, 251
Sunbelt South, 31

tall tales, 31, 127, 180–81, 186, 187, 195
Tate, Allen, 6, 107, 146
Tatum, Stephen, 250
Taylor, Charles, 181
Taylor, Helen, 17
Taylor, Peter, 31
"Tell-Tale Heart, The" (Poe), 213
tennis, 88–90
Thompson, Graham, 21
Thoreen, David, 85–86, 186–87
Thorpe, Thomas Bangs, 180
Tichi, Cecelia, 232
time-space compression (Harvey), 155
Tom Sawyer (Twain), 216
"Toward a Post-postpolitical Southern stud-
    ies" (J. Smith), 22, 23, 247, 260n1 (concl.)
Tower, Wells, 208
transnationalism, 20–21, 27–28, 29–30,
    108
trauma studies, 114
Trefzer, Annette, 20, 21, 23, 28, 183
True West (Handley and Lewis), 184, 192
Tunc, Tanfer Emin, 146
Twain, Mark, 31, 180

Unsettling the Literary West (Lewis),
    184
Updike, John, 42

V. (Pynchon), 40
Van Buskirk, Kathleen, 202
Van D'Elden Donaldson, Susan, 3, 19, 29,
    114, 252
Vanarsdall, Robert, 208
Vernon, Zackary, 201

Vice, Brad, 31
Vicksburg, MS, 169. See also Battle of
    Vicksburg
Vietnam War, 83–84, 85, 87–88, 91, 94, 133,
    166, 218, 223, 236
Vietnamese Americans in the South, 19
"Violence, the Body, and 'The South'" (Baker
    and Nelson), 18, 21, 109, 250

Ward, Brian, 17, 18–19
Ward, Jesmyn, 251
Warren, Kenneth, 22
Waste Land, The (Eliot), 211, 231, 234
Watts, Trent, 82
Waugh, Patricia, 4, 5, 177
Welty, Eudora, 31
West (American), 11–12, 24, 30, 184, 192, 255;
    American fantasy of "going West," 68, 218–
    19; Southern writers who "went West,"
    257n5; Westward mobility as freedom, 108,
    218–19
Weston, Ruth D., 35, 43, 72, 89–90, 94, 112–
    13, 115, 117, 167, 180, 186, 187, 214–15, 217,
    222, 229, 237
Whaley, Preston, 49
Whayne, Jeannie, 113
"Where is Southern Literature?" (Romine),
    15–16, 23, 26, 140
Where the New World Is (Bone), 18, 21, 23–24,
    26, 27–28
white guilt. See race and racism
White Masculinity in the Recent South
    (Watts), 82
white southern melancholy, 22–23, 29, 149,
    175, 248–49
white supremacy. See race and racism
Widiss, Benjamin, 107, 109, 112
Williams, Tennessee, 227
Williamson, Joel, 82
Wilson, Charles Raegan, 29
Wilson, Rob, 27
Wind Done Gone, The (Randall), 149
Windham, Donald, 258n7
Wittgenstein, Ludwig, 61

Wolfe, Tom, 224, 226–27, 240
Woodward, C. Vann, 6, 107–9, 113,
    140–41
Woodward, Richard, 210
Wright, Elizabeth, 174
Wyatt-Brown, Bertram, 115

Yaeger, Patricia, 19, 114, 243
Yoder, Edwin, 11, 244

Žižek, Slavoj, 23, 248, 252
zombie culture, 154, 242. *See also* casino
    capitalism

www.ingramcontent.com/pod-product-compliance
Lightning Source LLC
Chambersburg PA
CBHW030922150426
42812CB00046B/486

* 9 7 8 0 8 0 7 1 7 4 9 3 7 *